The Life of St Francis Xavier by John Dryden

John Dryden was born on August 9th, 1631 in the village rectory of Aldwincle near Thrapston in Northamptonshire. As a boy Dryden lived in the nearby village of Titchmarsh, Northamptonshire. In 1644 he was sent to Westminster School as a King's Scholar.

Dryden obtained his BA in 1654, graduating top of the list for Trinity College, Cambridge that year.

Returning to London during The Protectorate, Dryden now obtained work with Cromwell's Secretary of State, John Thurloe.

At Cromwell's funeral on 23 November 1658 Dryden was in the company of the Puritan poets John Milton and Andrew Marvell. The setting was to be a sea change in English history. From Republic to Monarchy and from one set of lauded poets to what would soon become the Age of Dryden.

The start began later that year when Dryden published the first of his great poems, Heroic Stanzas (1658), a eulogy on Cromwell's death.

With the Restoration of the Monarchy in 1660 Dryden celebrated in verse with Astraea Redux, an authentic royalist panegyric.

With the re-opening of the theatres after the Puritan ban, Dryden began to also write plays. His first play, The Wild Gallant, appeared in 1663 but was not successful. From 1668 on he was contracted to produce three plays a year for the King's Company, in which he became a shareholder. During the 1660s and '70s, theatrical writing was his main source of income.

In 1667, he published Annus Mirabilis, a lengthy historical poem which described the English defeat of the Dutch naval fleet and the Great Fire of London in 1666. It established him as the pre-eminent poet of his generation, and was crucial in his attaining the posts of Poet Laureate (1668) and then historiographer royal (1670).

This was truly the Age of Dryden, he was the foremost English Literary figure in Poetry, Plays, translations and other forms.

In 1694 he began work on what would be his most ambitious and defining work as translator, The Works of Virgil (1697), which was published by subscription. It was a national event.

John Dryden died on May 12th, 1700, and was initially buried in St. Anne's cemetery in Soho, before being exhumed and reburied in Westminster Abbey ten days later.

Index of Contents

THE LIFE OF ST FRANCIS XAVIER, OF THE SOCIETY OF JESUS, APOSTLE OF THE INDIES, AND OF JAPAN.

TO THE QUEEN.[1]

MADAM,

The reverend author of this life, in his dedication to his Most Christian Majesty, affirms, that France was owing for him to the intercession of St Francis Xavier. That Anne of Austria, his mother, after twenty years of barrenness, had recourse to heaven, by her fervent prayers, to draw down that blessing, and addressed her devotions, in a particular manner, to this holy apostle of the Indies. I know not, madam, whether I may presume to tell the world, that your majesty has chosen this great saint for one of your celestial patrons, though I am sure you will never be ashamed of owning so glorious an intercessor; not even in a country where the doctrine of the holy church is questioned, and those religious addresses ridiculed. Your majesty, I doubt not, has the inward satisfaction of knowing, that such pious prayers have not been unprofitable to you; and the nation may one day come to understand, how happy it will be for them to have a son of prayers ruling over them.[2] Not that we are wholly to depend on this particular blessing, as a thing of certainty, though we hope and pray for its continuance. The ways of Divine Providence are incomprehensible; and we know not in what times, or by what methods, God will restore his church in England, or what farther trials and afflictions we are yet to undergo. Only this we know, that if a religion be of God, it can never fail; but the acceptable time we must patiently expect, and endeavour by our lives not to undeserve. I am sure if we take the example of our sovereigns, we shall place our confidence in God alone; we shall be assiduous in our devotions, moderate in our expectations, humble in our carriage, and forgiving of our enemies. All other panegyrics I purposely omit; but those of Christianity are such, that neither your majesty, nor my royal master, need be ashamed of them, because their commemoration is instructive to your subjects. We may be allowed, madam, to praise Almighty God for making us happy by your means, without suspicion of flattery; and the meanest subject has the privilege of joining his thanksgiving with his sovereigns, where his happiness is equally concerned. May it not be permitted me to add, that to be remembered, and celebrated in after ages, as the chosen vessel, by which it has pleased the Almighty Goodness to transmit so great a blessing to these nations, is a secret satisfaction, which is not forbidden you to take; the blessings of your people are a prelibation of the joys in heaven, and a lawful ambition here on earth.

Your majesty is authorized, by the greatest example of a mother, to rejoice in a promised son. The blessed Virgin was not without as great a proportion of joy, as humanity could bear, when she answered the salutation of the angel in expressions, which seemed to unite the contradicting terms of calmness, and of transport: "Be it to thy hand-maid, according to thy word."

It is difficult for me to leave this subject, but more difficult to pursue it as I ought; neither must I presume to detain your majesty by a long address. The life of Saint Francis Xavier, after it had been written by several authors in the Spanish and Portuguese, and by the famous Padre Bartoli in the Italian tongue, came out at length in French, by the celebrated pen of Father Bohours, from whom I have translated it, and humbly crave leave to dedicate it to your patronage. I question not but it will undergo the censure of those men, who teach the people, that miracles are ceased. Yet there are, I presume, a sober party of the Protestants, and even of the most learned among them, who being convinced, by the concurring testimonies of the last age, by the suffrages of whole nations in the Indies and Japan, and by the severe scrutinies that were made before the act of canonization, will not dispute the truth of most matters of fact as they are here related; nay, some may be ingenuous enough to own freely, that to propagate the faith amongst infidels and heathens, such miraculous operations are as necessary now in those benighted regions, as when the Christian doctrine was first planted by our blessed Saviour and his apostles.

The honourable testimonies which are cited by my author, just before the conclusion of his work, and one of them in particular from a learned divine of the church of England,[3] though they slur over the mention of his miracles, in obscure and general terms, yet are full of veneration for his person. Farther than this I think it needless to prepossess a reader; let him judge sincerely, according to the merits of the cause, and the sanctity of his life, of whom such wonders are related, and attested with such clouds of witnesses; for an impartial man cannot but of himself consider the honour of God in the publication of his gospel, the salvation of souls, and the conversion of kingdoms, which followed from those miracles; the effects of which remain in many of them to this day.

But that it is not lawful for me to trespass so far on the patience of your majesty, I should rather enlarge on a particular reflection, which I made in my translation of this book, namely, that the instructions of the saint, which are copied from his own writings, are so admirably useful, so holy, and so wonderfully efficacious, that they seem to be little less than the product of an immediate inspiration. So much excellent matter is crowded into so small a compass, that almost every paragraph contains the value of a sermon. The nourishment is so strong, that it requires but little to be taken at a time. Where he exhorts, there is not an expression, but what is glowing with the love of God; where he directs a missioner, or gives instructions to a substitute, we can scarcely have a less idea than of a St Paul advising a Timothy, or a Titus. Where he writes into Europe, he inspires his ardour into sovereign princes, and seems, with the spirit of his devotion, even to burn his colleagues at the distance of the Indies.

But, madam, I consider that nothing I can say is worthy to detain you longer from the perusal of this book, in which all things are excellent, excepting only the meanness of my performance in the translation. Such as it is, be pleased, with your inborn goodness, to accept it, with the offer of my unworthy prayers for the lasting happiness of my gracious sovereign, for your own life and prosperity, together with the preservation of the son of prayers, and the farther encrease of the royal family; all which blessings are continually implored from heaven, by,

MADAM,
Your Majesty's most humble,
And most obedient subject and servant,
JOHN DRYDEN.

FOOTNOTES

1: Mary of Este, wife of James II.

2: The superstitious and, as it proved, fatal insinuation, that the birth of the Chevalier de St George was owing to the supernatural intercession of St Francis Xavier, was much insisted on by the Protestants as an argument against the reality of his birth. See the Introduction to "Britannia Rediviva," Vol. X. p. 285. In that piece, our author also alludes to this foolery: Hail, son of prayers, by holy violence Drawn down from heaven!--

3: The Reverend Richard Hackluyt, editor of the large collection of voyages to which Purchas' Pilgrim is a continuation.

THE AUTHOR'S ADVERTISEMENT TO THE READER

Having already presented you with the Life of St Ignatius, I thought myself obliged to give you that of St Francis Xavier. For, besides that it was just that the son should attend the father, it seemed to me, that these two saints being concerned so much together, the history of the apostle of India and Japan would give you a clearer knowledge of him who was founder of the Jesuits. I may add likewise, that many considerable persons, and particularly of the court, have testified so great a desire to see a complete history of St Xavier in our language, that I thought my labour would not be unacceptable to them; and that in satisfying my own private devotion, I might at the same time content the curiosity of others.

The writings out of which I have drawn this work, have furnished me with all I could desire for the perfection of it, in what regards the truth and the ornaments of this history: for without speaking of Turselline and Orlandino, I have diligently read Lucena and Bartoli; the first of which Wrote in Portuguese with this title, "The History of the Life of Father Francis Xavier, and of what was done in the Indies by the Religious of the Society of Jesus." He informs us, that he had in his hands the authentic copies of the informations which were made by order of John III. king of Portugal, concerning the actions of the blessed Father Xavier, and the originals of many letters, written from the Indies on that subject, which are to this day deposited in the archives of the university of Coimbra. As for Bartoli, who is so famous by his writings, and who is accounted amongst the best of the Italian authors, he has extracted from the archives of the Casa Professa at Rome, and from the acts of the canonization, what he relates of our saint in the first part of the History of the Society, intitled, Asia.

Though these two historians have in some sort collected all that can be said concerning St Francis Xavier, I omitted not to take a view of what others have written on that subject; and chiefly the book of Nieremberg, which bears for title, "_Claros Varones_, or Illustrious Men;" the History of India, by Maffeus, and that of Jarrio; the Church History of Japan, by Solia; the Castilian History of the Missions, which the Fathers of the Society have made to the East Indies, and the kingdoms of China and Japan, composed by Lewis de Gusman; and, lastly, the Portuguese History of the Travels of Ferdinand Mendez Pinto.

But seeing St Francis Xavier himself has written some parts of those accidents which have befallen him in India and Japan, I have faithfully copied his letters, and from thence have drawn those particulars which have much conduced to my information, and clearing of the truth. These letters have also furnished me with materials to make the narration appear more lively and moving, when you hear the saint himself speaking in his proper words, and mixing his own thoughts and reflections with his actions.

I had almost finished this my work, when I received from Spain and Italy two other lives of St Francis Xavier, which before that time I had not seen: the one very new, which was written in Italian by Father Joseph Massei; the other more ancient, written in Spanish by Father Francis Garcia. I found nothing in those two books which I had not observed in others; but read them with great pleasure, as being most exactly and elegantly written, each in their several tongue.

For what remains, amongst all those historians which I have cited, there is only the author of the new Italian Life, who has not followed the common error, in relation to the age of St Francis Xavier: for the rest of them not precisely knowing the year and day of his birth, have made him ten years older than he was; placing his nativity about the time when the passage to the East Indies was discovered by Vasco de Gama.

But Father Massei has taken his measures in that particular, from Father Poussines, that judicious person to whom we are owing for the new letters of St Xavier, and who has composed a dissertation in Latin, touching the year of our apostle's birth.

He produces, in the said treatise, a Latin paper, written in all appearance in the year 1585, and found in the records of the house of Don Juan Antonio, Count of Xavier. That paper,--wherein is treated of the ancestors and birth of the saint, and which very probably, as Poussines judges, is the minute of a letter sent to Rome, where Dr Navara then resided, to whom it refers you,--that paper, I say, has these words in it: _Non scitur certò annus quo natus est P. Franciscus Xaverius. Vulgo tamen invaluit, a quibusdam natum cum dici anno millesimo quadragintesimo nonagesimo-sexto_: which is to say, the year is not certainly known, in which Father Francis Xavier was born; but it is generally held, that some have reported he was born in the year 1496.

But it is to be observed, that these words, _Non scitur certò annus quo natus est P. Franciscus Xaverius_, are dashed out with the stroke of a pen. There is also a line drawn over these other words, _Natum eum dici millesimo, quadragintesimo, nonagesimo-sexto_: and this is written over head, _Natus est P. Franciscus Xaverius anno millesimo quingentesimo sexto_. Father Francis Xavier was born in the year 1506. There is also written in the margin, _Natus est die 7 Aprilis, anni 1506_. He was born on the 7th of April, 1506.

That which renders this testimony more authentic, is, that at the bottom of the letter, these words, in Spanish, are written by the same hand which corrected those two passages of which I spoke: _Hallo se la razon del tiempo que el S. P. Francisco Xavier nació, en un libro manual de su hermano el Capitan Juan de Azpilcueta: la qual sacò de un libro, de su padre Don Juan Jasso; viz_. "The time when the blessed Father Francis Xavier was born, is found in the journal of his brother Don Juan de Azpilcueta, who extracted it from the journal or manual of his father Don Juan Jasso." 'Tis on this foundation, that, before I had read the Life written by Father Massei, I had already closed with the opinion of Father Poussines.

As to the precise day of the father's death, I have followed the common opinion, which I take to be the most probable, in conformity to the bull of his canonization. For the historians who have mentioned it, agree not with each other, on what clay he died. 'Tis said in Herbert's Travels to the Indies and Persia, translated out of the English, "St Francis Xavier, the Jesuit of Navarre, died the 4th of December, 1552." Ferdinand Mendez Pinto, the Portuguese, affirms, that he died at midnight, on Saturday the 2d of December, the same year. A manuscript letter, pretended to be written by Anthony de Sainte Foy, companion to Xavier for the voyage of China, the truth of which I suspect, relates, that the Saint died on a Sunday night at two of the clock, on the 2d of December, 1552. Now 'tis most certain, that in the year 1552, the 2d of December fell on a Friday; so that it is a manifest mistake to say, that St Xavier died that year either on Saturday or Sunday the 2d of December.

I should apprehend, lest a life so extraordinary as this might somewhat shock the profaner sort of men, if the reputation of St Francis Xavier were not well established in the world, and that the wonderful things he did had not all the marks of true miracles. As the author who made the collection of them has well observed, the mission of the saint gives them an authority, even in our first conceptions of them: for being sent from God for the conversion of infidels, it was necessary that the faith should be planted in the East, by the same means as it had been through all the world, in the beginning of the church.

Besides which, never any miracles have been examined with greater care, or more judicially than these. They were not miracles wrought in private, and which we are only to believe on the attestation of two or three interested persons, such who might have been surprised into an opinion of them; they were ordinarily public matters of fact, avowed by a whole city or kingdom, and which had for witnesses the body of a nation, for the most part Heathen, or Mahometan. Many of these miracles have been of long continuance; and it was an easy matter for such who were incredulous, to satisfy their doubts concerning them. All of them have been attended by such consequences as have confirmed their truth, beyond dispute: such as were--the conversions of kingdoms, and of kings, who were the greatest enemies to Christianity; the wonderful ardency of those new Christians, and the heroical constancy of their martyrs. But after all, nothing can give a greater confirmation of the saint's miracles, than his saint-like life; which was even more wonderful than the miracles themselves. It was in a manner of necessity, that a man of so holy a conversation should work those things, which other men could not perform; and that, resigning himself to God, with an entire confidence and trust, in the most dangerous occasions, God should consign over to him some part of his omnipotence, for the benefit of souls.

THE LIFE OF ST FRANCIS XAVIER

BOOK I

His birth. His natural endowments, and first studies. His father purposes to recal him from his studies, and is diverted from that resolution. He continues his studies, and sets up a philosophy lecture. He is preserved from falling into heresy. His change of life. His retirement, and total conversion. He consecrates himself to God, by a vow. What happened to him in his journey to Venice. What he did at Venice. He goes to Rome, and from thence returns to Venice. He prepares himself to celebrate his first mass. He celebrates his first mass, and falls sick after it. St Jerome appears to him. He goes to Bolognia, and labours there with great success. He relapses into his sickness, and yet continues preaching. He is recalled to Rome by Father Ignatius, and labours there with great success. The occasion of the mission into the Indies. He is named for the mission of the Indies. God mysteriously reveals to him his intended mission to the Indies. He takes his leave of the Pope, and what his Holiness said to him. He departs from Rome. How he employed himself during his journey. His letter to Ignatius. Some remarkable accidents in his journey to Lisbon. He passes by the castle of Xavier without going to it. He arrives at Lisbon, and cures Rodriguez immediately after his coming. He is called to court. The manner of his life at Lisbon. He refuses to visit his uncle, the Duke of Navarre. The fruit of his evangelical labours. The reputation he acquired at Lisbon. They would retain him in Portugal. He is permitted to go to the Indies, and the king discourses with him before his departure. He refuses the provisions offered him for his voyage. He goes for the Indies, and what he said to Rodriguez at parting.

I have undertaken to write the life of a saint, who has renewed, in the last age, the greatest wonders which were wrought in the infancy of the church; and who was himself a living proof of Christianity. There will be seen in the actions of one single man, a new world converted by the power of his preaching, and by that of his miracles: idolatrous kings, with their dominions, reduced under the obedience of the gospel; the faith flourishing in the very midst of barbarism; and the authority of the Roman church acknowledged by nations the most remote, who were utterly unacquainted with ancient Rome.

This apostolical man, of whom I speak, is St Francis Xavier, of the society of Jesus, and one of the first disciples of St Ignatius Loyola. He was of Navarre; and, according to the testimony of Cardinal Antonia Zapata, who examined his nobility from undoubted records, he derived his pedigree from the kings of Navarre.

His father was Don Juan de Jasso, a lord of great merit, well conversant in the management of affairs, and who held one of the first places in the council of state, under the reign of King John III. The name of his mother was Mary Azpilcueta Xavier, heiress to two of the most illustrious families in that kingdom; for the chief of her house, Don Martin Azpilcueta, less famous by the great actions of his ancestors, than by his own virtue, married Juana Xavier, the only daughter and remaining hope of her family. He had by her no other child but this Mary of whom we spoke, one of the most accomplished persons of her time.

This virgin, equally beautiful and prudent, being married to Don Jasso, became the mother of many children; the youngest of whom was Francis, the same whose life I write. He was born in the castle of Xavier, on the 7th of April, in the year 1506. That castle, situated at the foot of the Pyrenean Mountains, seven or eight leagues distant from Pampeluna, had appertained to his mother's house for about two hundred and fifty years; his progenitors on her side having obtained it in gift from King Thibald, the first of that name, in recompence of those signal services which they had performed for the crown. 'Tis from thence they took the name of Xavier, in lieu of Asnarez, which was the former name of their family. This surname was conferred on Francis, as also on some of the rest of his brothers, lest so glorious a name, now remaining in one only woman, should be totally extinguished with her.

That Providence, which had selected Francis for the conversion of such multitudes of people, endued him with all the natural qualities which are requisite to the function of an apostle. He was of a strong habit of body, his complexion lively and vigorous, his genius sublime and capable of the greatest designs, his heart fearless, agreeable in his behaviour, but above all, he was of a gay, complying, and winning humour: this notwithstanding, he had a most extreme aversion for all manner of immodesty, and a vast inclination for his studies.

His parents, who lived a most Christian life, inspired him with the fear of God from his infancy, and took a particular care of his education. He was no sooner arrived to an age capable of instruction, than, instead of embracing the profession of arms, after the example of his brothers, he turned himself, of his own motion, on the side of learning; and, as he had a quick conception, a happy memory, and a penetrating mind, he advanced wonderfully in few years.

Having gained a sufficient knowledge in the Latin tongue, and discovered a great propensity to learning, he was sent to the university of Paris, the most celebrated of all Europe, and to which the gentlemen of Spain, Italy, and Germany, resorted for their studies.

He came to Paris in the eighteenth year of his age, and fell immediately on the study of philosophy. 'Tis scarcely credible with how much ardour he surmounted the first difficulties of logic. Whatsoever his inclinations were towards a knowledge so crabbed and so subtle, he tugged at it with incessant pains, to be at the head of all his fellow students; and perhaps never any scholar besides himself could join together so much ease, and so much labour.

Xavier minded nothing more, than how to become an excellent philosopher, when his father, who had a numerous family of children, and who was one of those men of quality, whose fortunes are not equal to their birth, was thinking to remove him from his studies, after having allowed him a competent maintenance for a year or two. He communicated these his thoughts to Magdalen. Jasso, his daughter, abbess of the convent of St Clare de Gandia, famous for the austerity of its rules, and established by some holy Frenchwomen of that order, whom the calamities of war had forced to forsake their native country, and to seek a sanctuary in the kingdom of Valencia.

Magdalen, in her younger days, had been maid of honour and favourite to the Catholic queen Isabella. The love of solitude, and of the cross, had caused her to forsake the court of Arragon, and quit for ever the pleasures of this world. Having chosen the most reformed monastery of Spain for the place of her retreat, she applied herself, Avith fervour, to the exercises of penitence and prayer; and became, even from her noviciate, a perfect pattern of religious perfection.

During the course of her life, she had great communications with God; and one day he gave her to understand, that she should die a sweet and easy death; but, on the contrary, one of her nuns was pre-ordained to die in strange torments. The intention of God was not thereby to reveal to the abbess what was really to happen, but rather to give her an opportunity of exercising an heroic act of charity. She comprehended what her heavenly Father exacted from her, and petitioned him for an exchange.

God granted to her what himself had inspired her to demand; and was pleased to assure her, by a new revelation, that he had heard her prayers. She made known to her ghostly father what had passed betwixt God and her, and time verified it: for the sister above mentioned died without sickness, and appeared in dying to have had a foretaste of the joys to come. On the other side, the abbess was struck with a terrible disease, which took all her body, as it were, in pieces, and made her suffer intolerable pains; yet even those pains were less cruel to her, than those inward torments which God at the same time inflicted on her. She endured all this with wonderful patience and resignation; being well assured, that in the whole series of these dispensations there was somewhat of divine.

For what remains concerning her, from the first years of her entry into a religious life, the gift of prophecy shone so visibly in her, that none doubted but that she was full of the spirit of God; and 'tis also probable, that she left a legacy of her prophetic gifts to her spiritual daughters. For, after her decease, the nuns of Gandia foretold many things, which afterward the event confirmed; as, amongst others, the unhappy success of the expedition to Algier; of which the Duke of Borgia, viceroy of Catalonia, gave the advertisement from them to Charles V. when he was making his preparations for that enterprize.

It was six years before the death of Magdalen, that Don Jasso, her father, writ to her concerning Xavier. After she had received the letter, she was illuminated from above; and, according to the dictates of that divine light, she answered Don Jasso, that he should beware of recalling her brother Francis, whatsoever it might cost him for his entertainment in the university of Paris. That he was a chosen vessel, preordained to be the apostle of the Indies, and that one day he should become a great pillar of the church.

These letters have been preserved for a long time afterwards, and have been viewed by many persons, who have deposed the truth judicially in the process of the canonization of the saint.

Don Jasso received this answer from his daughter as an oracle from heaven; and no longer thought of recalling his son from his studies.

Xavier, thereupon, continued his philosophy; and succeeded so well in it, that having maintained his thesis, at the end of his course, with a general applause, and afterwards taking his degree of master of arts, he was judged worthy to teach philosophy himself. His parts appeared more than ever in this new employment; and he acquired an high reputation in his public lectures on Aristotle. The praises, which universally were given him, were extremely pleasing to his vanity. He was not a little proud to have augmented the glory of his family by the way of learning, while his brothers were continually adorning it by that of arms; and he flattered himself, that the way which he had taken, would lead him onward to somewhat of greater consequence.

But God Almighty had far other thoughts than those of Xavier; and it was not for these fading honours that the Divine Providence had conducted him to Paris.

At the same time, when this young master of philosophy began his course, Ignatius Loyola, who had renounced the world, and cast the model of a learned society, wholly devoted to the salvation of souls, came into France to finish his studies, which the obstacles he found in Spain, after his conversion, had constrained him to interrupt.

He had not continued long in the university of Paris, before he heard talk of Xavier, and grew acquainted with him. Our new professor, who taught at the college of Beauvois, though he dwelt in the college of St Barbe, with Peter le Fevre, a Savoyard, was judged by Ignatius to be very proper for the preaching of the gospel, as well as his companion. To gain the better opportunity of insinuating himself into their acquaintance, he took lodgings with them, and was not wanting to exhort them to live up to the rules of Christianity.

Le Fevre, who was of a tractable nature, and was not enamoured of the world, resigned himself without opposition. But Xavier, who was of a haughty spirit, and whose head was filled with ambitious thoughts, made a fierce resistance at the first. The discipline and maxims of Ignatius, who lived in a mean equipage, and valued nothing but that poverty, made him pass for a low-minded fellow in the opinion of our young gentleman. And accordingly Xavier treated him with much contempt; rallying him on all occasions, and making it his business to ridicule him.

This notwithstanding, Ignatius omitted no opportunities of representing to him the great consequence of his eternal welfare, and urging the words of our blessed Saviour, "What profit is it to a man to gain the whole world, and to lose his own, soul?" but perceiving that he could make no impression on a heart where self-conceit was so very prevalent, and which was dazzled with vain-glory, he bethought, himself of assaulting him on the weaker side.

When he had often congratulated with him for those rare talents of nature with which he was endowed, and particularly applauded his great wit, he made it his business to procure him scholars, and to augment his reputation by the crowd of his auditors. He conducted them even to his chair; and in presenting them to their master, never failed to make his panegyric.

Xavier was too vain, not to receive, with a greedy satisfaction, whatever incense was given him of that kind: applause was welcome from whatever hands it came; and withal he was too grateful, not to acknowledge those good offices which were done him, by a person whom he had used so very ill: he was the more sensible of such a kindness, by being conscious to himself how little he had deserved it. He began to look with other eyes on him who had the appearance of so mean a creature; and at the same time was informed, that this man, of so despicable a presence, was born of one of the noblest families in Guypuscoa; that his courage was correspondent to his birth; and that only the fear of God had inspired him with the choice of such a life, so distant from his inclination, and his quality.

These considerations, in favour of Ignatius, led him to hearken, without repugnance, to those discourses which were so little suitable to his natural bent; as if the quality and virtue of him who made them, had given a new charm and weight to what he said.

While things were passing in this manner, Xavier's money began to fail him, as it frequently happens to foreigners, who are at a great distance from their own country; and Ignatius, who was newly returned from the voyages which he had made into Flanders and England, from whence he had brought back a large contribution of alms, assisted him in so pressing an occasion, and thereby made an absolute conquest of his affections.

The heresy of Luther began to spread itself in Europe: and it was an artifice of those sectaries, to procure proselytes in the Catholic universities, who, by little and little, might insinuate their new opinions into the scholars, and their masters. Many knowing men of Germany were come on that design to Paris, though under the pretence of seconding the intentions of Francis the First, who was desirous to restore learning in his kingdom. They scattered their errors in so dexterous a manner, that they made them plausible; and principally endeavoured to fasten on young scholars, who had the greatest reputation of wit. Xavier, who was naturally curious, took pleasure in these novelties, and had run into them of his own accord, if Ignatius had not withdrawn him. He gave an account of this very thing not long afterwards in a letter to his elder brother, Don Azpilcueta, of which Ignatius himself was the bearer; who made a voyage into Spain, for those reasons which I have set down in another place. And these are his words, which well deserve to be related.

"He has not only relieved me, by himself, and by his friends, in those necessities to which I was reduced; but, which is of more importance, he has withdrawn me from those occasions which I had to contract a friendship with young men of my own standing, persons of great wit, and well accomplished, who had sucked in the poison of heresy, and who hid the corruptions of their heart under a fair and pleasing outside. He alone has broken off that dangerous commerce in which my own imprudence had engaged me; and has hindered me from following the bent of my easy nature, by discovering to me the snares which were laid for me. If Don Ignatius had given me no other proof of his kindness, I know not how I could be able to return it, by any acknowledgments I could make: for, in short, without his assistance, I could not have defended myself from those young men, so fair in their outward carriage, and so corrupt in the bottom of their hearts."

We may conclude, from this authentic testimony, that Xavier, far from carrying the faith to the remotest nations of idolaters, was in danger to make shipwreck of his own; had he not fallen into the hands of such a friend as was Ignatius, who detested even the least appearance of heresy, and whose sight was sharp enough to discover heretics, how speciously soever they were disguised.

It was not sufficient to have only preserved Xavier from error, but it was farther necessary to wean him altogether from the world: these favourable dispositions which appeared in him, encouraged Ignatius to pursue his design, and gave him hope of a fortunate success. Having one day found Xavier more than ordinarily attentive, he repeated to him these words more forcibly than ever: "What will it profit a man to gain the whole world, and to lose his own soul?" After which he told him, that a mind so noble and so great as his, ought not to confine itself to the vain honours of this world; that celestial glory was the only lawful object of his ambition; and that right reason would require him to prefer that which was eternally to last, before what would vanish like a dream.

Then it was that Xavier began to see into the emptiness of earthly greatness, and found himself touched with the love of heavenly things. But these first impressions of grace had not all their effect immediately: he made frequent reflections within himself, of what the man of God had said to him; and it was not without many serious thoughts, and after many a hard struggling, that, being overcome at length by the power of those eternal truths, he took up a solid resolution, of living according to the maxims of the gospel, and of treading in his footsteps, who had made him sensible of his being gone astray.

He resigned himself therefore to the conduct of Ignatius, after the example of Le Fevre, who had already reformed his life, and was inflamed with the zeal of edifying others. The directions of a guide so well enlightened, made easy to Xavier the paths of that perfection which were hitherto unknown to him. He learnt from his new master, that the first step which a sincere convert is to make, is to labour in the subduing of his darling passion. As vainglory had the greatest dominion over him, his main endeavours, from the very beginning, were to humble himself, and to confound his own pride in the sense of his emptiness, and of his sins. But well knowing that he could not tame the haughtiness of the soul without mortifying the flesh, he undertook the conquest of his body, by haircloth, by fasting, and other austerities of penance.

When his time of vacancies was come, he performed his spiritual exercises, which his lectures of philosophy had till then hindered. Those very exercises I mean, which Ignatius, inspired of God, had composed at Manreze; and of which I have drawn the model, in the life of that holy founder of the society of Jesus.

He began his retirement with an extraordinary fervour, even to the passing of four days entire without taking any nourishment. His contemplations were wholly busied, day and night, on divine matters. And an ancient memorial assures us, that he went to his devotions with his hands and feet tied; either to signify, that he was desirous to do nothing, but by the inspiration of the Holy Spirit, or to give himself the same usage which was given to the man in the parable of the gospel; "who dared to appear in the wedding-room, without cloathing himself in wedding-garments."

By meditating at his leisure on the great truths of Christianity, and especially on the mysteries of our Saviour, according to the method of Ignatius, he was wholly changed into another man; and the humility of the cross appeared to him more amiable than all the glories of the world. These new insights caused him, without the least repugnance, to refuse a canonry of Pampeluna, which was offered him at that time, and was very considerable, both in regard of the profits and of the dignity. He formed also, during his solitude, the design of glorifying God by all possible means, and of employing his whole life for the salvation of souls.

On these foundations, having finished the course of philosophy which he read, and which had lasted three years and a half, according to the custom of those times, he studied in divinity, by the counsel of Ignatius, whose scholar he openly declared himself to be.

In the mean time, Ignatius, who found in himself an inward call to the Holy-Land, for the conversion of Jews and Infidels, discovered his intentions to Xavier, which he had already communicated to Le Fevre, and four other learned young men, who had embraced his form of life.

All the seven engaged themselves, by promise to each other, and by solemn vows to God Almighty, to forsake their worldly goods, and undertake a voyage to Jerusalem; or in case that, in the compass of a year, they could not find an accommodation of passing the seas, that they would cast themselves at the feet of our holy Father, for the service of the church, into whatever part of the world he would please to send them.

They made these vows at Montmartre, on the day of our Lady's assumption, in the year 1534. That holy place, which has been watered with the blood of martyrs, and where their bodies are still deposited, inspired a particular devotion into Xavier, and possessed him with a fervent desire of martyrdom.

Towards the end of the year following, he went from Paris, in the company of Le Fevre, Laynez, Salmeron, Rodriguez, Bobadilla, and three other divines, whom Le Fevre had gained in the absence of Ignatius, who, for important reasons, was obliged to go before, and who was waiting for them at Venice.

Somewhat before their departure, Xavier, who was sometimes too far transported by the fervency of his soul, had tied his arms and thighs with little cords, to mortify himself, for some kind of vain satisfaction which he took in out-running and over-leaping his young companions; for he was very active; and, amongst all the recreations used by scholars, he liked none but the exercises of the body.

Though the cords were very straight about him, yet he imagined they would not hinder him from travelling on foot. But he had scarcely begun his journey, when he was taken with extreme pains. He bore them as well as he was able; and dissembled them, till his strength failed him. His motion had swelled his thighs, and indented the cords so deep into his flesh, that they were hardly visible; insomuch that the chirurgeons, to whom his fellows discovered them, plainly said, that any incisions which could be made, would serve only to increase his pains, and that the ill was incurable.

In this dangerous conjuncture, Le Fevre, Laynez, and the rest, had recourse to Almighty God, and not in vain. Xavier waking the next morning, found the cords fallen down, the swelling wholly taken away from his thighs, and the marks of the cords only remaining on his flesh. They joined in actions of thanksgiving to the Almighty, for his providential care already shewn in their behalf; and though the ways were very rugged, in the inclemency of that season, yet they cheerfully pursued their journey.

Xavier was serviceable to his companions on all occasions, and was always beforehand with them in the duties of charity; whether it were, that, being naturally officious, and of a warm temper, he was more eager to employ himself for them; or that his health, miraculously restored, rendered him more obliging and charitable towards those by whose prayers it was recovered.

When they were arrived at Venice, their breathings were only after the holy places. Ignatius, whom they were ravished to see again, and whom they acknowledged for their common father, was of opinion, that while they were waiting the opportunity of going to receive the Pope's blessing for their voyage to Jerusalem, each of them should employ himself on works of charity, in the hospitals of the town.

Xavier, whose lot fell in the hospital of the incurable, was not satisfied only with busying himself all day, in dressing sick men's sores, in making their beds, and doing them more inferior service, but also passed whole nights in watching by them. But his care and pains were not confined to the succour of their bodies. Though he was wholly ignorant of the Italian tongue, he frequently spoke of God to them; and, above all things, exhorted the greatest libertines to repentance, by causing them to comprehend, in the best manner he was able, that though their corporal maladies were incurable, yet the diseases of their souls were not so; that how enormous soever our offences were, we ought always to rely on God's mercy; and that a desire of being sincerely converted, was only requisite in sinners for obtaining the grace of their conversion.

One of these sick alms-men had an ulcer, which was horrible to the sight, but the noisomeness of the stench was yet more insupportable; every one shunned the miserable creature, not enduring so much as to approach him; and Xavier once found a great repugnance in himself to attend him: but at the same time, he called to his remembrance a maxim of Ignatius, that we make no progress in virtue, but by vanquishing ourselves; and that the occasion of making a great sacrifice, was too precious to be lost. Being fortified with these thoughts, and encouraged by the example of St Catharine de Sienna, which came into his mind, he embraced the sick person, applied his mouth to the ulcer, surmounted his natural loathing, and sucked out the corruption. At the same moment his repugnance vanished; and after that, he had no farther trouble in the like cases: of so great importance it is to us, once to have thoroughly overcome ourselves.

Two months were passed away in these exercises of charity. After which he set forward on his journey to Rome with the other disciples of Ignatius, who himself stayed behind alone at Venice. They underwent great hardships in their way. It rained continually, and bread was often wanting to them, even when their strength was wasted. Xavier encouraged his companions, and sustained himself by that apostolic spirit with which God replenished him from that time forwards, and which already made him in love with pain and sufferings.

Being arrived at Rome, his first care was to visit the churches, and to consecrate himself to the ministry of the gospel, upon the sepulchre of the holy apostles. He had the opportunity of speaking more than once before the Pope: for the whole company of them being introduced into the Vatican, by Pedro Ortiz, that Spanish doctor whom they had formerly known at Paris, and whom the emperor had sent to Rome for the affair concerning the marriage of Catharine of Arragon, queen of England, Paul the Third, who was a lover of learning, and who was pleased to be entertained at his table with the conversation of learned men, commanded that these strangers, whose capacity he had heard so extremely praised, should be admitted to see him for many days successively; and that in his presence they should discourse concerning divers points of school-divinity.

Having received the benediction of our holy father for their voyage to the Holy Land, and obtained the permission for those amongst them who were not in sacred orders, to receive them, they returned to Venice. Xavier there made his vows of poverty and perpetual chastity, together with the rest, in the hands of Jeronimo Veralli, the Pope's nuncio; and having again taken up his post in the hospital of the incurable, he resumed his offices of charity, which his journey to Rome had constrained him to interrupt, and continued in those exercises till the time of his embarkment.

In the mean time, the war which was already kindled betwixt the Venetians and the Turk, had broken the commerce of the Levant, and stopt the passage to the Holy Land; insomuch, that the ship of the pilgrims of Jerusalem went not out that year, according to the former custom.

This disappointment wonderfully afflicted Xavier; and the more, because he not only lost the hope of seeing those places which had been consecrated by the presence and the blood of Jesus Christ, but was also bereft of an occasion of dying for his divine Master. Yet he comforted himself in reflecting on the method of God's providence; and at the same time, not to be wanting in his duty to his neighbour, he disposed himself to receive the orders of priesthood, and did receive them with those considerations of awful dread, and holy confusion, which are not easy to be expressed.

The town appeared to him an improper place for his preparation, in order to his first mass. He sought out a solitary place, where, being separated from the communication of man, he might enjoy the privacies of God. He found this convenience of a retirement near Monteselice, not far from Padua: it was a miserable thatched cottage, forsaken of inhabitants, and out of all manner of repair. Thus accommodated, he passed forty days, exposed to the injuries of the air, lying on the cold hard ground, rigidly disciplining his body, fasting all the day, and sustaining nature only with a little pittance of bread, which he begged about the neighbourhood; but tasting all the while the sweets of paradise, in contemplating the eternal truths of faith. As his cabin did not unfitly represent to him the stable of Bethlehem, so he proposed to himself frequently the extreme poverty of the infant Jesus, as the pattern of his own; and said within himself, that, since the Saviour of mankind had chosen to be in want of all things, they who laboured after him for the salvation of souls, were obliged, by his example, to possess nothing in this world.

How pleasing soever this loneliness were to him, yet, his forty days being now expired, he left it, to instruct the villages and neighbour-towns, and principally Monteselice, where the people were grossly ignorant, and knew little of the duties of Christianity.

The servant of God made daily exhortations to them, and his penitent aspect gave authority to all his words; insomuch, that only looking on his face, none could doubt but he was come from the wilderness to instruct them in the way to heaven. He employed himself during the space of two or three months in that manner: for, though there was no appearance that any vessel should set sail for the Holy Land, yet Ignatius and his disciples, who had obliged themselves to wait one year in expectation of any such opportunity, would not depart from the territories of the republic till it was totally expired, that they might have nothing to upbraid themselves, in relation to the vow which they had made.

Xavier being thus disposed, both by his retirement, and his exterior employments, at length said his first mass at Vicenza; to which place Ignatius had caused all his company to resort; and he said it with tears flowing in such abundance, that his audience could not refrain from mixing their own with his.

His austere, laborious life, joined with so sensible a devotion, which often makes too great an impression on the body, so much impaired the strength of his constitution, that he fell sick, not long after his first mass. He was carried into one of the own hospitals, which was so crowded, and so poor, that Xavier had in it but the one half of a wretched bed, and that too in a chamber which was open on every side. His victuals were no better than his lodging, and never was sick man more destitute of human succours. But, in requital, heaven was not wanting to him.

He was wonderfully devoted to St Jerome; and had often had recourse to that blessed doctor of the church for the understanding of difficult places in the scripture. The saint appeared to him one night, refulgent in his beams of glory, and gave him consolation in his sickness; yet, at the same time, declaring to him, that a far greater affliction than the present was waiting for him at Bolognia, where himself and one of his companions were to pass the winter; that some of them should go to Padua, some to Rome, others to Ferrara, and the remainder of them to Sienna.

This apparition fortified Xavier so much, that he recovered suddenly; yet whether he had some doubts concerning it, or was of opinion that he ought to keep it secret, he said nothing of it at that time. But that which then happened to him made it evident, that the vision was of God: for Ignatius, who was ignorant of what had been revealed to Xavier, having assembled his disciples, gave them to understand, that since the gate of the Holy Land was shut against them, they ought not any longer to defer the offering of their service to the Pope; that it was sufficient if some of them went to Rome, while the rest of them dispersed themselves in the universities of Italy, to the end, they might inspire the fear of God into the scholars, and gather up into their number some young students of the greatest parts. Ignatius appointed them their several stations, just as they had been foreshewn by St Jerome; and that of Bolognia fell to the share of Xavier and Bobadilla.

After their arrival at Bolognia, Xavier went to say a mass at the tomb of St Dominic; for he had a particular veneration for the founder of that order, whose institution was for the preaching of the gospel.

A devout virgin, whose name was Isabella Casalini, seeing him at the altar, judged him to be a man of God; and was led by some interior motion to speak to this stranger priest when his mass was ended. She was so much edified, and so satisfied with the discourse of Xavier, that she immediately informed her uncle, at whose house she lodged, of this treasure which she had discovered.

Jerome Casalini, who was a very considerable clergyman, both in regard of his noble blood, and of his virtue, went in search of this Spanish priest, upon the account which was given of him by his niece; and, having found him at the hospital, he importuned him so much to take a lodging in his house, that Xavier could not in civility refuse him. But the holy man would never accept of his table, of whose house he had accepted. He begged his bread from door to door according to his usual custom; and lived on nothing but the alms which was given him in the town.

Every day, after having celebrated the divine mysteries in St Lucy's church, of which Casalini was curate, he there heard the confessions of such as presented themselves before him: after which he visited the prisons and the hospitals, catechised the children, and preached to the people.

'Tis true, he spoke but very ill; and his language was only a kind of Lingua Franca, a confused medley of Italian, French, and Spanish: but he pronounced it with so much vehemence, and the matter of his sermons was so solid, that his ill accent and his improper phrases were past by. His audience attended to him, as to a man descended from above, and his sermon being ended, came to cast themselves at his feet, and make confession.

These continual labours, during a very sharp winter, threw him into a relapse of sickness, much more dangerous than the former; as it were to verify the prediction of St Jérome; for he was seized with a quartan ague, which was both malignant and obstinate; insomuch that it cast him into an extreme faintness, and made him as meagre as a skeleton. In the mean time, lean and languishing as he was, he ceased not to crawl to the public places, and excite passengers to repentance. When his voice failed him, his wan and mortified face, the very picture of death, seemed to speak for him, and his presence alone had admirable effects.

Jerome Casalini profited so well by the instructions and example of the holy man, that he arrived in a short space to a high degree of holiness: the greater knowledge he had of him, he the more admired him, as he himself related. And it is from this virtuous churchman chiefly, that we have this account of Xavier, that having laboured all the day, he passed the night in prayer; that on Friday saying the mass of the passion, he melted into tears, and was often ravished in his soul; that he spoke but seldom, but that all his words were full of sound reason, and heavenly grace.

While Xavier was thus employing his labours at Bolognia, he was recalled to Rome by Father Ignatius; who had already presented himself before the Pope, and offered him the service both of himself and his companions. Pope Paul the Third accepted the good will of these new labourers; enjoining them to begin their work in Rome, and preach under the authority of the Holy See. The principal churches were assigned them; and that of St Laurence in Damaso was allotted to Xavier.

Being now freed from his quartan ague, and his strength being again restored, he preached with more vigour and vehemence than ever.

Death, the last judgment, and the pains of hell, were the common subject of his sermons. He proposed those terrible truths after a plain manner, but withal so movingly, that the people, who came in crowds to hear him preach, departed out of the church in a profound silence; and thought less of giving praises to the preacher, than of converting their own souls to God.

The famine, which laid waste the city of Rome at that time, gave opportunity to the ten stranger-priests, to relieve an infinite number of miserable people, oppressed with want, and unregarded. Xavier was ardent above the rest, to find them places of accommodation, and to procure alms for their subsistence. He bore them even upon his shoulders to the places which were provided for them, and attended them with all imaginable care.

In the mean time, James Govea, a Portuguese, who had been acquainted with Ignatius, Xavier, and Le Fevre, at Paris, and who was principal of the college of Saint Barbe, when they lived together there, being come to Rome on some in portant business, for which he was sent thither by John III. King of Portugal, and seeing the wonderful effects of their ministry, wrote to the king, as he had formerly done from Paris, on the reports which were spread of them, that such men as these, knowing, humble, charitable, inflamed with zeal, indefatigable in labour, lovers of the cross, and who aimed at nothing but the honour of Almighty God, were fit to be employed in the East-Indies, to plant and propagate the faith. He adjoined, that if his majesty were desirous of these excellent men, he had only to ask them from the Pope, who had the absolute disposition of them.

John III., the most religious prince then living, wrote thereupon to his ambassador, Don Pedro Mascaregnas, and ordered him to obtain from his Holiness, six at least of those apostolic men, which had been commended to him by Govea. The Pope having heard the proposition of Mascaregnas, remitted the whole business to Father Ignatius, for whom he had already a great consideration, and who had lately presented to his Holiness the model of the new order, which he and his companions were desirous to establish.

Ignatius, who had proposed to himself no less a design than the reformation of the whole world, and who saw the urgent necessities of Europe, infected with heresy on every side, returned this answer to Mascaregnas, that often, which was their whole number, he could spare him at the most but two persons. The Pope approved this answer, and ordered Ignatius to make the choice himself. Thereupon Ignatius named Simon Rodriguez, a Portuguese, and Nicholas Bobadilla, a Spaniard. The first of these was, at that time, employed at Sienna, and the other in the kingdom of Naples, as they had been commissioned by the Holy Father. Though Rodriguez was languishing under a quartan ague, when he was recalled from Sienna, yet he failed not to obey the summons; and shortly after embarking on a ship of Lisbon which went off from Civita Vecchia, carried with him Paul de Camerin, who, some months before, had joined himself to their society.

As for Bobadilla, he was no sooner come to Rome, than he fell sick of a continued fever; and it may be said, that his distemper was the hand of heaven, which had ordained another in his stead for the mission of the Indies. For sometimes that which appears but chance, or a purely natural effect in the lives of men, is a disposition of the Divine Providence which moves by secret ways to its own proposed ends; and is pleased to execute those designs, by means as easy as they are powerful.

Mascaregnas, who had finished his embassy, and was desirous to carry with him into Portugal the second missioner who had been promised him, was within a day of his departure, when Bobadilla arrived. Ignatius seeing him in no condition to undertake a voyage, applied himself to God for his direction, in the choice of one to fill his place, or rather to make choice of him whom God had chosen; for he was immediately enlightened from above, and made to understand, that Xavier was that vessel of election. He called for him at the same instant, and being filled with the Divine Spirit, "Xavier," said he, "I had named Bobadilla for the Indies, but the Almighty has nominated you this day. I declare it to you from the vicar of Jesus Christ. Receive an employment committed to your charge by his Holiness, and delivered by my mouth, as if it were conferred on you by our blessed Saviour in person. And rejoice for your finding an opportunity, to satisfy that fervent desire, which we all have, of carrying the faith into remote countries. You have not here a narrow Palestine, or a province of Asia, in prospect, but a vast extent of ground, and innumerable kingdoms. An entire world is reserved for your endeavours, and nothing but so large a field is worthy of your courage and your zeal. Go, my brother, where the voice of God has called you; where the Holy See has sent you, and kindle those unknown nations, with the flame that burns within you."

Xavier, wholly confounded in himself with these expressions of Ignatius, with tears of a tender affection in his eyes, and blushing in his countenance, answered him, that he could not but be astonished, that he should pitch upon a man, so weak, and pusillanimous as himself, for an enterprize which required no less than an apostle: that nevertheless he was ready to obey the commands of heaven; and that he offered himself, with the whole power of his soul, to do and suffer all things for the salvation of the Indies. After which, giving leave to his internal joy to break out, and to diffuse itself, he more confidently said to Father Ignatius, that his desires were now accomplished; that for a long time he had sighed after the Indies without daring to declare it; and that he hoped, from those idolatrous nations, to have the honour of dying for Jesus Christ, which had been denied him in the Holy Land.

He added, in the height of these transports, that at length he saw that clearly, of which God had often given him a glimpse, under some mysterious figures. In effect, Xavier had frequently dreamed by night, that he carried on his shoulders a gigantic and very swarthy Indian; and opprest with this strong imagination, he groaned and sighed, in that uneasy slumber, as one out of breath, and labouring under an intolerable burden; insomuch that the noise of his groans and heavings waked those who were lodged in the same chamber; and, one night it happening that Father Laynez being awakened by it, asked him what it was that troubled him: Xavier immediately told his dream, and added, that it put him into a sweat, with big drops over all his body.

Besides this, he once beheld, either in a dream, or in a trance, vast oceans full of tempests and of rocks, desart islands, barbarous countries, hunger and thirst raging every where, nakedness, multiplicity of labours, with bloody persecution, and imminent dangers of death and of destruction. In the midst of this ghastly apparition, he cried aloud, "yet more, O my God, yet more!" and Father Simon Rodriguez heard these words distinctly; but however he importuned him to declare their meaning, he would discover nothing at that time, till embarking for the Indies, he revealed the mystery.

Such ideas, always present in his imagination, filled his familiar discourses with notions of a new world, and the conversion of infidels. While he was speaking on that subject, his face was on a fire, and the tears came into his eyes. This was testified of him by Father Jerome Dominic, who, before he entered into the Society, had conversed with him at Bolognia, where a strict friendship was made betwixt them.

As Xavier was advertised of this voyage to the Indies but the day before Mascaregnas departed, he had but time enough to piece up his cassock, bid his friends farewell, and go to kiss the feet of our Holy Father.

Paul III., overjoyed, that under his pontificate a gate should be opened to the gospel, in the Oriental Indies, received him with a most fatherly affection, and excited him to assume such thoughts, as were worthy of so high an undertaking; telling him for his encouragement, that the Eternal Wisdom is never failing to supply us with strength, to prosecute the labours to which it has ordained us, even though they should surpass all human abilities. He must, indeed, prepare himself for many sufferings; but the affairs of God succeeded not but by the ways of suffering, and that none could pretend to the honour of an apostleship, but by treading in the steps of the apostles, whose lives were but one continual cross, and a daily death; that heaven had employed him in the mission of St Thomas, the apostle of the Indies, for the conquest of souls; that it became him to labour generously, in reviving the faith in those countries, where it had been planted by that great apostle; and that if it were necessary for him to shed his blood, for the glory of Christ Jesus, he should account it his happiness to die a martyr.

It seemed that God himself had spoken by the mouth of his vicegerent, such impression had these words on the mind and heart of Xavier. They inspired into him a divine vigour; and in his answer to his Holiness, there shone through a profound humility such a magnanimity of soul, that Paul III. had from that very minute a certain presage of those wonderful events which afterwards arrived. Therefore the most Holy Father, having wished him the special assistance of God in all his labours, tenderly embraced him, more than once, and gave him a most ample benediction.

Xavier departed in the company of Mascaregnas the 15th of March, in the year 1540, without any other equipage besides his breviary. In giving his last adieu to Father Ignatius, he cast himself at his feet, and with all humility desired his blessing; and, in taking leave of Laynez, he put into his hands a small memorial, which he had written, and signed.

This memorial, which is still preserved at Rome, contains, that he approves, as much as depends on him, the rules and constitutions, which shall be drawn up, by Ignatius and his companions; that he elects Ignatius to be their general, and, in failure of him, Le Fevre; that he consecrates himself to God, by the three vows, of poverty, chastity, and obedience, in the Society of Jesus, when it shall be raised into a religious order, by the apostolical authority.

The conclusion of that affair was daily expected; and indeed it was happily finished, before the ending of the year, in that almost miraculous manner, as is related in the Life of St Ignatius.

His journey from Rome to Lisbon was all the way by land, and was above three months. Xavier had a horse allowed him, by order from the ambassador; but they were no sooner on their way, than he made him common. The Father often alighted to ease the servants who followed on foot; or exchanged his horse with others, who were not so well mounted. At the inns he was every man's servant, even to the rubbing of the horses, by an excess of humility, which, on those occasions, caused him to forget the dignity of his character. He resigned his chamber and his bed to those who wanted them; and never lodged but either on the ground, or on the litter in the stable. In the rest of his actions, ever cheerful, and pleasant in discourse, which made all men desirous of his company; but always mixing somewhat with that gaiety, which was edifying both to the masters and the servants, and inspired them alike with thoughts of piety.

They went by Loretto, where they rested at the least eight days; after which they continued their journey by Bolognia. From thence, Xavier wrote to Ignatius, in this manner:

"I received, on the holiday of Easter, the letter which you wrote and inclosed in the packet of my lord ambassador. God only knows my joy in receiving it. Believing, as I do, that we shall never entertain each other in this world, by any other way than that of writing, and that we shall never see each other but in heaven, it concerns us, that little time we have to live in this place of exile, to give ourselves the mutual consolation of frequent letters. The correspondence, on my part, shall be exactly kept; for being convinced, by the reasons which you gave me at our parting, that a commerce of this nature ought to be established, in a regular method, betwixt the colonies and the mother country, I have resolved, that in whatever parts of the world I shall reside, or any members of our Society with me, to maintain a strict communication with you, and with the fathers at Rome, and send you as large an account, as possibly I can, of any news concerning us. I have taken my opportunity of seeing the Cardinal of Invrea, as you gave me in command, and have discoursed at leisure with him. He received me with much goodness, and offered me, with great civility, his interest, for our common cause. In the midst of the discourse, which we had together, I threw myself at his feet, and kissed his hand, in the name of all our Society. As much as I can gather by his words, he extremely approves the manner of our living.

"As concerning my lord ambassador, he loads me with so many favours, that I should never conclude, if I began to relate them. And I know not how I could suffer the many good offices he does me, if I had not some hope of repaying him in the Indies, at the expence of my life itself. On Palm-Sunday I heard his confession, and after him many of his domestic servants; I communicated them afterwards, in the holy chapel of Loretto, where I said mass. I likewise confessed them, and gave them the communion, on Easter Sunday. My lord ambassador's almoner recommends himself to your good prayers, and has promised to bear me company to the Indies. I am more taken up with confessions here, than I was in Rome, at St Lewis. I heartily salute all our fathers; and if I name not every one of them in particular, I desire them to believe, 'tis neither from my want of memory, or affection.

"Your brother and servant in Jesus Christ, FRANCIS." _from Bolognia, March_ 31. 1540.

The whole town of Bolognia was in motion at the approach of Father Xavier: they were wonderfully affected to him, and in a manner esteemed him their apostle: both great and small were desirous of seeing him, and most of them discovered the state of their conscience to him; many of them proffered themselves to go along with him to the Indies; all of them shed tears at his departure, as thinking they should never more behold him.

Jerome Casalini, curate of St Lucy, who had lodged him the year before, was most particularly kind to him at his return: he obliged him to accept of his house once more; and his church became as it were the public rendezvous, where Xavier heard an infinite number of confessions.

In the rest of this long journey, there happened two or three passages, which were sufficiently remarkable. A domestic servant to the ambassador, who rode before as harbinger, to take up lodgings for the train, a violent and brutal man, being reprehended by his lord for having been negligent in his duty, fell into a horrible fit of passion, as soon as he was out of Mascaregnas his presence. Xavier heard him, but took no notice of it at that time, for fear of provoking him to any farther extravagance. But the next morning, when the same person set out before the company, according to his custom, he spurred after him at full speed. He found him lying under his horse, who was fallen with him from a precipice, the man sorely bruised, and the horse killed outright. "Wretched creature," said the father to him, "what had become of thee, if thou hadst died of this fall?" These few words made him sensible of his furious expressions, for which he sincerely asked pardon of Almighty God; and Xavier alighting, mounted him on his own horse, and walked on foot by him, to their lodging.

Another time, the gentleman of the horse attempting to pass a small river, which was very deep and rapid, the current carried away both man and horse, and the whole company gave him for lost. Xavier, moved with compassion for the danger of his soul, because, having had a call from heaven to enter into a religious life, he had not followed the motions of grace, but remained in the world, began to implore God in his behalf. The ambassador, who had a great kindness for him, joined in that devout action, and commanded the whole train to follow their example. They had scarcely opened their mouths for him, when the man and horse, who were both drowning, came again above water, and were carried to the bank. The gentleman was drawn out, pale in his countenance, and half dead. When he had recovered his senses, Xavier demanded of him, what thoughts he had, when he was at the point of perishing? He freely acknowledged, that the religious life, to which God had called him, then struck upon his soul; with dismal apprehensions, for having neglected the means of his salvation. He protested afterwards, as Xavier himself relates, in one of his letters, that, in that dreadful moment, the remorse of his conscience, and the sense of God's judgments on souls unfaithful to their vocation, were more terrible to him, than the horrors even of death itself. He spoke of eternal punishments, with expressions so lively and so strong, as if he had already felt them, and was returned from hell. He frequently said, (as the saint has assured us,) that, by a just judgment of eternal God, those who, during their life, made no preparations for their death, had not the leisure to think on God when death surprised them.

The ambassador, and all his people, doubted not, but the safety of this gentleman was to be ascribed to the merits of the saint: but Xavier himself believed it to be the pure effect of the ambassador's devotion; for thus he writes to father Ignatius concerning it--"Our Lord was pleased to give ear to the fervent prayers of his servant Mascaregnas, which he made with tears in his eyes, for the deliverance of the poor creature, whom he looked upon as lost; and who was taken from the jaws of death by a most evident miracle."

In passing over the Alps, the ambassador's secretary alighting to walk in a difficult way, which he could not well observe, by reason of the snows, his foot happened to slip on a sharp descent, and he rolled down into a precipice: he had tumbled to the very bottom, if, in falling, his clothes had not taken hold on one of the crags of the rock, where he remained hanging over the depths without ability, either to disengage himself, or get up again. Those who followed, made towards him, but the horror of that abyss stopt short the most daring: Xavier only made not the least demur; he descended the precipice, and lending his hand to the secretary, by little and little dragged him up.

Being gotten out of France, and having passed the Pyreneans, on the side of Navarre, when they were now approaching Pampeluna, Mascaregnas bethought himself, that Father Francis, for by that name Xavier was usually called, had not spoken one word of going to the castle of Xavier, which was but little distant from their road: he remembered him of it, and was even so importunate with him, as to say, that since he was about to leave Europe, and perhaps never more to see it, he could not in decency dispense with giving a visit to his family, and taking his last leave of his mother, who was yet living.

But all the arguments of Mascaregnas wrought no effect upon a man, who, having forsaken all things for the love of God, was of opinion, that he had nothing remaining in this world; and who also was persuaded, that flesh and blood are enemies to the apostolical spirit. He turned not out of the road, but only said to the ambassador, that he deferred the sight of his relations till he should visit them in heaven; that this transient view would be accompanied but with melancholy and sadness, the common products of a last farewell, but in heaven he should eternally behold them with pleasure, and without the least allay of sorrow.

Mascaregnas had already a high idea of Xavier's virtue; but this wonderful disengagement from the world yet more increased the esteem which he had of him; insomuch, that before they reached Portugal, he sent an express to King John III. with no other errand, than to inform him of the holiness of this second missioner to the Indies.

They arrived at Lisbon towards the end of June; and Xavier retired to the hospital of All Saints, where Rodriguez, who came by sea, had taken up his lodging. He found him much weakened with a quartan ague, which had not left him; and embraced him just at the moment when his fit was coming on him. But whether it were, that the extreme joy which Rodriguez found, so unexpectedly to see him, dissipated the humour which caused his disease, or that the embraces of Xavier had from that time an healing virtue; certain it is that the fit came not, and from thenceforward the sick man entirely recovered of that distemper.

Three or four days after, they were both called to court. The king and queen, who were in company together, received Xavier as a saint, on the report of Mascaregnas, and entertained him with all imaginable shews of kindness. They asked them diverse questions concerning their way of living; by what accident their new Society came to be formed; and what was the ground and ultimate design of it; and at last desired to be informed by them, from whence proceeded that strange persecution, which was raised in Rome against their body, which had made so great a noise over all Europe. Xavier made answer to all these demands in few words, but so very pertinently, as much satisfied both their majesties: they gave great approbation, (as himself relates in his letter from Lisbon to Ignatius,) to what he said, concerning the discipline of our houses, the quality of our ministry, and the spirit and model of our foundation.

In the midst of the conversation, the king sent for the Prince of Portugal, his son Don Juan, and the Infanta Maria, his daughter, that the two missioners might see them. And from thence his majesty took occasion of relating to them, how many children he had still living, and how many he had lost, which turned the discourse on the education of youth; and before the fathers were dismissed, the king recommended to their care, an hundred young gentlemen, who were bred at court.

Though an officer of the palace had orders to prepare an handsome lodging, with good accommodation, for Xavier and Rodriguez, they returned to their hospital, and there continued. They would not so much as receive their entertainment of diet, which was assigned them from court, but went the round of the city begging alms at their appointed hours, and lived in poverty, according to the manner of life which they had prescribed themselves.

The fleet not being to set sail till the next spring, and these apostolical persons not knowing what it was to live in idleness, Xavier was not satisfied only to instruct those young gentlemen in piety, whom the king had committed to his charge; he gave himself an employment, and did at Lisbon what he had done at Venice, Bolognia, and Rome, for the space of two years and more. But, besides that he assisted the sick in the hospital day and night, visited the prisoners every day, and catechised the children many times in the week, he often discoursed with the principal persons of the court, and engaged them in the spiritual exercises of Ignatius.

At first he preached not in the churches, judging, that the ministries of the gospel ought to begin with less public actions; and went not into the pulpit, without being first requested by the king, who one day sending for him to the palace, acquainted him with the desire he had to hear him preach; and told him, "That the Bishop of Lisbon was of opinion, that they ought not any longer to defer his public exhortations."

Father Simon Rodriguez laboured also on his part, in the service of his neighbour, according to the same method, and with the same spirit.

In the mean time, Martin d'Azpilcueta, surnamed the doctor of Navarre, who was uncle to Xavier, on the mother's side, and who was chief professor of divinity in the university of Coimbra, having heard the news of his nephew's arrival, wrote earnestly to the king, that it would please him to send Father Francis to him. He added, that in case the Father might have leave to remain with him till the departure of the fleet, he would oblige himself to make two new lectures, at his own expence, the one in canon-law, the other in mystical divinity. And farther, that in few years afterwards he would follow Xavier to the Indies, and preach the gospel in conjunction with him, to the eastern idolaters.

These letters prevailed nothing; the man, who had refused so much as to turn out of his way to see his mother, was bent against the taking of a journey, and forsaking his important business to visit one of his relations. The king retained Xavier at Lisbon, at the request of Xavier himself; and the father wrote a letter of excuse to the doctor of Navarre, who had written two to him full of tenderness and friendship. As that doct&r was unsatisfied with that kind of life, which his nephew had embraced, so Xavier resolved him, on that point, in this manner. "For what concerns our institute, of which so many reports are now raised, I have but one word, at present, to say of it. 'Tis of little consequence, illustrious doctor, to be judged by men, especially by such, who will needs be judging before they understand the matter, and know the merits of the cause."

As to his intention of going to the Indies, he desired him to think no farther of it; for thus Navarre relates that passage in his manual: "I had resolved to have ended my days in those parts, if Xavier, in consideration of my great age, had not thought me incapable of those labours which attend his mission: and if he had not written to me at his departure, that I should comfort myself for his absence, by the hope of seeing each other in the celestial kingdom."

Our two missioners laboured not in vain at Lisbon. From the very beginning of their ministry, devotion began to spread amongst the people. All men ran to the blessed sacrament, which before was never thought on but in Lent: and this holy custom diffused itself insensibly through all the towns of Portugal Many, who had deferred their conversion from time to time, now on the sudden gave themselves up to God, and even renounced the world. The most inveterate enemies were sincerely reconciled, and the most impudent harlots abandoned their prostitute way of living.

But this change of manners was most particularly apparent at the court: the king, who was truly religious, and full of goodness, was the first to declare himself against those vices which usually infect the palaces of princes. And that he might introduce a reformation by degrees, not only into his house, bat also dilate it through his whole kingdom, he obliged all the young courtiers to confess themselves once a week; for he said, "That if the lords and gentlemen would accustom themselves, from their tender years, to the service and fear of God, they would live with greater Christianity in their riper age: and if persons of quality came once to give good examples of religion, the commonalty, who form themselves according to their model, would not fail to regulate their manners; and therefore the reformation of all degrees in the kingdom consisted chiefly in the virtuous education of young noblemen."

The example of the prince and the young courtiers drew the rest; and thereupon Xavier writes to Ignatius in these terms:

"Nothing can be more regular than the court of Portugal: it resembles rather a religious society, than a secular court. The number of courtiers who come to confession, and are afterwards communicated, every eight days, is so very great, that we are in admiration of it," and are in perpetual thanksgiving for it. We are so taken up with hearing confessions, that if we were twice so many as we are, there would be employment more than enough for us. We are sitting on the confession-seat all the day long, and part of the night, though none but courtiers are permitted to come to us.

"I remember, that I observed, when the king was at Almerin, those who waited on him, from all parts of the kingdom, about their own affairs, as the custom is, were in great admiration at this new court-mode; and when they beheld the young gentlemen at the sacrament of the altar, every Sunday and holiday, with great reverence, they thought themselves in another world. But the greatest part of them imitating that which they admired, drew near to the tribunal of penance, and the holy table. Had we confessors enow to attend the crowds that come to court, no man would venture to apply himself to the king for any business, before he had been first with God, and were well with him."

The two labourers in God's harvest were so exhausted with their pains, that at length they were constrained to accept of the diet which was provided for them by the king's appointment; for they judged their time was better employed in the service of souls, than in begging their daily bread about the streets. Yet they omitted not to ask alms once or twice a-week, that they might not disuse themselves from the spirit of mortification and poverty. With these considerations, they reserved but little of what was sent them from the palace, and distributed the rest among the poor.

On the other side, the perpetual labour of confessions reduced them to preach but very seldom, for want of leisure. But, all things duly examined, they thought it of more consequence to God's service, to administer the sacrament of penance, than to preach the word; because the court of Portugal was furnished with able preachers, but was much wanting in judicious confessors; which was the very observation that Xavier made in the letter above cited.

These visible and wonderful operations caused the two missioners to be respected as men sent down from heaven, and replenished with the spirit of the Most High; insomuch that all men gave them the surname of apostles, which glorious title still remains with their successors in Portugal. The king, on all occasions, shewed them a most particular affection; and Xavier, ravished with so many expressions of his goodness to them, gives this account of it to Father Ignatius.

"Our whole society stands obliged to his majesty, for his singular favour to us; as well the rest of you at Rome, as we in Portugal. I am given to understand, from the ambassador Mascaregnas, that the king told him, he should be very glad, that all the members of our company might be gathered together, and established here; though on that condition he employed a good part of his revenue for our entertainment."

"This pious prince," says Xavier in another of his letters, "who has so tender an inclination for our society, and who wishes our advancement as much as if he were one of us, has thereby engaged us for ever to his service; and we should be guilty of a most horrible ingratitude, even to be unworthy of life, if we made not a public profession of our service to him, and if every day of our lives we endeavoured not to acknowledge, by our prayers, as far as our weakness will give us leave, all the favours of so generous a protector, and so magnificent a benefactor."

The Prince, Don Henry, who was nominated cardinal not long after, and in process of time came to the crown by the death of Don Sebastian, had not less affection for them than the king his brother. Being grand inquisitor, he gave the fathers an absolute power in his tribunal; and permitted them to discourse freely with all the prisoners of the Inquisition.

Some of the greatest quality in the court were so much edified with the apostolic life of Xavier and Rodriguez, that they were desirous to embrace their institute; as some learned persons of the city had already done. In short, every thing succeeded with them so, that Xavier had some apprehensions concerning this tide of happiness: He bemoaned it sometimes to himself, and said, that prosperity was always formidable, even in the most pious undertakings; that persecution was more desirable, and a much surer mark of Christ's disciples.

The two missioners appointed for the Indies lived in this manner; and impatiently waited for the proper season of navigation. But the king weighing in his mind the great good which they had done, in so short a time, both amongst the nobility and the common people, was desirous to retain them still in Portugal. It seemed reasonable to him, that the interest of his own kingdom ought to be dearer to him than that of foreign nations; and that these new labourers would produce a larger increase in Catholic countries, than amongst barbarians.

Yet that he might undertake nothing without mature deliberation, he called a council, and himself proposed it to them. All of them approved the king's opinion, excepting only the Prince Don Henry; who strongly urged, that Xavier and Rodriguez having been nominated for the new world, by the vicar of our Saviour, it was in a manner to disturb the order of Providence, if he thwarted their intended voyage; that the Indies were equally to be considered with Portugal itself, since they had been conquered by the Portuguese, and were annexed to the imperial crown; that those idolaters had better inclinations towards Christianity than was generally thought; and that they would come over to the faith of their own accord, when they should see amongst them disinterested preachers, free from avarice and ambition.

As the opinions of kings are always prevalent, the reasons of Don Henry were slighted; and it was concluded in council, that the two missioners should not depart the realm. This resolution afflicted them the more sensibly, because they both breathed after those eastern countries; their last recourse was to write to Rome, and interpose the mediation of Father Ignatius. He accordingly moved the Pope in their behalf; but his Holiness refused to make an absolute decision, and remitted the whole affair to Portugal: insomuch that Ignatius sent word to the two fathers, that the king was to them in the place of God, and that it was their duty to pay him a blind obedience. At the same time he also wrote to Don Pedro Mascaregnas, that Xavier and Rodriguez were wholly at the king's command; and that they should always remain in Portugal, in case his majesty desired it. Notwithstanding which, he thought a temperament might be found, which was, that Rodriguez might be retained in Portugal, and Xavier permitted to go for India.

The king was satisfied with this proposal of Ignatius; and believed it to be inspired by God himself. Xavier, transported with joy at the news of it, gave thanks to the Divine Goodness, which had chosen him anew for the mission of the Oriental parts, or rather which had executed its eternal purpose, notwithstanding human opposition.

The time of embarkment being come, he was called one day to the palace: the king discoursed fully with him concerning the present condition of the Indies, and recommended particularly to him the affairs of religion. He likewise gave him in charge, to visit the fortresses of the Portuguese, and take notice how God was served in them; and withal to give him an account of what more was requisite to be done for the establishment of Christianity in those new conquests; and to write frequently on that subject, not only to his ministers, but to his own person.

After this he presented him the four briefs, which had been expedited from Home the same year; in two of which, our Holy Father had constituted Xavier apostolical nuncio, and endued him with ample power for the extending and maintenance of the faith throughout the East; in the third, his Holiness recommended him to David Emperor of Ethiopia; and in the fourth, to all the princes who possessed the isles of the sea, or the continent from the Cape of Good Hope, even beyond the Ganges.

John III. had requested these briefs, and the Pope had freely granted them, with design thereby to make the mission of Father Francis the more illustrious and authentic. The father received them from the hands of the king with profound respect; saying, that as much as his weakness was capable of performing, he should endeavour to sustain the burden, which God and man had laid upon him.

Some few days before he went to sea, Don Antonio d'Ataida, count of Castagnera, who supervised the provisions of the naval army, advertised Xavier to make a note of what things were necessary for him in order to his voyage; assuring him from his majesty, that he should be furnished to his own desire. They want nothing, replied the father with a smile, who have occasion for nothing. I am much obliged to the king for his liberality, and to you for your care of me; but I owe more to the Divine Providence, and you would not wish me to distrust it.

The count of Castagnera, who had an express order from the king, to make a large provision for Father Xavier, was very urgent with him, and importuned him so strongly to take something, for fear, said he, of tempting Providence, which does not every day work miracles, that Xavier, not to appear either obstinate or, presumptuous, demanded some few little books of devotion, for which he foresaw he should have occasion in the Indies, and a thick eloth habit against the excessive colds, which are to be endured in doubling the Cape.

The count, amazed that the father asked for nothing more, besought him to make a better use of the king's offers; but seeing that all his intreaties prevailed nothing, "you shall not be master in every thing," said he, with some kind of heat, "and at the least you cannot possibly refuse a servant to attend you, because I am sure you cannot be without one." "So long as I have the use of these two hands," replied Xavier, "I will have no other servant." "But decency," rejoined the count, "requires, that you should have one, if it were but to maintain the dignity of your character. How shameful would it seem to behold an apostolical legate washing his own linen on the deck, and dressing his own victuals?" "I will take upon me for once," said Xavier, "to serve myself, and others too, without dishonouring my character. So long as I do no ill, I am in no fear of scandalizing my neighbour; nor of debasing that authority with which I am entrusted by the Holy See. They are these human considerations, and false notions of decencies and punctilios, which have reduced the church to that condition in which we now see it."

This positive answer stopped Castagnera's mouth; but afterwards, he gave great commendations of Xavier, and publicly said, "that he found it much more difficult to combat the denials of Father Francis, than to satisfy the craving desires of other men."

The day of his departure being come at length, and all things in a readiness to set sail, Xavier went to the port, with his two companions, whom he carried with him to the Indies; namely, Father Paul de Camerino, an Italian, and Francis Mansilla, a Portuguese, who was not yet in priests orders. Simon Rodriguez bore him company to the fleet; and then it was, that, embracing each other with much tenderness, "My brother," said Xavier, "these are the last words which I shall ever say to you: we shall see each other no more in this present world; let us endure our separation with patience; for most certain it is, that, being well united with our Lord, we shall be united in ourselves; and that nothing shall be able to divide us from the society which we have in Jesus Christ.

"As to what remains, I will, for your satisfaction," added he, "discover to you a secret, which hitherto I have concealed from your knowledge: You may remember, that when we lodged as chamber-fellows, in the hospital at Rome, you heard me crying out one night, 'yet more, O my Lord, yet more!' you have often asked what that exclamation meant; and I have always answered you, that you should not trouble yourself about it: I must now tell you, that I then beheld, (but whether sleeping or waking, God only knows,) all I was to suffer for the glory of Jesus Christ; our Lord infused into me so great a delight for sufferings, that not being able to satiate, myself with those troubles which he had presented to my imagination, I begged of him yet more; and that was the sense of what I pronounced with so much fervency, 'yet more, yet more!' I hope the Divine Goodness will grant me that in India, which he has foreshewn to me in Italy, and that the desires which he inspired into me shall be shortly satisfied."

After these words they embraced each other anew, and parted both of them in tears. When Rodriguez was returned on shore, they gave the signal of departure, and set sail. This was on the 7th of April, in the year 1541, under the command of Don Martin Alphonso de Sosa, viceroy of the Indies; a man of known integrity, and consummate experience in what related to those parts, where he had formerly lived for many years. He was desirous of Xavier's company, in the Admiral, which was called the St James. Xavier went aboard on his own birth-day, entering then on his six-and-thirtieth year. He had resided eight months entire at Lisbon; and forseven years, and somewhat more, had been the professed disciple of Ignatius Loyola.

THE LIFE OF ST FRANCIS XAVIE.

BOOK II

By what way he passes to the Indies. His employment in the ship. He arrives at Mozambique, and what he does there. He falls sick himself, and yet continues to serve the sick. His first prediction Verified by the success. He arrives at Melinda, and there confers with the Mahometans. He passes over to Socotora; his opinion concerning that people. He arrives at Goa. He visits the Bishop of the Indies. The estate of religion in the India at his arrival. His first work at Goa. The first fruits of his labours. His industry to gain the Concubinarians. He is told of the coast of Fishery, and goes thither. This coast is called in the maps La Pescaria. He works a miracle at Cape Comorin. He labours in the salvation of the Paravas. His manner of teaching the Christian faith. He establishes catechists and teachers of the faith to supply ids place. The fruit of his labours on the coast of Fishery. He makes use of children to cure the sick. The zeal of the children against idols and idolaters. The punishment of a pagan, who had despised the admonitions of Father Xavier. The original and character of the Brachmans. He treats with the Brachmans. The conference of Xavier with a famous Brachman. He works divers miracles. He declares himself against the Brachmans. The means whereby he destroyed idolatry. He returns to Goa, and for what reason. The beginning and establishment of the seminary of holy faith. The seminary of holy faith new named the College of St Paul. He returns to the coast of Fishery; his actions there. He goes to the relief of the Christians, on the coast of Fishery. He goes to the kingdom of Travancore, and there labours with great success. God communicates to him the gift of tongues. He is persecuted by the Brachmans. He goes to meet the army of the Badages, and puts them to flight. He prevails upon the king of Travancore to favour the gospel. He raises two from death.

While the Christian religion flourished in Asia, under the emperors of Constantinople, there were two ordinary passages, and both of them short enough towards the Indies: the one by Syria, over the Euphrates and the Persian Gulph; the other by Egypt, over the Arabian Gulph, commonly called the Red Sea. But after the Saracens had possessed themselves of those places, the European Christians finding those passages unsecure for travelling, sought out ways of a larger circuit, to avoid falling into the hands of their most mortal enemies.

The Portuguese were the first who bethought themselves of coasting all Africa, and one part of Arabia and Persia; by taking this compass, the Indies are distant from Portugal about four thousand leagues, and the passengers are constrained to suffer twice the scorching heats of the torrid zone, in going under the equinoctial line, which divides Africa almost in two equal parts.

Don Henry, son of King John I., the most skilful prince of that age in the mathematics, was he who attempted the discovery of those seas, and undertook to double the Cape of Good Hope, upon the account of traffic, which he desired to establish betwixt the crown of Portugal and the emperor of Ethiopia, commonly called Prester John. This enterprise having succeeded, the kings of Portugal, Alphonso V., John II., and Emanuel I., followed it so happily, that, by little and little, they completed the passage to the Indies.

This was the course that Father Xavier held with the fleet of Portugal. He found himself sufficient employment, during the time of the navigation: his first study was to put a stop to those disorders which are commonly occasioned by an idle life on ship-board; and he began with gaming, which is the only recreation, or rather the whole employment, of the seamen.

That he might banish games of chance, which almost always occasion quarrels and swearing, he proposed some little innocent diversions, capable of entertaining the mind, without stirring up the passions. But seeing that, in spite of his endeavours, they were bent on cards and dice, he thought it not convenient to absent himself, but became a looker on, that he might somewhat awe them by his presence; and when they were breaking out into any extravagance, he reclaimed them by gentle and soft reproofs. He shewed concernment in their gains, or in their losses, and offered sometimes to hold their cards.

There were at least a 'thousand persons in the Admiral, men of all conditions: the father made himself all to all, thereby to gain some to Jesus Christ; entertaining every man with such discourse as was most suitable to his calling. He talked of sea affairs to mariners, of war to the soldiery, of commerce to merchants, and of affairs of state to men of quality. His natural gaiety, and obliging humour, gained him a general esteem; the greatest libertines, and most brutal persons, sought his conversation, and were even pleased to hear him speak of God.

He instructed the seamen daily in the principles of religion, of which the greater part were wholly ignorant, or had at the best but a smattering of it; and preached to them on every holiday, at the foot of the main mast. All of them profited by his sermons, and in little time nothing was heard amongst them, which was offensive to the honour of God, or that wounded Christian charity; or touched upon obsceneness, or ill manners. They had a profound veneration for him; with one word only, he appeased their quarrels, and put an end to all their differences.

The viceroy, Don Martin Alphonso de Sosa, invited him from the very first clay to eat at his table; but Xavier humbly excused it, with great acknowledgments, and during all the voyage lived only on what he begged about the ship.

In the mean time, the insufferable colds of Cabo Verde, and the excessive heats of Guinea, together with the stench of the fresh waters, and putrifaction of their flesh provisions under the line, produced many dangerous distempers. The most common was a pestilential fever, accompanied with a kind of cancer, which bred in the mouth, and ulcerated all the gums; the sick being crowded together, spread the infection amongst themselves; and as every one was apprehensive of getting the disease, they had been destitute of all succour, if Father Francis had not taken compassion on them. He wiped them in their sweats, he cleansed their ulcers, he washed their linen, and rendered them all the most abject services; but, above all things, he had care of their consciences, and his principal employment was to dispose them to a Christian death.

These were his perpetual employments; being at the same time himself seized with continued fits of vomiting, and extreme languishments, which lasted two whole months. For his ease and refreshment, Sosa caused him to be accommodated with a larger cabin than was first appointed for him: he accepted of it, but it was only to lodge in it those who were most desperately ill; as for himself, he lay bare upon the deck, without other pillow than the tackling.

He received also the dishes which the viceroy sent him from his table, and divided them amongst those who had most need of nourishment. So many actions of charity gained him the surname of the Holy Father from thenceforward, which continued to him all his life, even, amongst Mahometans and idolaters.

While Xavier employed his time in this manner, the navy following its course, met with rocks and tempests, and contrary tides. After five months of perpetual navigation, it arrived at Mozambique, towards the end of August.

Mozambique is a kingdom situated on the eastern coasts of Africa, inhabited by negroes; a barbarous people, but less savage than their neighbours the Cafres, by reason of the trade which they continually maintain with the Ethiopians and Arabs. There is no port on all the shore to secure shipping from the winds; only one little island is shaped into a haven, both convenient and safe.

This isle, which is but a mile distant from the main land, bears the name of Mozambique, together with the whole kingdom. It was formerly subject to the Saracens, and a Xeriffe Moor commanded it; but since, the Portuguese have made themselves masters of it, and built a fort, to secure the passage of their vessels, and refresh their sea-beaten men, who commonly stay there for some time.

The army under Sosa was constrained to winter in this island, not only because the season was far spent, but also because the sick passengers could no longer support the incommodities of the sea. The place notwithstanding was not very proper for infirm persons, for the air is unwholesome; which proceeds from hence, that the sea overflowing the low-lands of the isle, at the spring tides, the mass of waters there gathered and inclosed is corrupted by the heats; for which reason, the inhabitants are commonly short-lived, but more especially strangers; upon which occasion, Mozambique is generally called the sepulchre of the Portuguese. Besides the intemperance of the air, at the same time, an infectious disease was raging in the country.

Being come ashore, Sosa gave immediate orders to carry the sick of every ship to the hospital, which is in the island, of which the kings of Portugal are founders. Father Xavier followed them; and, with the assistance of his two companions, undertook to attend them all. The undertaking was beyond his strength; but the soul sustains the body of apostolical men, and charity can do all things.

Animated with this new fervour, he went from chamber to chamber, and from bed to bed, giving remedies to some, and administering the last sacrament to others. Every one desired to have him by him; and all acknowledged, that only the sight of his countenance availed them more than a thousand medicines.

Having passed the day in continual labour, he watched all night with dying men, or laid himself down by those who were in most danger, to steal a short unquiet slumber, which was interrupted almost every moment: at the least complaint, or even at a sigh, he was awake, and ran to their relief.

So many fatigues at the length overwhelmed nature, and he fell sick himself of a fever, so violent, and so malignant, that he was blooded seven times in a little space, and was three days in a delirium. At the beginning of his sickness, many were desirous to have withdrawn him from the hospital, where the contagion was frightful, and offered him their own lodgings. He constantly refused their offers, and told them, "That, having made a vow of poverty, he would live and die amongst the poor."

But when the violence of his distemper was somewhat abated, the saint forgot himself to think on others. Sometimes, not being able to sustain his body, and burning with his fever, he visited his dear patients, and attended them as much as his weakness would permit him. The physician having one day met him, going hither and thither as his charity called him, in the middle of his fit, after having felt his pulse, plainly told him, that in all the hospital, there was not one man in more danger than himself, and prayed him that he would take some small repose, and but give himself a breathing time until his fever were on the declension.

"I will punctually obey you," replied the father, "when I have satisfied one part of my duty which calls upon me; it concerns the salvation or a soul, and there is no time to be lost on such an occasion." Immediately he ordered to be carried to his own bed a poor ship-boy, who lay stretched out on a little straw, with a burning fever upon him, without speech or knowledge. The youth was no sooner placed upon the saint's bed, but he came to himself: Xavier made use of the opportunity, and laying himself by the sick person, who had led a most dissolute life, exhorted him so strongly all that night to abominate his sins, and to rely on the mercy of Almighty God, that he saw him die in great contrition, mixed with saving hope.

After this, the father kept the promise which he had made to the physician, and took a greater care of his own preservation; insomuch that his fever abated by degrees, and at length left him of itself; but his strength was not yet recovered, when the navy put to sea again. The viceroy, who began to find himself indisposed, would make no longer stay upon a place so much infected, nor attend the recovery of his people, to continue his voyage. He desired Xavier to accompany him, and to leave Paul de Camerino, and Francis Mansilla, to attend the sick in the hospital; where indeed they both, performed their duty as became them.

Thus having made a six months residence on Mozambique, they embarked once more on the 15th of March, and in the year 1542. But they went not aboard the St James, in which they came thither, changing her for a lighter vessel, which made better sail.

It is here proper to observe, that the father, according to the report of the passengers who came with him from Portugal to Mozambique, began to manifest that spirit of prophecy, which he had to the end of his days in so eminent a degree. For hearing those of the St James commend that ship, as a vessel of the strongest built, and the best equipped of all the fleet, he said in express words, that she would prove unfortunate. And in effect, that ship, which the viceroy left behind him at Mozambique, in the company of some others, pursuing her course afterwards to the Indies, was driven against the rocks, and dashed in pieces towards the island of Salseta.

The galeon, which carried Sosa and Xavier, had the wind so favourable, that in two or three days she arrived at Melinda, on the coast of Africa, towards the equinoctial line. It is a town of Saracens, on the sea side, in a flat country, well cultivated, planted all along with palm-trees, and beautified with fair gardens. It has a large enclosure, and is fortified with walls, after the European fashion. Though the building is Moresque, the houses notwithstanding are both pleasantand convenient. The inhabitants are warlike, they are black, and go naked; excepting only that they are covered with a kind of an apron of cotton or linen, from the waist to the mid thigh. And indeed the heat of their climate will permit them to wear no more; Melinda being distant from the line but three degrees and some few minutes.

They have always maintained a good correspondence with the Portuguese, by reason of the commerce established betwixt them. The flag of Portugal was no sooner seen, but the Saracen king came down to the port, attended by the most honourable persons of his court, to receive the new governor of the Indies. The first object which presented itself to Father Francis when he stept ashore, drew tears from his eyes; but they were tears of joy and pity mingled together. The Portuguese having there a constant trade, and now and then some of them happening to die, are allowed a burying-place near the town, full of crosses set upon their graves, according to ihe custom of the Catholics: and above the rest there was a very large one of hewn stone placed in the middle, and all over gilded.

The saint ran to it, and adored before it; receiving an inward consolation, to behold it raised so high, and, as it were, triumphing amongst the enemies of Jesus Christ. But at the same time, he was sensibly afflicted, that this sign of our salvation served less to edify the living, than to honour the memory of the dead. And lifting up his hands to heaven, he besought the Father of all mercies to imprint in the hearts of the infidels, that cross, which they had suffered to be planted on their ground.

His next thoughts prompted him to confer of religion with the Moors, that he might endeavour to shew them the extravagances of the Mahometan belief, and gain an opportunity of revealing to them the eternal truths of Christian faith. One of the principal inhabitants, and wonderfully bigotted to his sect, prevented him, and immediately demanded of him, if piety were not wholly extinguished in the towns of Europe, as it was in Melinda. "For, to confess the truth," said he, "of seventeen mosques which we have, fourteen are quite forsaken; there are but three remaining, at which we pay our devotions; and even those three are but little visited, and by few persons.

"This proceeds, without all question," added the Mahometan, "from some enormous sin, but what it is, I know not: and whatsoever reflections I can make, I am not able to find what has drawn upon us so dreadful a misfortune." "There is nothing more clear," replied Xavier; "God, who detests the prayer of infidels, has permitted a worship to moulder away, which is displeasing to him; and gives you thence to understand, that he condemns your sect." The Saracen was not satisfied with this reason, nor with any other argument which Xavier used against the Alcoran. While they were thus disputing, a Caciz, or doctor of the law, joined company with them, having made the same complaint concerning the mosques, how little they were frequented, and how cold was grown the devotion of the people. "I have taken my measures," said he, "and if in two years Mahomet comes not in person to visit the congregations of the faithful, who acknowledge him for God's true prophet, I will certainly look out for some other religion." Xavier took pity on the folly of the Caciz, and endeavoured all he could to convert him at that instant from Mahometanism; but he could not prevail upon an obstinate mind, blinded with the opinion of its own reason; and therefore the father acquiesced in the decrees of that Providence, which has fixed the times and revolutions for the conversion of infidels and sinners.

Having left Melinda, where they continued but few days, and still coasting Africa, they cast anchor at Socotora, which is beyond Cape Guardafu, and over against the Strait of Mecca. The Moors of that country call it the Isle of Amazons; and the reason they allege is, because it is governed by women. The inhabitants believe their isle to be the earthly paradise; which notwithstanding, there is scarcely to be found in all the world, a spot of ground less deserving that glorious title. The air is in a perpetual sultry heat, the soil is dry and barren, and, excepting only for the aoes which is there produced, and is indeed the best which grows in those eastern parts, even the name of Socotora would not be mentioned. It is not certainly known what religion they profess, so monstrous is their belief. They hold from the Saracens the worship of Mahomet, from the Jews the use of circumcision and sacrifices, and yet give themselves the name of Christians. The males bear the name of some or other of the apostles, the most part of the women are called Mary, and yet they have no knowledge of baptism. They adore the cross, and hang it in little about their necks. They chiefly venerate St Thomas; and it is an ancient tradition amongst them, that this holy apostle, in going to the Indies, was cast by a tempest on their coast; that being come ashore, he preached Jesus Christ to those of Socotora; and that from the wreck of that ship which brought him thither, they built a chapel in the middle of their island.

The condition of these islanders sensibly afflicted Father Xavier; yet he despaired not of reducing them to a right understanding of the faith, because, as barbarous as they were, they still preserved some footsteps of Christianity amongst them. Having no knowledge of their tongue, which bears not the least resemblance to any of our European languages, and is also wholly different from the Ethiopian and Arabic, at the first he was constrained to testify his sorrow to them by dumb signs, for their ignorance and errors. Afterwards, whether it were that some one amongst them understood the Portuguese, and served as interpreter to all the rest, or that counting from this very time he began to receive from above, the first fruits of the gift of tongues, which was so abundantly bestowed on him in the Indies on sundry occasions, he spoke to them concerning the necessity of baptism, and let them know, that there was no possibility of salvation without a sincere belief in Jesus Christ: but that the faith allowed of no mixture, and that to become Christians, they must of necessity cease to be Jews or Mahometans.

His words made a wonderful impression on the souls and hearts of those barbarians: some of them made him presents of their wild fruits, in token of their good will; others offered him their children to be baptised; all promised him to receive baptism themselves, and to lead the life of true Christians, on condition he would remain with them. But when they beheld the Portuguese galleon ready to depart, they ran in crowds to the water-side, and besought the holy man, with tears in their eyes, not to forsake them.

So moving a spectacle wrought compassion in Xavier; he was earnest with the viceroy for leave to stay upon the isle, at least till the arrival of the vessels, which he had left at Mozambique, But he could obtain no part of his request: and Sosa told him, that heaven having designed him for the Indies, it was to be wanting to his vocation if he endeavoured this exchange, and stopped in the beginning of his race; that his zeal would find a more ample field, wherein to exercise itself, than in Socotora, and people of better inclination than those islanders, naturally inconstant, and as ready to forsake the faith, as they were easy to receive it.

Xavier submitted to these reasons of the viceroy, which on this occasion seemed to interpret to him the good pleasure of Almighty God. Instantly they hoisted sail; but the saint was pierced with sorrow to behold those poor creatures, who followed him with their eyes, and held up their hands from afar to him; while the vessel was removing into the deep, he turned his head towards them, breathing out profound sighs, and looking mournfully upon them. But that he might leave nothing upon his conscience to upbraid him concerning the Socotorins, he engaged himself solemnly before Almighty God to return to them, so soon as possibly he could; or in case he could not, to procure for them some preachers of the gospel, to instruct them in the way of their salvation.

This last part of his navigation was not long. After having crossed the sea of Arabia, and part of that which belongs to India, the fleet arrived at the port of Goa, on the 6th of May, in the year 1542, being the thirteenth month since their setting out from the port of Lisbon.

The town of Goa is situated on this side of the Ganges, in an island bearing the same name. It is the capital city of the Indies, the seat of the bishop and the viceroy, and the most considerable place of all the East for traffic. It had been built by the Moors forty years before the Europeans had passed into the Indies; and in the year 1510, Don Alphonso de Albuquerque, surnamed the Great, took it from the infidels, and subjected it to the crown of Portugal.

At that time was verified the famous prophecy of St Thomas the apostle, that the Christian faith, which he had planted in divers kingdoms of the East, should one day flourish there again; which very prediction he left graven on a pillar of living stone, for the memory of future ages. The pillar was not far distant from the walls of Meliapore, the metropolis of the kingdom of Coromandel; and it was to be read in the characters of the country, that when the sea, which was forty miles distant from the pillar, should come up to the foot of it, there should arrive in the Indies white men and foreigners, who should there restore the true religion.

The infidels had laughed at this prediction for a long time, not believing that it would ever be accomplished, and indeed looking on it as a kind of impossibility that it should; yet it was accomplished, and that so justly, that when Don Vasco de Gama set foot on the Indies, the sea, which sometimes usurps upon the continent, and gains by little and little on the dry land, was by that time risen to the pillar, so as to bathe its lower parts.

Yet it may be truly said, that the prophecy of St Thomas had not its full effect, till after the coming of Father Xavier; according to another prediction of that holy man Peter de Couillan, a religious of the Trinity, who, going to the Indies with Vasco de Gama, in quality of his ghostly father, was martyred by the Indians on the seventh of July 1497, forty-three years before the beginning of the Society of Jesus, who being pierced through with arrows, while he was shedding his blood for Christ, distinctly pronounced these following words: "In few years there shall be born in the church of God, a new religious order of clergymen, which shall bear the name of Jesus: and one of its first fathers, conducted by the Spirit of God, shall pass into the most remote countries of the East Indies, the greatest part of which shall embrace the orthodox faith, through the ministry of this evangelical preacher."

This is related by Juan de Figueras Carpi, in his history of the order of the redemption of captives, from the manuscripts of the Trinity Convent in Lisbon, and the memoirs of the king of Portugal's library.

After Xavier was landed, he went immediately to the hospital, and there took his lodging, notwithstanding the instances of the viceroy, who was desirous to have had him in his palace. But he would not begin his missionary function, till he had paid his respects to the Bishop of Goa; whose name was Juan d'Albuquerque, of the order of St Francis, a most excellent person, and one of the most virtuous prelates which the church has ever had.

The father having informed him of the reasons for which his Holiness and the king of Portugal had sent him to the Indies, presented to him the briefs of Pope Paul III., at the same time declaring to him, that he pretended not to use them without his approbation and good-liking: after this, he cast himself at his feet, and desired his blessing.

The prelate, edified with the modesty of the father, and struck with that venerable air of sanctity which appeared in his countenance, took him up immediately, and embraced him with great tenderness. Having often kissed the briefs, he restored them to the father, with these words: "An apostolical legate, sent from the vicar of Jesus Christ, has no need of receiving his mission from any other hand; use freely that power, which the holy seat has conferred upon you; and rest assured, that if the Episcopal authority be needful to maintain, it shall never be wanting to you."

From that moment they contracted a most sacred friendship, whose union was so strict, that ever after they seemed to have but one heart and one soul: insomuch that Father Xavier undertook not any thing without consulting the bishop first; and the bishop, on his side, imparted all his designs to Father Xavier: and it is almost incredible, how much this holy correspondence contributed to the salvation of souls, and exaltation of the faith.

Before we pass farther, it is of consequence to know the estate of religion at that time in the Indies. It is true, that, according to the prophecy of St. Thomas, they who discovered the East Indies, had new planted Christianity in some parts of them, where all was in a manner quite forgotten. But ambition and avarice, in short time after, cooled the zeal of these new conquerors; instead of extending the kingdom of Jesus Christ, and of gaining souls to him, they thought of nothing more than of enlarging their dominion, and enriching themselves. It happened also, that many Indians newly converted to the faith, being neither cultivated by wholesome instructions, nor edified by good examples, forgot insensibly their baptism, and returned to their ancient superstitions.

And if any amongst them kept constant to his Christianity, and declared himself a believer, the Mahometans, who were uppermost in many places along the coast, and very wealthy, persecuted him with great cruelty, without any opposition on the part of the Portuguese governor or magistrates. Whether the power of Portugal were not yet sufficiently established, or that interest was predominant over justice and religion, this cruel usage deterred the new Christians fom professing Jesus Christ, and was the reason, that, amongst the infidels, all thoughts of conversion were laid aside.

But what yet appears more wonderful, the Portuguese themselves lived more like idolaters than Christians. For, to speak somewhat more particularly of their corrupt manners, according to the relation which was sent to King John III. of Portugal from the Indies, by a man in power, and worthy of belief; some few months before the arrival of Father Xavier, every man kept as many mistresses as he pleased, and maintained them openly in his own house, even in the quality of lawful wives. They bought women, or took them away by force, either for their service, or to make money of them. Their masters taxed them at a certain sum by the day, and, for fault of payment, inflicted on them ail sorts of punishment; insomuch, that those unhappy creatures, not being able sometimes to work out the daily rate imposed on them, were forced upon the infamous traffic of their bodies, and became public prostitutes, to content the avarice of their masters.

Justice was sold at the tribunals, and the most enormous crimes escaped from punishment, when the criminals had wherewithal to corrupt their judges.

All methods for heaping up money were accounted lawful, how indirect soever, and extortion was publicly protest. Murder was reckoned but a venial trespass, and was boasted as a piece of bravery.

The Bishop of Goa, to little purpose, threatened them with the wrath of heaven, and the thunder of excommunications. No dam was sufficient for such a deluge; their hearts were hardened against spiritual threatening and anathemas; or, to speak more properly, the deprivation of sacraments was no punishment to such wicked wretches, who were glad to be rid of them.

The use of confessions, and the communion, were in a manner abolished; and if any one by chance was struck with a remorse of conscience, and desired to reconcile himself to God, at the foot of a priest, he was constrained to steal to his devotions by night, to avoid the scandal to his neighbour.

So strange a depravation of manners proceeded from these causes. Its rise was taken from the licence of arms, which permit, and almost authorize, the greatest disorders in a conquered country. The pleasures of Asia, and the commerce of infidels, aided not a little to debauch the Portuguese, as starched and regular as they naturally are. The want of spiritual directors contributed largely to this growing mischief. There were not four preachers, in all the Indies, nor any one priest without the walls of Goa; insomuch, that in many fortified places whole years were passed without hearing a sermon or a mass.

Behold a draught, not unresembling the face of Christianity in this new world, when Father Xavier arrived in it.

The author of the relation from whence mine is copied, seems to have had some kind of foresight of his coming; for, in the conclusion of his memorial, he prays Almighty God, and earnestly desires the king of Portugal, to send some holy man to the Indies, who might reform the manners of the Europeans, by his apostolic instructions, and his exemplary virtues.

As for the Gentiles, the life they led resembled that of beasts rather than of men. Uncleanness was risen to the last excess amongst them; and the least corrupt were those who had no religion. The greatest part of them adored the devil under an obscene figure, and with ceremonies which modesty forbids to mention. Some amongst them changed their deity every day; and the first living creature which happened to meet them in the morning was the object of their worship, not excepting even dogs or swine. In this they were uniform, that they all offered bloody sacrifices to their gods; and nothing was more common, than to see bleeding infants on the altars, slaughtered by the hands of their own parents.

Such manifold abominations inflamed the zeal of Father Xavier. He wished himself able at the same time, to have applied remedies to them all; yet thought himself obliged to begin with the household of faith, according to the precept of St Paul; that is to say, with the Christians: and amongst them he singled out the Portuguese, whose example was like to be most prevalent with the baptised Indians. Behold in what manner he attempted this great enterprise of reformation.

To call down the blessing of heaven on this difficult employment, he consecrated the greatest part of the night to prayers, and allowed himself at the most but four hours of sleep; and even this little repose was commonly disturbed: for, lodging in the hospital, and lying always near the sick, as his custom had been at Mozambique, his slumber was broken by their least complaint, and he failed not to rise to their relief.

He returned to his prayers at break of day, after which he celebrated mass. He employed the forenoon in the hospitals, particularly in that of the lepers, which is in one of the suburbs of Goa. He embraced those miserable creatures one after the other, and distributed amongst them those alms which he had been begging for them from door to door. After this he visited the prisons, and dealt amongst them the same effects of charity.

In coming back, he made a turn about the town, with his bell in his hand, and gave a loud summons to the fathers of families, that, for the love of God, they would send their children and their slaves to catechism.

The holy man was convinced in his heart, that if the Portuguese youth were well instructed in the principles of religion, and formed betimes to the practice of good life, Christianity, in a little time, would be seen to revive in Goa; but in case the children grew up without instruction or discipline, there was no remaining hope, that they who sucked in impiety and vice, almost with their milk, should ever become sincere Christians.

The little children gathered together in crowds about him, whether they came of their own accord, through a natural curiosity, or that their parents sent them, out of the respect which they already had for the holy man, howsoever vicious themselves. He led them to the church, and there expounded to them the apostles' creed, the commandments of God, and all the practices of devotion which are in use amongst the faithful.

These tender plants received easily the impressions which the father made on them, and it was through these little babes that the town began to change its face. For, by daily hearing the man of God, they became modest and devout; their modesty and devotion was a silent censure of that debauchery which appeared in persons of riper age. Sometimes they even reproved their fathers, with a liberty which had nothing of childish in it, and their reproofs put the most dissolute libertines to the blush.

Xavier then proceeded to public preaching, whither all the people flocked; and to the end that the Indians might understand, as well as the Portuguese, he affected to speak that language in a gross and clownish dialect, which passed at that time amongst the natives of the country. It was immediately seen what power a preacher, animated by the spirit of God, had over the souls of perverted men. The most scandalous sinners, struck with the horror of their crimes, and the fear of eternal punishment, were the first who came to confession. Their example took away from others the shame of confessing; insomuch, that every one now strove who should be foremost to throw himself at the father's feet, knocking their breasts, and bitterly lamenting their offences.

The fruits of penitence accompanying these tears, were the certain proofs of a sincere conversion. They cancelled their unlawful bonds and covenants of extortion; they made restitution of their ill-gotten goods; they set at liberty their slaves, whom they had opprest, or had acquired unjustly; and lastly, turned away their concubines, whom they were unwilling to possess by a lawful marriage.

The saint acted with the concubinarians almost in the same manner as our Saviour dealt with the publicans and harlots. Far from treating them severely, the deeper they were plunged in that darling vice, the more tenderly he seemed to use them. On all occasions he declared himself their friend; he made them frequent visits, without fear of being upbraided with so infamous a conversation. He invited himself sometimes to eat with them; and then, assuming an air of gaiety, he desired the master to bring down the children to bear him company. When he had a little commended their prettiness, he asked to see their mother, and shewed her the same countenance, as if he had taken her for an honest woman. If she were beautiful or well shaped, he praised her, and said "she looked like a Portuguese:" after which; in private conversation, "you have," said he to her master, "a fair slave, who well deserves to be your wife." But if she were a swarthy, ugly Indian, "Good God!" he cried out, "what a monster do you keep within your doors! and how are you able to endure the sight of her?" Such words, spoken in all appearance without design, had commonly their full effect: the keeper married her whom the saint had commended, and turned off the others.

This so sudden a change of manners was none of those transient fits of devotion, which pass away almost as soon as they are kindled; piety was established in all places, and they who formerly came to confession once a year, to speak the best of it, now performed it regularly once a month. They were all desirous of confessing themselves to Father Xavier; so that, writing from Goa to Rome on that subject, he said, "That if it had been possible for him to have been at once in ten places, he should not have wanted for employment." His catechising having had that wonderful success which we have mentioned, the Bishop Don John d'Albuquerque ordained, that, from thenceforward, the children should be taught the Christian doctrine, in all the churches of the town. The gentlemen and merchants applied themselves to the regulation of their families, and banishment of vice. They gave the father considerable sums of money, which he distributed in their presence, in the hospitals and prisons. The viceroy accompanied the saint thither once a week, to hear the complaints of the prisoners, and to relieve the poor. This Christian practice was so pleasing to the king of Portugal, John III, that afterwards he writ to Don John de Castro, governor of the Indies, expressly ordering him to do that once a month, which Don Martin Alphonso de Sosa never failed of doing every week; in short, the Portuguese of Goa had gained such an habitude of good life, and such an universal change of manners had obtained amongst them, that they seemed another sort of people.

This was the state of affairs, when Michael Vaz, vicar general of the Indies, a man of rare virtue, and wonderful zeal for the propagation of the faith, gave Xavier to understand, that on the Oriental coast, which lies extended from Cape Comorin to the Isle of Manar, and is called the coast of Fishery, there were certain people called Paravas, that is to say, fishers, who had caused themselves to be baptized some time since, on occasion of succours which had been given them by the Portuguese against the Moors, by whom they were cruelly opprest; that these people had nothing more of Christianity than baptism, and the name, for want of pastors to instruct them; and that it would be a work well-pleasing in the sight of God to accomplish their conversion. He concealed not from him, that the land was barren, and so destitute of the conveniences of life, that no stranger was willing to settle there; that interest alone drew the merchants thither, in the season of pearl-fishing, and otherwise the heats were insupportable.

There could not have been made to Xavier a proposition more according to his heart's desire. He offered himself, without the least hesitation, to go and instruct that people; and he did it so much the more freely, because his presence was no longer so necessary at Goa, where piety was now grown into a habit, by a settled form of five months standing.

Having received the benediction of the bishop, he embarked about the midst of October, in the year 1542, in a galiot, which carried the new captain of Comorin; and took with him two young ecclesiastics of Goa, who had a tolerable insight into the language of the Malabars, which is spoken in the coast of Fishery. Sosa offered to have furnished him with money for all his occasions; but apostolic men have no greater treasures than their poverty, nor any fund more certain than that of Providence. He accepted only a pair of shoes, to defend him in some measure from the burning sands upon the coasts; and, at parting, desired the viceroy to send him his two companions, who were left behind at Mozambique, so soon as they should arrive at Goa.

The Cape of Cornorin is at the distance of about six hundred miles from Goa. It is a high promontory, jutting out into the sea, and facing the isle of Ceylon. The Father being there arrived, immediately fell in with a village of idolaters. He could bear to go no farther without preaching the name of Jesus to the Gentiles; but all he could declare, by the mouth of his interpreters, signified nothing; and those pagans plainly told him, that they could not change their faith without consent of the lord of whom they held. Their obstinacy, however, was of no long continuance; and that Omnipotence, which had pre-ordained Xavier to the conversion of idolaters, would not that his first labours should be unsuccessful.

A woman of the village had been three days in the pains of childbirth, and had endured great torments, without being eased, either by the prayers of the Brachmans, or any natural remedies. Xavier went to visit her, accompanied by one of his interpreters; "and then it was," says he, in one of his letters, "that, forgetting I was in a strange country, I began to call upon the name of the Lord; though, at the same time, I could not but remember, that all the earth is equally his, and all its inhabitants are belonging to him."

The Father expounded to the sick woman the principles of our faith, and exhorted her to repose her trust in the God of the Christians. The Holy Ghost, who, by her means, had decreed to save that people, touched her inwardly; insomuch, that being asked if she believed in Jesus Christ, and if she desired to be baptized? she answered, yes; and that she spake from the bottom of her heart. Xavier then read the gospel to her, and baptized her:--she was immediately delivered of her child, and perfectly recovered. This visible miracle immediately filled that poor cabin with astonishment and gladness: The whole family threw themselves at the Father's feet, and asked to be instructed; and, being sufficiently taught, not one amongst them but received baptism. This news being blown abroad through all the country, the chief of the place had the curiosity to see a person so wonderful in his works and in his words. He preached to them the words of eternal life, and convinced their reason of the truth of Christianity; but convinced though they were, they durst not, as they said, become Christians, without the permission of their prince.

There was at that time in the village an officer, sent expressly from the prince to collect a certain annual tribute. Father Xavier went to see him, and expounded so clearly to him all the law of Jesus Christ, that the pagan presently acknowledged there was nothing in it which was ill; and after that gave leave to the inhabitants to embrace it. There needed no more to a people, whom nothing but fear withheld from it; they all offered themselves to be baptized, and promised thenceforth to live in Christianity.

The holy man, encouraged by so happy a beginning, followed his way with more cheerfulness, and came to Tutucurin, which is the first town belonging to the Paravas. He found, in effect, that this people, excepting only their baptism, which they had received, rather to shake off the Moorish yoke than to subject themselves to that of Jesus Christ, were wholly infidels; and he declared to them the mysteries of our faith, of which before they had not received the least tincture. The two churchmen who accompanied him served him in the nature of interpreters; but Xavier, reflecting within himself, that these churchmen frequently altered those things which passed through their mouths, and that our own words, when spoken by ourselves, have more vigour in them, bethought himself of finding some expedient, whereby to be understood without the assistance of another. The way he took, was to get together some people of the country, who understood the Portuguese language, and to join them with the two ecclesiastics who were knowing in the Malabar. He consulted both parties for many days together, and, drudging at his business, translated into the Paravas tongue, the words of the sign of the cross, the apostles' creed, the commandments, the Lord's prayer, the salutation of the angel, the confiteor, the salve regina, and, in fine, the whole catechism.

The translation being finished, the Father got, without book, what he could of it, and took his way about the villages of the coast, in number thirty, about half of which were baptized, the rest idolaters.

"I went about, with my bell in my hand," says he himself, "and gathering together all I met, both men and children, I instructed them in the Christian doctrine. The children learnt it easily by heart in the compass of a month; and when they understood it, I charged them to teach it their fathers and mothers, all of their own family, and even their neighbours.

"On Sundays I assembled the men and women, little boys and girls, in the chapel; all came to my appointment with an incredible joy, and most ardent desire to hear the word of God. I began with the confessing God to be one in nature, and trine in Persons; I afterwards repeated distinctly, and with an audible voice, the Lord's prayer, the angelical salutation, and the apostles' creed. All of them together repeated after me; and it is hardly to be imagined what pleasure they took in it. This being done, I repeated the creed singly; and, insisting on every particular article, asked, if they certainly believed it? They all protested to me, with loud cries, and their hands across their breasts, that they firmly believed it. My practice is, to make them repeat the creed oftener than the other prayers; and I declare to them, at the same time, that they who believe the contents of it are true Christians.

"From the creed I pass to the ten commandments, and give them to understand, that the Christian law is comprised in those ten precepts; that he who keeps them all according to his duty is a good Christian, and that eternal life is decreed to him; that, on the contrary, whoever violates one of these commandments is a bad Christian, and that he shall be damned eternally in case he repent not of his sin. Both the new Christians and the pagans admire our law as holy, and reasonable, and consistent with itself.

"Having done as I told you, my custom is, to repeat with them the Lord's prayer, and the angel's salutation. Once again we recite the creed; and at every article, besides the Paternoster and the Ave Maria, we intermingle some short prayer; for having pronounced aloud the first article, I begin thus, and they say after me,--' Jesus, thou son of the living God, give me the grace to believe firmly this first article of thy faith, and with that intention we offer thee that prayer of which thou thyself art author.' We add,--' Holy Mary, mother of our Lord Jesus Christ, obtain for us, from thy beloved Son, to believe this article, without any doubt concerning it.' The same method is observed in all the other articles; and almost in the same manner we run over the ten commandments. When we have jointly repeated the first precept, which is, to love God, we pray thus: 'O Jesu Christ, thou Son of the living God, grant us thy grace to love thee above all things!' and immediately after we say the Lord's prayer; then immediately we subjoin: 'O holy Mary, mother of Jesus, obtain for us, from thy Son, that we may have the grace to keep this first commandment.' After which we say the Ave Maria. We observe the same method through the other nine commandments, with some little variation, as the matter requires it.

"These are the things which I accustom them to beg of God in the common prayers; omitting not sometimes to assure them, that if they obtain the thing for which they pray, even that is a means for them to obtain other things more amply than they could demand them.

"I oblige them all to say the confiteor, but principally those who are to receive baptism, whom I also enjoin to say the belief. At every article, I demand of them, if they believe it without any scruple; and when they have assured me, that they do, I commonly make them an exhortation, which I have composed in their own language,--being an epitome of the Christian faith, and of the necessary duties incumbent on us in order to our salvation. In conclusion, I baptize them, and shut up all in singing the salve regina, to implore the assistance of the blessed Virgin."

It is evident, by what we have already said concerning the instruction of the Paravas, that Xavier had not the gift of tongues when he began to teach them: But it appears also, that, after he had made the translation, which cost him so much labour, he both understood and spoke the Malabar tongue, whether he had acquired it by his own pains, or that God had imprinted the species of it in his mind after a supernatural manner. It is at least probable, that, being in the Indies when he studied any tongue, the Holy Spirit seconded his application, and was in some sort his master; for it is constantly believed, that in a very little time he learnt the most difficult languages, and, by the report of many persons, spoke them so naturally, that he could not have been taken for a foreigner.

Father Xavier having, for the space of a month, instructed the inhabitants of one village, in the manner above said, before he went farther, called together the most intelligent amongst them, and gave them in writing what he had taught, to the end, that as masters of the rest, on Sundays and Saints-days, they might congregate the people, and cause them to repeat, according to his method, that which they had learnt formerly.

He committed to these catechists, (who in their own tongue are called Canacopoles,) the care of the churches, which he caused to be built in peopled places; and recommended to them the ornament of those sacred buildings, as far as their poverty would allow. But he was not willing to impose this task on them, without some kind of salary; and therefore obtained from the viceroy of the Indies, a certain sum for their subsistence, which was charged upon the annual tribute, payable to the crown of Portugal, from the inhabitants of that coast.

It is hardly to be expressed, what a harvest of souls was reaped from his endeavours; and how great was the fervour of these new Christians. The holy man, writing to the fathers at Rome, confesses himself, that he wanted words to tell it. He adds, "That the multitude of those who had received baptism, was so vast, that, with the labour of continual christenings, he was not able to lift up his arms; and that his voice often failed him, in saying so many times over and over, the apostles' creed, and the ten commandments, with a short instruction, which he always made concerning the duties of a true Christian, before he baptized those who were of age."

The infants alone, who died after baptism, amounted, according to his account, to above a thousand. They who lived, and began to have the use of reason, were so affected with the things of God, and so covetous of knowing all the mysteries of faith, that they scarcely gave the father time to take a little nourishment, or a short repose. They sought after him every minute; and he was sometimes forced to hide himself from them, to gain the leisure of saying his prayers, and his breviary.

By the administration of these children, who were so fervently devout, he performed divers extraordinary works, even many of those miraculous cures, which it pleased God to perate by his means. The coast of Fishery was never so full of diseases, as when the father was there. It seemed, as he himself has expressed it in a letter, that God sent those distempers amongst that people, to draw them to him almost in their own despite. For coming to recover on an instant, and against all human appearance, so soon as they had received baptism, or invoked the name of Jesus Christ, they clearly saw the difference betwixt the God of the Christians and the pagods, which is the name given in the Indies, both to the temples and the images of their false gods.

No one fell sick amongst the Gentiles, but had immediate recourse to Father Xavier. As it was impossible for him to attend them all, or to be in many places at the same time, he sent there Christian children where he could not go himself. In going from him, one took his chaplet, another his crucifix, a third his reliquiary, and all being animated with a lively faith, dispersed themselves through the towns and villages. There gathering about the sick as many people as they could assemble, they repeated often the Lord's prayer, the creed, the commandments, and all they had learnt by heart of the Christian faith; which being done, they asked the sick, "If he believed unfeignedly in Jesus Christ, and if he desired to be baptized?" When he had answered "Yes," they touched him with the chaplet, or crucifix belonging to the father, and he was immediately cured.

One day, while Xavier was preaching the mysteries of faith to a great multitude, some came to bring him word from Manapar, that one of the most considerable persons of that place was possessed by the devil, desiring the father to come to his relief. The man of God thought it unbecoming of his duty to break off the instruction he was then making. He only called to him some of those young Christians, and gave them a cross which he wore upon his breast; after which he sent them to Manapar with orders to drive away the evil spirit.

They were no sooner arrived there, than the possessed person fell into an extraordinary fury, with, wonderful contortions of his limbs, and hideous yellings. The little children, far from being terrified, as usually children are, made a ring about him, singing the prayers of the church. After which they compelled him to kiss the cross; and at the same moment, the devil departed out of him. Many pagans there present, visibly perceiving the virtue of the cross, were converted on the instant, and became afterwards devout Christians.

These young plants, whom Xavier employed on such occasions, were in perpetual disputations with the Gentiles, and broke in pieces as many idols as they could get into their power; and sometimes burnt them, throwing their ashes into the air. When they discovered any bearing the name of Christianity, and yet keeping a pagod in reserve to adore in secret, they reproved them boldly; and when those rebukes were of no effect, they advertised the holy man, to the end, he might apply some stronger remedy. Xavier went often in their company, to make a search in those suspected houses; and if he discovered any idols, they were immediately destroyed.

Being informed, that one who was lately baptized, committed idolatry sometimes in private, and that the admonitions which he had received were useless, he bethought himself to frighten him; and in his presence commanded the children to set fire to his house, that thereby he might be given to understand, how the worshippers of devils deserved eternal burning like the devils. They ran immediately to their task, taking the command in a literal sense, which was not Xavier's intention. But the effect of it was, that the infidel, detesting and renouncing his idolatry, gave up his pagods to be consumed by fire, which was all the design of the holy man.

Another infidel was more unhappy; he was one of the first rank in Manapar; a man naturally violent and brutal. Xavier one day going to visit him, desired him, in courteous words, that he would listen to what he had to say to him concerning his eternal welfare. The barbarian vouchsafed not so much as to give him the hearing, but rudely thrust him out of his house, saying, "That if ever he went to the Christians' church, he was content they should shut him out." Few days after, he was assaulted by a troop of armed men, who designed to kill him: all he could do was to disengage himself from them, and fly away. Seeing at a distance a church open, he made to it as fast as he could run, with his enemies at his heels pursuing him. The Christians, who were assembled for their exercises of devotion, alarmed at the loud cries they heard, and fearing the idolaters were coming to plunder the church, immediately shut their doors, insomuch that he, who hoped for safety in a holy place, fell into the hands of murderers, and was assassinated by them, without question by a decree of the divine justice, which revenged the saint, and suffered the wretch to be struck with that imprecation which he had wished upon himself.

These miracles, which Xavier wrought by the means of children, raised an admiration of him, both amongst Christians and idolaters; but so exemplary a punishment caused him to be respected by all the world: and even amongst the Brachmans there was not one who did not honour him. As it will fall in our way to make frequent mention of those idol-priests, it will not be from our purpose to give the reader a description of them.

The Brachmans are very considerable amongst the Indians, both for their birth and their employment. According to the ancient fables of the Indies, their original is from heaven. And it is the common opinion, that the blood of the gods is running in their veins. But to understand how they were born, and from what god descended, it is necessary to know the history of the gods of that country, which in short is this:

The first, and lord of all the others, is Parabrama; that is to say, a most perfect substance, who has his being from himself, and who gives being to the rest. This god being a spirit free from matter, and desirous to appear once under a sensible figure, became man; by the only desire which he had to shew himself, he conceived a son, who came out at his mouth, and was called Maiso. He had two others after him, one of them whose name was Visnu, was born out of his breast, the other called Brama, out of his belly. Before he returned to his invisibility, he assigned habitations and employments to his three children. He placed the eldest in the first heaven, and gave him an absolute command over the elements and mixed bodies. He lodged Visnu beneath his elder brother, and established him the judge of men, the father of the poor, and the protector of the unfortunate. Brama had for his inheritance the third heaven, with the superintendance of sacrifices, and other ceremonies of religion. These are the three deities which the Indians represent by one idol, with three heads growing out of one body, with this mysterious signification, that they all proceed from the same principle. By which it may be inferred, that in former times they have heard of Christianity; and that their religion is an imperfect imitation, or rather a corruption of ours.

They say that Visnu has descended a thousand times on earth, and every time has changed his shape; sometimes appearing in the figure of a beast, sometimes of a man, which is the original of their pagods, of whom they relate so many fables.

They add, that Brama, having likewise a desire of children, made himself visible, and begot the Brachmans, whose race has infinitely multiplied. The people believe them demi-gods, as poor and miserable as they are. They likewise imagine them to be saints, because they lead a hard and solitary life; having very often no other lodging than the hollow of a tree, or a cave, and sometimes living exposed to the air on a bare mountain, or in a wilderness, suffering all the hardships of the weather, keeping a profound silence, fasting a whole year together, and making profession of eating nothing which has had life in it.

But after all, there was not perhaps a more wicked nation under the canopy of heaven. The fruit of those austerities which they practice in the desert, is to abandon themselves in public to the most brutal pleasures of the flesh, without either shame or remorse of conscience. For they certainly believe, that all things, how abominable soever, are lawful to be done, provided they are suggested to them by the light which is within them. And the people are so infatuated with them, that they believe they shall become holy by partaking in their crimes, or by suffering any outrage from them.

On the other side, they are the greatest impostors in the world; their talent consists in inventing new fables every day, and making them pass amongst the vulgar for wonderful mysteries. One of their cheats is to persuade the simple, that the pagods eat like men; and to the end they may be presented with good cheer, they make their gods of a gigantic figure, and are sure to endow them with a prodigious paunch. If those offerings with which they maintain their families come to fail, they denounce to the people, that the offended pagods threaten the country with some dreadful judgment, or that their gods, in displeasure, will forsake them, because they are suffered to die of hunger.

The doctrine of these Brachmans is nothing better than their life. One of their grossest errors is to believe that kine have in them somewhat of sacred and divine; that happy is the man who can be sprinkled over with the ashes of a cow, burnt by the hand of a Brachman; but thrice happy be, who, in dying, lays hold of a cow's tail, and expires with it betwixt his hands; for, thus assisted, the soul departs out of the body purified, and sometimes returns into the body of a cow. That such a favour, notwithstanding, is not conferred but on heroic souls, who contemn life, and die generously, either by casting themselves headlong from a precipice, or leaping into a kindled pile, or throwing themselves under the holy chariot wheels, to be crushed to death by the pagods, while they are carried in triumph about the town.

We are not to wonder, after this, that the Brachmans cannot endure the Christian law; and that they make use of all their credit and their cunning to destroy it in the Indies. Being favoured by princes, infinite in number, and strongly united amongst themselves, they succeed in all they undertake; and as being great zealots for their ancient superstitions, and most obstinate in their opinions, it is not easy to convert them.

Father Xavier, who saw how large a progress the gospel had made amongst the people, and that if there were no Brachmans in the Indies, there would consequently be no idolaters in all those vast provinces of Asia, spared no labour to reduce that perverse generation to the true knowledge of Almighty God. He conversed often with those of that religion, and one day found a favourable occasion of treating with them: Passing by a monastery, where above two hundred Brachmans lived together, he was visited by some of the chiefest, who had the curiosity to see a man whose reputation was so universal. He received them with a pleasing countenance, according to his custom; and having engaged them by little and little, in a discourse concerning the eternal happiness of the soul, he desired them to satisfy him what their gods commanded them to do, in order to it after death. They looked a while on one another without answering. At length a Brachman, who seemed to be fourscore years of age, took the business upon himself, and said in a grave tone, that two things brought a soul to glory, and made him a companion to the gods; the one was to abstain from the murder of a cow, the other to give alms to the Brachmans. All of them confirmed the old man's answer by their approbation and applause, as if it had been an oracle given from the mouths of their gods themselves.

Father Xavier took compassion on this their miserable blindness, and the tears came into his eyes. He rose on the sudden, (for they had been all sitting,) and distinctly repeated, in an audible tone, the apostles' creed, and the ten commandments, making a pause at the end of every article, and briefly expounding it, in their own language; after which he declared to them what were heaven and hell, and by what actions the one and other were deserved.

The Brachmans, who had never heard any thing of Christianity before, and had been listening to the father with great admiration, rose up, as soon as he had done speaking, and ran to embrace him, acknowledging, that the God of the Christians was the true God, since his law was so conformable to the principles of our inward light. Every one of them proposed divers questions to him; if the soul were immortal, or that it perished with the body, and in case that the soul died not, at what part of the body it went out; if in our sleep we dreamed we were in a far country, or conversed with an absent person, whether the soul went not out of the body for that time; of what colour God was, whether black or white; their doctors being divided on that point, the white men maintaining he was of their colour, the black of theirs: the greatest part of the pagods for that reason being black.

The father answered all their questions in a manner so suitable to their gross understanding, which was ignorant alike of things divine and natural, that they were highly satisfied with him. Seeing them instructed and disposed in this sort, he exhorted them to embrace the faith of Jesus Christ, and gave them to understand, that the truth being made known to them, ignorance could no longer secure them from eternal punishment.

But what victory can truth obtain over souls which find their interest in following error, and who make profession of deceiving the common people? "They answered," said the saint in one of his letters, "that which many Christians answer at this day, what will the world say of us if they see us change? And after that, what will become of our families, whose only subsistence is from the offerings which are made to the pagods? Thus, human interest, and worldly considerations, made the knowledge of the truth serve only to their greater condemnation."

Not long afterwards, Xavier had another conference with a Brachman, who lived in the nature of an hermit. He passed for the oracle of the country, and had been instructed in his youth at one of the most famous academies of the East. He was one of those who was knowing in their most hidden mysteries, which are never intrusted by the Brachmans, but to a certain select number of their wise men. Xavier, who had heard speak of him, was desirous to see him; and he, on his side, was as desirous to see Xavier. The intention of the saint was to try, in bringing over this Brachman, if he could gain the rest, who were proud of being his disciples.

After the first civilities which commonly pass betwixt two men, who mutually covet an acquaintance, and know each other by reputation, the discourse fell upon religion; and the Brachman found in himself, at the very first, so great an inclination for Xavier, that he could not conceal from him those secrets which a religious oath had bound him never to disclose to any. He confest plainly to him, that the idols were devils, and that there was only one God, creator of the world, and that this God alone deserved the adoration of men: that those who held the rank of wisdom amongst the Brachmans, solemnized the Sunday in his honour as a holiday; and that day they only said this prayer, "O God, I adore thee at this present, and for ever:" that they pronounced those words softly, for fear of being overheard, and to preserve the oath which they had made, to keep them secret. "In fine," said he, "it is to be read in our ancient writings, that all the false religions should one day cease, and the whole world should observe one only law."

The Brachman having disclosed these mysteries to Father Xavier, desired him, in his turn, to reveal to him what was most mysterious in the Christian law; and to engage him to deal the more freely with him, and without the least disguise, swore, that he would inviolably, and for ever, keep the secret. "I am so far," said the father, "from obliging you to silence, that I will inform you of nothing you desire to know, but on condition that you shall publish in all places what I tell you." The Brachman having given him his word, he began to instruct him by these words of Jesus Christ; "He who will believe, and be baptized, shall be saved." This he expounded to him at large; at the same time, declaring to him how baptism was necessary to salvation: and passing from one article of faith to another, he placed the truth of the gospel in so advantageous a light before him, that the Brachman declared upon the place he would become a Christian, provided he might be so in secret; and that he might have a dispensation from some certain duties of Christianity.

This so wicked a disposition made him unworthy of the grace of baptism; he remained unconverted. Notwithstanding which, he desired to have in writing the apostles' creed, together with our Saviour's words, which had been expounded to him.

He saw Father Xavier a second time, and told him he had dreamed he was baptized, and that afterwards he became his companion, and that they travelled together preaching the gospel in far countries; but this dream had no effect, and the Brachman would never promise to teach the people, that there was one only God, creator of the world, "or fear," says he, "that if he broke that oath which obliged him to secrecy, the devil should punish him with death."

Thus the master, though convinced, yet not submitting, the scholars all stood out; and in the sequel, of so great a multitude of idol-priests, not one embraced the Christian doctrine from the heart. Nevertheless, Xavier, in their presence, wrought many miracles which were capable of converting them. Having casually met a poor creature all naked, and full of ulcers from head to foot, he washed him with his hands, drank part of the water wherewith he had washed him, and prayed by him with wonderful fervency; when he had ended his prayer, the flesh of the diseased person was immediately healed, and appeared as clean as that of an infant.

The process of the saint's canonization makes mention of four dead persons, to whom God restored their life, at this time, by the ministry of his servant. The first was a catechist, called Antonio Miranda, who had been stung in the night by one of those venomous serpents of the Indies, whose stings are always mortal. The second was a child, who fell into a pit, and was drowned. The two others were a young man and a maid, whom a pestilential fever had carried off after a short sickness.

But these miracles, which gave to the father the name of saint among the Christians, and caused him to be called the God of Nature amongst the Gentiles, had no other effect upon the Brachmans than to harden their hearts, and blind their understandings. Xavier, despairing of their conversion, thought himself bound to publish all their wicked actions, and bring them into disrepute. And he performed it so successfully, that those men, who were had in veneration by the people, came to be despised by all the world; insomuch, that even the children laughed at them, and publicly upbraided them with their cheats. They began at first to threaten the people, according to their custom, with the anger of their pagods; but seeing their menaces turned to scorn, they made use of another artifice, to regain their credit.

What malice soever they harboured in their hearts against Father Xavier, they managed it so well, that, to see their conduct, they might have been taken for his friends. They made him visits; desired him to have some kindness for them; they gave him many commendations; they presented him sometimes with pearls and money. But the father was inexorable; and for their presents, he returned them without so much as looking on them.

The decrying of those idol-priests contributed not a little to the destruction of idolatry through all that coast. The life which Xavier led, contributed full as much. His food was the same with that of the poorest people, rice and water. His sleep was but three hours at the most, and that in a fisher's cabin on the ground: for he had soon made away with the mattress and coverlet, which the viceroy had sent him from Goa. The remainder of the night he passed with God, or with his neighbour.

He owns himself, that his labours were without intermission; and that he had sunk under so great hardships, if God had not supported him. For, to say nothing of the ministry of preaching, and those other evangelical functions, which employed him day and night, no quarrel was stirring, no difference on foot, of which he was not chosen umpire. And because those barbarians, naturally choleric, were frequently at odds, he appointed certain hours, for clearing up their misunderstandings, and making reconciliations. There was not any man fell sick, who sent not for him; and as there were always many, and for the most part distant from each other, in the scattering villages, his greatest sorrow was, that he could not be present with them all. In the midst of all this hurry, he enjoyed those spiritual refreshments and sweets of heaven, which God only bestows on souls, who regard nothing but the cross; and the excess of those delights was such, that he was often forced to desire the Divine Goodness to moderate them; according to what himself testifies in a letter to his father Ignatius, though written in general terms, and in the third person.

Having related what he had performed in the coast of the Fishery, "I have no more to add," says he, "concerning this country, but only that they who come hither to labour in the salvation of idolaters, receive so much consolation from above, that if there be a perfect joy on earth, it is that they feel." He goes on, "I have sometimes heard a man saying thus to God, O my Lord, give me not so much comfort in this life; or if, by an excess of mercy, thou wilt heap it on me, take me to thyself, and make me partaker of thy glory, for it is too great a punishment to live without the sight of thee."

A year and more was already past since Xavier had laboured in the conversion of the Paravas; and in all this time, his two companions, Paul de Camerine, and Francis Mansilla, were not come to his assistance, though they had been arrived at Goa some months since. The number of Christians daily multiplying to a prodigy, and one only priest not being sufficient to cultivate so many new converts in the faith, or advance them in Christian piety, the saint thought it his duty to look out for succour. And besides, having selected some young men, well-natured, and of a good understanding, qualified for the studies of divinity, and human sciences, who being themselves well modelled, might return with him to instruct their countrymen; he was of opinion, that he ought to conduct them himself, without deferring his voyage any longer.

On these considerations he put to sea, on his return, about the conclusion of the year 1543; and having got to Cochin by mid-January, he arrived at Goa not long after. For the better understanding of what relates to the education of those young Indians, whom Xavier brought, it will be necessary to trace that matter from its original.

Before the coming of Father Francis to the Indies, Christianity had made but little progress in those countries; and of an infinite number of Pagans, inhabiting the isle of Goa, and the parts adjoining, scarce any man thought of forsaking his idolatry. In the year 1541, James de Borba, a Portuguese preacher and divine, whom king John III. had sent to India, searching out the cause of so great a misfortune, found, that it was not only because the Europeans could not easily learn the Indian tongue, but also, because if an Indian happened to be converted, they exercised no charity towards him; and that the children of the faithful, who died poor, were destitute of succour in their wants.

He gave notice of this to the grand vicar, Michael Vaz, to the auditor general, Pedro Fernandez, to the deputy-governor, Rodriguez de Castel Blanco, and to the secretary of state, Cosmo Annez, who were all of them his particular friends, and virtuous men. These being in the government, considered of the means to remedy the growing evil, the foundation of which had been discovered to them by Borba; and he himself excited the people to be instrumental in so good a work. For, one day preaching, he passionately bemoaned the damnation of so many Indians, and charged it on the conscience of his auditory, that the salvation of that idolatrous people depended, in some sort, on them. "I pretend not," said he, "that you should go yourselves to the conquest of souls, nor learn barbarous languages on purpose, to labour in the conversion of Gentiles. What I beg of you, in the name of Jesus Christ, is, that each of you would contribute something towards the maintenance of the new Christians. You will perform by that, what it is not in your power to do by the preaching of the gospel; and gain, by your temporal goods, those immortal souls, for which the Saviour of the world has shed his blood."

The Holy Spirit, who had inspired his tongue, gave efficacy to his words, by touching the hearts of those who heard them. Many of them being joined together, it was resolved to form a company, which should provide for the subsistence of those young Indians newly converted; and that society at first was called, the Brotherhood of St Mary of the Light, (or Illumination,) from the name of that church where the fraternity assembled, to regulate that new establishment.

It is true, that, as great works are not accomplished all at once, in the beginning of this, there was only founded a small seminary, for the children of Goa, and those of the neighbourhood; but the revenues were increased so much afterwards by the liberality of Don Estevan de Gama, governor of the Indies, and by the bounty of John III., king of Portugal, that all the idolatrous children, who turned Christians, of what country soever, were received into it.

There was also a fund sufficient for the building a fair house and a magnificent church in a larger plot: and the seminary, over which Borba presided, was then called, the Seminary of Holy Faith.

Matters being thus disposed, above threescore children, of divers kingdoms, and nine or ten different languages, were assembled, to be educated in piety and learning. But it was soon perceived, that these children wanted masters, capable of instructing and forming them, according to the intention of the institute. God Almighty had pre-ordained the seminary of holy faith, for the Society of Jesus; and it was by a particular disposition of the Divine Providence, that the same year, wherein the seminary was established, brought over the sons of Ignatius to the Indies.

Accordingly, when Xavier first arrived at Goa, Borba offered him the conduct of this new establishment, and used his best endeavours to engage him in it. Xavier, who found an inward call to something more important, and who already was conceiving in his mind the conversion of a heathen world, would not coop himself up within a town, but in his secret intentions, designed one of his companions for that employment, which was presented to himself. In the meantime, Borba wrote into Portugal, to Simon Rodriguez, and earnestly desired from him some fathers of the new society, "for whom" he said, "the Almighty had prepared a house in the new world, before their coming."

During these transactions, Paul de Camerin and Francis Mansilla arrived at Goa, from Mozambique: Borba retained them both in the seminary, by permission from the viceroy; and that was the reason why they followed not Father Xavier to the coast of Fishery.

Xavier put into the seminary those young Indians whom he had brought along with him; and whatever want he had otherwise of his companions, he gave the charge of the Seminarists to Father Paul de Camerin, at the request of Borba, who had the chief authority in the seminary. For it was not till the year 1548, after the death of Borba, that the company possess it in propriety, and without dependence. It then received the name of a college, and was called the college of St Paul, from the title of the church, which was dedicated to the conversion of the apostle of the Gentiles. From thence it also proceeded, that the Jesuits were called in that country, the fathers of St Paul, or the fathers Paulists, as they are called in that country even at this day.

Father Xavier remained but a little time at Goa; and returned with all expedition to his Paravas, with the best provision of gospel labourers, which he could make. He was then desirous of sending a missioner of the company to the isle of Socotora, not being in circumstances of going thither in person; for he had not forgotten the promise, which he made to God in behalf of that people, when he left them. But the small number of companions which he had, was not sufficient for the Indies; and it was not till three or four years afterwards that he sent Father Alphonso Ciprian to Socotora.

Besides Mansilla, who had not yet received the order of priesthood, he carried with him to the coast of Fishery two priests, who were Indians by nation, and one Biscayner, called John Dortiaga. When they were arrived there, he visited all the villages with them; and taught them the method of converting idolaters to the faith, and of confirming those who were already Christians, in it. After which, having assigned to each of them a division at his particular province in the coast, he entered farther into the country; and, without any other guide than the spirit of God. penetrated into a kingdom, the language of which was utterly Unknown to him, as he wrote to Mansilla in these, terms.

"You may judge, what manner of life Head here, by what I shall relate to you. I am wholly ignorant of the language of the people, and they understand as little of mine; and I have no interpreter. All I can perform, is to baptize children, and serve the sick, an employment easily understood, without the help of an interpreter, by only minding what they want."

This was the preaching by which he declared Jesus Christ, and made the Christian law appear amiable in that kingdom. For amongst those barbarians, who reduce all humanity to the notion of not being inhuman, and who acknowledge no other duties of charity, than forbearing to do injuries, it was a thing of admiration, to see a stranger, who, without any interest, made the sufferings of another man his own; and performed all sorts of services to the poor, as if he had been their father, or their slave. The name of the country is neither known, nor the fruits which these works of charity produced. It is only certain, that the saint continued not there any long time; and that a troublesome affair recalled him to the coast of Fishery, when it was least in his intentions to return.

The Badages, who are a great multitude of robbers, in the kingdom of Bisnagar, idolaters, and enemies of the Christian name, naturally fierce, always quarrelling amongst themselves, and at war with their neighbours, after they had seized, by force of arms, on the kingdom of Pande, which is betwixt Malabar and the coasts of Fishery, made an irruption into the said coast, in the absence of Xavier. The Paravas were under a terrible consternation at the sight of those robbers, whose very name was formidable to them, not daring so much as to gather into a body, nor to hazard the first brunt of war. They took flight, and abandoned their country, without any other thought than of saving their lives. In order to which, they threw themselves by heaps into their barks, some of them escaping into little desart islands, others hiding amongst the rocks and banks of sand, betwixt Cape Comorin, and the Isle of Ceylon. These were the places of their retreat, together with their wives and children, while the Badages overran the coast, and destroyed their country.

But what profits it to have escaped the sword, when, they must die of hunger? Those miserable creatures, exposed to the burning heats of the sun, wanted nourishment in their isles, and on their rocks, and numbers of them daily perished.

In the mean time, the news of this excursion of the robbers, and the flight of the Christians, was spread about, and Xavier heard it in the country where he then resided. The misfortunes of his dear Paravas touched him in the most tender part. He made haste to their relief; and, having been informed that they were pressed with famine, he passed speedily to the western coast, and earnestly solicited the Portuguese to supply them in this their extreme necessity. He obtained twenty barks, laden with all manner of provision, and himself brought it to their places of retreat, where the poor Paravas, as many as were left alive of them, were languishing without hope of comfort, and expecting death to end their misery.

The sight of the holy man, whom all of them regarded as their common father, caused them to forget some part of their misfortune, and seemed to restore them to life. He gave them all imaginable consolation; and, when they had somewhat recovered their strength, he brought them back to their habitations, from whence the Badages were retired. Those plunderers had swept all away, and the Christians were more poor than ever; he therefore procured alms for them, and wrote a letter earnestly to the Christians of another coast, to supply their brethren in distress.

The Paravas being resettled by degrees, Xavier left them under the conduct of the missioners, whom he had brought for them, and turned his thoughts elsewhere. He was desirous to have carried the sound of the gospel into the more inland countries, which had never heard of Jesus Christ; yet he forbore it at that time, upon this account, that in those kingdoms where there were no Portuguese to protect the new Christians, the idolaters and Saracens would make war on them, or constrain them to renounce their Christianity to buy their peace.

Returning therefore by the western coasts, which were in the possession of the Portuguese, he travelled by land, and on foot, according to his custom, towards the coast of Travancore, which beginning from the point of Comorin, lies extended thirty leagues along by the sea, and is full of villages.

Being come thither, and having, by the good offices of the Portuguese, obtained permission from the king of Travancore to publish the law of the true God, he followed the same method which he had used at the Fishery; and that practice was so successful, that all that coast was converted to Christianity in a little space of time, insomuch, that forty-five churches were immediately built. He writes himself, "That in one month he baptized, with his own hand, ten thousand idolaters; and that, frequently, in one day, he baptized a well peopled village." He says also, "that it was to him a most pleasing object, to behold, that so soon as those infidels had received baptism, they ran, vying with each other to demolish the temples of the idols."

It was at that time, properly speaking, when God first communicated to Xavier the gift of tongues in the Indies; according to the relation of a young Portuguese of Coimbra, whose name was Vaz, who attended him in many of his travels, and who being returned into Europe, related those passages, of which himself had been an eye witness. The holy man spoke very well the language of those barbarians, without having learnt it, and had no need of an interpreter when he instructed. There being no church which was capable of containing those who came to hear him, he led them into a spacious plain, to the number of five or six thousand persons, and there getting up into a tree, that he might the farther extend his voice, he preached to them the words of eternal truth. There it was also, that to the end the compass of the plain might serve in the nature of a church, he sometimes celebrated the divine mysteries under the sails of ships, which were spread above the altar, to be seen on every side.

The Brachmans could not suffer the worship of the pagods to be abandoned in this manner; but were resolved to be revenged on the author of so strange an alteration. In order to execute their design, they secretly engaged some idolaters to lie in wait for him, and dispatch him privately. The murderers lay in ambush more than once, and in the silence of the night endeavoured to shoot him with their arrows. But divine Providence would not suffer their malice to take place; of all their arrows, one only wounded him, and that but slightly; as it were rather to give him the satisfaction of shedding some blood in testimony of the faith, than to endanger his life.

Enraged and desperate for having missed their aim, they sought him everywhere; and not finding him, they set fire on three or four houses, where they thought he might possibly be lodged. The man of God was constrained one day to hide in the covert of a forest, and passed the following night upon a tree, to escape the fury of his enemies, who searched the whole forest to have found him. There was a necessity sometimes that the faithful should keep guard about him day and night, and to that purpose they placed themselves in arms about the house where he was retired.

In the meantime, the Badages, who had ravaged the coast of Fishery the year before, animated of themselves against the Christians, and perhaps pushed forward by the devils, who saw their empire decaying day by day, excited also by the desire of glory, and above all things by the hope of booty, entered into the kingdom of Travancore, on the side of one of those mountains-which confine on the cape of Comorin. Their former success had rendered them so haughty and so insolent, that they flattered themselves with an imagination that every thing would bend before them. But not having now to do, as they had before, with simple fishers, they were come in good order, and well armed, under the conduct of the Naiche, or lord of Modure, a valiant and experienced captain.

The inhabitants of the maritime villages took fright at the noise of an hostile army; and retiring, for the most part with great haste and confusion into the inland country, carried even to the court the news of the invasion.

The king of Travancore, whom the Portuguese call the Great Monarch, because indeed he is the most powerful of all the kings of Malabar, collecting his army with all speed, put himself at the head of it, and marched towards the enemy. The battle, in all appearance, was likely to be bloody, and the victory seemed assured to those vagabond robbers, who were more in number, and better disciplined.

Father Xavier, so soon as he understood that the Badages were drawing near, falling prostrate on the ground, "O Lord," said he; "remember that thou art the God of mercies, and protector of the faithful: give not up to the fury of these wolves that flock, of which thou hast appointed me the pastor; that these new Christians, who are yet so feeble in the faith, may not repent their embracing it, and that the infidels may not have the advantage of oppressing those, who repose their confidence in none but thee."

His prayer being ended, he arose, and inspired with a more than human courage, which made him incapable of fear, he takes a troop of fervant Christians, and, with a crucifix in his hand, runs with them towards the plain, where the enemies were marching in battalia. When he arrived within distance of being heard, he stopped and said to them, in a threatening voice, "I forbid you, in the name of the living God, to pass farther, and on his part, command you to return the way you came."

These few words cast a terror into the minds of those soldiers who were at the head of the army; they remained confounded, and without motion. They, who marched after them, seeing the foremost advanced not, asked the reason of it; answer was returned from the first ranks, that they had before their eyes an unknown person habited in black, of a more than human stature, of a terrible aspect, and darting fire from his eyes. The most hardy were desirous to satisfy themselves concerning what was told them; they were seized with amazement at the sight, and all of them fled with a precipitate confusion.

The new Christians who had followed Xavier, ran to declare to the neighbouring villages this wonderful event. The fame of it was suddenly spread abroad, and the king, who was marching towards the enemy with great speed, heard the report of it on his way. He caused Xavier to be brought into his presence, and embraced him as the redeemer of Travancore; and after he had publicly thanked him for so eminent a service, he said thus to him: "I am called the Great Monarch; and, from henceforth, you shall be called the Great Father."

The saint gave the king to understand, that it was only Jesus Christ to whom he ought to pay his acknowledgments; and, as for himself, he ought only to be regarded as a weak instrument, who could do nothing of his own power. The Pagan king comprehended nothing of his meaning; and the two vices which are the common obstacles to the conversion of the great, that is to say, the concupiscence of the flesh, and pride of heart, hindered him afterwards from embracing of the faith; which notwithstanding, he caused an edict to be published throughout his kingdom, whereby all men were commanded to obey the Great Father, as they would his proper person; and that whoever desired to be a Christian, might be so without any apprehension of danger to ensue. He went so far as even to call Xavier his brother; and bestowed on him large sums of money, all which the servant of God employed in charities on the poor.

An edict so favourable to the law of our belief, made many Christians even in the court, though contrary to the example of the prince. But the miraculous actions of Xavier finished the conversion of the whole kingdom. Besides his curing all sorts of diseases, he raised four persons from the dead, two women and two men. The act of canonization relates no more of the resurrection of the women, but the bare matter of fact, without any circumstances; but the resurrection of the men is related at large, of which the substance is in the ensuing account.

Xavier preached in one of the maritime villages of Travancore, called Coulan, near Cape Comoriu. Some were converted by his first sermons; but the greater party remained in their ancient superstition, after having often heard him. The most obstinate, it is true, listened to him with delight, and found the maxims of the gospel to be most conformable to the light of reason: but the pleasure which they took in hearing, produced nothing; and they satisfied themselves with admiring the Christian law, without troubling themselves to follow it.

The father one day finding, that he spoke to them of God without working any thing upon their hearts, prayed fervently to the Almighty in their behalf; and, with his eyes lifted up to heaven, his countenance more than ordinarily inflamed, and with abundance of tears, besought him to take pity on those obstinate idolaters. "O Lord," said he, "all hearts are in thy hands; thou canst bend, as it pleases thee, the most stubborn, and soften the most obdurate; do that honour, on this day, to the blood and the name of thy beloved Son." Scarcely had he ended his prayer, when he was assured it was answered:

turning himself to his audience, with the air of one inspired, "Well," said he, "since you will not believe me on my word, behold that which will make me be believed. What testimony do you desire from me, of those truths which I have declared to you?" At the same instant he recalled to his remembrance, that a man had been there buried the day before. Then resuming his discourse in the same tone that he began it, "Open," said he, "the sepulchre which you closed yesterday, and bring out the body; but observe carefully, whether he who was buried be truly dead."

The most incredulous ran hastily to take up the corpse; far from finding any the least sign of life, they perceived it began to putrify with a noisome scent. They took off the linen in which he was wrapped, and laid the dead man at the feet of the father, who was come to the place of burial. The barbarians gazed with astonishment on the dead body, and impatiently expected the event. The saint fell upon his knees, and, after a short prayer, addressing himself to the dead, "I command thee," said he, "in the holy name of the living God, to arise, for the confirmation of that religion which I preach." At these words, the dead arose of himself, and appeared not only living, but vigorous, and in perfect health. All who were present cried out, with a loud voice, "That the God of the Christians was omnipotent; and that the law which the great Father preached was true." In consequence of which, they threw themselves at his feet, desired baptism, and received it on the place.

The other dead person whom the apostle raised to life, was a young man, and a Christian, who died at Mutan, on the same coast, betwixt Carjapatan and Alicale. He had been dead above four-and-twenty hours, of a pestilential fever. Xavier met the corpse by chance, as they were carrying it to the grave. The parents of the dead man, who were of the greatest quality in all the country, accompanied the funeral pomp, with all their kindred, according to the custom of that nation. As comfortless as they were, yet upon sight of the saint, they recovered courage, and, embracing his knees, implored him to restore their son to life; being persuaded, that what was not to be effected by the power of nature, would cost him only a word speaking. Xavier, moved by their affliction, and excited by their faith, begged the assistance of the Most High, made the sign of the cross, and threw holy water on the dead, after which he took him by the hand, raised him up in the name of the Lord, and restored him living to his father and mother.

To preserve the memory of an action so wonderful and so authentic, the parents of the man they raised erected a great cross on the place where the miracle was done; and were accustomed afterwards to go often thither, and pray to God before it. These resurrections were so famous through all the country, and made so great impressions on the souls of the inhabitants, that the people came thronging from all parts to behold the great Father, and to receive baptism from his hands; insomuch, that the whole kingdom of Travancore was Subjected to Christ Jesus in few months; and the king, with some few of his chief courtiers, were the only remaining idolaters in the land, by a terrible judgment of Almighty God, who sometimes abandons princes to their unruly passions, and departs from the great, while he communicates himself to those of the lowest quality.

BOOK III.

He writes into Europe for a supply of missioners. The saint's letter to the doctors of Sorbonne. Ambassadors from the isle of Manar to the saint. He sends a missioner to the isle of Manar. The constancy of the Christians of Manar. A miraculous cross, and its effects. The enterprise of Xavier against the persecutor. New motives for his journey to Cambaya. He persuades Michael Vaz to go to Portugal. His letter to the king of Portugal. The success of the voyage undertaken by Michael Vaz. He converts a debauched Portuguese. He engages the viceroy of the Indies to make war on the king of Jafanatapan. Divers predictions of the saint. He goes to join the Portuguese fleet, and raises one from the dead. He frees the island of Manar from the plague. The enterprise of Jafanatapan defeated. He designs the voyage of Macassar, and the conversion of many kingdoms. He goes to the sepulchre of St Thomas, to consult God concerning his voyage to Macassar. What happened to him in his passage to Meliapor. He comes to Meliapor; the monuments which he there finds of the apostle St Thomas. He is threatened by devils, and afterwards beaten by them. He learns the will of God concerning his design. The conversions which he makes at Meliapor. He brings a great sinner to repentance. Divers wonderful events which encrease his fame. He persuades a rich merchant to evangelical perfection. The new convert falls from grace, and becomes suspected to the Saint. His charity to a soldier, who had lost all his money at play. He arrives at Malacca; a digression concerning it. In what condition he found the town, and what he did in order to reform it. He labours with success at Malacca. He revives a dead maid. He receives letters from Europe by the new missioners who are sent him. He defers the voyage to Macassar, and designs another. He foreknows, and foretels the ruin of Malacca. He goes to Amboyna, and what happens to him in his voyage. He arrives at Amboyna: What he performs there. He converts the idolaters and Moors of Amboyna. A Spanish fleet arrives at Amboyna. He assists the Spanish fleet during the contagion amongst them. He passes into divers islands. He recovers his crucifix, which was fallen into the sea. He foretels the holy death of a new convert. He goes to the island of Ulate, and the miracle there wrought by him. He goes to the Moluccas. What happens to him in his way. He declares to the people the death of John Araus. He makes many converts at Ternate. Conversion of a queen at Ternate. He hears of the isles del Moro. Great endeavours are used to dissuade the saint from going to the isles del Moro. He complains of those who make opposition to his voyage to the isle Del Moro. He goes for the isle Del Moro, and writes to Rome. God reveals to him what is doing in a distant island. He arrives at Del Moro; the condition in which he found it. He gains the inhabitants of the isle Del Moro. He speaks to them of hell. He exhorts them to repentance. He says mass in the midst of an earthquake. He is admired by the barbarians. He is persecuted by a cruel and savage people. His sufferings in the isle Del Moro; and the consolations which he there received. He goes for Goa; and the reason that induced him. He returns to Ternate. His proceedings at Ternate. He endeavours the conversion of the king of Ternate. What hindered the king of Ternate's conversion. He labours with great fruit in the court of Ternate. He leaves to the islanders a Christian instruction written with his own hand. The counsel he gave the Ternatines at parting. He renews his labours at Amboyna. He is endued with the supernatural knowledge of some things. A cross, erected by Xavier, becomes famous. The constancy of the Christians in Amboyna.

The reputation of Xavier was not confined to the kingdom of Travancore; it was spread abroad through all the Indies; and the God of the Christians, at the same time, was had in so great veneration, that the most idolatrous nations sent to desire the saint, that he would come and give them baptism. His joy was infinite, to find the Gentiles, of their own free motion, searching after the way of eternal life; but, on the other side, he was afflicted that he was not sufficient alone to instruct so many vast countries as were gone astray from it.

Seeing the harvest so great, and the labourers so few, he wrote earnestly to Father Ignatius in Italy, and to Simon Rodriguez in Portugal, for a supply of missioners. He had such transports of zeal on that occasion, as to say, in one of his letters, "I have often thoughts to run over all the universities of Europe, and principally that of Paris, and to cry aloud to those who abound more in learning than, in charity, Ah, how many souls are lost to heaven through your default! It were to be wished, that those people would apply themselves as diligently to the salvation of souls, as they do to the study of sciences; to the end they might render to Almighty God a good account of their learning, and the talents which he has bestowed on them. Many, without doubt, moved with thoughts like these, would make a spiritual retreat, and give themselves the leisure of meditating on heavenly things, that they might listen to the voice of God. They would renounce their passions, and, trampling under foot all worldly vanities, would put themselves in condition of following the motions of the divine will. They would say, from the bottom of their hearts, behold me in readiness, O my Lord; send me wheresoever thou shalt please, even to the Indies, if thou commandest me.

"Good God, how much more happily would those learned men then live, than now they do! with how much more assurance of their salvation! and, in the hour of death, when they are ready to stand forth before the dreadful judgment-seat, how much greater reason would they have, to hope well of God's eternal mercy, because they might say, O Lord, thou hast given me five talents, and behold I have added other five.

"I take God to witness, that, not being able to return into Europe, I have almost resolved to write to the university of Paris, and namely to our masters, Cornet and Picard, that millions of idolaters might be easily converted, if there were more preachers, who would sincerely mind the interests of Jesus Christ, and not their own concernments."

It is pity that his letter to the doctors of Sorbonne is irrecoverably lost; for certain it is, he wrote to them from the midst of the Indies, to engage them to come, and preach the gospel. And for this we have the testimony of Don John Derada, one of the chief magistrates of the kingdom of Navarre, who, studying at Paris, saw the letter sent from Father Xavier, admired the apostolical charity with which it was replenished, and took a copy of it, as did also many divines, to whom it was directed.

Amongst those idolatrous nations, which breathed after baptism, and desired to be instructed, the Manarois were the first, who made a deputation to the saint.

The isle of Manar is situate towards the most northern point of Ceylon, and at the head of the sands of Remanancor. It has a very convenient port, and is a place of great traffic. But the soil is so sandy and so dry, that it produces nothing, unless in some few places, which also are cultivated with much care and labour. For Manar has no resemblance to Ceylon, though placed so near it: Ceylon being the most delicious and most fruitful part of all the East; where the trees are always green, and bear fruits and flowers in every season; where there are discovered mines of gold and silver, crystal, and precious stones; which is encompassed with forests of ebony, cinnamon, and cocoa; and where the inhabitants live to an extreme old age, without any of the incommodities which attend it, The wonder is, that, being distant from the equinoctial but six degrees, the air is temperate and pure, and the rains, which water it from heaven regularly once a month, joined with the springs and rivers which pass through it, refresh the ground in a greater measure than the scorching heats can parch it.

Father Xavier was employed in establishing Christianity in Travancore, when he received this embassy from Manar. As he could not forsake an infant church without a reasonable apprehension of its ruin, he sent to Manar one of the priests whom he had left on the coast of Fishery. And God so blessed the labours of that missioner, that the Manarois not only became Christians, but died generously for the faith; and this was the occasion of their martyrdom.

The isle of Manar was at that time under the dominion of the king of Jafanatapan; for by that name the northern part of Ceylon is called. This prince had usurped the crown from his elder brother, and enslaved his subjects. Above all things, he was an implacable enemy of the Christian faith; though in appearance he was a friend to the Portuguese, whose forces only could set bounds to his tyranny. When he understood that the Manarois were converted to Christianity, he entered into that fury of which tyrants only can be capable; for he commanded, that his troops should immediately pass over into the island, and put all to the sword, excepting only the idolaters. His orders were punctually executed; and men, women, and children, were all destroyed, who had embraced the Christian faith.

It was wonderful to behold, that the faithful being examined, one by one, concerning their religion, and no more required for the saving of their lives, than to forsake their new belief, there was not one amongst them, who did not openly declare himself a Christian. The fathers and mothers answered for the newly baptized infants, who were not able to give testimony of their faith; and offered them to the death, with a resolution, which was amazing to their executioners. Six or seven hundred of these islanders gave up their lives for the name of Jesus Christ; and the principal place which was consecrated by so noble blood, from Pasim, which it was called before, now took the name of the Field of Martyrs.

This dreadful massacre, far from abolishing the Christian law, served only to render it more flourishing. The tyrant had even the shame of seeing his officers and domestic servants forsake their ancient superstition in despite of him. But what most enraged him, was the conversion of his eldest son. This young prince, inspired of God, caused himself to be instructed by a Portuguese merchant, who had dealings at the court; which yet could not be so secretly performed, but that the king had notice of it. At the first news, he cut his throat, and threw the body into the fields, to serve for food to savage beasts.

But Heaven permitted not, that a death which was so precious in the sight of God, should be without honour in the sight of men, The Portuguese merchant buried his disciple by night; and on the next morning, there appeared a beautiful cross, printed on the ground, which covered the body of the martyr. The spectacle extremely surprised the infidels. They did what they were able, to deface, and (if I may so say) to blot out the cross, by treading over it, and casting earth upon it. It appeared again the day following, in the same figure, and they once more endeavoured to tread it out. But then it appeared in the air, all resplendent with light, and darting its beams on every side. The barbarians who beheld it, were affrighted; and, being touched in their hearts, declared themselves Christians. The king's sister, a princess naturally virtuous, having privately embraced the faith, instructed both her own son, and her nephew, who was brother to the martyr. But, while she directed them in the way of heaven, she took care to preserve them from the cruelty of the tyrant. To which purpose she addressed herself to the merchant above mentioned, and intrusting him with the lives of the two princes, ordered him to convey them to the seminary of Goa.

This Portuguese managed all things so discreetly, with the concurrence of the princess, that he escaped out of the island, with the two princes, undiscovered. He took his way by the kingdom of Travancore, that he might behold Father Xavier, and present to him these two illustrious new converts. The father received them as angels descended from above, and gave immortal thanks to God, for so noble a conquest. He fortified them in the faith, gave them excellent instructions, and promised so to mediate in their favour, with the viceroy of the Indies, that they should have no occasion of repenting themselves for having abandoned all things for the sake of Jesus Christ.

When the king of Jafanatapan had notice of the flight of his son and nephew, he broke out into new fury against the Christians, and put to death great numbers of them. Being apprehensive that his brother, from whom he had usurped the crown, and who now led a wandering life, might possibly change his religion also, and beg protection from the Portuguese, he sent officers round about, with orders to bring him into his hands, or, at the least, to bring back his head. But he failed of getting him in his power either alive or dead; for this unhappy prince, attended by ten horsemen, having passed to Negapatan, came by land to Goa, after having suffered extreme hardships, in a journey of more than two hundred leagues.

Father Xavier, who was informed of all these proceedings, thought it necessary to make advantage of these favourable opportunities without loss of time. He considered with what perfection Christians might live in a kingdom where they died so generously for the faith, with so imperfect a knowledge of it. On the other side, he judged, that if the injustice and cruelty of the tyrant remained unpunished, what an inducement it might be to other idolatrous kings, for them to persecute the new converts in their turn; that the only means for repairing the past, and obviating future mischiefs, was to dispossess the tyrant of the crown, which he so unjustly wore, and restore it to his brother, to whom it rightfully belonged; that, for these considerations, recourse ought to be had to the Portuguese to engage them, by a principle of religion, to take arms against the usurper of the kingdom, and the persecutor of the Christians.

In order to this, the father caused Mansilla to be recalled from the coast of Fishery; and having intrusted him with the care of christianity in Travancore, took his way by land to Cambaya, where the viceroy of the Indies then resided.

Besides these reasons, relating to the king of Jafanatapan, the saint had other motives which obliged him to take this journey. The greatest part of the Europeans, who were in the Indies, and chiefly the officers of the crown of Portugal, lived after so infamous a manner, that they made the Christian faith appear odious, and scandalised alike both the idolaters and the faithful.

The public worship of the pagods was tolerated at Goa, and the sect of the Brachmans daily increased in power; because those Pagan priests had bribed the Portuguese officers. The people professed heathenism freely, provided they made exact payments of their tribute, as if they had been conquered only for the sake of gain. Public offices were sold to Saracens, and the Christian natives stood excluded, for want of money, which does all things with corrupt ministers. The receivers of the king's revenues, who were to pay the Paravas of the coast of Fishery, constrained those poor fishers to deliver their pearls almost for nothing; and thus the exaction of a lawful tribute, in the constitution, became tyranny and oppression in the management. Men were sold like beasts, and Christians enslaved to Pagans at cheap pennyworths. To conclude, the king of Cochin, an idolater, but tributary to the crown of Portugal, was suffered to confiscate the goods of his subjects, who had received baptism.

Father Francis was wonderfully grieved to perceive, that the greatest hindrance to the growth of Christianity, in those vast dominions of Asia, proceeded only from the Christians. He bewailed it sometimes to God, in the bitterness of his heart; and one day said, "That he would willingly return to Portugal to complain of it to the king, not doubting, but so religious and just a prince would order some remedy for this encroaching evil, if he had notice how it spread."

Xavier had taken the way of Cochin, along by the sea coast. He arrived there the 16th of December, 1544, where he happened to meet with Michael Vaz, vicar-general of the Indies. In acquainting him with the reasons of his journey, he made him sensible, that the weakness of the government was the principal cause of the avarice and violence of the officers; that Don Alphonso de Sosa was indeed a religious gentleman, but wanted vigour; that it was not sufficient to will good actions, if, at the same time, he did not strongly oppose ill ones; in a word, that it was absolutely necessary for the king of Portugal to be informed of all the disorders in the Indies, by a person who was an eye-witness of them, and whose integrity was not liable to suspicion. Vaz immediately entered into the opinions of the father, and his zeal carried him to pass himself into Portugal, in a vessel which was just ready to set sail. Xavier praised God for those good intentions; and wrote a letter by him to King John the Third, the beginning of which I have here transcribed:--

"Your Majesty ought to be assured, and often to call into your mind, that God has made choice of you, amongst all the princes of the world, for the conquest of India, to the end he may make trial of your faith, and see what requital you will make to him for all his benefits. You ought also to consider, that, in conferring on you the empire of a new world, his intention was, not so much that you should fill your coffers with the riches of the East, as that you should have an opportunity of signalizing your zeal, by making known to idolaters, through the means of those who serve you, the Creator and Redeemer of mankind."

The saint, after this beginning, gave the king to understand the good intentions of Michael Vaz, and the ill conduct of the Portuguese, who were in the government of the Indies. He suggested to him the means of putting a stop to those disorders, and advised him, above all things, not only to recommend, by letters, the interest of religion, but rigorously to punish all those officers, who were wanting to their duty in that respect; "for there is danger," said he, "that when God shall summon your Majesty to judgment, that will then come to pass which you least expect, and which is not to be avoided; there is danger, great Prince, that you may then hear these words of an offended God. Why have you not punished those who, under your authority, have made war against me in the Indies, you who have punished them so severely, when they were negligent in gathering your revenues? Your cause will be little helped by your return of this answer to Jesus Christ;--Lord, I have not wanted yearly to recommend, by letters to my subjects, all that concerns thy honour and thy service. For, doubt not, it will be thus answered;--But your orders were never put in execution, and you left your ministers, at their own disposal, to do whatever they thought good.

"I therefore beg your Majesty, by that fervent zeal which you have for the glory of our Lord, and by the care which you have always testified of your eternal salvation, to send hither a vigilant and resolute minister, who will bend his actions to nothing more than to the conversion of souls; who may act independently to the officers of your treasury; and who will not suffer himself to be led and governed by the politics of worldly men, whose foresight is bounded with the profit of the state. May your Majesty be pleased a little to inspect your incomes from the Indies, and, after that, look over the expences which are made for the advancement of religion; that, having weighed all things equally on either side, you may make a judgment, if that which you bestow bears any proportion with that which you receive; and then, perhaps, you will find a just subject to apprehend, that, of those immense treasures, which the Divine Goodness has heaped upon you, you have given to God but an inconsiderable pittance.

"For what remains, let not your Majesty defer any longer the payment of so just a debt, to so bountiful a giver, nor the healing of so many public wounds. What remedy soever you can apply, what diligence soever you can make, all will be too little, and of the latest. The sincere and ardent charity of my heart, towards your Majesty, has constrained me to write to you in this manner, especially when my imagination represents to me, in a lively sort, the complaints which the poor Indians send up to heaven, that out of so vast a treasure, with which your estate is enriched by them, you employ so little for their spiritual necessities." The letter ended, in begging this favour of Almighty God, "that the king, in his lifetime, might have those considerations, and that conduct, which he would wish to have had when he was dying."

Michael Vaz negotiated so well with King John the Third, pursuant to the instructions of Father Xavier, that he obtained another governor of the Indies, and carried back such orders and provisions, signed by his Majesty's own hand, as were in a manner the same which the father had desired.

These orders contained, That no toleration should be granted for the superstition of the infidels in the isle of Goa, nor in that of Salseta; that they should break in pieces all the pagods which were there, and make search, in the houses of the Gentiles, for concealed idols, and whosoever used or made them should be punished according to the quality of his crime; that as many of the Brachmans as were found to oppose the publication of the gospel, should be banished; that out of a yearly rent of three thousand crowns, charged on a mosque at Bazain, a subsistence should be made for the poor, newly converted from idolatry; that hereafter no public employment should be given to Pagans; that no exaction should remain unpunished; that no slaves should henceforth be sold, either to Mahometans or Gentiles; that the pearl fishing should only be in the hands of Christians, and that nothing should be taken from them, without paying them the due value; that the king of Cochin should not be suffered to despoil or oppress the baptized Indians; and, last of all, that if Sosa had not already revenged the murder of the Christians in Manar, who were massacred by the king of Jafanatapan's command, Castro, who succeeded in his place, should not fail to see it done.

To return to Father Xavier;--he put to sea at Cochin, and sailed towards Cambaya. In the ship there was a Portuguese gentleman, much a libertine, and one of those declared atheists who make a boast of their impiety. This was motive enough for the holy man to make acquaintance with him. He kept him company, and was even so complaisant as to entertain him with pleasant conversation. The Portuguese was much delighted with his good humour, and took pleasure in hearing him discourse on many curious subjects. But if Xavier offered to let fall a word concerning the salvation of his soul, he laughed at it, and would hear no more. If the father mildly reproved him for his profane and scandalous way of living, he flew out into a fury against the holy practice of the church, and swore he would never more come to confession.

These ill inclinations did not at all discourage Xavier from his undertaking. He treated this hardened sinner after the manner that physicians use a patient raving in his sickness, with all manner of compassion and soft behaviour. In the meantime, they came to an anchor before the port of Cananor, and, going ashore together, they took a walk into a wood of palm-trees which was near their place of landing. After they had made a turn or two, the saint stripped himself to the waist, and taking a discipline, pointed at the ends with wire, struck so hard and so often on his naked body, that, in a very little time, his back and shoulders were all bloody. "It is for your sake," said he to the gentleman who accompanied him, "that I do what you see, and all this is nothing to what I would willingly suffer for you. But," added he, "you have cost Christ Jesus a much dearer price. Will neither his passion, his death, nor all his blood, suffice to soften the hardness of your heart?" After this, addressing himself to our blessed Saviour, "O Lord," said he, "be pleased to look on thy own adorable blood, and not on that of so vile a sinner as myself." The gentleman, amazed and confounded, both at once, at such an excess of charity, cast himself at the feet of Xavier, beseeching him to forbear, and promising to confess himself and totally to change his former life. In effect, before they departed out of the wood, he made a general confession to the father, with sincere contrition for his sins, and afterwards lived with the exemplary behaviour and practice of a good Christian.

Being returned to the port, they went again on shipboard, and continued their voyage to Cambaya. When they were arrived at that place, Xavier went to wait on the viceroy, and easily persuaded him to what he desired, in reference to Jafanatapan; for, besides that Sosa reposed an entire confidence in

Father Xavier, and was himself zealous for the faith, the expedition, which was proposed to him, was the most glorious that the Portuguese could undertake, since the consequence of it was to punish a tyrant, to dispossess an usurper, and to restore a lawful king.

The viceroy, therefore, wrote letters, and dispatched couriers, to the captains of Comorin and of the Fishery, commanding them to assemble all the forces they could make at Negapatan, and make a sudden irruption into the tyrant's country, without giving him time to provide for his defence. He gave them also in charge to take the tyrant alive, if possibly they could, and put him into the hands of Father Francis, who desired his conversion, not his death, and hoped the blood of the martyrs of Manar might obtain the forgiveness of his crimes.

Xavier, encouraged by these hopes, returned towards Cochin, where he proposed to himself to follow his ministerial vocation, while the preparations of war were making. Coming back by Cananor, he lodged in the house of a Christian, who himself was religious, but his son debauched, and subject to all sorts of vices. The good man, sensibly afflicted at the ill conduct of his graceless son, wept day and night; and Xavier began at first to comfort him, saying, those vices were ordinary in youth, and riper age would reclaim him from them. Having done speaking, he stood mute awhile, and recollected himself; then, suddenly lifting up his eyes to heaven, "Know," said he, "that you are the most happy father in the world. This libertine son, who has given you so many disquiets, shall one day change his manners, he shall be a religious of the order of St Francis, and at last shall die a martyr." The event verified the prediction. The young man afterwards took the habit of St Francis, and went to preach the faith in the kingdom of Cande,[1] where he received martyrdom from the barbarians.

[1: Cande is a kingdom in the island of Ceylon.]

Father Xavier, being come back to Cochin, was very kindly received by the secretary of state, Cosmo Annez, his intimate friend, who was there on some important business. Being one day together, and talking familiarly, Xavier asked Annez, if the year had been good for the Portugal merchants? Annez answered him, that it could not have been better: that not long since, seven vessels had been sent off, which were now in their passage to Europe, and richly laden. He added, that himself had sent the king of Portugal a rare diamond, which had cost six thousand ducats at Goa, and Avould be worth more than thirty thousand at Lisbon. Xavier had a farther curiosity to enquire, which of the ships had carried the diamond; and Annez told him, it was the ship called the Atoghia, and that he had entrusted the jewel to John Norogna, who was captain of the ship.

Xavier then entered into a profound meditation; and after he had kept silence for some time, all on the sudden thus replied; "I could have wished that a diamond of so great value had not been entrusted to that ship." "And for what reason?" answered Annez; "is it not because the Atoghia has once formerly sprung a leak? but, father, she is now so well refitted, that she may be taken for a new vessel." The saint explained himself no farther; and Annez, upon a second consideration, began to conjecture, both from the father's words, and afterwards from, his silence, that there was some danger in the matter, whereupon he desired him to recommend that ship to the protection of almighty God; "for in conclusion," said he, "the Atoghia cannot be lost without a very considerable damage to me. I have had no order," said he, "to buy that diamond; so that in case it should miscarry, the loss will be wholly mine."

Sitting one day together at the table, and Xavier observing Annez to be in great concernment, "give thanks to God," said he, "your diamond is safe, and at this very time in the hands of the queen of Portugal." Annez believed Xavier on his word; and understood afterwards, by letters from Norogna, that the ship opened in the midst of her voyage, and let in so much water, that being upon the point of sinking, the mariners had resolved to have forsaken her, and thrown themselves into the sea, but after having cut down the main mast, they changed their thoughts without any apparent reason; that the leak stopped of itself, and the ship pursuing her course, with only two sails, arrived safely in the port of Lisbon.

The man of God remained about three months in Cochin, and towards the end of May set sail for Negapatan, where the Portuguese fleet was now in a readiness. Passing by the Isle of De las Vaccas, which is near the flats of Ceylon, towards the north, he raised to life a Saracen's child, which is all that is known of that miracle. He was desirous in his passage to see the isle of Manar, where so many Christians had been massacred for the faith; and going ashore, he often kissed the ground, which had been sprinkled with the blood of martyrs at Pasim. While he rejoiced at the happy destiny of the dead, he had cause to be afflicted for the misfortune of the living: a contagious disease laid waste the island, and there died an hundred every day.

When the Manarois had notice, that the great father, so famous in the Indies, was at Pasim, they assembled together, above three thousand of them, for the most part Gentiles, and being come to the village, besought him humbly to deliver them from the pestilence.

Xavier asked three days, wherein to implore of God, for that which they had begged from him. During all which time, he only offered up to our Lord, and set before him the merits of those blessed martyrs, who had suffered for his name at Pasim. Before those days were ended, his prayers were heard, the plague ceased, and all the sick were restored to health at the same moment. So visible a miracle wrought on all of them to believe in Jesus Christ; and the apostle baptized them with his own hand. He could make no longer stay with them; for the naval army then expected him, and his presence was necessary to encourage the soldiers, and mind the captains of the performance of their duty.

He passed over from Manar to Negapatan; but there he found all things in a far different condition from what he hoped. The Portuguese navy diminished daily; and the commanders, who at the beginning had been so zealous for the Holy War, were now the first to condemn it. It was in vain for him to set before their eyes the honour of their nation, and that of God: interest did so blind their understanding, that they forgot they were either Portuguese or Christians: behold, in short, what overthrew so glorious an expedition.

While they were equipping the fleet, it happened that a Portuguese vessel, coming from the kingdom of Pegu, and laden with rich merchandise, was driven by tempest upon the coast of Jafanatapan. The king made seizure of it, and possessed himself of all within it, according to the custom of the barbarians. The captain and the ship's company foreseeing, that if, in this conjuncture, war should be made against the heathen prince, they should never be able to retrieve their wealth out of his hands, corrupted the officers of the fleet with large presents, to desist from their undertaking. Thus the tyrant, whom Father Xavier designed to drive out from his ill-gotten kingdom, was maintained in it, by the covetousness of Christians; or rather by the secret decrees of Providence, which sometimes permits the persecutors of the church to reign in peace, to the end a trial may be made of such as dare to continue constant in their faith.

As holy men resign their will to that of God, Xavier wholly abandoned the enterprize of Jafanatapan, and thought only of returning to the kingdom of Travancore. Being now on sea, he cast back his eyes on the Isle of Ceylon, which he saw from far; and cried out, lamenting for it, "Ah! Unhappy island, with how many carcases do I behold thee covered, and what rivers of blood are making inundations on all sides of thee!" These words were prophetical of what happened afterwards, when on Constantine de Braganza at one time, and Don Hurtado de Mendoca at another, destroyed all those islanders with the sword; and the king of Jafanatapan being himself taken, together with his eldest son, was put to death in his own palace; as if the divine justice had not deferred the death of this persecutor, but only to render it more terrible, and more memorable.

Father Xavier was very desirous of returning to Travancore; but the winds blew so contrary, that they always drove him from the coast. By this he judged that God had called him to some other place; and thereupon formed a resolution of carrying the light of the gospel from isle to isle, and from kingdom to kingdom, even to the utmost limits of the East. The news he heard, during his navigation, caused him suddenly to cast his thoughts on an island situate under the equinoctial, betwixt the Moluccas and Borneo, stretched in length two hundred leagues from north to south, and divided into sundry kingdoms, called by the geographers Celebes, by the historians Macassar, from the names of the two capital cities, of the two principal kingdoms; as to the rest, well peopled, and abounding in all sorts of riches.

It was related to him, that about the year 1531, two brothers, both idolaters, as were all the inhabitants of Macassar, going on their private business to Ternate, the chief of the Moluccas, had some conference, relating to religion, with the governor, Antonio Galvan, a Portuguese, one of the most famous warriors of his age, and celebrated in history both for his piety and valour: that having learnt from him the vanity of their idols, they embraced the Christian faith, and at their baptism took the names of Antonio and Michael: that being returned into their country, they themselves taught publicly the faith of Jesus Christ: that all their countrymen, with one accord, sent their ambassadors to the governor of Ternate, desiring him to send them some to instruct them in the principles of faith; and that the heads of this embassy were the two brothers, known to Galvan: that these ambassadors found a very kind reception; and that for want of a priest, Galvan gave them a soldier for their teacher, whose name was Francis de Castro; a man knowing in religion, and of exemplary piety. In conclusion, that Castro, who was thus chosen to instruct that people, embarking for Macassar, was driven by a tempest another way.

Besides this, Xavier was likewise informed, that not long before, a Portuguese merchant, called Antonio Payva, going to Macassar in the name of Ruys Vaz Pereyra, captain of Malacca, for a ship's lading of sandal, a precious wood growing in that island, the king of Supa, which is one of the kingdoms of Macassar, came in person to see him, and asked divers questions relating to the Christian faith: that this honest merchant, better acquainted with his traffic than his religion, yet answered very pertinently, and discoursed of the mysteries of faith after so reasonable a manner, that the king, then threescore years of age, was converted, with all his family and court: that another king of the same island, called the king of Sion, followed his example; and that these two princes, who were solemnly baptized by the hand of Payva, not being able to retain him with them, desired him to send them some priests, who might administer the sacraments, and baptize their subjects.

These pious inclinations appeared to Father Xavier as an excellent groundwork for the planting of the gospel. He wept for joy at the happy news; and adored the profound judgments of the Divine Providence, which, after having refused the grace of baptism to the king of Travancore, when all his subjects had received it, began the conversion of Sion and of Supa by that of their sovereigns. He even believed, that his evangelical ministry exacted from him, to put the last hand to the conversion of those kingdoms.

In the mean time, he thought it his duty, that, before he resolved on the voyage of Macassar, he should ask advice from heaven concerning it; and to perform it as he ought, it came into his mind to implore the enlightnings of God's spirit at the sepulchre of St Thomas, the ancient founder, and first father of Christianity in the Indies, whom he had taken for his patron and his guide, in the course of all his travels. He therefore resolved to go in pilgrimage to Meliapor, which is distant but fifty leagues from Negatapan, where the wind had driven him back. And embarking in the ship of Michael Pereyra, on Palm-Sunday, which fell that year, 1545, on the 29th of March, they shaped their course along-the coasts of Coromandel, having at first a favourable wind; but they had not made above twelve or thirteen leagues, when the weather changed on a sudden, and the sea became so rough, that they were forced to make to land, and cast anchor under covert of a mountain, to put their ship into some reasonable security. They lay there for seven days together, in expectation of a better wind; and all that time the holy man passed in contemplation, without taking any nourishment, either of meat or drink, as they observed who were in the vessel with him, and as James Madeira, who was a witness of it, has deposed in form of law. He only drank on Easter-Eve, and that at the request of the said Madeira, a little water, in which an onion had been boiled, according to his own direction. On that very day, the wind came about into a favourable quarter, and the sea grew calm, so that they weighed anchor, and continued their voyage.

But Xavier, to whom God daily imparted more and more of the spirit of prophecy, foreseeing a furious tempest, which was concealed under that fallacious calm, asked the pilot, "If his ship were strong enough to endure the violence of bad weather, and ride out a storm?" The pilot confessed she was not, as being an old crazy vessel. "Then," said Xavier, "it were good to carry her back into the port." "How, Father Francis," said the pilot, "are you fearful with so fair a wind? you may assure yourself of good weather by all manner of signs, and any little bark may be in safety." It was in vain for the saint to press him farther, not to believe those deceitful appearances; neither would the passengers follow his advice, but they soon repented of their neglect. For far they had not gone, when a dreadful wind arose, the sea was on a foam, and mounted into billows. The ship was not able to withstand the tempest, and was often in danger of sinking, and the mariners were constrained to make towards the port of Negapatan, from whence they set out, which, with much ado, they at length recovered.

The impatience of Father Xavier to visit the tomb of the apostle St Thomas, caused him to make his pilgrimage by land; and he travelled with so much ardour, through the rough and uncouth ways, that in few days he arrived at Meliapor.

That city is now commonly known by the name of St Thomas; because that blessed apostle lived so long in it, and there suffered martyrdom. If we will give credit to the inhabitants, it was once almost swallowed by the sea; and for proof of this tradition, there are yet to be seen under water, the ruins of great buildings. The new town of Meliapor was built by the Portuguese; near the walls there is a hill, which they called the Little Mount, and in it a grotto, wherein they say St Thomas hid himself during the persecution. At the entry of this cave there is a cross cut in the rock; and at the foot of the mountain there arises a spring, the waters of which are of such virtue, that sick people drinking of them are ordinarily cured.

From this small ascent you pass to a higher and much larger mountain, which seems formed by nature for a lonely contemplative life; for on one side it looks upon the sea, and on the other is covered with old trees, always green, which at once make a fruitful and a pleasing object. Hither St Thomas retired to pray with his disciples; and here it was also that he was slain by a Brachman with the thrust of a spear.

The Portuguese, who rebuilt Meliapor, found on the top of the mountain a little chapel, of stonework, all in ruins. They were desirous to repair it, in memory of the holy apostle; and, as they were rummaging all about, even to the foundations of it, they drew out a white marble, whereon was a cross, with characters graved round about it, which declared, "That God was born of the Virgin Mary; that this God was eternal; that the same God taught his law to his twelve apostles; and that one of them came to Meliapor with a palmer's staff in his hand; that he built a church there; that the kings of Malabar, Coromandel, and Pandi, with many other nations, submitted themselves to the law preached by St Thomas, a man holy and penitent."

This marble, of which we make mention, having on it divers stains of blood, the common opinion is, that the apostle suffered martyrdom upon it. Howsoever it be, the marble was placed upon the altar when the chapel was rebuilt; and the first time that a solemn mass was said there, the cross distilled some drops of blood, in the sight of all the people; which also happened many times in the following years, on the day whereon his martyrdom is celebrated.

When Xavier was come into the town, the vicar of Meliapor, who had heard speak of him as a successor of the apostles, and a man sent from God, for the conversion of the Indies, came to offer him a lodging in his house. The father accepted of it, because it was adjoining to the church, wherein were kept the relicks of St Thomas; and that he could easily step from thence by night, to consult the will of God concerning his intended voyage to Macassar.

In effect, as soon as the vicar was laid to sleep, for they were lodged in the same chamber, Xavier rose as softly as he could, and went to the church, through a church-yard which parted it from the house. The vicar perceived it, and advertised Xavier, that this passage was not over-safe by night, and that horrible phantoms had been often seen in it. The saint believed this only said to frighten him, and hinder him from rising before day; so he continued his usual prayers; but it was not long before he found that the advice was true: for, the nights ensuing, as he passed through the church-yard, he saw those dreadful spectres, which endeavoured to have stopped him; yet he saved himself from them, and even laughed at them as vain illusions.

The demons are too proud to bear contempt without revenge, when God permits them. One night, when the saint was at his devotions before the image of the blessed Virgin, they assaulted him in great numbers, and beat him so violently, that he was all over bruised, and forced to keep his bed for some days together. He said nothing of his adventure to the vicar; but it was discovered by a young man of Malabar, who lodged near the church, and was awakened with the noise; rising from his bed, he heard the blows distinctly, and what Father Xavier said to the holy Virgin, invoking her assistance against the infernal powers, insomuch, that the vicar, to whom the young man had related the words which he had heard, sometimes repeated them to Xavier with an inoffensive kind of raillery.

The servant of God having recovered some little strength, returned to the church, and there continued all the night. What rage soever the devils had against him, they durst no more attempt his person, nor so much as endeavour to affright him. They only made a noise to distract him in his prayers; and one time, disguised in the habit of canons, they counterfeited so well the midnight matins, that he asked the vicar, "Who were those chanters who sung so admirably?"

But the favours which Xavier received from heaven, made him large amends for all the injuries of hell; for though the particulars of what passed betwixt God and him were kept secret, it is known, at least in regard of the principal affair, for which he consulted God, that he had an interior light, which gave him clearly to understand, that he was commanded to pass to the more southern islands, and to labour in their conversion. The Christian, strength, with which he found himself animated at the same time, caused all the dangers, which naturally he might apprehend, to disappear, as is manifest by what he wrote from Meliapor on that occasion, to two of his friends at Goa, Paul de Camerin, and James Borba, of whom we have made so frequent mention.

"I hope that God will confer many favours on me in this voyage; since, through his infinite mercy, I have learned, with so much spiritual joy, that it is his holy pleasure I should go to those kingdoms of Macassar, where so many Christians have been made in these latter years. For what remains, I am so much resolved on executing what our Lord has revealed to me, that if I should be wanting on my part, I should go, to my thinking, in direct opposition to his orders, and render myself unworthy of his favour, both in this life and in the next. If I cannot find this year any Portuguese vessel bound for Malacca, I will embark myself on any ship belonging to the Gentiles or the Saracens. I repose, withal, so great a confidence in God, for the love of whom I undertake this voyage, that if there should only pass this way some little bark of Malacca, I should go aboard without the least deliberation. All my hope is in God; and I conjure you by his love, to remember always in your prayers so great a sinner as myself."

Though his intentions in coming to Meliapor were only to receive the instructions of heaven in his solitude, yet he employed some part of his time in the good of others. His holy life gave a lustre and value to his discourse; and the sight of him alone was of efficacy to touch the heart. The people had received it as a maxim, "That whoever followed not the counsel of Father Francis, should die an enemy of God." And they related the unhappy end of some sinners, who, being urged by Xavier to make a speedy repentance, had deferred the work of their conversion. This popular opinion contributed much to the change of manners in the town; and the fear of a disastrous death served frequently to break off in one moment the criminal commerce of many years.

There was in Meliapor a Portuguese gentleman, who lived a debauched and scandalous life. His house was a seraglio, in little; and the greatest part of his business was making a collection of beautiful slaves. Xavier went one day to visit him about dinner time: "Are you willing," said the Father, "that we should begin an acquaintance by dining together?" The Portuguese was somewhat discomposed, both at the visit and the compliment; yet he forced himself into good humour, and made shew of being very glad of the honour which the Father had done him. While they were at table, Xavier spoke not one word to him concerning his debauchery, and only entertained him with ordinary talk, though they had been served by young damsels whose habit was not over modest, and whose air was very impudent. He continued in the same way he had began, after they were risen from dinner, and, in conclusion, took his leave, without making him the least reproach.

The gentleman, surprised at the conduct of Father Francis, believed his silence to be a bad omen to him; and that he had nothing else to expect but an unhappy death, and a more unhappy eternity. In this thought, he went with all diligence to find the Father, and falling down before him, "Your silence," said he, "has spoken powerfully to my heart: I have not enjoyed one moment of repose since you parted from me: Ah, Father, if my everlasting damnation be not already fixed, I put myself into your hands; do with me what you shall judge necessary for the salvation of my soul, behold me ready to pay you a blind obedience."

Xavier embraced him; and after he had given him to understand that the mercies of the Lord are infinite, that it is our duty never to despair, that he who sometimes refuses to sinners the hour of repentance, always grants pardon to the penitent; he caused him to put away those occasions of his sin, and disposed him to a general confession, the fruit of which was a chaste and Christian life.

In short, the Father did what he could desire to be done at Meliapor; and witnesses of known integrity have deposed on oath, that he left the town so different from what it was, at his coming thither, that it was hardly to be known for the same place; which also gave him so entire a satisfaction, that giving it a thousand benedictions, he said that there was not in all the Indies a more Christian town. And at the same time he prophecied, that one day it should become flourishing and wealthy; which prediction was accomplished some few years afterward.

Though all these conversions drew the public veneration on Father Francis, it seemed that God took pleasure in making the name of his servant yet more illustrious, by certain wonderful events. A merchant of Meliapor being just ready to embark for Malacca, went to take his leave of him. In receiving his blessing, he begged of him some little token of his friendship. The Father, who was very poor, could find nothing to give him but the chaplet which was hanging at his neck: "This chaplet,"[1] said he to the merchant, "shall not be unprofitable to you, provided you repose your trust in the Virgin Mary." The merchant went away in full assurance of the divine protection, and without fear of pirates, winds, or rocks; but God would make a trial of his faith. He had already almost crossed, without the least hazard, the great gulph which is betwixt Meliapor and Malacca, when suddenly there blew a furious storm, the sails were torn, the rudder broken, and the mast came by the board, and the vessel afterwards being driven against the rocks, was split: The greatest part of the seamen and passengers were drowned; some of them held upon the rocks, where they were cast away, and the merchant himself was of that number; but, being upon the wide sea, and not having wherewithal to supply nature, to avoid dying by hunger, they took a resolution which only despair could have inspired; having gathered up some floating planks of their wrecked vessel, and joining them together the best they could, they put themselves upon them, and abandoned their safety to the mercy of the waves, without other hope than of lighting on some current which might possibly carry them on shore.

[1: Or beads.]

The merchant, full of confidence in the blessed Virgin, had still preserved the chaplet of Xavier, and feared not drowning while he held it in his hand. The float of planks was hardly adrift upon the waves, when he found he was transported out of himself, and believed he was at Meliapor with Father Francis. Returning from his extacy, he was strangely surprised to find himself on an unknown coast, and not to see about him the companions of his fortunes, nor the planks to which he had entrusted his life. He understood, from some people who casually came that way, that it was the coast of Negapatan, and, in a transport mixed with joy and amazement, he told them, in how miraculous a manner God had delivered him from death.

Another Portuguese, by profession a soldier, called Jerome Fernandez de Mendoza, received a considerable assistance from Xavier, in a different manner, but full as marvellous. Fernandez, having put off from the coast of Coromandel, in a ship belonging to him, wherein was all his wealth, to go to another coast more westward, was taken near the cape of Comorin, by the Malabar pirates, equally covetous and cruel. To save his life, in losing his goods, he threw himself into the sea, and was happy enough, in spite of his ill fortune, to swim to land, on the coast of Meliapor. Meeting there Father Francis, he related his misfortune to him, and begged an alms. The father was almost sorry, at that time, for his being so poor himself, that he had not wherewithal to relieve the miserable man; yet he put his hand into his pocket, as if he were searching there for something, but finding nothing, he lifted up his eyes to heaven, and afterwards turning to Fernandez, with looks full of compassion, "have courage, brother," said he to him, "heaven will provide for you." After which, walking forward four or five paces, he once more put his hands into his pockets, and pulled out fifty pieces of gold: "receive," added he, "what heaven sends you; make use of it, but speak not of it." The surprise and joy of Fernandez were so great, that it was impossible for him to keep silence. He published, in all places, the bounty of his benefactor; and the pieces of gold were found to be so pure and fine, that it was not doubted but they were miraculous.

But perhaps nothing is more admirable, than what passed betwixt the Father and John Duro, or Deyro, as some have called him. He was a man of about five-and-thirty years of age, who had formerly borne arms; afterwards became a merchant and owner of a ship, very wealthy and fortunate in all his traffic; all which notwithstanding, he was ill satisfied with the world, uneasy to himself, unquiet in the midst of all his wealth, and persuaded that God alone could content his soul. He went one day to see the holy man, and told him, that for many years he had a desire of changing his condition, and of serving God as perfectly as he was able, but that two reasons had always hindered him: the one was, that he never yet could meet with any person, who was capable of shewing him the way of perfection; the other was, that he was afraid of falling into poverty. He added, that he was now out of pain concerning those two points. That for the first, he hoped he should walk surely in the way of heaven, having so able a guide as he; and for the second, he had got sufficiently for his maintenance in an honest and comfortable way, during the remainder of his life. He begged leave of Father Xavier, that he might follow him, and promised, on all occasions, to defray his charges.

The Father made Deyro understand, how far he was yet from the kingdom of heaven; that, to arrive at perfection, he must perform what our Saviour counselled the young man, who seemed willing to follow him, that is to say, he must practise these words in the literal sense, "sell all thou hast, and give it to the poor." Deyro, thus undeceived, immediately desired the Father to take all his goods, and distribute them amongst the poor; but the Father would neither do what Deyro had proposed to him, nor permit that he should himself dispose of any thing, before he had made confession to him. Foreseeing, without doubt, that being so rich, he should be obliged to make restitution of some part of that which he had gained.

The confession of the merchant was three days in making; after which, having sold his ship and his merchandise, he restored what he had got unjustly, and gave great alms. And in consequence of this, under the direction of the saint, he gave himself to the exercises of piety and penitence, thereby to lay a solid foundation of that perfection to which he aspired.

But these fair beginnings were not attended with any answerable fruit; and that spirit of retirement, of mortification, and of poverty, was soon extinguished in a man accustomed to the turmoils of the world, who had always lived in plenty, and who passionately loved his profit. He returned to the thoughts of his former condition, and having recovered some jewels, and bought a small vessel in secret, he set himself to follow his former way of living.

When he was just on the point of setting sail, a catechist, called Antonio, came and told him, that Father Xavier desired to speak with him. Deyro, who thought of nothing more than of making his escape, and who had not entrusted his design to the knowledge of any person, made as if he took him for another. But Antonio persisting in it, that it was himself whom the Father meant, he durst not dissemble any longer, and went to find him; resolved, however, of denying all, as thinking the Father at most could have but a bare suspicion of his change and intended flight. He therefore assumed an air of confidence, and presented himself boldly before the saint; but God had given him knowledge of Deyro's intentions.

"You have sinned," said Xavier, as soon as he beheld him; "you have sinned." These few words so deeply struck him, that he threw himself at the feet of the Father, all trembling, and crying out, "it is true, my Father, I have sinned:" "Penitence then, my son," replied the Father, "penitence!" Deyro confessed himself immediately, went to sell off his ship, and distributed all the money to the poor. He returned afterwards, and put himself once more under the conduct of the Father, with a firm resolution of following his counsels more sincerely, and of serving God more faithfully.

How unfeigned soever the repentance of Deyro seemed, Xavier had no confidence in it; and these new fervours were suspected by him. He would not receive him into the company of Jesus, which requires solid spirits, and such as are firm to their vocation.

Yet he refused not to admit him for his companion, in quality of a catechist, and carried him with him to Malacca: for having continued four months at Meliapor, he parted thence in September 1545, notwithstanding the tears of the people, who were desirous of retaining him; and held the course of Malacca, designing from thence to pass to Macassar.

Before he went on board, he wrote to Father Paul de Camerine at Goa, that when the fathers of the society, who were daily expected from Portugal, should arrive, two of those new missioners should accompany the princes of Jafanatapan, whensoever the Portuguese should think fit to re-establish the lawful king. For there was a report, that the expedition should be renewed, which a base interest had set aside. But this project was not put in execution; and both the princes died, one after the other, in less than two years after their conversion, which was only profitable to their souls. While the ship that carried Xavier was crossing the Gulph of Ceylon, an occasion of charity was offered to the saint, which he would not suffer to escape. The mariners and soldiers passed their time, according to their custom, in playing at cards. Two soldiers set themselves to it, more out of avarice than pleasure, and one of them played with such ill fortune, that he lost not only all his own money, but the stock which others had put into his hands to traffic for them. Having nothing more to lose, he withdrew, cursing his luck, and blaspheming God. His despair prevailed so far over him, that he had thrown himself into the sea, or run upon the point of his sword, if he had not been prevented. Xavier had notice of these his mad intentions and execrable behaviour, and immediately came to his relief. He embraced him tenderly, and said all he could to comfort him; but the soldier, who was still in the transports of his fury, thrust him away, and forbore not even ill language to him. Xavier stood recollected for some time, imploring God's assistance and counsel; then went and borrowed fifty royals of a passenger, brought them to the soldier, and advised him once more to try his fortune. At this the soldier took heart, and played so luckily, that he recovered all his losses with great advantage. The saint, who looked on, took out of the overplus of the winnings, what he had borrowed for him; and seeing the gamester now returned to a calm temper, wrought upon him so successfully, that he, who before refused to hear him, was now overpowered by his discourse, never after handled cards, and became exemplary in his life.

They arrived at Malacca the 25th of September. As this is one of those places in the Indies, where the saint, whose life I write, had most business, and whither he made many voyages, it will not be unprofitable to say somewhat of it. It is situate beyond the gulph of Bengal, towards the head of that great peninsula, which, from the mouth of the Ara, is extended to the south, almost to the equinoctial line; and is of two degrees and a half of elevation, over against the island of Sumatra, which the ancients, who had not frequented this channel, believed to be joined to the continent.

Malacca was under the dominion of the kings of Siam, until the Saracens, who traded thither, becoming powerful, first made it Mahometan, then caused it to revolt against the lawful prince, and set up a monarch of their own sect, called Mahomet. There was not, at that time, any more famous mart town than this, and where there was a greater concourse of different nations. For, besides the people of Guzuratte, Aracan, Malabar, Pegu, Sumatra, Java, and the Moluccas, the Arabs, the Persians, the Chinese, and the Japonians, trafficked there; and accordingly the town lay extended all along by the sea side, for the convenience of trade.

Amongst all the nations of Asia there is not any more inclined to pleasure; and this seems chiefly to proceed from the mild temper of the air. For there is an eternal spring, notwithstanding the neighbourhood of the line. The inhabitants follow the natural bent of their complexion; their whole business is perfumes, feasts, and music; to say nothing of carnal pleasures, to which they set no bound. Even the language which they speak participates of the softness of the country: It is called the Malaya tongue, and, of all the orient, it is the most delicate and sweet of pronunciation.

Don Alphonso Albuquerque conquered Malacca in the year 1511, and thirty thousand men, with eight thousand pieces of artillery, and an infinite number of elephants and ships, were not able to defend it. It was taken by force, at the second assault, by eight hundred brave Portuguese, seconded by some few Malabars. It was given up to pillage for three days; and the Moor king, after all his endeavours, was forced to fly with only fifty horsemen to attend him. The Portuguese built a citadel, which the succeeding governors took care to fortify; yet not so strongly, as to be proof against the attempts of the barbarians, who many times attacked it, and half ruined it.

As soon as Xavier came on shore, he went to visit the governor of the town, to inform him of his intended voyage to Macassar. The governor told him, that he had lately sent thither a priest of holy life, with some Portuguese soldiers, and that he expected to hear of them very suddenly: that, in the mean time, he was of opinion, that the Father and his companion should stay at Malacca, till the present condition of the Christians in Macassar were fully known. Xavier gave credit to the governor, and retired to the hospital, which he had chosen for the place of his abode. The people ran in crowds to behold the countenance of that great apostle, whose fame was spread through all the Indies, and over all the East. The parents showed him to their children; and it was observed, that the man of God, in caressing those little Portuguese, called every one of them by their proper names, as if he had been of their acquaintance, and were not a stranger newly come on shore.

For what remains, he found the town in a most horrible corruption of manners. The Portuguese who lived there, at a distance both from the Bishop and the viceroy of the Indies, committed all manner of crimes, without fear of laws, either ecclesiastical or civil. Avarice, intemperance, uncleanness, and forgetfulness of God, were every where predominant; and the habit only, or rather the excess and number of their vices, distinguished the Christians from the unbelievers.

This terrible prospect of a sinful town, gave Xavier to comprehend, that his stay in Malacca was necessary, and might possibly turn to a good account; but before he would undertake the reformation of a town so universally corrupted, he employed some days in serving of the sick; he passed many nights in prayer, and performed extraordinary austerities.

After these preparatives, he began his public instructions, according to the methods which he had frequently practised at Goa. Walking the streets at evening with his bell in his hand, he cried, with a loud voice, "Pray to God for those who are in the state of mortal sin;" and by this, he brought into the minds of sinners, the remembrance and consideration of their offences. For, seeing the ill habits of their minds, and that the disease was like to be inflamed, if violent remedies were applied, he tempered more than ever the ardour of his zeal. Though he had naturally a serene countenance, and was of a pleasing conversation, yet all the charms of his good humour seemed to be redoubled at Malacca, insomuch, that his companion, John Deyro, could not but wonder at his gaiety and soft behaviour.

By this procedure, the apostle gained the hearts of all and became in some manner, lord of the city. At the very first, he rooted out an established custom, which permitted the young maids to go in the habit of boys whenever they pleased, which occasioned a world of scandal. He drove out of doors the concubines, or turned them into lawful wives, according to his former method. As for the children, who had no knowledge of God, and who learnt songs of ribaldry and obsceneness as soon as they began to speak, he formed them so well in a little time, that they publicly recited the Christian doctrine, and set up little altars in the streets, about which they sung together the hymns of the Catholic church. But that in which he was most successful, was to restore the practice of confession, which was almost entirely lost. But now men and women crowded the tribunal of holy penitence, and the Father was not able to supply the necessities of so many.

He laboured in the knowledge of the Malaya tongue, which is spoken in all the isles beyond Malacca, and is as it were the universal language. His first care was to have a little catechism translated into it, being the same he had composed on the coast of Fishery; together with a more ample instruction, which treated of the principal duties of Christianity. He learnt all this without book; and, to make himself the better understood, he took a particular care of the pronunciation.

With these helps, and the assistance of interpreters, who were never wanting to him at his need, he converted many idolaters, as also Mahometans and Jews; amongst the rest, a famous rabbi, who made a public adjuration of Judaism. This rabbi, who before had taken for so many fables, or juggling tricks, all those wonders which are reported to have been done by Xavier, now acknowledged them for truths by the evidence of his own eyes: for the saint never wrought so many miracles as at Malacca. The juridical depositions of witnesses then living, have assured us, that all sick persons whom he did but touch, were immediately cured, and that his hands had an healing virtue against all distempers. One of his most famous cures, was that of Antonio Fernandez, a youth not above fifteen years of age, who was sick to death. His mother, a Christian by profession, but not without some remainders of paganism in her heart, seeing that all natural remedies were of no effect, had recourse to certain enchantments frequently practised amongst the heathens, and sent for an old sorceress, who was called Nai. The witch made her magical operations on a lace braided of many threads, and tied it about the arm of the patient. But instead of the expected cure, Fernandez lost his speech, and was taken with such violent convulsions, that the physicians were called again, who all despaired of his recovery. It was expected every moment he should breath his last, when a Christian lady, who happened to come in, said to the mother of the dying youth, "Why do you not send for the holy Father? he will infallibly cure him." She gave credit to her words, and sent for Xavier. He was immediately there: Fernandez, who had lost his senses, and lay gasping in death, began to cry out, and make violent motions, so soon as the Father had set his foot within the doors; but when he came into the room, and stood before the youth, he fell into howlings and dreadful wreathings of his body, which redoubled at the sight of the cross that was presented to him. Xavier doubted not but there was something of extraordinary in his disease, nor even that God, for the punishment of the mother, who had made use of diabolical remedies, had delivered her son to the evil spirits. He fell on his knees by the bed-side, read aloud the passion of our Lord, hung his reliquiary about the neck of the sick person, and sprinkled him with holy water. This made the fury of the devil cease; and the young man, half dead, lay without motion as before. Then Xavier rising up, "get him somewhat to eat," said he, and told them what nourishment he thought proper for him. After which, addressing himself to the father of the youth, "when your son," added he, "shall be in condition to walk, lead him yourself, for nine days successively, to the church of our Lady of the Mount, where to-morrow I will say mass for him." After this he departed, and the next day, while he was celebrating the divine sacrifice, Fernandez on the sudden came to himself, spoke very sensibly, and perfectly recovered his former health.

But how wonderful soever the cure of this youth appeared in the eyes of all men, the resurrection of a young maid was of greater admiration. Xavier was gone on a little journey, somewhere about the neighbourhood of Malacca, to do a work of charity when this girl died. Her mother, who had been in search of the holy man during her daughter's sickness, came to him after his return, and throwing herself at his feet all in tears, said almost the same words to him which Martha said formerly to our Lord, "That if he had been in town, she, who was now dead, had been alive; but if he would call upon the name of Jesus Christ, the dead might be restored to life." Xavier was overjoyed to behold so great faith in a woman, who was but lately baptized, and judged her worthy of that blessing which she begged. After having lifted up his eyes to heaven, and silently prayed to God some little space, he turned towards her, and said to her, with much assurance, "Go, your daughter is alive." The poor mother seeing the saint offered not to go with her to the place of burial, replied, betwixt hope and fear, "That it was three days since her daughter was interred." "It is no matter," answered Xavier, "open the sepulchre, and you shall find her living." The mother, without more reply, ran, full of confidence, to the church, and, in presence of many persons, having caused the grave-stone to be removed, found her daughter living.

While these things passed at Malacca, a ship from Goa brought letters to Father Xavier from Italy and Portugal; which informed him of the happy progress of the society of Jesus, and what it had already performed in Germany for the public service of the church. He was never weary of reading those letters; he kissed them, and bedewed them with his tears, imagining himself either with his brethren in Europe, or them present with himself in Asia. He had news at the same time, that there was arrived a supply of three missioners, whom Father Ignatius had sent him; and that Don John de Castro, who succeeded Alphonso de Sosa, in the government of the Indies, had brought them in his company. These missioners were Antonio Criminal, Nicholas Lancilotti, and John Beyra, all three priests; the two first Italians, and the last a Spaniard: apostolical men, and of eminent virtue, particularly Criminal, who, of all the children of Ignatius, was the first who was honoured with the crown of martyrdom. Xavier disposed of them immediately, commanding, by his letters, "That Lancilotti should remain in the seminary of holy faith, there to instruct the young Indians in the knowledge of the Latin tongue, and that the other two should go to accompany Francis Mansilla on the coast of Fishery."

For himself, having waited three months for news from Macassar, when he saw the season proper for the return of the ship, which the Governor of Malacca had sent, was now expired, and that no vessel was come from those parts, he judged, that Providence would not make use of him at present, for the instruction of those people, who had a priest already with them. Nevertheless, that he might be more at hand to succour them, whenever it pleased God to furnish him with an occasion, it was in his thoughts to go to the neighbouring islands of that coast, which were wholly destitute of gospel ministers.

God Almighty at that time revealed to him the calamities which threatened Malacca; both the pestilence and the war, with which it was to be afflicted in the years ensuing; and the utter desolation, to which it should one day be reduced for the punishment of its crimes. For the inhabitants, who, since the arrival of the Father, had reformed their mariners, relapsed insensibly into their vices, and became more dissolute than ever, as it commonly happens to men of a debauched life, who constrain themselves for a time, and whom the force of ill habits draws backward into sin. Xavier failed not to denounce the judgments of God to them, and to exhort them to piety, for their own interest. But his threatenings and exhortations were of no effect: and this it was that made him say of Malacca the quite contrary of what he had said concerning Meliapor, that he had not seen, in all the Indies, a more wicked town.

He embarked for Amboyna the 1st of January, 1546, with John Deyro, in a ship which was bound for the Isle of Banda. The captain of the vessel was a Portuguese; the rest, as well mariners as soldiers, were Indians; all of them almost of several countries, and the greatest part Mahometans, or Gentiles. The saint converted them to Jesus Christ during the voyage; and what convinced the infidels of the truth of Christianity, was, that when Father Xavier expounded to them the mysteries of Christianity in one tongue, they understood him severally, each in his own language, as if he had spoken at once in many tongues.

They had been already six weeks at sea, without discovering Amboyna; the pilot was of opinion they had passed it, and was in pain concerning it, not knowing how to tack about, because they had a full fore-wind. Xavier perceiving the trouble of the pilot, "Do not vex yourself," said he, "we are yet in the Gulph; and to-morrow, at break of day, we shall be in view of Amboyna." In effect, at the time mentioned, the next morning, they saw that island. The pilot being unwilling to cast anchor, Father Xavier, with some of the passengers, were put into a skiff, and the ship pursued its course. When the skiff was almost ready to land, two light vessels of pirates, which usually cruised on that coast, appeared on the sudden, and pursued them swiftly. Not hoping any succour from the ship, which was already at a great distance from them, and being also without defence, they were forced to put off from shore, and ply their oars towards the main sea, insomuch that the pirates soon lost sight of them. After they had escaped the danger, they durst not make to land again, for fear the two vessels should lie in wait to intercept them at their return. But the Father assured the mariners, they had no further cause of fear: turning therefore towards the island, they landed there in safety, on the 16th of February.

The Isle of Amboyna is distant from Malacca about two hundred and fifty leagues; it is near thirty leagues in compass, and is famous for the concourse of merchants, who frequent it from all parts. The Portuguese, who conquered it during the time that Antonio Galvan was governor of Ternate, had a garrison in it; besides which, there were in the island seven villages of Christians, natives of the place, but without any priest, because the only one in the island was just dead. Xavier began to visit these villages, and immediately baptized many infants, who died suddenly after they were christened. "As if," says he himself in one of his letters, "the Divine Providence had only so far prolonged their lives, till the gate of heaven were opened to them."

Having been informed, that sundry of the inhabitants had retired themselves from the sea-side into the midst of the woods, and caves of the mountains, to shelter themselves from the rage of the barbarians, their neighbours and their enemies, who robbed the coasts, and put to the sword, or made slaves of all who fell into their hands, he went in search of those poor savages, amidst the horror of their rocks and forests; and lived with them as much as was necessary, to make them understand the duties of Christianity, of which the greatest part of them was ignorant.

After having instructed the faithful, he applied himself to preach the gospel to the idolaters and Moors; and God so blessed the endeavours of his servant, that the greatest part of the island became Christians. He built churches in every village, and made choice of the most reasonable, the most able, and the most fervent, to be masters over the rest, till there should arrive a supply of missioners. To which purpose he wrote to Goa, and commanded Paul de Camerine to send him Francis Mansilla, John Beyra, and one or two more of the first missioners which should arrive from Europe: he charged Mansilla, in particular, to come. His design was to establish in one of those isles a house of the company, which should send out continual supplies of labourers, for the publication of the gospel, through all that Archipelago.

While Xavier laboured in this manner at Amboyna, two naval armies arrived there; one of Portugal with three ships, the other of Spaniards with six men of war. The Spaniards were come from Nueva Espagna, or Mexico, for the conquest of the Moluccas, in the name of the emperor Charles the Fifth, as they pretended; but their enterprise succeeded not. After two years cruising, and long stay with the king of Tidore, who received them, to give jealousy to the Portuguese, who were allied to the king of Ternate, his enemy, they took their way by Amboyna, to pass into the Indies, and from thence to Europe. They were engaged in an unjust expedition against the rights of Portugal, and without order from Charles the Fifth; for that emperor, to whom King John the Third addressed his complaints thereupon, disavowed the proceedings of his subjects, and gave permission, that they should be used like pirates.

Yet the Portuguese proceeded not against them with that severity. But it seems that God revenged their quarrel, in afflicting the Spaniards with a contagious fever, which destroyed the greatest part of their fleet. It was a sad spectacle to behold the mariners and soldiers, lying here and there in their ships, or on the shore, in cabins, covered only with leaves. The disease which consumed them, kept all men at a distance from them; and the more necessity they had of succour, the less they found from the people of the island.

At the first report which came to Xavier of this pestilence, he left all things to relieve them; and it is scarce to be imagined, to what actions his charity led him on this occasion. He was day and night in a continual motion, at the same time administering to their bodies and their souls; assisting the dying, burying the dead, and interring them even with his own hands. As the sick bad neither food nor physic, he procured both for them from every side; and he who furnished him the most, was a Portuguese, called John d'Araus, who came in his company from Malacca to Amboyna. Nevertheless the malady still increasing day by day, Araus began to fear he should impoverish himself by these charities; and from a tender-hearted man, became so hard, that nothing more was to be squeezed out of him. One day Xavier sent to him for some wine, for a sick man who had continual faintings: Araus gave it, but with great reluctance, and charged the messenger to trouble him no more; that he had need of the remainder for his own use; and when his own was at an end, whither should he go for a supply? These words were no sooner related to Father Francis, than inflamed with a holy indignation, "What," says he, "does Araus think of keeping his wine for himself, and refusing it to the members of Jesus Christ! the end of his life is very near, and after his death all his estate shall be distributed amongst the poor." He denounced death to him with his own mouth; and the event verified the prediction, as the sequel will make manifest.

Though the pestilence was not wholly ceased, and many sick were yet aboard the vessels, the Spanish fleet set sail for Goa, forced to it by the approach of winter, which begins about May in those quarters. Father Xavier made provisions for the necessities of the soldiers, and furnished them, before their departure, with all he could obtain from the charity of the Portuguese. He recommended them likewise to the charity of his friends at Malacca, where the navy was to touch; and wrote to Father Paul de Camerine at Goa, that he should not fail to lodge in the college of the company, those religious of the order of St Augustin, who came along with the army from Mexico, and that he should do them all the good offices, which their profession, and their virtue, claimed from him.

After the Spaniards were departed, Xavier made some little voyages to places near adjoining to Amboyna; and visited some islands, which were half unpeopled, and desart, waiting the convenience of a ship to transport him to the Moluccas, which are nearer to Macassar than Amboyna. One of those isles is Baranura, where he miraculously recovered his crucifix, in the manner I am going to relate, according to the account which was given of it by a Portuguese, called Fausto Rodriguez, who was a witness of the fact, has deposed it upon oath, and whose juridical testimony is in the process of the saint's canonization.

"We were at sea," says Rodriguez, "Father Francis, John Raposo, and myself, when there arose a tempest, which alarmed all the mariners. Then the Father drew from his bosom a little crucifix, which he always carried about him, and leaning over deck, intended to have dipt it into the sea; but the crucifix dropt out of his hand, and was carried off by the waves. This loss very sensibly afflicted him, and he concealed not his sorrow from us. The next morning we landed on the island of Baranura; from the time when the crucifix was lost, to that of our landing, it was near twenty-four hours, during which we were in perpetual danger. Being on shore, Father Francis and I walked along by the sea side, towards the town of Tamalo, and had already walked about 500 paces, when both of us beheld, arising out of the sea, a crab-fish, which carried betwixt his claws the same crucifix raised on high. I saw the crab-fish come directly to the Father, by whose side I was, and stopped before him. The Father, falling on his knees, took his crucifix, after which the crab-fish returned into the sea. But the Father still continuing in the same humble posture, hugging and kissing the crucifix, was half an hour praying with his hands across his breast, and myself joining with him in thanksgiving to God for so evident a miracle; after which we arose, and continued on our way." Thus you have the relation of Rodriguez.

They staid eight days upon the island, and afterwards set sail for Rosalao, where Xavier preached at his first coming, as he had done at Baranura. But the idolaters, who inhabited these two islands, being extremely vicious, altogether brutal, and having nothing of human in them besides the figure, gave no credit to his words; and only one man amongst them, more reasonable than all the rest, believed in Jesus Christ. Insomuch, that the holy apostle, at his departure from Rosalao, took off his shoes, and shook off the dust, that he might not carry any thing away with him, which belonged to that execrable land.

Truly speaking, the conversion of that one man was worth that of many. The saint gave him in baptism his own name of Francis; and foretold him, that he should die most piously, in calling upon the name of Jesus. The prophecy was taken notice of, which has recommended the fame of this new convert to posterity, and which was not accomplished till after forty years. For this Christian, forsaking his barbarous island, and turning soldier, served the Portuguese, on divers occasions, till in the year 1588 he was wounded to death in a battle given by Don Sancho Vasconcellos, governor of Amboyna, who made war with the Saracen Hiamo. Francis was carried off into the camp; and many, as well Indians as Portuguese, came about him, to see the accomplishment of the prediction, made by the blessed Francis Xavier. All of them beheld the soldier dying, with extraordinary signs of piety, and crying, without ceasing, "Jesus, assist me!"

The island of Ulate, which is better peopled, and less savage than those of Baranura and Rosalao, was not so deaf nor so rebellious to the voice of the holy man. He found it all in arms, and the king of it besieged in his town, ready to be surrendered, neither through want of courage, nor of defendants, but of water; because the enemy had cut off the springs, and there was no likelihood of rain; insomuch, that during the great heats, both men and horses were in danger of perishing by thirst.

The opportunity appeared favourable to Father Xavier, for gaining the vanquished party to Jesus Christ, and perhaps all the conquerors. Full of a noble confidence in God, he found means to get into the town; and being presented to the king, offered to supply him with what he most wanted. "Suffer me," said he, "to erect a cross, and trust in the God, whom I come to declare to you. He is the Lord and Governor of nature, who, whenever he pleases, can open the fountains of heaven, and water the earth. But, in case the rain should descend upon you, give me your promise, to acknowledge his power, and that you, with your subjects, will receive his law." In the extremity to which the king was then reduced, he consented readily to the Father's conditions; and also obliged himself, on the public faith, to keep his word, provided Xavier failed not on his part of the promised blessing. Then Xavier causing a great cross to be made, set it up, on the highest ground of all the town; and there, on his knees, amongst a crowd of soldiers, and men, women, and children, attracted by the novelty of the sight, as much as by the expected succour, he offered to God the death of his only son, and prayed him, by the merits of that crucified Saviour, who had poured out his blood for the sake of all mankind, not to deny a little water, for the salvation of an idolatrous people.

Scarcely had the saint begun his prayer, when the sky began to be overcast with clouds; and by that time he had ended it, there fell down rain in great abundance, which lasted so long, till they had made a plentiful provision of water. The enemy, now hopeless of taking the town, immediately decamped; and the king, with all his people, received baptism from the hand of Father Xavier. He commanded also, that all the neighbouring islands, who held of him should adore Christ Jesus, and engaged the saint to go and publish the faith amongst them. Xavier employed three months and more in these little voyages; after which, returning to Amboyna, where he had left his companion, John Deyro, to cultivate the new-growing Christianity, and where he left him also for the same intention, embarked on a Portuguese vessel, which was setting sail for the Moluccas.

That which is commonly called by the name of the Moluccas, is a country on the Oriental Ocean, divided into many little islands, situated near, the equator, exceeding fruitful in cloves, and famous for the trade of spices. There are five principal islands of them, Ternate, Tidor, Motir, Macian, and Bacian. The first of these is a degree and a half distant from the equinoctial to the north, the rest follow in the order above named, and all five are in sight of one another. These are those celebrated islands, concerning which Ferdinand Magellan raised so many disputes amongst the geographers, and so many quarrels betwixt Spain and Portugal. For the Portuguese having discovered them from the east, and the Spaniards from the west, each of them pretended to inclose them, within their conquests, according to the lines of longitude which they drew.

Ternate is the greatest of the Moluccas, and it was on that side that Father Xavier took his course. He had a gulph to pass of ninety leagues, exceedingly dangerous, both in regard of the strong tides, and the uncertain winds, which are still raising tempests, though the sea be never so calm. The ship which carried the Father was one of those vessels, which, in those parts, are called caracores, of a long and narrow built, like gallies, and which use indifferently sails and oars. Another vessel of the same make carried a Portuguese, called John Galvan, having aboard her all his goods. They set out together from Amboyna, keeping company by the way, and both of them bound for the port of Ternate.

In the midst of the gulph, they were surprised with a storm, which parted them so far, that they lost sight of each other. The caracore of Xavier, after having been in danger of perishing many times, was at length saved, and recovered the port of Ternate by a kind of miracle: as for that of Galvan, it was not known what became of her, and the news concerning her was only brought by an evident revelation.

The first saint's day, when the Father preached to the people, he stopped short in the middle of his discourse, and said, after a little pause, "Pray to God for the soul of John Galvan, who is drowned in the gulph." Some of the audience, who were friends of Galvan, and interested in the caracore, ran to the mariners, who had brought the Father, and demanded of them, if they knew any certain news of this tragical adventure? They answered, "that they knew no more than that the storm had separated the two vessels." The Portuguese recovered courage at those words, and imagined that Father Francis had no other knowledge than the seamen. But they were soon undeceived by the testimony of their own eyes; for three days after, they saw, washed on the shore, the corpse of Galvan, and the wreck of the vessel, which the sea had thrown upon the coast.

Very near this time, when Xavier was saying mass, turning to the people to say the Orate Fratres, he added, "pray also for John Araus, who is newly dead at Amboyna." They who were present observed punctually the day and hour, to see if what the Father had said would come to pass: ten or twelve days after, there arrived a ship from Amboyna, and the truth was known not only by divers letters, but confirmed also by a Portuguese, who had seen Araus die at the same moment when Xavier exhorted the people to pray to God to rest his soul. This Araus was the merchant which refused to give wine for the succour of the sick, in the Spanish fleet, and to whom the saint had denounced a sudden death. He fell sick after Xavier's departure; and having neither children nor heirs, all his goods were distributed amongst the poor, according to the custom of the country.

The shipwreck of Galvan, and the death of Araus, gave great authority to what they had heard at Ternate, concerning the holiness of Father Francis, and from the very first gained him an exceeding reputation. And indeed it was all necessary; I say not for the reformation of vice in that country, but to make him even heard with patience by a dissolute people, which committed, without shame, the most enormous crimes, and such as modesty forbids to name.

To understand how profitable the labours of Father Xavier were to those of Ternate, it is sufficient to tell what he has written himself: "That of an infinite number of debauched persons living in that island when he landed there, all excepting two had laid aside their wicked courses before his departure. The desire of riches was extinguished with the love of pleasures. Restitutions were frequently made, and such abundant alms were given, that the house of charity, set up for the relief of the necessitous, from very poor, which it was formerly, was put into stock, and more flourishing than ever."

The change of manners, which was visibly amongst the Christians, was of no little service to the conversion of Saracens and idolaters. Many of those infidels embraced Christianity. But the most illustrious conquest of the saint, was of a famous Saracen lady, called Neachile Pocaraga, daughter to Almanzor, king of Tidore, and wife to Boliefe, who was king of Ternate, before the Portuguese had conquered the island. She was a princess of great wit and generosity, but extremely bigotted to her sect, and a mortal enemy to the Christians, that is to say, to the Portuguese. Her hatred to them was justly grounded; for, having received them into her kingdom with great civility, and having also permitted them to establish themselves in one part of the island, for the convenience of their trade, she was dealt with so hardly by them, that, after the death of the king, her husband, she had nothing left her but the bare title of a queen; and by their intrigues, the three princes, her sons, lost the crown, their liberty, and their lives. Her unhappy fortune constrained her to lead a wandering life, from isle to isle. But Providence, which would accomplish on her its good designs, brought her back at last to Ternate, about the time when Xavier came thither. She lived there in the condition of a private person, without authority, yet with splendour; and retaining still in her countenance and behaviour, somewhat of that haughty air, which the great sometimes maintain, even in their fetters.

The saint gained access to her, and found an opportunity of conversing with her. In his first discourse, he gave her a great idea of the kingdom of God; yet withal informed her, that this kingdom, was not difficult to obtain; and that being once in possession of it, there was no fear of being after dispossessed. Insomuch, that the Saracen princess, who had no hopes remaining of aught on earth, turned her thoughts and her desires towards heaven. It is true, that, as she was endued with a great wit, and was very knowing in the law of Mahomet, there was some need of argumentation; but the Father still clearing all her doubts, the dispute only served to make her understand more certainly the falseness of the Alcoran, and the truth of the gospel. She submitted to the saint's reasons, or rather to the grace of Jesus Christ, and was publicly baptized by the apostle himself, who gave her the name of Isabella.

He was not satisfied with barely making her a Christian. He saw in her a great stock of piety, an upright heart, a tenderness of mind, inclinations truly great and noble, which he cultivated with admirable care, and set her forward, by degrees, in the most sublime and solid ways of a spiritual life: So that Neachile, under the conduct of Father Xavier, arrived to a singular devotion; that is to say, she grew humble and modest, from disdainful; and haughty as she was, mild to others, and severe to herself, suffering her misfortunes without complaint of injuries; united to God in her retirements, and not appearing publicly, but to exercise the deeds of charity to her neighbour; but more esteemed and honoured, both by the Indians and Portuguese, than when she sat upon the throne, in all the pomp and power of royalty.

During the abode which Xavier made in Ternate, he heard speak of certain isles, which are distant from it about sixty leagues eastward; and which take their name from the principal, commonly called the Isle del Moro. It was reported to him, that those islanders, barbarians as they were, had been most of them baptized, but that the faith had been abolished there immediately after it was introduced, and this account he heard of it.

The inhabitants of Momoya, which is a town in the Isle del Moro, would never embrace the law of Mahomet, though all the neighbouring villages had received it. And the prince, or lord of that town, who chose rather to continue an idolater, than to become a Mahometan, being molested by the Saracens, had recourse to the governor of Ternate, who was called Tristan d'Atayda, promising, that himself and his subjects would turn Christians, provided the Portuguese would take them into their protection. Atayda receiving favourably those propositions of the prince of Momoya, the prince came in person to Ternate, and desired baptism; taking then, the name of John, in honour of John III., king of Portugal. At his return to Momoya, he took along with him a Portuguese priest, called Simon Vaz, who converted many idolaters to the faith. The number of Christians, thus daily increasing more and more, another priest, called Francis Alvarez, came to second Vaz, and both of them laboured so happily in conjunction, that the whole people of Momoya renounced idolatry, and professed the faith of Jesus Christ.

In the mean time, the Portuguese soldiers, whom the governor of Ternate had promised to send, came from thence to defend the town against the enterprizes of the Saracens. But the cruelty which he exercised on the mother of Cacil Aerio, bastard son to King Boliefe, so far exasperated those princes and the neighbouring people, that they conspired the death of all the Portuguese, who were to be found in those quarters. The inhabitants of Momoya, naturally changeable and cruel, began the massacre by the murder of Simon Vaz, their first pastor; and had killed Alvarez, whom they pursued with flights of arrows to the sea side, if accidentally he had not found a bark in readiness, which bore him off, all wounded as he was, and saved him from the fury of those Christian barbarians.

The Saracens made their advantage of these disorders, and mastering Mamoya, changed the whole religion of the town. The prince himself was the only man, who continued firm in the Christian faith, notwithstanding all their threatening, and the cruel usage which he received from them. Not long after this, Antonio Galvan, that Portuguese, who was so illustrious for his prudence, his valour, and his piety, succeeding to Tristan d'Atayda in the government of Ternate, sent to the Isle del Moro a priest, who was both able and zealous, by whose ministry the people were once more reduced into the fold of Christ, and the affairs of the infidels were ruined. But this priest remained not long upon the island, and the people, destitute of all spiritual instructions, returned soon after, through their natural inconstancy, to their original barbarism.

In this condition was the Isle del Moro when it was spoken of to Father Xavier; and for this very reason, he determined to go, and preach the gospel there, after he had stayed for three months at Ternate. When his design was known, all possible endeavours were used to break it. His friends were not wanting to inform him, that the country was as hideous as it was barren: That it seemed accursed by nature, and a more fitting habitation for beasts than men: That the air was so gross, and so unwholesome, that strangers could not live in the country: That the mountains continually vomited flakes of fire and ashes, and that the ground itself was subject to terrible and frequent earthquakes. And besides, it was told him, that the people of the country surpassed in cruelty and faithlessness all the barbarians of the world: That Christianity had not softened their manners; that they poisoned one another; that they fed themselves with human flesh; and that, when any of their relations happened to die, they cut off his hands and feet, of which they made a delicate ragou: That their inhumanity extended so far, that when they designed a sumptuous feast, they begged some of their friends to lend them an old unprofitable father, to be served up to the entertainment of their guests, with promise to repay them, in kind, on the like occasion.

The Portuguese and Indians, who loved Xavier, added, that since those savages spared not their own countrymen and their parents, what would they not do to a stranger, and an unknown person? That they were first to be transformed into men, before they could be made Christians. And how could he imprint the principles of the divine law into their hearts, who had not the least sense of humanity? Who should be his guide through those thick entangled forests, where the greatest part of them were lodged like so many wild beasts; and when, by rare fortune, he should atchieve the taming of them, and even convert them, how long would that conversion last? at the longest, but while he continued with them: That no man would venture to succeed him in his apostleship to those parts, for that was only to be exposed to a certain death; and that the blood of Simon Vaz was yet steaming. To conclude, there were many other isles, which had never heard of Jesus Christ, and who were better disposed to receive the gospel.

These reasons were accompanied with prayers and tears; but they were to no purpose, and Xavier was stedfast to his resolution. His friends perceiving they could gain nothing upon him by intreaties, had recourse, in some measure, to constraint; so far as to obtain from the governor of Ternate a decree, forbidding, on severe penalties, any vessel to carry the Father to the Isle del Moro.

Xavier then resented this usage of his friends, and could not forbear to complain publicly of it. "Where are those people," said he, "who dare to confine the power of Almighty God, and have so mean an apprehension of our Saviour's love and grace? Are there any hearts hard enough to resist the influences of the Most High, when it pleases him to soften and to change them? Can they stand in opposition to that gentle, and yet commanding force, which can make the dry bones live, and raise up children to Abraham from stones? What! Shall he, who has subjected the whole world to the cross, by the ministry of the apostles, shall he exempt from that subjection this petty corner of the universe? Shall then the Isle del Moro be the only place, which shall receive no benefit of redemption? And when Jesus Christ has offered to the eternal Father, all the nations of the earth as his inheritance, were these people excepted out of the donation? I acknowledge them to be very barbarous and brutal; and let it be granted they were more inhuman than they are, it is because I can do nothing of myself, that I have the better hopes of them. I can do all things in Him who strengthens me, and from whom alone proceeds the strength of those who labour in the gospel."

He added, "That other less savage nations would never want for preachers; that these only isles remained for him to cultivate, since no other man would undertake them." In sequel, suffering himself to be transported with a kind of holy choler, "If these isles," pursued he, "abounded with precious woods and mines of gold, the Christians would have the courage to go thither, and all the dangers of the world would not be able to affright them; they are base and fearful because there are only souls to purchase: And shall it then be said, that charity is less daring than avarice? You tell me they will take away my life, either by the sword or poison; but those are favours too great for such a sinner as I am to expect from heaven; yet I dare confidently say, that whatever torment or death they prepare for me, I am ready to suffer a thousand times more for the salvation of one only soul. If I should happen to die by their hands, who knows but all of them might receive the faith? for it is most certain, that since the primitive times of the church, the seed of the gospel has made a larger increase in the fields of paganism, by the blood of martyrs, than by the sweat of missioners."

He concluded his discourse, by telling them, "That there was nothing really to fear in his undertaking; that God had called him to the isles del Moro; and that man should not hinder him from obeying the voice of God." His discourse made such impressions on their hearts, that not only the decree against his passage was revoked, but many offered themselves to accompany him in that voyage, through all the dangers which seemed to threaten him.

Having thus disengaged himself from all the incumbrances of his voyage, he embarked with some of his friends, passing through the tears of the people, who attended him to the shore, without expectation of seeing him again. Before he set sail, he wrote to the Fathers of the company at Rome, to make them acquainted with his voyage.

"The country whither I go," says he in his letter, "is full of danger, and terrible to strangers, by the barbarity of the inhabitants, and by their using divers poisons, which they mingle with their meat and drink; and it is from hence that priests are apprehensive of coming to instruct them: For myself, considering their extreme necessity, and the duties of my ministry, which oblige to free them from eternal death, even at the expence of my own life, I have resolved to hazard all for the salvation of their souls. My whole confidence is in God, and all my desire is to obey, as far as in me lies, the word of Jesus Christ: 'He who is willing to save his life shall lose it, and he who will lose it for my sake shall find it.' Believe me, dear brethren, though this evangelical maxim, in general, is easily to be understood, when the time of practising it calls upon us, and our business is to die for God, as clear as the text seems, it becomes obscure; and he only can compass the understanding of it, to whom God, by his mercy, has explained it; for then it will be seen, how frail and feeble is human nature. Many here, who love me tenderly, have done what possibly they could to divert me from this voyage; and, seeing that I yielded not to their requests, nor to their tears, would have furnished me with antidotes; but I would not take any, lest, by making provision of remedies, I might come to apprehend the danger; and also, because, having put my life into the hands of Providence, I have no need of preservatives from death: for it seems to me, that the more I should make use of remedies, the less assurance I should repose in God."

They went off with a favourable wind, and had already made above an hundred and fourscore miles, when Xavier, on the sudden, with a deep sigh, cried out, "Ah, Jesus, how they massacre the poor people!" saying these words, and oftentimes repeating them, he had turned his countenance, and fixed his eyes towards a certain part of the sea. The mariners and passengers, affrighted, ran about him. Inquiring what massacre he meant, because, for their part, they could see nothing; but the saint was ravished in spirit, and, in this extacy, God had empowered him to see this sad spectacle.

He was no sooner come to himself, than they continued pressing him to know the occasion of his sighs and cries; but he, blushing for the words which had escaped him in his transport, would say no more, but retired to his devotions. It was not long before they beheld, with their own eyes, what he refused to tell them: Having cast anchor before an isle, they found on the shore the bodies of eight Portuguese, all bloody; and then comprehended, that those unhappy creatures had moved the compassion of the holy man. They buried them in the same place, and erected a cross over the grave; after which they pursued their voyage, and in little time arrived at the Isle del Moro.

When they were come on shore, Xavier went directly on to the next village. The greatest part of the inhabitants were baptized; but there remained in them only a confused notion of their baptism; and their religion was nothing more than a mingle of Mahometanism and idolatry.

The barbarians fled at the sight of the strangers, imagining they were come to revenge the death of the Portuguese, whom they had killed the preceding years. Xavier followed them into the thickest of their woods; and his countenance, full of mildness, gave them to believe, that he was not an enemy who came in search of them. He declared to them the motive of his voyage, speaking to them in the Malaya tongue: For though in the Isle del Moro there were great diversity of languages, insomuch, that those of three leagues distance did not understand each other in their island tongues, yet the Malaya was common to them all.

Notwithstanding the roughness and barbarity of these islanders, neither of those qualities were of proof against the winning and soft behaviour of the saint. He brought them back to their village, using all expressions of kindness to them by the way, and began his work by singing aloud the Christian doctrine through the streets; after which he expounded it to them, and that in a manner so suitable to their barbarous conceptions, that it passed with ease into their understanding.

By this means he restored those Christians to the faith, who had before forsaken it; and brought into it those idolaters who had refused to embrace it when it was preached to them by Simon Vaz and Francis Alvarez. There was neither town nor village which the Father did not visit, and where those new converts did not set up crosses and build churches. Tolo, the chief town of the island, inhabited by twenty-five thousand souls, was entirely converted, together with Momoya.

Thus the Isle del Moro was now to the holy apostle the island of Divine Hope,[1] as he desired it thenceforth to be named; both because those things which were there accomplished by God himself, in a miraculous manner, were beyond all human hope and expectation; and also because the fruits of his labours surpassed the hopes which had been conceived of them, when his friends of Ternate would have made him fear that his voyage would prove unprofitable.

To engage these new Christians, who were gross of apprehension, in the practice of a holy life, he threatened them with eternal punishments, and made them sensible of what hell was, by those dreadful objects which they had before their eyes: For sometimes he led them to the brink of those gulphs which shot out of their bowels vast masses of burning stones into the air, with the noise and fury of a cannon; and at the view of those flames, which were mingled with a dusky smoke that obscured the day, he explained to them the nature of those pains, which were prepared in an abyss of fire, not only for idolaters and Mahometans, but also for the true believers, who lived not according to their faith. He even told them, the gaping mouths of those flaming mountains were the breathing places of hell; as appears by these following words, extracted out of one of his letters on that subject, written to his brethren at Rome: "It seems that God himself has been pleased, in some measure, to discover the habitation of the damned to people had otherwise no knowledge of him."

1:_Divina Esperanya_.]

During their great earthquakes, when no man could be secure in any place, either in his house, or abroad in the open air, he exhorted them to penitence; and declared to them, that those extraordinary accidents were caused, not by the souls of the dead hidden under ground, as they imagined, but by the devils, who were desirous to destroy them, or by the omnipotent hand of God, who adds activity to natural causes, that he may imprint more deeply in their hearts the fear of his justice and his wrath.

One of those wonderful earthquakes happened on the 29th of September; on that day, consecrated to the honour of St Michael, the Christians were assembled in great numbers, and the Father said mass. In the midst of the sacrifice, the earth was so violently shaken, that the people ran in a hurry out of the church. The Father feared lest the altar might be overthrown, yet he forsook it not, and went through with the celebration of the sacred mysteries, thinking, as he said himself, that the blessed archangel, at that very time, was driving the devils of the island down to hell; and that those infernal spirits made all that noise and tumult, out of the indignation which they had to be banished from that place where they had held dominion for so many ages.

The undaunted resolution of Father Xavier amazed the barbarians; and gave them to believe, that a man who remained immovable while the rocks and mountains trembled, had something in him of divine; but that high opinion which most of them had conceived of him, gave him an absolute authority over them; and, with the assistance of God's grace, which operated in their souls while he was working by outward means, he made so total a change in them, that they who formerly, in respect of their manners, were like wolves and tygers, now became tractable and mild, and innocent as lambs.

Notwithstanding this, there were some amongst them who did not divest themselves fully, and at once, of their natural barbarity; either to signify, that divine grace, how powerful soever, does not work all things in a man itself alone, or to try the patience of the saint. The most rebellious to God's spirit were the Javares,--a rugged and inhuman people, who inhabit only in caves, and in the day-time roam about the forests. Not content with not following the instructions of the Father, they laid divers ambushes for him; and one day, while he was explaining the rules of morality to them out of the gospel, by a river side, provoked by the zeal wherewith he condemned their dissolute manners, they cast stones at him with design to kill him. The barbarians were on the one side of him, and the river on the other, which was broad and deep; insomuch, that it was in a manner impossible for Xavier to escape the fury of his enemies: but nothing is impossible to a man whom heaven protects. There was lying on the bank a great beam of wood; the saint pushed it without the least difficulty into the water, and placing himself upon it, was carried in an instant to the other side, where the stones which were thrown could no longer reach him.

For what remains, he endured in this barren and inhospitable country all the miseries imaginable, of hunger, thirst, and nakedness. But the comforts which he received from heaven, infinitely sweetened all his labours; which may be judged by the letter he wrote to Father Ignatius. For, after he had made him a faithful description of the place, "I have," said he, "given you this account of it, that from thence you may conclude, what abundance of celestial consolations I have tasted in it. The dangers to which I am exposed, and the pains I take for the interest of God alone, are the inexhaustible springs of spiritual joys; insomuch, that these islands, bare of all worldly necessaries, are the places in the world, for a man to lose his sight with the excess of weeping; but they are tears of joy. For my own part, I remember not ever to have tasted such interior delights; and these consolations of the soul, are so pure, so exquisite, and so perpetual, that they take from me all sense of my corporeal sufferings."

Xavier continued for three months in the Isle del Moro; after which, he repassed to the Moluccas, with intention from thence to sail to Goa; not only that he might draw out missioners from thence, to take care of the new Christianity which he had planted in all those isles, and which he alone was not sufficient to cultivate, but also to provide for the affairs of the company, which daily multiplied in this new world.

Being arrived at Ternate, he lodged by a chapel, which was near the Port, and which, for that reason, is called "Our Lady of the Port." He thought not of any long stay in that place, but only till the ship which was intended for Malacca should be ready to set out. The Christians, more glad of his return, because they had despaired of seeing him again, begged of him to continue longer with them, because Lent was drawing near; and that he must, however, stay all that holy time, in the island of Amboyna, for the proper season of navigation to Malacca. The captain of the fortress of Ternate, and the brotherhood of the Mercy, engaged themselves to have him conducted to Amboyna, before the setting out of the ships. So that Xavier could not deny those people, who made him such reasonable propositions; and who were so desirous to retain him, to the end they might profit by his presence, in order to the salvation of their souls.

He remained then almost three months in Ternate; hearing confessions day and night, preaching twice on holidays, according to his custom; in the morning to the Portuguese, in the afternoon to the islanders newly converted; catechising the children every day in the week, excepting Wednesday and Friday, which he set apart for the instruction of the Portuguese wives. For, seeing those women, who were either Mahometans or idolaters by birth, and had only received baptism in order to their marrying with the Portuguese, were not capable of profiting by the common sermons, for want of sufficient understanding in the mysteries and maxims of Christianity; he undertook to expound to them the articles of faith, the commandments, and other points of Christian morality. The time of Lent was passed in these exercises of piety, and penitence, which fitted them for the blessed sacrament at Easter. All people approached the holy table, and celebrated that feast with renewed fervour, which resembled the spirit of primitive Christianity.

But the chief employment of Father Xavier was to endeavour the conversion of the king of Ternate, commonly called king of the Moluccas. This Saracen prince, whose name was Cacil Aerio, was son to king Boleife, and his concubine, a Mahometan, and enemy to the Portuguese, whom Tristan d'Atayda, governor of Ternate, and predecessor of Antonio Galvan, caused to be thrown out of a window, to be revenged of her. This unworthy and cruel usage might well exasperate Cacil; but fearing their power, who had affronted him in the person of his mother, and having the violent death of his brothers before his eyes, he curbed his resentments, and broke not out into the least complaint. The Portuguese mistrusted this over-acted moderation, and affected silence; and according to the maxim of those politicians, who hold, that they who do the injury should never pardon, they used him afterwards as a rebel, and an enemy, upon very light conjectures, Jordan de Treitas, then governor of the fortress of Ternate. a man as rash and imprudent as Galvan was moderate and wise, seized the person of the prince, stript him of all the ornaments of royalty, and sent him prisoner to Goa, in the year 1546, with the Spanish fleet, of which we have formerly made mention.

The cause having been examined, in the sovereign tribunal of Goa, there was found nothing to condemn, but the injustice of Treitas: Cacil was declared innocent; and the new viceroy of the Indies, Don John de Castro, sent him back to Ternate, with orders to the Portuguese, to replace him on the throne, and pay him so much the more respect, by how much more they had injured him. As for Treitas, he lost his government, and being recalled to Goa, was imprisoned as a criminal of state.

The king of Ternate was newly restored, when Xavier came into the isle for the second time. King Tabarigia, son of Boleife, and brother to Cacil, had suffered the same ill fortune some years before. Being accused of felony, and having been acquitted at Goa, where he was prisoner, he was also sent back to his kingdom, with a splendid equipage; and the equity of the Christians so wrought upon him, that he became a convert before his departure.

Xavier was in hope, that the example of Tabarigia would make an impression on the soul of Cacil after his restoration, at least if any care were taken of instructing him; and the hopes or the saint seemed not at the first to be ill grounded. For the barbarian king received him with all civility, and was very affectionate to him, insomuch that he could not be without his company. He heard him speak of God whole hours together; and there was great appearance, that he would renounce the Mahometan religion.

But the sweet enchantments of the flesh are often an invincible obstacle to the grace of baptism. Besides a vast number of concubines, the king of Ternate had an hundred women in his palace, who retained the name and quality of wives. To confine himself to one, was somewhat too hard to be digested by him. And when the Father endeavoured to persuade him, that the law of God did absolutely command it; he reasoned on his side, according to the principles of his sect, and refined upon it in this manner: "The God of the Christians and of the Saracens is the same God; why then should the Christians be confined to one only wife, since God has permitted the Saracens to have so many?"

Yet sometimes he changed his language; and said, that he would not lose his soul, nor the friendship of Father Xavier, for so small a matter. But, in conclusion, not being able to contain himself within the bounds of Christian purity, nor to make the law of Jesus Christ agree with that of Mahomet, he continued fixed to his pleasures, and obstinate in his errors. Only he engaged his royal word, that in case the Portuguese would invest one of his sons in the kingdom of the Isles del Moro, he would on that condition receive baptism.

Father Xavier obtained from the viceroy of the Indies whatever the king of Ternate had desired; but the barbarian, far from keeping his promise, began from thenceforward a cruel persecution against his Christian subjects. And the first strokes of it fell on the Queen Neachile, who was dispossessed of all her lands, and reduced to live in extreme poverty during the remainder of her days. Her faith supported her in these new misfortunes; and Father Xavier, who had baptized her, gave her so well to understand how happy it was to lose all things and to gain Christ, that she continually gave thanks to God for the total overthrow of her fortune.

In the mean time, the labours of the saint were not wholly unprofitable in the court of Ternate. He converted many persons of the blood-royal; and, amongst others, two sisters of the prince, who preferred the quality of Christians, and spouses of Christ Jesus, before all earthly crowns; and chose rather to suffer the ill usage of their brother, than to forsake their faith.

Xavier, seeing the time of his departure drawing near, composed, in the Malaya tongue, a large instruction, touching the belief and morals of Christianity. He gave the people of Ternate this instruction written in his own hand, that it might supply his place during his absence. Many copies were taken of it, which were spread about the neighbouring islands, and even through the countries of the East. It was read on holidays in the public assemblies; and the faithful listened to it, as coming from the mouth of the holy apostle.

Besides this, he chose out some virtuous young men for his companions in his voyage to Goa, with design to breed them in the college of the company, and from thence send them back to the Moluccas, there to preach the gospel. These things being thus ordered, and the caracore, winch was to carry him to Amboyna, in readiness, it was in his thoughts to depart by night, in the most secret manner that he could, not to sadden the inhabitants, who could not hear of his going from them without a sensible affliction. But whatsoever precautions he took, he could not steal away without their knowledge. They followed him in crowds to the shore; men, women, and children, gathering about him, lamenting his loss, begging his blessing, and beseeching him, with tears in their eyes, "That since he was resolved on going, he would make a quick return."

The holy man was not able to bear these tender farewells without melting into tears himself. His bowels yearned within him for his dear flock; and seeing what affection those people bore him, he was concerned lest his absence might prejudice their spiritual welfare. Yet reassuring himself, by considering the providence of God, which had disposed of him another way, he enjoined them to meet in public every day, at a certain church, to make repetition of the Christian doctrine, and to excite each other to the practice of virtue. He charged the new converts to learn by heart the exposition of the apostles' creed, which he had left with them in writing; but that which gave him the greatest comfort was, that a priest, who was there present, promised him to bestow two hours every day in instructing the people, and once a-week to perform the same to the wives of the Portuguese, in expounding to them the articles of faith, and informing them concerning the use of the sacraments.

After these last words, Father Xavier left his well-beloved children in Jesus, and immediately the ship went off. At that instant an universal cry was raised on the shore; and that last adieu went even to the heart of Father Xavier.

Being arrived at Amboyna, he there found four Portuguese vessels, wherein were only mariners and soldiers, that is to say, a sort of people ill instructed in the duties of Christianity, and little accustomed to put them in practice, in the continual hurry of their life. That they might profit by that leisure which they then enjoyed, he set up a small chapel on the sea-side, where he conversed with them, sometimes single, sometimes in common, concerning their eternal welfare. The discourses of the saint brought over the most debauched amongst them; and one soldier, who had been a libertine all his life, died with such evident signs of true contrition, that being expired, Father Xavier was heard to say, "God be praised, who has brought me hither for the salvation of that soul;" which caused people to believe, that God Almighty had made a revelation of it to him.

By the same supernal illumination, he saw in spirit one whom he had left in Ternate in the vigour of health, now expiring in that place; for preaching one day, he broke off his discourse suddenly, and said to his auditors, "Recommend to God, James Giles, who is now in the agony of death;" the news of his death came not long after, which entirely verified the words of Xavier.

The four ships continued at Amboyna but twenty days, after which they set sail towards Malacca. The merchant-ship, which was the best equipped and strongest of them, invited the saint to embark in her; but he refused, out of the horror which he had for those enormous crimes which had been committed in her. And turning to Gonsalvo Fernandez, "This ship," said he, "will be in great danger; God deliver you out of it." Both the prediction and the wish of the saint were accomplished; for the ship, at the passage of the Strait of Saban, struck against a hidden rock, where the iron-work of the stern was broken, and little wanted but that the vessel had been also split; but she escaped that danger, and the rest of the voyage was happily performed.

The Father staying some few days longer on the isle, visited the seven Christian villages which were there; caused crosses to be set up in all of them, for the consolation of the faithful; and one of these crosses, in process of time, became famous for a great miracle, of which the whole country was witness.

There was an extreme drought, and a general dearth was apprehended. Certain women, who before their baptism were accustomed to use charms for rain, being assembled round about an idol, adored the devil, and performed all the magic ceremonies; but their enchantments were of no effect. A devout Christian woman knowing what they were about, ran thither, and having sharply reprehended those impious creatures, "As if," said she, "having a cross so near us, we had no expectations of succour from it; and that the holy Father had not promised us, that whatsoever we prayed for at the foot of that cross, should infallibly be granted." Upon this, she led those other women towards a river-side, where Xavier had set up a cross with his own hands, and falling down with them before that sacred sign of our salvation, she prayed our Saviour to give them water, to the shame and confusion of the idol. At the same moment the clouds began to gather on every side, and the rain poured down in great abundance. Then, all in company, they ran to the pagod, pulled it down, and trampled it under their feet; after which they cast it into the river, with these expressions of contempt, "That though they could not obtain from him one drop of water, they would give him enough in a whole river."

A faith thus lively, answered the hopes which the saint had conceived of the faithful of Amboyna. He compared them sometimes to the primitive Christians; and believed their constancy was of proof against the cruelty of tyrants. Neither was he deceived in the judgment he made of them; and they shewed themselves, when the Javeses, provoked by their renouncing the law of Mahomet, came to invade their island. While the Saracen army destroyed the country, six hundred Christians retired into a castle, where they were presently besieged. Though they were to fear all things from the fury of the barbarians, yet what they only apprehended was, that those enemies of Jesus Christ might exercise their malice against a cross which was raised in the midst of all the castle, and which Father Xavier had set up with his own hands. To preserve it, therefore, inviolable from their attempts, they wrapt it up in cloth of gold, and buried it in the bottom of the ditch. After they had thus secured their treasure, they opened the gate to the unbelievers, who, knowing what had been done by them, ran immediately in search of the cross, to revenge upon it the contempt which had been shown to Mahomet. But not being able to find it, they turned all their fury upon those who had concealed it, and who would not discover where it was.

Death seemed to have been the least part of what they suffered. The Mahometan soldiers cut off one man's leg, another's arm, tore out this man's eyes, and the other's tongue. So the Christians died by degrees, and by a slow destruction, but without drawing one sigh, or casting out a groan, or shewing the least apprehension; so strongly were they supported in their souls by the all-powerful grace of Jesus Christ, for whom they suffered.

Xavier at length parted from Amboyna; and probably it was then, if we consider the sequel of his life, that he had the opportunity of making the voyage of Macassar.

For though it be not certainly known at what time he visited that great island, nor the fruit which his labours there produced, it is undoubted that he has been there; and, in confirmation of it, we have, in the process of his canonization, the juridical testimony of a Portuguese lady of Malacca, called Jane Melo, who had many times heard from the princess Eleonar, daughter to the king of Macassar, that the holy apostle had baptized the king her father, the prince her brother, and a great number of their subjects.

But at whatsoever time he made this voyage, he returned to Malacca, in the month of July, in the year 1547.

BOOK IV.

_He arrives at Malacca, and there meets three missioners of the company. His conduct with John Deyro. Deyro has a vision, which God reveals to Xavier. The actions of the saint at Malacca. The occasion of the king of Achen's enterprise against Malacca. The preparation of the barbarians for the siege of Malacca. The army of Achen comes before Malacca; its landing and retreat. The letter of the general of Achen to the governor of Malacca. Xavier's advice to the governor of Malacca. They follow his counsel. They prepare to engage the enemy. He exhorts the soldiers and captains to do their duty. The fleet sets out, and what happened at that time. He upbraids the governor with his diffidence. He foretels what is suddenly accomplished. The Portuguese fleet goes in search of the enemy. Troubles in Malacca concerning their fleet. A new cause of consternation. The true condition of the fleet. The soldiers are encouraged by their general to fight. The naval fight betwixt the Portuguese and the Achenois. The Achenois defeated. The saint declares the victory to the people of Malacca. The certain news of the victory is brought. The return of the victorious fleet. Anger arrives at Malacca, when the saint was ready to depart from it. Divers adventures of Anger. Anger is brought to the Father, who sends him to Goa. Xavier calms a tempest. He writes to the king of Portugal. His letter full of zeal, discretion, and charity. He desires the king to send him some preachers of the society. He writes to Father Simon Rodriguez. He sends an account to the Fathers at Rome of his voyages. He receives great comfort from the fervency of the new converts. He stays at Manapar, and what he performed there. The rules which he prescribes to the missioners of the fishing coast. He pusses over to the isle of Ceylon; his actions there. He departs for Goa, and finds the viceroy at Britain. He obtains whatever he demands of the viceroy. He concerts a young gentleman, who was very much debauched. He fixes the resolution of Cosmo de Torrez to enter into the society. He instructs Anger anew, and causes him to be farther taught by Torrez. He hears news from Japan, and designs a voyage thither to preach the gospel. He undertakes the conversion of a soldier. He converts the soldier, and what means he uses to engage him to penance. He assists the viceroy of the Indies at his death. He applies himself more than ever to the exercises of an interior life. He returns to his employment in the care of souls at Goa. He receives supplies from Europe: the arrival of Father Gasper Barzæus. He goes to the fishing coast; his actions there. He speaks to the deputy-governor of the Indies, concerning his voyage to Japan. All endeavours are used to break the Father's intended voyage to Japan. He slights the reasons alleged against his voyage to Japan. He writes to Father

Ignatius, and to Father Rodriguez. He constitutes superiors to superintend the society in India during his absence, and the orders which he leaves them. He sends Gasper Barzæus to Ormuz. He gives instructions and orders to Barzæus. He recommends to him the perfecting of himself. He charges him to instruct the children himself. He recommends the poor to him. He recommends the prisoners to him. His advice concerning restitutions. He prescribes him some precautions in his dealings with his friends. He recommends to him the practice of the particular Examen. He exhorts him to preach, and gives him rules for preaching. He institutes him in the way of correcting sinners. He prescribes him a method, for administering the sacrament of penance. He continues to instruct him on the subject of confession. He instructs him how to deal with those who want faith, concerning the blessed sacrament. He instructs how to deal with penitents. He recommends to him, the obedience due to ecclesiastical superiors. He commands him to honour the governor. He gives him advice concerning his evangelical functions. He orders him to write to the Fathers of the society at Goa. He counsels him to inform himself of the manner of the town at his arrival. He recommends to his prayers the souls in purgatory. He exhorts him not to shew either sadness or anger. He prescribes him the time of his functions. He gives him instructions, touching the conduct of such as shall be received into the society. He teaches him the methods of reducing obstinate sinners. He advises him to find out the dispositions of the people, before he treats with them. He counsels him to learn the manners and customs of the people. He gives him counsel concerning reconciliations. He instructs him in the way of preaching well. What he orders him concerning his subsistance, and touching presents. What he orders him in reference to his abode. He goes for Japan. He arrives at Malacca, and what he performs there. His joy for the success of his brethren in their functions. He receives a young gentleman into the society. The instructions which he gives to Bravo. The news which he hears from Japan. He disposes himself for the voyage of Japan more earnestly than ever. He goes from Malacca to Japan; and what happens to him in the way_.

Xavier found at Malacca three missioners of the company, who were going to the Moluccas, in obedience to the letters he had written. These missioners were John Beyra, Nugnez Ribera, and Nicholas Nugnez, who had not yet received priests' orders. Mansilla came not with them, 'though he had precise orders for it; because he rather chose to follow his own inclinations, in labouring where he was, than the command of his superior, in forsaking the work upon his hands. But his disobedience cost him dear. Xavier expelled him out of the society, judging, that an ill brother would do more hurt, than a good labourer would profit the company.

These three missioners above mentioned had been brought to the Indies in the fleet, by Don Perez de Pavora, with seven other sons of Ignatius; part of whom was already left at Cape Comorine, and the fishing coast, to cultivate those new plants of Christianity, which were so beloved by Father Xavier. Now the ships which were bound for the Moluccas, being not in a readiness to sail before the end of August, Beyra, Ribera, and Nugnez, had all the intermediate time, which was a month, to enjoy the company of the saint, in which space they were formed by him for the apostolic function. For himself, he remained four months at Malacca, in expectation of a ship to carry him to Goa; and during all that time, was taken up with continual service of his neighbour.

He had brought with him, from Amboyna, his old companion, John Deyro. Though Deyro was in his attendance, yet he was not a member of the society, for the causes already specified, and deserved not to be of it, for those which follow. Some rich merchants having put into his hands a sum of money, for the subsistence of the Father, he concealed it from him. Xavier, who lived only on the alms which were daily given him, and who hated money as much as his companion loved it, looked on this action of Deyro as an injury done to evangelical poverty; and the resentment which he had of it, caused him to forget his usual mildness to offenders. Not content to make him a sharp reprimand, he confined him to a little desart isle not far distant from the port; enjoining him, not only continual prayer, but fasting upon bread and water, till he should of his own accord recal him. Deyro, who was of a changeable and easy temper, neither permanent in good, nor fixed in ill, obeyed the Father, and lived exactly in the method which was prescribed.

He had one night a vision, whether awake or sleeping has not been decided by the juridical informations of the Father's life. It seemed to him, that he was in a fair temple, where he beheld the Blessed Virgin, on a throne all glittering with precious stones. Her countenance appeared severe; and he, making his approaches to her, was rejected with indignation, as unworthy to be of the company of her son. After which she arose from the throne, and then all things disappeared. Deyro being recalled from his solitude some time after, said nothing of his vision to Father Xavier, to whom God had revealed it. He even denied boldly to have seen any, though the Father repeated it to him, with all the circumstances. Xavier, more scandalised than ever with this procedure of Deyro, refused all farther communication with a man, who was interested, and insincere. He rid his hands of him, but withal foretold him, "That God would be so gracious to him, as to change his evil inclinations, and that hereafter he should take the habit of St Francis." Which was so fully accomplished, that when the informations were taken in the Indies, concerning the holiness and miracles of Xavier, Deyro then wore the habit of St Francis, and lived a most religious life.

After the three missioners were gone for the Moluccas, Xavier alone bore the whole burden of the work. The knowledge which the Portuguese and Indians had of his holiness, made all men desirous of treating with him, concerning the business of their conscience. Not being able to give audience to all, many of them were ill satisfied, and murmured against him: but since their discontent and murmurs proceeded from a good principle, he comforted himself, and rather rejoiced than was offended, as he says himself expressly in his letters. His ordinary employment was preaching to the Christians and Gentiles, instructing and baptising the catechumens, teaching children the Christian doctrine, visiting the prisoners and the sick, reconciling enemies, and doing other works of charity.

While the saint was thus employed, there happened an affair, which much increased his reputation in all the Indies. For the understanding of the whole business, it will be necessary to trace it from its original.

Since the conquest of Malacca by the Portuguese, the neighbouring princes grew jealous of their power, and made many attempts to drive that nation out of the Indies, which came to brave them at their own doors. Thereupon, they set on foot many great armies, at divers times, but always unsuccessfully; and learning, by dear-bought experience, that multitudes can hardly prevail against true valour.

These disgraces provoked the Sultan Alaradin, king of Achen, instead of humbling him. Achen is the greatest kingdom of the island of Sumatra, distant about twelve leagues from the _terra firma_ of Malacca. This prince was a Mahometan, an implacable enemy of the Christians by his religion, and of the Portuguese by interest of state. Yet he durst not immediately assault the fortress of Malacca. All his fury was spent in cruizing about the coasts, with a strong fleet, thereby to break the trade of the Portuguese, and hinder the succours which they had from Europe. His design was then to attack the town, when it should be bare of defendants, and unprovided of stores of victuals: but to compass his enterprize, he was to assure himself of a port, which was above Malacca towards the north, which might serve for a convenient retreat to his fleet; and had also occasion for a fortress, to secure himself from the enemy. He therefore made himself master of that port, and ordered the building of a citadel.

As for his preparations of war, he made them so secretly, that the Portuguese had neither any news, nor even the least suspicion of them. Five thousand soldiers, trained up in wars, and well-experienced in naval fights, were chosen out for this glorious expedition; and five hundred of them, called Orabalons, were the flower of the whole nobility, and accordingly wore bracelets of gold, as a distinguishing mark of their high extraction. There was besides a great number of Janisaries newly arrived at the court of Achen, who served as volunteers, and were eager of shewing their courage against the Christians. The fleet consisted of sixty great ships, all well equipped and manned, without reckoning the barks, the frigates, and the fire-ships. It was commanded by the Saracen, Bajaja Soora, a great man of war, and so famous for his exploits in arms, that his prince had honoured him with the title of King of Pedir, in reward for his taking Malacca even before he had besieged the town.

There was no other intelligence of this at Malacca, but what the army of Achen brought itself. They came before the place, and entered the port on the 9th of October, in the year 1547, about two o'clock in the morning, resolved to assault it while they were favoured by the darkness. They began by a discharge of their artillery, and sending in their fire-ships against the Portuguese vessels. After which the most daring of them landed, ran without any order against that part of the wall which they believed weakest, filled up part of the ditch, and mounted the ladders with a furious assault. They found more resistance than they expected: the garrison, and the inhabitants, whom the shouts and artillery of the barbarians had at first affrighted, recovering courage through the imminence of danger, and the necessity of conquering or dying, ran upon the rampart, and vigorously repulsed the assailants; overthrowing their ladders, or tumbling their enemies headlong from them, insomuch that not a man of them entered the town, and great numbers of them lay dead or dying in the ditch.

Soora comforted himself for the ill success of his assault, by the execution which his fire-ships and cannon had done. All the vessels within the port were either burnt or disabled. And the rain which immediately fell, served not so much to extinguish the flames, as the violent wind which then arose contributed to kindle them. Those of Achen, proud of that action, appeared next morning on their decks, letting fly their pompous streamers, and shouting, as if already they were victorious. But their insolence was soon checked; the cannon from the fortress forced them to retire as far off as the isle of Upe. In the mean time, seven poor fishermen, who had been out all night about their employment, and were now returning to the town, fell into an ambuscade of the Infidels, were taken, and brought before the general. After he had cut off their ears and noses, he sent them back with a letter, directed to Don Francisco de Melo, governor of Malacca, of which these were the contents:

"I Bajaja Soora, who have the honour to carry in vessels of gold the rice of the Great Souldan, Alaradin, king of Achen, and the territories washed by the one and the other sea, advertise thee to write word to thy king, that, in despite of him, I am casting terror into his fortress by my fierce roaring, and that I shall here abide as long as I shall please. I call to witness of what I declare, not only the earth, and all nations which inhabit it, but all the elements, even to the heaven of the moon; and pronounce with these words of my mouth, that thy king is a man of no reputation nor courage; that his standards, now trampled under foot, shall never be lifted up again without his permission who has conquered him; that, by the victory already by us obtained, my king has under his royal foot the head of thine; that from this day forward he is his subject and his slave; and, to the end, that thou thyself mayest confess this truth, I defy thee to mortal battle, here on the place of my abode, if thou feelest in thyself sufficient courage to oppose me."

Though the letter of Soora was in itself ridiculous, and full of fustian bravadoes, according to the style of the barbarians, yet it put the governor and officers of the fortress to a shrewd demur; for how should they accept the challenge without ships to fight him, and how could they refuse it with their honour? A council of war was summoned to deliberate on this weighty and nice affair, when Father Xavier came amongst them. He had been saying mass at the church of our Lady Del Monte; so called, from its being built on a mountain near the city, and dedicated to the blessed Virgin. Don Francisco, who had sent for him to consult him in this troublesome business, gave him the general of Achen's letter to peruse, and demanded his advice what was to be done on this occasion.

The saint, who knew the king of Achen's business was not only to drive the Portuguese out of Malacca, but also, and that principally, to extirpate Christianity out of all the East; having read the letter, lifted up his eyes to heaven, and answered without the least pause, that the affront was too great to be endured; that the honour of the Christian religion was more concerned in it than that of the crown of Portugal: If this injury should be dissembled, to what audaciousness would the enemy arise, and what would not the other Mahometan princes attempt after this example? In conclusion, that the challenge ought to be accepted, that the infidels might see the King of Heaven was more powerful than their king Alaradin.

"But how," said the governor, "shall we put to sea, and on what vessels, since, of eight gally-foysts which we had in port, there are but four remaining, and those also almost shattered in pieces, and half burned; and, in case we could refit them, what could they perform against so numerous a fleet?" "Suppose," answered Xavier, "the barbarians had twice so many ships, are not we much stronger, who have heaven on our side; and how can we choose but overcome, when we fight in the name of our Lord and Saviour?"

No man was so bold to contradict the man of God; and they all went to the arsenal. There they found a good sufficient bark, of those they call catur, besides seven old foysts, fit for nothing but the fire. Duarte de Bareto, who by his office had the superintendance of their naval stores, was commanded to fit out these foysts with all expedition. But he protested it was not in his power; for, besides that the kings magazines were empty of all necessaries for the equipping of them, there was no money in the treasury for materials.

The governor, who had no other fund, was ready to lose courage, when Xavier, by a certain impulse of spirit, suddenly began to embrace seven sea captains there present, who were of the council of war. He begged of them to divide the business amongst them, and each of them apart to take care of fitting out one galley: At the same time, without waiting for their answer, he assigned every man his task. The captains durst not oppose Xavier, or rather God, who inclined their hearts to comply with the saint's request. Above an hundred workmen were instantly employed on every vessel; and in four days time the seven gallies were in condition for fighting. Melo gave the catur to Andrea Toscano, a man of courage, and well versed in sea affairs. He divided amongst the seven captains an hundred and fourscore soldiers, chosen men, and appointed Francis Deza admiral of the fleet. Xavier was desirous to have gone along with them, but the inhabitants, who believed all was lost if they lost the Father, and who hoped for no consolation but from him alone in case the enterprize should not succeed, made such a disturbance about it, that, upon mature deliberation, it was resolved to keep him in the town.

The day before their embarkment, having called together the soldiers and the captains, he told them that he should accompany them in spirit; and that while they were engaging the barbarians, he would be lifting up his hands to heaven for them: That they should fight valiantly, in hope of glory, not vain and perishable, but solid and immortal: That, in the heat of the combat, they should cast their eyes on their crucified Redeemer, whose quarrel they maintained, and, beholding his wounds themselves, should not be afraid either of wounds or death; and how happy should they be to render their Saviour life for life.

These words inspired them with such generous and Christian thoughts, that, with one voice, they made a vow to fight the infidels to their last drop of blood. This solemn oath was so moving to Xavier, that it drew tears from him: he gave them all his blessing; and, for their greater encouragement, named them, "The Band of our Saviour's Soldiers:" in pursuit of which, he heard every man's confession, and gave them the communion with his own hand.

They embarked the clay following with so much cheerfulness, that it seemed to presage a certain victory. But their joy continued but a moment. They had scarcely weighed anchor, when the admiral split, and immediately went to the bottom, so that they had hardly time to save the men. The crowd of people, who were gathered together on the shore to see them go off, beheld this dismal accident, and took it for a bad omen of the expedition; murmuring at the same time against Father Xavier, who was the author of it, and casting out loud cries to recal the other vessels. The governor, who saw the people in an uproar, and apprehended the consequences of this violent beginning, sent in haste to seek the Father. The messenger found him at the altar, in the church of our Lady Del Monte, just ready to receive the blessed sacrament: he drew near to whisper the business to him, but the Father beckoned him with his hand to keep silence, and retire. When mass was ended, "Return," said Xavier, without giving the man leisure to tell his message, "and assure the governor from me, that he has no occasion to be discouraged for the loss of one vessel." By this the saint made known, that God had revealed to him what had happened. He continued some time in prayer before the image of the Virgin; and these words of his were overheard: "O my Jesus, the desire of my heart, regard me with a favourable eye; and thou, holy Virgin, be propitious to me! Lord Jesus," he continued, "look upon thy sacred wounds, and remember they have given us a right to ask of thee every thing conducing to our good."

His prayers being ended, he goes to the citadel: The governor, alarmed with the cries and murmurs of the people, could not dissemble his disturbance, but reproached the Father for having engaged them in this enterprize. But Xavier upbraided him with his distrust of God; and said, smiling, to him, "What! are you so dejected for so slight an accident?" After which, they went in company to the shore, where the soldiers belonging to the admiral stood in great consternation for the hazard they had run so lately. The Father reassured them, and exhorted them to remain constant in their holy resolution, notwithstanding their petty misadventure: he remonstrated to them, that heaven had not permitted their admiral to sink, but only to make trial of their faith; neither had themselves been saved from shipwreck, but only that they might perform their vow. In the mean time, the governor held it necessary to summon the great council. All the officers of the town, and the principal inhabitants, were of opinion to give over an enterprize, which, as they thought, was begun rashly, and could have no fortunate conclusion. But the captains and soldiers of the fleet, encouraged by the words of the holy man, and inspired with vigour, which had something in it of more than human, were of a quite contrary judgment. They unanimously protested, that they had rather die than violate that faith, which they had solemnly engaged to Jesus Christ. "For the rest," said they, "what have we more to fear this day than we had yesterday? our number is not diminished, though we have one vessel less, and we shall fight as well with six foysts, as we should with seven. But, on the other side, what hopes ought we not to conceive, under the auspices and promise of Father Francis?"

Then Xavier taking the word, "The lost galley shall be soon made good," said he with a prophetic voice; "before the sun goes down, there shall arrive amongst us two better vessels than that which perished; and this I declare to you from Almighty God." This positive prediction amazed the whole assembly, and caused them to put off the determination of the affair until the day ensuing. The remaining part of the day was passed with great impatience, to see the effect of the Father's promise. When the sun was just on the point of setting, and many began to fear the accomplishment of the prophecy, in the very minute marked out by the Father, they discovered, from the clock-house of our Lady del Monte, two European ships, which were sailing directly from the north. Melo sent out a skiff immediately to hail them, being informed that they were Portuguese vessels, one belonging to James Soarez Gallego, and the other to his son Balthazar, who came from the kingdom of Patan, but who took the way of Pegu, without intentions of casting anchor at Malacca, to avoid paying customs. He went in search of Father Francis, who was at his devotions in the church del Monte, and told him, that his prophecy would be accomplished to little purpose, if the ships came not into the port. Xavier took it upon himself to stop them; and, going into the skiff which had hailed them, made directly to the two vessels. The masters of the ships, seeing the man of God, received him with respect. He made them understand the present juncture of affairs, and earnestly besought them, by the interests of their religion, and their country, to assist the town against the common enemy of the Christian name, and the crown of Portugal. And to engage them farther, by their particular concernment, he let them see the danger into which they were casting themselves, in case they should obstinately pursue their voyage; and that they were going, without consideration, to precipitate themselves into the hands of the barbarians.

They yielded to the reasons of the Father; and the next morning entered the port amidst the shouts and acclamations of the people. After this, there was no farther dispute of fighting the enemy; and the most timorous came about to the opinion of the captains and the soldiers.

All things being in a readiness to set sail, the admiral, Francis Deza, received the flag from the hands of Xavier, who had solemnly blessed it, and mounted the ship of his brother George Deza, instead of his own, which was already sunk. The rest of the captains, who had been on shore, returned on ship-board; and, with the two newly arrived vessels, the whole fleet consisted of nine, their number also being increased by fifty men; they were in all two hundred and thirty Portuguese. The fleet went out of port the 25th of October, with strict orders from the general not to pass beyond the Pulo Cambylan, which is the farthest bounds of the kingdom of Malacca on the west. His reason was, that since they were so much inferior in strength to the enemy, who vastly outnumbered them in men and shipping, their glory consisted in driving them from off their coasts, and not in farther pursuit of them: That what hope soever we have in God, yet it becomes us not to tempt him, because heaven is not accustomed to give a blessing to rashness and presumption.

Thus setting out full of assurance and of joy, they arrived in four days at Pulo Cambylan, without having any news of the enemy, notwithstanding their endeavours to find him out. The admiral, in obedience to the governor, was thinking to return; though the courage of his soldiers prompted them to pass beyond the bounds prescribed them, and to go in search of the barbarians into whatsoever corner of the world they were retired. The admiral, I say, was disposed to have gone back, when the moon suddenly went into an eclipse. It was one of the greatest which had ever been observed, and seemed to them to prognosticate the total defeat of the Mahometans. But the same night there arose so violent a wind, that they were forced to stay upon their anchors for the space of three-and-twenty days successively. Their provisions then beginning to grow short, and the wind not suffering them to turn to the coast of Malacca, they resolved on taking in fresh provisions at Tenasserim, towards the kingdom of Siam.

In the mean time, all things were in confusion at Malacca. The hopes which Father Xavier had given the people, supported them for some few days. But seeing a month was now expired, without any intelligence from the fleet, they believed it was either swallowed by the waves, or defeated by the Achenois, and that none had escaped to bring the news. At the same time, the Saracens reported confidently, they had it from good hands, that the fleets had met, that the Achenois had cut in pieces all the Portuguese, and had sent the heads of their commanders as a present to their king. This bruit was spread through all the town, and was daily strengthened after the rate of false rumours, which are full of tragical events. The better to colour this report, they gave the circumstances of time and place, and the several actions of the battle. The sorcerers and soothsayers were consulted by the Pagan women, whose husbands and sons were in the fleet; and they confirmed whatever was related in the town. It came at last to a public rising against Xavier; and the governor himself was not wholly free from the popular contagion.

But Xavier, far from the least despondence in the promises of God, and of the knowledge he had given him concerning the condition of the fleet, with an erected countenance assured, they should suddenly see it return victorious. Which notwithstanding, he continued frequent in his vows and prayers; and at the end of all his sermons, recommended to their devotions the happy return of their desired navy. Their spirits were so much envenomed and prejudiced against him, that many of them treated him with injurious words; while he was rallied by the more moderate, who were not ashamed to say, his prayers might be of use for the souls of the soldiers, who were slain in fight, but were of little consequence to gain a battle which was lost.

Some fresh intelligence, which arrived from Sumatra, increased the disorders and consternation of the town. The king of Bintan, son to that Mahomet, whom Albuquerque the Great had despoiled of the kingdom of Malacca, sought for nothing more than an opportunity of reconquering what his father had lost by force of arms. Seeing the town now bare of soldiers, and hearing that the Achenois had beaten the Portuguese, he put to sea, with three hundred sail, and put in at the river of Muar, within six leagues of Malacca, towards the west.

That he might the better execute his design, by concealing it, he wrote from thence to the governor Melo, "That he had armed a fleet against the king of Patan, his enemy, but that having been informed of the defeat of the Portuguese, he was come as a friend and brother of the king of Portugal, to succour Malacca, against the king of Achen, who would not fail to master the town, if the course of his victories was not stopped; that therefore he desired only to be admitted into the place before it came into the possession of the conqueror; after which he had no farther cause of apprehension."

Melo, whom the constancy of Father Xavier had reassured, discovered the snare which was laid for him; and tricked those, who had intended to circumvent him. He answered the king of Bintan, "That the town had no need of relief, as being abundantly provided both of men and ammunition: That so great a conqueror as he, ought not to lay aside an expedition of such importance, nor to linger by the way: That, for themselves, they were in daily expectation of their fleet; not defeated, according to some idle rumours concerning it, but triumphant, and loaden with the spoils of enemies: That this report was only spread by Saracens, whose tongues were longer than their lances:" For these were the expressions which he used.

The Mahometan prince, judging by the governor's reply, that his artifice was discovered; and that, in reason, he ought to attempt nothing till it were certainly known what was become of the two fleets, kept himself quiet, and attended the success.

To return to the Christian navy: Before they could get to Tenasserim, their want of fresh water forced them to seek it nearer hand, at Queda, in the river of Parlez; where being entered, they perceived by night a fisher-boat, going by their ships. They stopped the boat, and the fishermen being examined, told them, "That the Achenois were not far distant; that they had been six weeks in the river; that they had plundered all the lowlands, and were now building a fortress." This news filled the Portuguese with joy; and Deza, infinitely pleased to have found the enemy, of whom he had given over the search, putting on his richest apparel, fired all his cannon, to testify his joy; without considering that he spent his powder to no purpose, and that he warned the barbarians to be upon their guard. What he did with more prudence, was to send three gallies up the river, to discover the enemy, and observe their countenance, while he put all things in order for the fight, The three foysts, in their passage, met with four brigantines, which the enemies had detached, to know the meaning of the guns which they had heard. Before they had taken a distinct view on either side, the three foysts had grappled each a brigantine, and seized her; the fourth escaped. The soldiers put all the enemies to the sword, excepting six, whom they brought off, together with the brigantines. These prisoners were all put to the question; but whatsoever torments they endured, they could not at first get one syllable out of them, either where the enemy lay, or what was the number of his men, or of his ships. Two of them died upon the rack, and other two they threw overboard; but the remaining couple, either more mortified with their torments, or less resolute, being separated from each other, began at last to open: And told the same things apart; both where the Achenois were lying, and that their number was above ten thousand, reckoning into it the mariners, which were of more consideration than the soldiers; that the king of the country, where now they lay, had been constrained to avoid a shameful death, by flight; that having massacred two thousand of the natives, and made as many captives, they were building a citadel, on the passage which the ships ordinarily make from Bengal to Malacca; and that their design was not only to block up that road, but to murder all the Christians who should fall into their hands.

This report inflamed anew the zeal and courage of the soldiers. The admiral was not wanting to encourage them to fight. Entering into a skiff, with his drawn sword, he went from vessel to vessel, exhorting his men to have Christ crucified before their eyes, while they were in fight, as Father Francis had enjoined them; and ever to keep in mind the oath which they had taken; but, above all things, to have an assured hope of victory, from the intercession of the holy Father, who had promised it.

All unanimously answered, "That they would fight it out to death; and should be happy to die in defence of their religion." Deza, animated by this their answer, posted himself advantageously on the river, so as to be able from thence to fall upon the enemy, without endangering his little fleet, to be encompassed by their numbers.

The Achenois no sooner were informed by their brigantine of the Portuguese navy, than they put themselves into a condition of attacking it. They were not only insolent by reason of their strength, but provoked also by the late affront they had received in their brigantines; so that, full of fury, without the least balancing of the matter, they set sail with all their navy, excepting only two vessels, and two hundred land soldiers, which were left in guard of two thousand slaves, and all their booty. Having the wind for them, and coming down the river, they were carried with such swiftness, that Deza was hardly got aboard the admiral, when he heard their drums, and their yelling shouts, which re-echoed from the shores and neighbouring mountains. They were divided into ten squadrons, and each of them composed of six vessels, excepting only the first, which consisted but of four, but those the strongest of the fleet. The admiral, on which the king of Pedir was on board, was in the first squadron, and with him were three Turkish gallions.

That fury, which transported the barbarians, caused them, at the first sight of the Portuguese navy, to discharge against it their whole artillery; but they aimed so ill, that they did them little or no mischief. Immediately after, the two admirals met, and stemmed each other. They engaged on either side with so much resolution, that the advantage was not seen, till a shot was made from the vessel of John Soarez, and out of the cannon called the camel It took place so justly, that Soora's vessel sunk to rights. The three gallions which were in front with him, on the same time, immediately changed their order, and left off fighting, to save their general, and the principal lords of his retinue. But these gallions, which were across the stream, and took up half the breadth of it, stopped their own vessels, which followed file by file; insomuch, that those of the second rank striking against the first, and those of the third against the second, they fell foul on each other, with a terrible confusion.

The Portuguese seeing the army of the enemy, on a heap together, without being able to disengage their ships, encompassed them, and battered them with their cannon. They discharged every tier, three rounds successively, and so to purpose, that they sunk nine great ships, and disabled almost all the rest. Then four of the Portuguese foysts set upon six Mahometans, which the cannon had used more favourably than the rest; the soldiers boarded them with their swords in their hands, and calling on the name of Jesus, in less than half an hour they destroyed above 2000 men. The fright and the disorder of the enemy was redoubled, at the sight of this slaughter, and at the thundering of the guns, which did such dreadful execution; insomuch, that the Achenois leaped into the river of their own accord, chusing rather to die in that manner, than by the hands of the Christians.

Their general being taken up, when he was just drowning, and drawing new courage from despair, endeavoured to have heartened up the remainder of those who were about him. But having himself received a musket-shot, he lost all manner of resolution, and made away with only two vessels. The five hundred gentlemen Orobalans were either slain or drowned, with all the Janisaries. None escaped, but those who followed Soora in his flight. On the side of the Christians there were twenty-six slain, of whom four only were Portuguese by nation The spoil was great; for, besides the two guard-ships which came into the power of the conquerors, and wherein was all the pillage which the enemy had gained, they took at least forty-five vessels, which might again be made serviceable. There was found amongst the spoils a prodigious quantity of Saracen and Turkish arms; 300 pieces of cannon of all sorts; and, what was yet more pleasing, sixty-two pieces of ordnance, whereon were graven the arms of Portugal, and which had been lost in divers wars, returned at length to the possession of their lawful lord and owner.

The king of Parlez no sooner had notice of the enemy's defeat, than, issuing out of the woods where he lay concealed, he came with 500 men, and fell upon the workmen, who, by Soora's orders, were building a fortress, and on the soldiers appointed for their guard. Having cut them in pieces, he went to visit Captain Deza, and congratulated the valour of the Portuguese, and their success. He owned the preservation of his kingdom to their arms; and offered, by way of acknowledgment, a yearly tribute to the king of Portugal.

Deza immediately ordered a frigate to carry the news of his victory to Malacca; but it was fully known in that city, with all its circumstances, before the frigate was sent off, and thus it happened.

Father Xavier, preaching in the great church, betwixt nine and ten of the clock on Sunday morning, which was the 4th of January, according to the old calendar, at the same time when the two fleets were actually engaged, stopped short on the sudden, and appeared transported out of himself, so manifest a change appeared, both in his countenance, and his whole person. Having somewhat recovered himself, instead of following his discourse, inspired with a divine impulse, he declared to his audience the encounter, and shock of the two navies, but in a mysterious and figurative manner.

The assembly, not comprehending their preacher's meaning, were of opinion that he was distracted; still as the fight grew warmer, and the engagement came to be more close, he seemed to be more and more inflamed, with all the motions of a man inspired, and speaking still prophetically. At the length, fixing his eyes on the crucifix that was before him, he said, with tears in his eyes, accompanied with sighs, but with an audible and distinct voice, "Ah Jesus, thou God of my soul, and Father of all mercies, I most humbly implore thee, by the merits of thy sacred passion, not to forsake those who fight thy battle!" After these words, he hung down his head, as overwearied, and leaned upon his pulpit, without farther speaking. Having continued in that posture for some time, he sprung up, on the sudden, and said aloud, with all the motions of joy, which he could not master, "My brethren, Jesus Christ has vanquished for you. At this moment, while I am speaking, the soldiers of his blessed name have completed their victory, by the entire defeat of the enemy's navy. They have made a great slaughter, and we have lost but four of our Portuguese. You shall receive the news of it on Friday next, and may shortly expect the return of your victorious fleet."

How incredible soever this appeared, yet Melo, and the principal persons of the town there present, gave credit to it, without the least scruple; considering the manner of his speaking, and his air, which had somewhat of divine in it, and bore the testimony of its truth. Yet the wives and mothers of the absent soldiers, apprehending still it might be false, and fearing the more, the more they desired it should be true, the Father assembled them all in the afternoon, at the church of our Lady del Monte, and there repeated so distinctly the whole series of what he had said in the morning, that they durst no longer doubt of it.

Even in the beginning of the week, they had almost evident signs of the victory, by the news which came of the king of Bintan; who having sent on all sides to be informed, whether the Portuguese had been defeated, being advertised from the river of Parlez of what had passed, forsook Muar, and retired with expedition, bewailing the misfortune of his allies, and ashamed of his ill-timed enterprize.

The frigate dispatched away by Deza, under the conduct of Emanuel Godigno, arrived exactly on the day mentioned by the saint. The fleet followed shortly after, and made a triumphant entry into the port, with trumpets sounding, and a general discharge of all their artillery. The town received them with repeated shouts of welcome; and Father Francis, who was at the head of the people on the shore, held forth a crucifix in his hand, to give both the inhabitants and soldiers to understand, that they owed their victory to Christ alone.

Both the one and the other joining their voices, gave solemn thanks to the Saviour of mankind; but they also broke out into the praises of the saint, upon the truth of his predictions, and could not hold from publishing, that it was he who had obtained from heaven this wonderful success.

The burden of these praises did no less hasten the saint's intended voyage to Goa, than the necessity of those affairs which called him thither. He had remained four months together at Malacca, since his return from the Moluccas, and was just on his departure, when the ships, which early come from China, arrived in the port. A Japonese, whose name was Anger, came with these vessels, expressly to see Xavier. He was about thirty-five years of age, rich, nobly born, and one whose life had been sufficiently libertine. The Portuguese, who two years before had made the discovery of Japan, had been acquainted with him at Cangoxima, the place of his birth, and understood, from his own mouth, that, having been much troubled with the remembrance of the sins of his youth, he had retired himself amongst the solitary Bonzes; but that neither the solitude, nor the conversation of those heathen priests, had been able to restore him the tranquillity of his soul, and that thereupon he had returned into the world, more disquieted than ever with his remorse of conscience.

Some other Portuguese merchants, who at that time came to Cangoxima, and who had seen Father Francis at Malacca, the first voyage he had made thither, made an intimate acquaintance and friendship with Anger. And this Japonese, discovering to them the perplexity of his soul, which augmented daily more and more, they told him that in Malacca there was a religious man, eminent for his holy life, well experienced in the conduct of souls, and most proper to settle his perplexed conscience; and that if he would try this remedy, they would facilitate the means to him, and bring him to the saint, of whom they had spoken: That it was Father Francis Xavier, their friend, the refuge of sinners, and comforter of troubled minds.

Anger found himself possessed with a strong desire of going to see the holy man; but the length of the voyage, which was 800 leagues, the dangers of a tempestuous sea, and the considerations of his family, somewhat cooled him. A troublesome affair, which he had upon his hands at the same time, at length resolved him. For, having killed a man in a quarrel, and being pursued by justice, he could not find a more secure retreat than the ships of Portugal, nor a surer way of preserving his life, than to accept the offer they had made him.

Alvarez Vaz, who had most importuned him to take this voyage, and who had many times offered to bring him to Father Xavier, had not yet finished all his business, when this Japonese came to take sanctuary in his ship. He therefore gave him letters of recommendation to another Portuguese, called Ferdinand Alvarez, who was at another port of Japan, and who was suddenly to set sail for Malacca.

Anger departed by night, attended by two servants. Being arrived at the port, and enquiring for Ferdinand Alvarez, he lighted accidentally on George Alvarez, who was just ready to weigh anchor. This George was a wealthy merchant, a man of probity, and who had an extreme affection for the Father. He received the letters of Alvarez as if they had been addressed to himself, took the three Japonians into his ship, entertained them with all kindness, and brought them to Malacca; taking great satisfaction in the good office he should do in presenting them to the man of God, who might, perhaps, make them the first Christians of their country. But the misfortune was, that they missed the Father, who was just gone for the Moluccas. Anger, more disquieted in a foreign land than he had been at home, and despairing of ever seeing him, whom he had so often heard of from his friends, had it in his thoughts to have returned to Japan, without considering the danger to which he exposed himself, and almost forgetting the murder which had caused his flight, according to the custom of criminals, who blind themselves in those occasions, and whom divine justice oftentimes brings back to the same place where they had committed their offence. Whereupon, he went again to sea, and having made some little stay in a port of China, he pursued his voyage. Already some Japonian islands were in sight, when there arose a furious tempest, which endangered the sinking of the ship, and which in four days brought him back into the same port of China, from whence he had set out. This was to Anger a favourable effect of God's providence; for the same hand which drives the guilty to the precipice, sometimes preserves them from falling into it, and pulls them back, after a miraculous manner.

The Japonese, very happily for himself, met there Alvarez Vaz, just ready to set sail for Malacca. The Portuguese, who loved Anger, reproved him for his impatience, and offered to reconduct him to the place which he had so abruptly left; withall telling him, that, according to all appearances, the Father by this time was returned from the Moluccas. Anger, who still carried about him a troubled conscience, and thereby was easily induced to any proposition which tended to compose it, followed the advice of Vaz, and returned with him.

Coming on shore, he there found George Alvarez, the same person who had brought him the first time to Molucca. Alvarez, surprised to see him once again, told him, that Father Xavier was returned from the Moluccas, and immediately brought Anger to his presence. The Father, who foresaw, not only that this Japonian should be the first Christian of that kingdom, but also, by his means, the gospel should be preached in it, was transported with joy at the first sight of him, and embraced him with exceeding tenderness. The sight of the saint, and his embracements, gave such consolations to Anger, that he no longer doubted of receiving an entire satisfaction from him. Understanding, in some measure, the Portuguese language, Xavier himself assured him, that the disquiets of his mind should be dissipated, and that he should obtain that spiritual repose, in search of which he had undertaken so long a voyage; but that before he could arrive to it, it concerned him first to understand and practise the law of the true God, who alone could calm the troubles of his heart, and set it in a perpetual tranquillity. Anger, who desired nothing so much as to have his conscience in repose, and who was charmed with the great goodness of the Father, offered himself to be directed in all things by him. The servant of God instructed him in the principles of faith, of which his friends, the Portuguese, had already given him some knowledge, as far as men of their profession were capable of teaching him. But to the end his conversion might be more solid, he thought it convenient to send him and his servants to the seminary of Goa, there to be more fully taught the truths and practice of Christianity before their baptism. The Father had yet a further purpose in it, that these first fruits of Japonian Christianity should be consecrated to God by the Bishop Don John d'Albuquerque, in the capital city of the Indies.

Since in his voyage to Goa he was to visit the fishing coast, he would not take the three Japonians with him, and gave the care of conducting them to George Alvarez. He only wrote by them to the rector of the College of St Paul, giving him orders to instruct them with all diligence. He put on board the ship of another Portuguese, called Gonsalvo Fernandez, twenty or thirty young men whom he had brought from the Moluccas, in order to their studies in the same college; after which, himself embarked in another vessel, which went directly for Cochin.

In passing the Strait of Ceylon, the ship which carried Xavier was overtaken with the most horrible tempest which was ever seen. They were constrained, at the very beginning of it, to cast overboard all their merchandize; and the winds roared with so much violence, that the pilot not being able to hold the rudder, abandoned the vessel to the fury of the waves. For three days and nights together they had death continually present before their eyes; and nothing reassured the mariners but the serene countenance of Father Xavier amidst the cries and tumults in the ship. After he had heard their confessions, implored the help of heaven, and exhorted all of them to receive, with an equal mind, either life or death from the hand of God, he retired into his cabin. Francis Pereyra, looking for the man of God in the midst of the tempest, to have comfort from him, found him on his knees before his crucifix, wholly taken up and lost to all things but to God. The ship, driven along by an impetuous current, already struck against the sands of Ceylon, and the mariners gave themselves for lost, without hope of recovery; when the Father coming out of his cabin, asked the pilot for the line and plummet, with which he was accustomed to fathom the sea; having taken them, and let them down to the bottom of the ocean, he pronounced these words: "Great God, Father, Son, and Holy Ghost, have mercy on us!" At the same moment the vessel stopped, and the wind ceased; after which they pursued their voyage, and happily arrived at the port of Cochin on the 21st of January, 1548.

There the Father gave himself the leisure of writing divers letters into Europe, by a vessel of Lisbon, which was just in readiness to set sail. The first was to the King of Portugal, John III.: the letter was full of prudent counsels concerning the duties of a king: he advertised him anew, that his majesty should be guilty before God of the evil government of his ministers, and that one day an account must be given of the salvation of those souls which he had suffered to perish, through neglect of application, or want of constancy in his endeavours; but he did it with all manner of precaution, and softened his expressions with Christian charity.

"I have long deliberated," said he, "whether I should certify your majesty of the transactions of your officers in the Indies, and what ought further to be done for the establishment of our faith. On the one side, the zeal of God's service, and his glory, encouraged me to write to you: on the other, I was diverted from that resolution by the fear I had of writing to no purpose; but, at the same time, I concluded, that I could not be silent without betraying my ministerial function: and it also seemed to me, that God gave me not those thoughts without some particular design; which probably was, that I might communicate them to your majesty; and this opinion, as the more likely, has at length prevailed with me. Nevertheless, I always feared, that if I should freely give you all my thoughts, my letter would only serve for evidence against you at the hour of your death, and would augment against your majesty the rigour of the last judgement, by taking from you the excuse of ignorance. These considerations gave me great anxieties, and your majesty will easily believe me: For, in fine, my heart will answer for me, that I desire not to employ all my strength, or even my life itself, for the conversion of the Indians, out of any other prospect than to free your majesty's conscience, as much as in me lies, and to render the last judgment less terrible to you. I do in this but that which is my duty; and the particular affection which you bear our Society well deserves that I should sacrifice myself for you."

After he had informed his majesty, how much the jealousies and secret divisions of his officers had hindered the progress of the gospel, he declares, that he could wish the king would bind himself by a solemn oath, to punish severely whosoever they should be who should occasion any prejudice to the farther propagation of faith in the Indies; and farther assured him, that if such who had the authority in their hands were made sensible, that their faults should not escape punishment, the whole Isle of Ceylon, all Cape Comorine, and many kings of Malabar, would receive baptism in the space of one year; that as many as were living in all the extent of the Indies would acknowledge the divinity of Jesus Christ, and make profession of his doctrine, if those ministers of state, who had neglected the interests of the faith, had been deprived of their dignities and their revenues.

After this he petitions the king to send him a supply of preachers, and those preachers to be of the Society, as judging them more proper than any others for the new world. "I beg and adjure your majesty," says he, "by the love you bear to our blessed Lord, and by the zeal wherewith you burn for the glory of the Divine Majesty, to send next year some preachers of our Society to your faithful subjects of the Indies: For I assure you, that your fortresses are in extreme want of such supplies; in garrison, and to the new Christians established in the towns and villages depending on them. I speak by experience; and that which I have seen with my own eyes obliges me to write concerning it. Being at Malacca, and at the Moluccas, I preached every Sunday, and all saints' days twice; and was forced upon it, because I saw the soldiers and people had great need of being frequently taught the word of God.

"I preached then, in the morning, to the Portuguese at mass: I went again into the pulpit in the afternoon, and instructed their children, their slaves, and idolaters newly converted, accommodating my discourse to the measure of their understanding, and expounding to them the principal points of Christian doctrine, one after another. Besides which, one day in the week, I assembled in the church the wives of the Portuguese, and catechised them on the articles of faith, on the sacraments of penance, and the eucharist. Much fruit would be gathered in a few years, if the same method were constantly observed in all places. I preached also, every day, in the fortresses, the principles of religion, to the sons and daughters of the soldiers, to their servants of both sexes; in fine, to the natives of the country, who were born Christians: and these instructions had so good effect, that they totally renounced the superstitions and sorceries which were in use amongst those stupid and ignorant new converts.

"I descend into all these petty circumstances, to the end your majesty may judge, according to your prudence, what number of preachers may be necessary here; and that you may not forget to send many to us: for if the ministry of preaching be not more exercised amongst us, we have reason to apprehend, that not only the Indians, who have embraced the faith, will leave it, but that the Portuguese also may forget the duties of Christianity, and live afterwards like Heathens."

As Father Simon Rodriguez, who governed the Society in Portugal, had great credit at the court, Father Xavier writ to him at the same time, desiring him, he would support his demands with his interest. He recommended to him in especial manner, "That he would make choice of those preachers, who were men of known virtue, and exemplary mortification." He subjoined, "If I thought the king would not take amiss the counsel of a faithful servant, who sincerely loves him, I should advise him to meditate one quarter of an hour every day, on that divine sentence, 'What does it profit a man to have gained the world, and to lose his soul?' I should counsel him, I say, to ask of God the understanding and taste of those words, and that he would finish all his prayers with the same words, 'What will it profit a man, to gain the world, and to lose his soul? 'Tis time," said Xavier, "to draw him out of his mistake, and to give him notice, that the hour of his death is nearer than he thinks: that fatal hour, when the King of kings, and Lord of lords, will summon him to judgment, saying to him these dreadful words, 'Give an account of your administration.' For which reason, do in such manner, my dear brother, that he may fulfil his whole duty; and that he may send over to the Indies all needful supplies, for the increase of faith."

Xavier also wrote from Cochin to the fathers of the society at Rome; and gave them an account, at large, of his voyages to Malacca, to Amboyna, to the Moluccas, and the Isle del Moro; with the success which God had given to his labours. But he forgot not the relation of his danger in the Strait of Ceylon, and made it in a manner which was full of consolation to them.

"In the height of the tempest," said he in his letter, "I took for my intercessors with God, the living persons of our society, with all those who are well affected to it; and joined to these, all Christians, that I might be assisted with the merits of the spouse of Christ, the holy Catholic Church, whose prayers are heard in heaven, though her habitation be on earth: afterwards I addressed myself to the dead, and particularly to Piere le Fevre, to appease the wrath of God. I went through all the orders of the angels, and the saints, and invoked them all. But to the end that I might the more easily obtain the pardon of my innumerable sins, I desired for my protectress and patroness, the most holy Mother of God, and Queen of Heaven, who, without difficulty, obtains from her beloved Son whatsoever she requests. In conclusion, having reposed all my hope in the infinite merits of our Lord and Saviour Jesus Christ, being encompassed with this protection, I enjoyed a greater satisfaction, in the midst of this raging tempest, than when I was wholly delivered from the danger.

"In very truth, being, as I am, the worst of all men, I am ashamed to have shed so many tears of joy, through an excess of heavenly pleasure, when I was just upon the point of perishing: insomuch, that I humbly prayed our Lord, that he would not free me from the danger of my shipwreck, unless it were to reserve me for greater dangers, to his own glory and his service. For what remains, God has often shewn me, by an inward discovery, from how many perils and sufferings I have been delivered, by the prayers and sacrifices of those of the society, both such as labour here on earth, and such who enjoy the fruits of their labours in the heavens. When I have once begun the mention of our society, I can never leave; but the departure of the vessels constrains me to break off: and behold what I have judged most proper for the conclusion of my letter. If I ever forget thee, O Society of Jesus, let my right hand be unprofitable to me, and may I even forget the use of it! _Si oblitus unquam fuero tui, Societas Jesu, oblivioni detur dextera meu_. I pray our Lord Jesus Christ, that since, during the course of this miserable life, he has gathered us into his society, he would reunite us in a blessed eternity, in the company of saints, who behold him in his glory."

After he had written these letters, and given some time to the service of his neighbour, he took the way of Comorine, doubled the Cape a second time, and arrived at the coast of Fishery. The Paravas, who were his first children in Jesus Christ, were overjoyed at the sight of their saint, and good Father, as they called him. All the villages came to meet him, singing the Christian doctrine, and praising God for his return. The satisfaction of the saint was not less than theirs: but above all things his consolation was unspeakable to see the number of Christians so much augmented, by the labours of his brethren. There were in that place many of the society, of whom the chief were Antonio Criminal, Francis Henriquez, and Alphonso Cyprian; for Father Xavier having written from Amboyna for the greatest number of missioners whom they could spare, towards the cultivation of those new plants at the coast of Fishery, all those who came from Portugal, after his own arrival in the Indies, went thither, excepting the three who went to the Moluccas, and two who stayed at Goa, for the instruction of the youth.

The fervency of those new converts did not less edify Xavier than their number. In visiting a certain village, they shewed him a young man, a native of the country, who, having embarked in company of a Portuguese, had been cast, by tempest, on the coast of Malabar. The Saracens, who inhabit that place, having murdered the Portuguese, would have forced his companion to renounce his faith. Thereupon they brought him into a mosque, where they promised him great store of money and preferments, in case he would forsake the law of Jesus Christ, and take up that of their prophet Mahomet. But seeing their promises could not prevail, they threatened him with death, and held their naked weapons over his head to fright him; but neither could they shake his resolution with that dreadful spectacle: then they loaded him with irons, and used him with extraordinary cruelty, till a Portuguese captain, informed of it, came suddenly upon them with a troop of soldiers, and rescued the young man out of their hands. Xavier embraced him many times, and blessed Almighty God, that his faith was imprinted so lively in the heart of a barbarian. He heard also, with great satisfaction, of the constancy of some slaves, who, having fled from the houses of their Portuguese masters, and living amongst Gentiles, far from being corrupted with the superstitions of the Infidels, complied exactly with the obligations of their baptism, and lived in a most religious manner. It was reported to him of these slaves, that when any of them died, they suffered not his body to be burnt, according to the custom of the Pagans, neither would they leave it without sepulture; but buried it according to the ceremonies of the church, and set up a cross over the grave.

Though these infidels, whom they served, did not hinder them from continuing in Christianity, and that every one of them in particular was resolved to persevere in his faith, even in the midst of idolatry, yet they had a longing desire to return into the company of the faithful, where they might be supplied with those spiritual succours which they wanted, and lead a life yet more conformable to their belief: so that as soon as they had the news of Father Xavier's return, who had baptized the greatest part of them, they came to desire him, that he would make their peace with their masters, whom they had left to free themselves from slavery, and declared, that they were content once more to lose their liberty in prospect of the salvation of their souls. Xavier received them with open arms, as his well-beloved children, and afterwards obtained their pardon.

After he had visited all the villages, he made some stay at Manapar, which is not far distant from Cape Comorine. As the only end which he proposed to himself, was to plant the gospel in the Indies, and that in order to it he must there establish the society, he began to regulate all things according to the principles, and in the spirit of Father Ignatius, general of the order. Having reassembled all the labourers in the gospel of that coast, he examined their several talents and virtues, in familiar conversation with them, by causing them to give an account of what passed betwixt God and them in their own hearts. After he had assigned to each of them the places which were most convenient for them, both in regard of their bodily strength, and of their spiritual endowments, he constituted Father Antonio Criminal superior of all the rest: and to the end they might be more capable of serving that people, he ordered every one of them, with all possible care, to apply himself to the study of the Malabar language, which obtains through all that coast. Upon this account, he commanded Father Francis Henriquez to reduce that tongue into the rules of art, and to compose an exact grammar of it, according to the method of the Greek and Latin grammars. The work seemed impossible, especially to one who was newly come from Europe, and who had little knowledge in the Indian tongues; nevertheless Henriquez compassed it in a small time, which was apparently a miracle of obedience. In the mean while, Xavier judging that the exposition of the Christian doctrine, which he had made for those of Molucca, might be of use to his dear Paravas, ordered a Malabar priest, who was well versed in the Portuguese, to translate it into his own language. But to the end that the conduct of the missioners might be uniform, and that the same spirit might animate all of them, besides the instructions which he gave them by word of mouth, he gave them the following rules in writing.

In the first place, "Wherever the lot of your ministry shall fall, be mindful of baptising infants newly born, and perform it yourselves, without trusting the care of it to any other person: there is nothing at present of more importance. Do not wait till the parents bid you come; as they may easily neglect it, it behoves you to run through all the villages, to enter into the houses, and to christen all the infants you can find.

"After the great concernment of giving baptism, you ought to be careful of nothing more than of entering those little children into the principles of faith, who are grown capable of instruction. Not being able to be in all places, you shall cause the Canacapoles, and the teachers of the catechism, to perform their duty, and religiously to observe the customs established. To which purposes, when you visit the villages, to take an account of what passes there, assemble the masters, with their scholars, and know from the children, in the presence of those who are accustomed to instruct them, what they have learned, or forgotten, since your last visit; this will double the ardency of the scholars, and the diligence of their teachers.

"On Sundays, gather the men together in the church to repeat their prayers; and observe well, whether the Pantagatins, or chief of the people, are there present. You are to expound the prayers which they repeat, and reprove them for the vices then in fashion, which you are to make them comprehend, by using familiar examples. In fine, you are to threaten the more stubborn sinners with the wrath of God; and tell them, that if they do not reform their lives, their days shall be shortened by all manner of diseases; that the Pagan kings shall enslave them, and that their immortal souls shall become fuel to the everlasting flames of hell.

"When you come to any place, you shall inform yourselves what quarrels are stirring in it, and who are the parties; after which, you shall endeavour to reconcile them. These reconciliations are to be made in the church; where it will be fitting to assemble all the women on Saturdays, as the men on Sundays.

"When the Malabar priest shall have translated the exposition of the creed, you shall take copies of it, which you shall cause to be carefully read to the women on Saturdays, to the men on Sundays. If you are there present, you shall read it yourselves, and add to the exposition what you think convenient for the farther clearing it.

"Distribute to the poor those collections which are made for them in the churches, by the charity of the congregation; and beware of taking any part of them for your own uses.

"Fail not every Saturday and Sunday to put the faithful in mind of giving you notice when any one falls sick, to the end you may visit them; and give them to know, that if they do not advertise you, and that the sick person dies, you will not allow him burial amongst Christians, in punishment of their neglect.

"When you visit the sick, take especial care that they repeat to you the apostles' creed in their mother tongue. Interrogate them on every article, and ask them if they believe sincerely. After this, make them say the confiteor, and the other Catholic prayers, and then read the gospel over them.

"For the burial of the dead, you shall assemble the children; and, coming out of the church with them, the cross being at the head of the procession, you shall sing the Christian doctrine, coming and going. You shall say the prayers of the church at the house of the dead person, and before he is put into the ground. You shall also make a short exhortation to the assembly before the corpse, upon the necessity of death, the amendment of life, and the practice of virtue.

"You shall give notice to the men on Sunday, and to the women on Saturday, to bring their sick children into the church, that you may read the gospel over them for their cure; and that the parents from thence may receive increase of faith, and respect to the temples of our Lord.

"You shall yourselves determine all litigious causes; and, if you cannot end them on the place, defer them to the next Sunday; and, after divine service, cause them to be expedited by the principal inhabitants of the place. Yet I will not that these sort of affairs should take up too much of your time, nor that you prefer the care of your neighbour's temporal concernments before works of charity, which respect the salvation of souls; and am of opinion, that when any important business of that kind shall happen, you should remit it to the Portuguese commandant.

"Do all things in your power to make yourselves beloved by those people; for by that you will be able to do more good upon them, than by being feared. Decree no punishment against any person but by the advice of Father Antonio Criminal; and, if the commandant of the Portuguese be present, do nothing without his order. In case any man or woman shall make a pagod, or idol, banish them from the village, if Father Criminal consent to it. Testify great affection to the children who frequent the Christian schools; pardon, and wink at their faults sometimes, lest a severe usage should fright them from us.

"In presence of a Portuguese, abstain from reproving and condemning the natives of the country who are Christians; on the contrary, commend and excuse them on all occasions; for, considering how lately they have embraced the faith, and what assistance is wanting to them to live like good Christians, it is only to be admired that they are not more vicious.

"Be serviceable in all you can to the Malabar priests, in what relates to their spiritual advantage; take care that they confess themselves, and say mass, and give good examples, and write nothing against them to any person whatsoever.

"Live so well with the Portuguese commandants, that no misunderstanding be ever perceived betwixt you and them. For the rest of the Portuguese, use all sort of means to make them your friends: Have never any quarrel with any of them, though they should bring you into law, or quarrel with you without the least provocation on your part. If they use the new Christians hardly, oppose them, but with much mildness; and, if you find your opposition may be likely to succeed, make your complaint to the Portuguese commandant, with whom I once again beseech you never to have any difference.

"Let your conversation with the Portuguese be always confined to spiritual subjects; of death, of judgment, of purgatory, of hell, of the frequentation of sacraments, and the exact observation of God's commandments; for, if you never speak to them but concerning these matters, they will never rob you of those hours which are set apart for your function.

"Fail not to write to Goa, to the fathers and brothers of our society, giving them an account of the fruit of your labours, and proposing to them what you think may be to the advancement of piety. You shall write also to the bishop, but with much reverence and submission, as to the common father, and pastor-general of this new world.

"What, above all things, I recommend to you, and which I can never sufficiently repeat, is, that whatsoever voyage you make, and wheresoever you shall be, you shall endeavour to gain the love of all people, by your good offices and fair demeanour, by which means you will have greater opportunities for the gaining of souls, which God Almighty grant you all the grace to do, and abide for ever with you."

Things being thus regulated on the coast of Fishery, the Father would pass into the isle of Ceylon before his return to Goa. His design was to gather the fruit of that precious blood which two years before was shed by the king of Jafanatapan; or, at least, to see what inclination those people had to receive the gospel, who had heheld the constancy of the martyrs. Indeed, the death of the two young princes converted, who pretended to the crown of Jafanatapan, destroyed almost all hopes of planting Christianity in that isle. Notwithstanding which, Xavier converted the king of Candè, who is one of the kings of Ceylon. After which he went to the tyrant, who had treated the Christians with so much cruelty, to try if he could work him, though against all human appearances, to suffer the law of Jesus Christ to be preached in his dominions, and to bring him also to be a Christian.

As reasons of state prevail most with princes, so the Father represented to this infidel, that his throne could never he established but by the arms of the Portuguese; that, if he once contracted with them a strict alliance, he had nothing farther to apprehend, either from his enemies or his subjects. The barbarian, who feared all things, both from within and from without, forgetting that Don Alphonso de Sosa would have made war upon him in favour of the two baptized princes, hearkened to the propositions of peace, and even permitted the Father to explain to him the mysteries of the Christian faith. The instructions of the saint wrought so much upon the tyrant, that being changed, in a very short space of time, he promised to embrace the faith, and labour to bring his subjects into it; offering for the pledge of his word, to put his kingdom into the hands of the king of Portugal, and to pay him such tribute as should be thought fitting, without any farther demand in his own behalf, than of two things. The one was, that the governor of the Indies should conclude a firm alliance with him, as he had clone with other Indian kings, who had made themselves vassals to the crown of Portugal; the other, that, in order to hinder those revolts and troubles which might arise from the change of religion, he might have a company of Portuguese soldiers, to be entertained at his own charges.

Father Xavier, well satisfied to have thus succeeded beyond his expectations, set sail for Goa, with an ambassador of the infidel king, and arrived there on March the 20th, in the year 1548. Understanding there, that the viceroy Don John de Castro was at Bazain, towards the gulph of Cambaya, he embarked anew, notwithstanding that the season was improper for navigation; as judging that a business of such consequence could not be too soon concluded, and that delays frequently ruined the most hopeful affairs. Castro had never seen Xavier, but all he had heard related of him, gave him an earnest longing to behold him. He received him with all those honours which are due to a saint at the first meeting, and willingly accepted what the king of Jafanatapan had offered, on the conditions above mentioned; but he retained for some time the man of God, both to hear him preach, and to consult him on some difficult affairs, where the interests of state and those of religion were joined together.

In the mean time, he designed Antonio Monis Barreto, a man of authority, and very brave, for the garrison of Jafanatapan, with an hundred soldiers, well disciplined, and worthy of such an officer. At the same time he ordered a magnificent entertainment for the ambassador, who remained at Goa; and that if any of his train would receive baptism, no cost should be spared at that solemnity. But the king of Jafanatapan failed afterwards in fidelity, both to God and man; and in all probability, it was that failure which drew the last misfortunes on his person and his kingdom.

The stay which Xavier made at Bazain was not unprofitable to a young man of quality, who was much debauched, called Rodrigue Segueyra, whom he had known two years before. For Segueyra having committed a murder at Malacca, when the Father made his first voyage to the town, retired into the hospital, to avoid the pursuit of justice. There it was that the Father knew him, and grew into his familiarity, by his engaging ways of mildness and courtesy, which always succeeded with him. When he had gained the affection of Segueyra, he spoke to him of eternity with so much power, that the young gentleman entered into serious thoughts, and made a general confession to him. Xavier, to engage him the more in the ways of goodness, and to free him from that confinement of the hospital, where his crimes had forced him to take sanctuary, made up the business with his adversaries, and obtained his pardon from the governor of Malacca; but seeing the soft and dissolute manner of living in Malacca was capable of ruining all his good intentions, he advised him to leave the Indies, and return into Europe. Segueyra, who was sensible of his own weakness, and desired to save his soul, promised the Father to obey him, and put himself into a condition of executing his promise. In effect, he took the way of Goa, with design from thence to go for Portugal. But being made a receiver of the public revenues by the viceroy Don John de Castro, he thought no more of Portugal, but relapsed into his first debauches.

Xavier was wholly lost to his remembrance when he happened to meet him at Bazain. The sight of the Father surprised him at first, and almost confounded him; but straight recovering, he came up boldly to him, and took his hand, to have kissed it according to his former custom. The Father, as courteous and civil as he was, yet thrust him back sternly enough; yet, mollifying himself a little, "How, my son," said he, "are you still in the Indies? Were you not advised to leave Malacca, and return to Portugal?"

The Portuguese, in great disorder, and not knowing how to excuse himself, laid all the blame upon the governor, who had detained him, in some sort, against his will. "But," replied Xavier, with a holy indignation, "is it the governor who has obliged you to lead the life of a beast, and to continue for two years without going to confession? However it be," continued the Father, "know, that we two shall never be well with one another, so long as you are upon ill terms with God." At these words, Segueyra, pierced with a lively sorrow, asked pardon of the Father for his breach of promise, and his unfaithfulness to the Divine Grace. He confessed himself the same day; and wholly changed his life, under his direction, whom God had sent to bring him back into a better way.

Don John de Castro, who was desirous of profiting by the Father's counsels for the regulation of his own life, would have been glad to have retained him longer; but, seeing him resolved on going, gave him leave to depart; yet, begging him at the same time, that he would pass the winter at Goa, that, after his own return thither, he might use his assistance in the affairs of his conscience.

The Father returned very seasonably for the good of Cosmo de Torrez, a Spanish priest, and native of Valentia, one of the greatest wits, and most knowing persons of that age. Torrez was embarked on the fleet which came from Mexico to the Molucca islands; and which having sailed over so many seas to little purpose, stayed at Amboyna, as we have already related. He there met Xavier, and was so charmed with his manner of life, that he had thoughts of becoming his disciple. But, besides that the labours which are inseparable from the ministry apostolical somewhat shocked him, he judged, that he ought to undertake nothing but by the counsel of the bishop of the Indies; insomuch, that he left Amboyna without forming any resolution, and even without opening himself to Father Xavier.

When the Spanish fleet was arrived at Goa, he presented himself to the bishop, who, being in want of spiritual substitutes, gave him one of the chief vicariats of his diocese. Torrez was of opinion, that God required nothing farther of him; and for the space of four or five months, performed all the functions of that office, which the bishop had given him in charge. But the continual disquiets of his soul rendered him suspicious of his own condition, and brought him to believe, that God had punished him, for not following the new apostle of the East.

Being one day much troubled in his mind, he went to the college of St Paul, and opened himself to Father Lancilotti, desiring him to unfold to him the nature of that institute, with which he was so much taken, by seeing Father Xavier at Amboyna. As some interior motions had of late pushed him on to the performance of somewhat that was great, and of suffering all things for the glory of Jesus Christ, he found the institute of Ignatius so conformable to the present dispositions of his soul, that, without farther balancing the matter, he was resolved to go through the spiritual exercises, to fit himself for the change of his condition. From the second day, he received such light, and so much comfort from above, that he believed himself in heaven already. He could not sufficiently admire, that those plain and easy truths, which he had often read without any taste of them, should make such lively impressions in him, as now they did. And he discovered this to Lancilotti, with expressions full of astonishment. Nevertheless, being affrighted at the prospect of a perpetual engagement, and perhaps tempted by the devil, he could not settle to it, and was every day more and more irresolute.

Xavier arrived just at that point of time. He had scarcely seen Torrez, when behold a man, fixed on the sudden, and resolved, and pressing to be received amongst the children of Ignatius. The apostle received him, and took pains himself to form him, according to the spirit of the society. He also admitted some Portuguese, who had great talents for the mission, and were inflamed with the zeal of souls.

They lived together in the college of St Paul, where that fervour reigned, not only amongst the Jesuits, but also amongst those of the seminary, whose number increased daily. The Japonese, Anger, was amongst them, leading a most regular life, and breathing after that baptism, which had been deferred till the return of the holy man.

Xavier did not satisfy himself with having instructed him anew; he consigned him over to the care of Torrez, who fully explained to him all the mysteries of faith. Anger, with his two servants, who received the same instruction, were at length solemnly baptized, on Whitsunday, by the bishop of Goa, Don John d'Albuquerque; so that the church began to take possession of the most remote nation in the world, on the same day of Pentecost, when the Holy Spirit, descending on the apostles, gave them their mission to carry the gospel to all the people of the earth.

Anger was desirous to be named Paul de Sainte Foi, in memory of the college belonging to the Society of Jesus, where he had received the particular knowledge of the divine law, which was sometimes called the College of St Paul, and sometimes the Seminary of the Holy Faith. One of his servants took the name of John, and the other of Anthony. In receiving baptism, he received the peace of soul which he never could obtain before; and writ word of it to Rome, the same year, in a letter to Father Ignatius, dated November the 25th.

But to the end, that the new converts might have the true principles of Christian morality, and that their behaviour might be answerable to their belief, Father Xavier intrusted Torrez with giving them the spiritual exercises of the society.

During the thirty days that these Japonians were in retirement, it is not to be expressed, what celestial illuminations, what holy thoughts, what interior delights, the Holy Spirit infused into them. Anger could speak of nothing but of God; and spoke of Him with so much fervency, that it seemed even to burn him up. The mystery of the passion moved him above all the rest; and he was so ravished with the goodness of God, so possessed with love, in considering a God crucified, that he breathed nothing but martyrdom, and the salvation of his brethren. So that he was often heard to cry out, in the midst of his devotions, "How glad should I be to die for thee, O my God! O my dear Japonians, how much are you to be lamented, and what compassion do you raise in me!"

The master and servants came out of their retirement with so much ardour, that Xavier wrote into Europe, that he was animated by their example to the service of God, and that he could not look on them without blushing at his own cowardice.

In conversing with them, he understood what he had formerly learnt by hearsay, from George Alvarez, and other Portuguese, that the empire of Japan was one of the most populous in the world; that the Japonese were naturally curious, and covetous of knowledge, and withal docible, and of great capacity; that being generally ingenious, and very rational, if they were instructed in the morals of Christianity, they would easily submit to them; and that, if the preachers of the gospel lived according to gospel rules, the whole nation would subject itself to the yoke of Jesus Christ, not perhaps so readily at first, but in process of time, and after clearing of their doubts.

There needed no more to induce Xavier to carry the faith into Japan. The mildness, the civility, and the good parts of the three baptized Japonians, made him conceive a high opinion of all the rest; and the Portuguese merchants newly returned from Japan, confirmed it so fully to him, that in these three he had the pattern of the whole nation, that he doubted not, but that the Christian religion would make an admirable progress there. But that which Anger told him, that there were in his country many monasteries of Heathen priests; that some of them led their lives in solitude and contemplation; that every monastery had its superior, who was a person venerable for his age and learning; that they came abroad from their lonely abode once a week, with mortified looks, and uncouth habits, to preach to the people; that, in their sermons, they drew such lively figures of hell, that the women wept, and cried out at those dismal representations: All this, I say, appeared to Xavier as so many doors and inlets for the faith; and he praised God, that, by the admirable conduct of his providence, which secretly manages the salvation of men, the spirit of lies had thus prepared the ways for the spirit of truth.

He adored also the wisdom of the same Providence, which, taking the occasion of a man who fled from justice, and sought repose for his troubled conscience, had led three Japonians from their native country, and brought them to Goa, that they might serve for guides to a missioner; but, that these guides might be the more serviceable, he thought fit they should learn to read and write in the Portuguese language. Anger, whom from henceforth we shall name Paul de Sainte Foy, was easily instructed in all they taught him; for, besides that he was of a quick and lively apprehension, he had so happy a memory, that he got by heart almost all the gospel of St Matthew, which Father Cosmo de Torrez had expounded to him before his baptism.

In the mean time, Don John de Castro was rigging out a fleet, with design to possess himself of Aden, one of the strongest towns of Arabia Felix, and situated at the foot of a high mountain, which reached even to the sea by a narrow tongue of earth. This port is of great importance to shut up the passage of the Indies to the Turks and Saracens, who go thither by the Red Sea; and from this consideration it was, that Albuquerque the Great endeavoured to have mastered it in the year 15_13_, but the vigorous resistance of the Achenois forced him to forsake the siege. After that time, they were desirous, of their own accord, to have delivered it up to the Portuguese, thereby to free themselves from the tyranny of the Turks. Yet it was not then done, through the fault of a captain called Soarez, who, having no orders to take possession of the town, was so weak a politician as to refuse it when it was offered to the crown of Portugal.

That people, whom the Turk used worse than ever, testified the same inclination under the government of Castro; and it was on that occasion that he sent a fleet towards the Strait of Mecca, under the command of his son Alvarez de Castro. Eight foysts of Goa, full of soldiers, set out for the expedition of Aden. Amongst these there was one very brave fellow, renowned for his military actions, but blackened with all sorts of crimes, and more infamous by his debauched manners, than known by his valour. He seemed a kind of savage beast, who had no more of man in him than the bare figure, nor any thing of a Christian besides the name. Above eighteen years he had abstained from confession; and that he once presented himself to the bishop of Goa, was less to reconcile himself to God, than to take off the imputation of being either a Mahometan or an idolater.

Father Xavier had cast an eye upon this wretch, and waited only an opportunity to labour in so difficult a conversion. Understanding that this soldier was embarking on one of the foysts, which were going to join the fleet, he went out of the college of St Paul, at the first notice of it, taking nothing with him besides his breviary, and entered into the same vessel. It was believed by those who saw the Father, that he had orders from the viceroy to accompany his son Alvarez; and every one was glad of it, excepting only he, for whose sake he came. He drew near the soldier, and when they had weighed anchor, began to make acquaintance with him, and grew familiar to that degree, that the rest of the soldiers, who were less debauched, could not sufficiently admire it; and some of them said of Xavier, what a Pharisee said formerly of our Lord, "If this man were indeed a prophet, he would discern what manner of man he was, in whom he takes so much delight."

These discourses did not at all daunt the Father. He saw his soldier playing whole nights together, for he was a great gamester. He took no notice of his extravagancies, and sometimes heard him swear without seeming to regard it. Only one day he said to him, that gaming required a composed spirit, and if he took not the better heed, that passion, which he had in play, would make him lose.

The soldier, brutal as he was, grew insensibly to have a kindness for a man, who was so much concerned in his advantages, and took pleasure in hearing him discourse not only of war, and sea affairs, but also of religion and morality. In conclusion, he made some reflections on the horror of his life, and felt even some remorse of conscience for it. Being one day together with the Father, in a private part of the ship, Xavier asked him, to whom he had confessed himself before he went on shipboard? "Ah Father," said the soldier, "I have not been at confession these many years!" "And what do you imagine would become of you," said the holy man, "supposing you should be killed in this action, and in the condition you now are?" "I would once have confessed myself," replied the soldier, "at least for fashion and decency, but the vicar of Goa would not so much as hear me, but told me I was a reprobate, and deserved nothing but hell-fire." "The vicar was, in my opinion," said Xavier, "somewhat too severe, to treat you in that manner. He had perhaps his reasons for that usage, and I have mine to treat you otherwise. For indeed the mercies of our Lord are infinite, and God would have us as indulgent to our brethren, as he himself is to us. Thus, when the sins, of which you find yourself guilty, are a thousand times more numerous and more crying than they are, I shall have the patience to hear them all, and shall make no difficulty of giving you absolution, provided you take those thoughts and resolutions which I shall endeavour to infuse into you."

By these words he brought the soldier to a general confession. He disposed him for it, by causing him to recal into his memory his past life, and drawing him into the particulars of those sins, which a man of his character and profession might possibly have committed. While they were upon these terms, the ship cast anchor at the port of Ceylon for refreshment. Many of the fleet went on shore, and, amongst the rest, the Father and the soldier. They went together to a wild solitary place; there the soldier made his confession with abundance of tears, resolved to expiate his crimes, with whatsoever penance the Father should enjoin him, were it never so rigorous. But his confessor gave him only a paternoster and an ave to say. Whereat the penitent being much amazed, "from whence proceeds it, my Father," said he, "that, being so great a sinner as I am, you have given me so light a penance?" "Be content," answered Xavier; "O my son, we shall appease the divine justice:" and at the same instant, he withdrew into a wood, while the soldier performed his penance. There he did what he had formerly done on the like occasion: he bared his shoulders, and disciplined himself so rigorously, that the soldier heard the noise of the strokes, and came running to him, beholding the Father all in blood; and rightly judging what was the motive of so strange an action, he snatched the discipline out of his hands, and crying out, "it was the criminal who ought to endure the punishment, and not the innocent to bear the pains of sin;" he immediately stripped himself, and chastised his body with all his strength. Xavier oftentimes embraced him, and declared, that it was for his sake alone that he came on shipboard. So having given him wholesome admonitions to confirm him in the grace of God, he left him, and returned to Goa in the first vessel which went out of the port where they made the stay. As for the soldier, he followed the fleet; and after the expedition of Aden was ended, he entered into religion, chusing one of the most austere orders, where he lived and died in extraordinary holiness.

Not long after the Father was returned to Goa, the governor Don John de Castro returned also; but very ill of a hectic fever, which had been consuming him for some months before. Finding himself in a daily decay of health and strength, and doubting not the end of his life was near approaching, he quite laid aside all business, and substituted others to supply his place; after which his thoughts were wholly employed on death, and the great concernments of eternity. He had many long conversations with Father Xavier on that subject, and refused to see any one but him. During these transactions, a ship which came from Lisbon brought letters to the viceroy from the king of Portugal, who gave great praises to his management, and continued him for three years longer in the government of the Indies. As Don John was much beloved, so on this occasion public rejoicings were made over all the town. But the sick viceroy, hearing the discharge of the artillery, and seeing almost from his bed the bonfires that were made, could not forbear laughing at it, though he was almost in the agonies of death. "How deceitful and ridiculous is this world," said he, "to present us with honours of three years continuance, when we have but a moment more to live!" The Father assisted him, even to the last drawing of his breath; and had the consolation to behold a great man of this world, expiring with the thoughts of a saint in holy orders.

Xavier being master of himself, in some manner, after the disease of Don John de Castro, who had desired him not to stir from Goa, during the winter, had thoughts of visiting once more the coast of Fishery before his voyage to Japan; his resolutions of which, he had not hitherto declared. But the incommodities of the season hindered him; for at one certain time the sands so choke up the channels of the isle, that no ship can either go out of the port, or enter into it.

In waiting until the navigation became free, the saint applied himself particularly to the exercises of a spiritual Life, as it were to recover new strength after his past labours, according to the custom of apostolical men, who, in the communications which they have with God, refresh themselves after the pains which they have taken with their neighbour.

Then it was, that, in the garden of Saint Paul's college, sometimes in walking, at other times in retiring into a little hermitage, which was there set up, he cried out, "It is enough, O my Lord, it is enough!" and that he opened his cassock before his breast, to give a little air to those flames which burnt within him, by which he declared, that he was not able to support the abundance of heavenly consolations; and at the same time gave us to understand, that he would have rather chosen to suffer any torments for the service of God, than to have enjoyed all those spiritual delights; so that his true meaning, was a prayer to God, that he would please to reserve for him those pleasures in another life, and in the mean time, would not spare, to inflict on him any pains or sufferings in this present world.

These interior employments did not hinder him from the labours of his ministerial vocation, nor from succouring the distressed in the hospitals and prisons. On the contrary, the more lively and ardent the love of God was in him, the more desirous He was to bring it forth, and kindle it in others. His charity caused him often to relinquish the quiet of solitude, and the delights of prayer; therein following the principle of his Father Ignatius, that it was necessary to forsake God for God.

The season began to be more moderate, and Xavier was disposing himself to set sail for the Cape of Comorine, when a Portuguese vessel arrived from Mozambique, which brought in her live missioners of the society. The most considerable of these missioners, and of five others which came along with the fleet, was Caspar Barzæus, a Fleming by nation. Father Francis had already heard speak of him, as an excellent labourer, and a famous preacher; but his presence, and the testimony of all the ship, gave the saint such great ideas of his merit, that he looked on him from thenceforward as an apostle of the eastern countries.

He passed five days with these new companions, on the fourth of which he caused Father Gaspar to preach before him, that he might see his talent for the pulpit; and discovered in him all the qualities of a perfect preacher. Many Portuguese gentlemen, who had been much edified by the virtues and conversation of Barzæus during all the navigation, which had been exceeding dangerous, came and fell at the feet of Xavier, desiring that he would please to receive them into the society. The captain of the ship, and the governor of one of the chief citadels, which the Portuguese enjoy in India, were of the number. He admitted some of them before his departure, and deferred the rest till his return; but he would that all of them should perform the spiritual exercises of Father Ignatius.

At length Xavier embarked, on the 9th of September, for the fishing coast. There he comforted and confirmed the faithful, who were continually persecuted by the Badages, those mortal and irreconcileable enemies of the Christian name. He also encouraged the gospel labourers of the society, who, for the same reason, went in daily hazard of their lives. Having understood, that Father Francis Henriquez, who cultivated the Christianity of Travancore, was somewhat dissatisfied, and believed he lost his time, because some of those new converts, shaken either by the promises or threatenings of a new king, who hated the Christians, had returned to their former superstitions, he writ him letters of consolation, desiring him to be of good courage, and assuring him, that his labours were more profitable than he imagined; that when all the fruit of his zeal should be reduced to the little children who died after baptism, God would be well satisfied of his endeavours, and that, after all, the salvation of one only soul ought to comfort a missioner for all his pains; that God accounted with us for our good intentions; and that a servant of his was never to be esteemed unprofitable, who laboured in his vineyard with all his strength, whatever his success might prove.

Father Xavier was not content to have fortified the missioners, both by word and writing, in his own person; he desired of Father Ignatius, that he would also encourage them with his epistles, and, principally, that he would have the goodness to write to Henry Henriquez, a man mortified to the world, and laborious in his ministry.

Having ordered all things in the coast of Fishery, he returned by Cochin, where he staid two months; employing himself, without ceasing, in the instruction of little children, administering to the sick, and regulating the manners of that town. After which he went to Bazain, there to speak with the deputy-governor of the Indies, Don Garcia de Saa, whom Don John de Castro had named, upon his death-bed, to supply his place. The Father was desirous to obtain his letters of recommendation to the governor of Malacca, that, in virtue of them, his passage to Japan might be made more easy.

It is true, the news he received, that the Chinese, ill satisfied with the Portuguese, had turned them out of their country, seemed to have broken all his measures, because it was impossible to arrive at the isles of Japan, by the way of Malacca, without touching at some port of China; but it is the property of apostolical zeal, to make no account of those seeming impossibilities, which appear in the greatest undertakings.

When Xavier was come back to Goa, and it was known that he designed a voyage to Japan, his friends made use of all their endeavours to divert him from it. They first set before him the length of the way, which was thirteen hundred leagues; the certain and inevitable dangers to which he must expose his life, not only by reason of pirates, which continually infest those seas, and murder all who come into their hands, but also for the rocks, unknown to the most skilful pilots, and of certain winds called Typhons, which reign from China even to Japan, in a vast extent of sea. They said, "That those impetuous hurricanes were used to whirl a vessel round, and founder it at the same moment; or else drive it with fury against the rocks, and split it in a thousand pieces." They added, "If, by miracle, he should happen to escape the pirates, and avoid the tempests, yet he could promise no manner of safety to himself in the ports of China, from whence the Portuguese were expelled; and, for what remained, if he were possessed with an unsatiable zeal, there were other vast kingdoms of the East, where the light of the gospel had not shone; that even in the neighbourhood of Goa there were isles remaining, and territories, of idolaters: that he might go thither in God's name, and leave the thoughts of those remote islands, which nature seemed to have divided from the commerce of mortals; and where the power of the Portuguese not being established, Christianity could not be able to maintain itself against the persecution of the Pagans."

Xavier was so well persuaded that God would have him travel to Japan, that he would not listen, to the reasons of his friends. He laughed at their fears, and told them, "That perhaps he should not be more unfortunate than George Alvarez, or Alvarez Vaz, who had performed the voyage of Japan, in spite of all those pirates, and those hurricanes, with which they would affright him." This he said smiling; after which, resuming a serious air, "Verily," said he, "I am amazed that you would endeavour to hinder me from going for the good of souls, whither you yourselves would go out of the sordid consideration of a small transitory gain; and must plainly tell you, I am ashamed of your little faith. But I am ashamed for myself, that you have prevented me in going thither first, and cannot bear that a merchant should have more courage than a missioner." In conclusion, he told them, "That having so often experienced the care of Providence, it would be an impiety to distrust it; that it had not preserved him from the swords of the Badages, and the poisons of the Isle del Moro, to abandon him in other dangers; that India was not the boundary of his mission; but that in coming thither, his design had always been, to carry the faith even to the utmost limits of the world."

He then wrote to Father Ignatius, to give him an account of his intended voyage, and of the thoughts of his heart concerning it. "I cannot express to you," said he, "with what joy I undertake this long voyage. For it is all full of extreme dangers; and he, who out of four ships can preserve one, thinks he has made a saving voyage. Though these perils are surpassing all I have hitherto proved, yet I am not discouraged a jot the more from my undertaking; so much the Lord has been pleased to fix it in my mind, that the cross shall produce great fruits in those countries, when once it shall be planted there."

He wrote at the same time to Father Simon Rodriguez, and some passages of the letter well describe the disposition of the holy man. "There are arrived here some ships from Malacca, who confirm the news, that all the ports of China are armed, and that the Chinese are making open war with Portugal; which notwithstanding, my resolutions still continue for Japan; for I see nothing more sweet or pleasing in this world, than to live in continual dangers of death, for the honour of Jesus Christ, and for the interests of the faith. It being indeed the distinguishing character of a Christian, to take more pleasure in the hardships of the cross, than in the softness of repose."

The apostle, being upon the point of his departure for Japan, established Father Paul de Camerine, superior-general in his place, and Father Antonio Gomez, rector of the seminary at Goa. At the same time he prescribed rules to both of them, in what manner they should live together, and how they should govern their inferiors.

Behold, in particular, what he recommended to Father Paul: "I adjure you," said he, "by the desire you have to please our Lord, and by the love you bear to Father Ignatius, and all the society, to treat Gomez, and all our fathers and brothers, who are in the Indies, with much mildness; not ordering them to do any thing without mature deliberation, and in modest terms, without any thing of haughtiness or violence. Truly, considering the knowledge I have of all the labourers of the society, at this present day employed in the new world, I may easily conclude, they have no need of any superior; nevertheless, not to bereave them of the merit of obedience, and because the order of discipline so requires, I have thought convenient to set some one above the rest, and have chosen you for that purpose, knowing, as I do, both your modesty and your prudence. It remains that I command and pray you, by that voluntary obedience which you have vowed to our Father Ignatius, to live so well with Antonio Gomez, that the least appearance of misunderstanding betwixt you may be avoided, nay, and even the least coldness; but, on the contrary, that you may he always seen in a holy union, and conspiring, with all your strength, to the common welfare of the church.

"If our brethren, who are at Comorine in the Moluccas, or otherwhere, write to you, that you would obtain any favour for them from the bishop or the viceroy, or demand any spiritual or temporal supplies from you, leave all things, and employ yourselves entirely to effect what they desire. For those letters which you shall write to those unwearied labourers, who bear the heat and burden of the day, beware that there be nothing of sharpness or dryness in them; rather be careful of every line, that even every word may breathe nothing but tenderness and sweetness.

"Whatsoever they shall require of you for their diet, their clothing, for their preservation of health, or towards their recovery of it, furnish them liberally and speedily; for it is reasonable you should have compassion on them, who labour incessantly, and without any human consolation. What I have said, points chiefly to the missioners of Comorine and the Moluccas. Their mission is the most painful, and they ought to be refreshed, lest they sink under the burden of the cross. Do then in such manner, that they may not ask you twice for necessaries. They are in the battle, you are in the camp; and, for my own part, I find those duties of charity so just, so indispensible, that I am bold to adjure you in the name of God, and of our Father Ignatius, that you would perform your duties with all exactness, with all diligence, and with all satisfaction imaginable."----

Father Xavier, since his return, had sent Nicholas Lancilotti to Coulan, Melchier Gonzales to Bazain, and Alphonso Cyprian to Socotora. Before his departure, he sent Gasper Barzæus to Ormuz, with one companion, who was not yet in orders. This famous town, situate at the entry of the Persian Gulph, was then full of enormous vices, which the mingle of nations and different sects had introduced. The saint had thoughts of going thither himself, to prepare the way for other missioners; according to his own maxims, to send none of the priests to any place, which he knew not first by his own experience. But the voyage of Japan superseded that of Ormuz.

How great soever his opinions were of the prudence and virtue of Father Gasper, yet he thought fit to give him in writing some particular instructions, to help him in the conduct of that important mission. I imagine those instructions would not be unpleasing to the reader; I am sure, at least, they will not be unprofitable to missioners; and for that reason I shall make a recital of them. You shall behold them, neither altered, nor in that confusion which they are in other authors; but faithfully translated from the copy of a manuscript extant in the archives of Goa.

"1. Above all things, have care of perfecting yourself, and of discharging faithfully what you owe to God, and your own conscience. For by this means you will become most capable of serving your neighbour, and of gaining souls. Take pleasure in the most abject employments of your ministry; that, by exercising them, you may acquire humility, and daily advance in that virtue.

"Be sure yourself to teach the ignorant those prayers, which every Christian ought to have by heart; and lay not on any other person an employment so little ostentatious Give yourself the trouble of hearing the children and slaves repeat them word by word after you. Do the same thing to the children of the Christian natives of the country: they who behold you thus exercised, will be edified by your modesty; and as modest persons easily attract the esteem of others, they will judge you proper to instruct themselves in the mysteries of the Christian religion.

"You shall frequently visit the poor in the hospitals, and from time to time exhort them to confess themselves, and to communicate; giving them to understand, that confession is the remedy for past sins, and the communion a preservative against relapses; that both of them destroy the cause of the miseries of which they complain, by reason that the ills they suffer, are only the punishment of their offences. On this account, when they are willing to confess, you shall hear their confessions, with all the leisure you can afford them. After this care taken of their souls, you are not to be unmindful of their bodies; but recommend the distressed, with all diligence and affection, to the administrators of the hospital, and procure them, by other means, all relief within your power.

"You shall also visit the prisoners, and excite them to make a general confession of their lives. They have more need than others to be stirred up to it, because among that sort of people there are few to be found, who ever made an exact confession. Pray the Brotherhood of Mercy to have pity on those wretches, and labour with the judges for their enlargement; in the mean time, providing for the most necessitous, who oftentimes have not wherewithal to subsist.

"You shall serve, and advance what lies in you, the Brotherhood of Mercy. If you meet with any rich merchants, who possess ill-gotten goods, and who, being confessed, are willing to restore that which appertains not to them, though of themselves they entrust you with the money for restitutions, when they are ignorant to whom it is due, or that their creditors appear not--remit all those sums into the hands of the Brotherhood of Mercy, even though you know of some necessitous persons, on whom such charities might be well employed.

"Thus you shall not expose yourself to be deceived by those wicked men, who affect an air of innocence and poverty, and who cannot so easily surprise the Brotherhood, whose principal application is to distinguish betwixt counterfeits and those who are truly indigent.

"And, besides, you will gain the more leisure for those functions, which are yours in a more especial manner, which are devoted to the conversion of souls, and shall employ your whole time therein, some of which must otherwise be taken up in the distribution of alms, which cannot be performed without much trouble and distraction. In fine, by this means, you shall prevent the complaints and suspicions of a sort of people who interpret all things in the worst meaning, and who might perhaps persuade themselves, that, under the pretence of paying other men's debts, you divert the intention of the money given, and employ in your own uses some part of what was entrusted with you.

"Transact in such manner, with secular persons, with whom you have familiarity or friendship, as if you thought they might one day become your enemies: by this management of yourself, you will neither do nor say any thing of which you may have reason to repent you, and with which they may upbraid you in their passion. We are obliged to these precautions, by the sons of a corrupt generation, who are continually looking on the children of light with mistrustful and malignant eyes.

"You ought not to have less circumspection in what relates to your spiritual advancement; and assure yourself you shall make a great progress in contemning of yourself, and in union with God, if you regulate all your words and actions by prudence. The Examen, which we call particular, will assist you much in it. Fail not of doing it twice a day, or once at least, according to our common method, whatsoever business you have upon your hands.

"Preach to the people the most frequently that you can, for preaching is an universal good; and amongst all evangelical employments, there is none more profitable: but beware of advancing any doubtful propositions, on which the doctors are divided: take for the subject of your sermons clear and unquestionable truths, which tend of themselves to the regulation of manners: set forth the enormity of sin, by setting up that infinite Majesty which is offended by the sinner: imprint in souls a lively horror of that sentence, which shall be thundered out against reprobates at the last judgment: represent, with all the colours of your eloquence, those pains which the damned are eternally to suffer. In fine, threaten with death, and that with sudden death, those who neglect their salvation; and who, having their conscience loaded with many sins, yet sleep in security, as if they had no cause of fear.

"You are to mingle with all these considerations that of the cross, and the death of the Saviour of mankind; but you are to do it in a moving pathetical manner; by those figures which are proper to excite such emotions, as cause in our hearts a deep sorrow for our sins, in the presence of an offended God, even to draw tears from the eyes of your audience. This is the idea which I wish you would propose to yourself, for preaching profitably.

"When you reprove vices in the pulpit, never characterise any person, especially the chief officers or magistrates. If they do any thing which you disapprove, and of which you think convenient to admonish them, make them a visit, and speak to them in private, or, when they come of themselves to confession, tell them at the sacred tribunal of penance, what you have to say to them: but never advertise them in public of it; for that sort of people, who are commonly proud and nice of hearing, instead of amendment by public admonitions, become furious, like bulls who are pricked forward by a goad: moreover, before you take upon you to give them private admonition, be careful to enter first into their acquaintance and familiarity.

"Make your admonition either more gentle or more strong, according as you have more or less access to them: but always moderate the roughest part of your reproof, with the gaiety of your air, and a smiling countenance; by the civility of well-mannered words, and a sincere protestation that all you do is but an effect of the kindness you have for them. It is good also to add respectful submissions to the pleasingness of your discourse, with tender embraces, and all the marks of that consideration and goodwill you have for the person of him whom you thus correct. For, if a rigid countenance, and harsh language, should accompany reproof, which of itself is hard of digestion, and bitter to the taste, it is not to be doubted but men, accustomed to flatteries, will not endure it; and there is reason to apprehend, that a burst of rage against the censor, will be all the fruit of the reprimand.

"For what concerns confession, behold the method which I judge the fittest for these quarters of the East, where the licence of sin is very great, and the use of penance very rare. When a person, hardened in a long habit of vice, shall come to confession, exhort him to take three or four days time of preparation, to examine his conscience thoroughly; and for the assistance of his memory, cause him to write down the sins which he has observed in all the, course of his life, from his childhood to that present time. Being thus disposed, after he has made his confession, it will not be convenient that you should be too hasty in giving him absolution. But it will be profitable to him to retire two or three days, and abstain from his ordinary conversation and dealings with men, and to excite himself to sorrow for his sins, in consideration of the love of God, which will render his sacramental absolution of more efficacy to him. During that little interval of retirement, you shall instruct him in the way of meditation, and shall oblige him to make some meditations from the first week of exercises. You shall counsel him to practise some mortification of his body; for example, to fast, or to discipline himself, which will help him to conceive a true sorrow for his offences, and to shed the tears of penance. Besides this, if the penitents have enriched themselves by sinister ways, or if, by their malicious talk, they have blasted the reputation of their neighbour, cause them to make restitution of their ill-gotten goods, and make reparations of their brethren's honour, during the space of those three days. If they are given to unlawful love, and are now in an actual commerce of sin, cause them to break off those criminal engagements, and forsake the occasions of their crime. There is not any time more proper to exact from sinners those duties, the performance of which is as necessary as it is difficult; for when once their fervour is past away, it will be in vain to demand of them the execution of their promise; and perhaps you will have the trouble of seeing them fall back into the precipice, for want of removing them to a distance from it.

"In administering the sacrament of penance, take heed of discouraging those who begin to discover the wounds of their souls to you, by appearing too rashly and too hastily severe. How enormous soever their sins may be, hear them, not only with patience, but with mildness; help out even their bashfulness, by testifying to them your compassion, and not seeming to be amazed at what you hear. Insinuate into them, that you have heard in confession sins of a much more crying nature: and, lest they should despair of pardon for their faults, speak to them of the infinite mercies of the Lord.

"When they declare a crime in such a manner that you may perceive they are in trouble how to speak, interrupt them, by letting them know, that their sin is not altogether so great as they may think; that by God's assistance you can heal the most mortal wounds of the soul; bid them go on without any apprehension, and make no difficulty of telling all. You will find some of them, whom either the weakness of their age or sex will hinder from revealing to you their most shameful sins. When you perceive that bashfulness has tied their tongue, be before-hand with them; and, by the way of a charitable prevention, let them know, that they are neither the first, nor the only persons, who have fallen into disorder; that those things which they want the confidence to tell you, are little in comparison of what you have heard from others on the same subject. Impute some part of their offence to the corruption of nature, to the violence of the temptation, and to the unhappiness they had to be engaged in such occasions and pressing circumstances, where their fall was almost unavoidable. In fine, I must advertise you, that to remove from such persons that unseasonable shame-facedness which keeps them silent; from such persons, I say, whom the devil has made as bashful after a crime as they were impudent before it, it may be necessary sometimes to discover to them, in general, the frailties of our own past lives. For what can a true and fervent charity refuse, for the safety of those souls who have been redeemed with the blood of Jesus Christ! But to understand when this is proper to be done, how far to proceed, and with what precautions, is what the interior spirit, and your experience, must teach you, in those particular conjunctures.

"You will ordinarily meet with some Christians who believe not the truth of the holy sacrament of the altar, either by not frequenting it, or by their conversation with Pagans, Mahometans, and Heretics, or by the scandal which is given them by some Christians, and principally (which I speak with shame and sorrow) by such priests whose life is not more holy than that of the people. For beholding some of them approaching the altar without any preparation, assisting at it without modesty and reverence, they imagine that Jesus Christ is not, as we say he is, in the sacrifice of the mass; for if he were there present, he would never suffer such impure hands to touch him. Make it your business, that those misbelieving Christians should propose to you all their doubts, and discover to you all their imaginations, which being known, then prove to them the real presence of Jesus Christ, by all those reasons which are capable of establishing it; and shew them, that the surest means for them to come out of their errors, and leave their vices, is often to approach that sacrament, with suitable preparations to it.

"Though your penitents may be well prepared for confession, think not, when they shall declare their sins, that your business is done. You must dive into the bottom of their conscience, and, by examination, draw out of them what themselves know not. Ask then of them, by what ways, and in what manner, they make advantage of their money; what are their principles, and what their practice, in their sales, in their borrowing, and in all their business. You shall find usury reigning throughout their traffic; and that they who have no stings of conscience, in relation to unjust dealings, have by indirect ways scraped together the greatest part of their estates. But in things where money has to do, many are so hardened, that, being charged with rapine, they have either no scruple concerning it, or so very light, that it never breaks their sleep.

"Use particularly this method towards the governors, the treasurers, the receivers, and other officers belonging to the revenue. Whensoever they present themselves before you in the sacred tribunal, interrogate that sort of people, by what means they grow so rich? what secret they have to make their offices and employments bring them in such mighty sums? If they are shy of telling you, turn and wind them every way, and the most mildly that you can, make them speak, in spite of themselves. You shall soon discover their tricks, and secret ways of management, by which an inconsiderable number of those they call men of business, divert, to their own private advantages, what was designed for the public profit. They buy up commodities with the king's money, that, by selling them again, they may be able to make up their accounts: And by taking up all the commodities in the port, they put the people upon a necessity of buying at their price, that is, at most intolerable rates.

"Too often also, they make men languish at the treasury, with long delays, and cunning shifts, or some other captious trick; men, I say, to whom the exchequer is owing, that they may be driven to compound with those sharks of state for half their due, and let them go off with the other half. This open robbery, this manifest villainy, those gentlemen call, by a mollified name, 'the fruits of their industry.' When you have squeezed out of them the confession of these monopolies, and the like, by wire-drawing them, with apt questions, you will come more easily to the knowledge of their ungodly gains, and what they ought to make restitution of to their neighbour, in order to their being reconciled to God, than if in general you should interrogate them concerning their injustice. For example, demand of them, what persons they have wronged? they will immediately answer, that their memory upbraids them not with wronging any man; and behold the reason! Custom is to them in the place of law; and that which they see done before them every day, they persuade themselves may be practised without sin. As if custom can authorize, by I know not what kind of prescription, that which is vicious and criminal in its own nature. You shall admit of no such right, but shall declare to such people, that if they will secure their conscience, they must restore what they possess unjustly.

"Remember especially, to obey the vicar of the bishop. When you are arrived at Ormuz, you shall go to wait on him, and, falling on your knees before him, you shall humbly kiss his hand. You shall neither preach, nor exercise any other employment of our institute, without his permission; above all things, have no difference with him for any whatsoever cause; on the contrary, endeavour, by all submissions, and all possible services, to gain his friendship, in such sort, that he may be willing to be taught by you, to make the meditations of our spiritual exercises, at least those of the first week. Use almost the same method with all the other priests; if you cannot persuade them to retire for a month, according to our custom, engage them to a retreat of some few days, and fail not to visit them every day, during that recess, to explicate to them the subjects of those meditations.

"Pay a great respect to the person of the governor, and make it apparent, by the most profound submissions, how much you honour him. Beware of any difference with him, on whatsoever occasion, even though you should observe, that he performs not his duty in matters of importance; but after you perceive, that your demeanour has instated you in his favour and good graces, go boldly to visit him;

and after you have testified the concernment you have for his safety and his honour, by a principle of good will to him, then declare, with all modesty and softness of expression, the sorrow you have to see his soul and reputation endangered, by what is reported of him in the world.

"Then you shall make known to him the discourse of the people; you shall desire him to reflect on the bad consequences of such reports; that they may possibly be put in writing, and go farther than he would willingly they should, if he bethinks him not in time of giving satisfaction to the public. Nevertheless, take not this upon you before you are in some sort satisfied of his good disposition, and that it appears probable to you that your advertisement may sort to good effect.

"Be yet more cautious in charging yourself with bearing to him the complaints of particular persons; and absolutely refuse that commission, by excusing yourself on your evangelical functions, which permit you not to frequent the palaces of the great, nor to attend whole days together for the favourable minutes of an audience, which is always difficult to obtain. You shall add, that when you should have the leisure to make your court, and that all the doors of the palace were open to you at all hours, you should have little hopes of any fruit from your remonstrances; and that if the governor be such a man as they report, he will have small regard to you, as being no way touched, either with the fear of God, or the duties of his own conscience.

"You shall employ, in the conversion of infidels, all the time you have free from your ordinary labours which indispensably regard Christians. Always prefer those employments which are of a larger extent to those which are more narrowly confined. According to that rule, you shall never omit a sermon in public, to hear a private confession; you shall not set aside the catechising, which is appointed every day, at a certain hour, to visit any particular person, or for any good work of the like nature. For the rest, an hour before catechism, either you or your companion shall go to the places of most concourse in the town, and invite all men, with a loud voice, to come and hear the exposition of the Christian doctrine.

"You shall write, from time to time, to the college of Goa, what functions you exercise for the advancement of God's glory, what order you keep there, and what blessing God gives on your endeavours. Have care that your relations be exact, and such that our Fathers at Goa may send them into Europe, as so many authentic proofs of what you perform in the East, and of what success it shall please God to bestow on the labours of our little Society. Let nothing slip into those accounts which may reasonably give offence to any man; nothing that may seem improbable; nothing which may not edify the reader, and give him occasion to magnify the name of God.

"When you are come to Ormuz, I am of opinion that you should see particularly those who are of greatest reputation for their probity, the most sincere, and who are most knowing in the manners of the town. From such, inform yourself exactly what vices are most reigning in it, what sorts of cheats; enter most into contracts, and societies of commerce, that so understanding all things thoroughly and truly, you may have your words and reasons in a readiness, to instruct and reprove those who, being guilty of covert usuries, false bargaining, and other wicked actions, so common in a place which is filled with such a concourse of different nations, shall treat with you in familiar conversation, or in sacramental confession.

"You shall walk the streets every night, and recommend the souls of the dead to the prayers of the living; but let those expressions which are used by you be proper to move the compassion of the faithful, and to imprint the thoughts of religion in the bottom of their souls. You shall also desire their prayers to God for such as are in mortal sin, that they may obtain the grace of coming out of so deplorable a condition.

"Endeavour at all times to make your humour agreeable: keep a gay and serene countenance, without suffering the least shadow of choler or sadness to appear in it; otherwise those who come to visit you will never open their hearts to you, and will not repose all that confidence in you which it is necessary they should have, to the end they may profit by your discourse. Speak always with civility and mildness, even in your reprehensions, as I have already told you; and when you reprove anyone, do it with so much charity, that it may be evident the fault displeases you, and not the person.

"On Sundays and saints' days you shall preach at two o'clock in the afternoon, at the church of the Misericordia, or in the principal church of the town; sending first your companion about the streets, with his bell in his hand, to invite the people to the sermon.

"If you had not rather perform that office in your own person, you shall carry to church that exposition of the apostles' creed which I have put into your hands, and the practice, which I have composed, how to pass the day in Christian duties. You shall give copies of that practice to those whose confessions you hear; and shall enjoin them, for their holy penance, to do for certain days that which is contained in it. By this means they shall accustom themselves to a Christian life, and shall come to do, of their own accord, by the force of custom, that which they did at the first only by the command of their confessor. But, foreseeing that you cannot have copies enough for so many people, I advise you to have that practice written out in a fair large hand, and expose it in some public place, that they who are willing to make use of it may read and transcribe it at their own convenience.

"They who shall be desirous of being received into the society, and whom you shall judge to be proper for it, you may send them to Goa with a letter, which shall point out their design, and their talents for it, or else you may retain them with you. In this last case, after you have caused them to perform the spiritual exercises for a month together, you shall make a trial of them, in some such manner as may edify the people without exposing them to be ridiculous. Order them, therefore, to serve the sick in the hospitals, and to debase themselves to the meanest and most distasteful offices. Make them visit the prisoners, and teach them how to give comfort to the miserable. In fine, exercise your novices in all the practices of humility and mortification; but permit them not to appear in public in extravagant habits, which may cause them to be derided by the multitude;--suffer it not, I say, far from imposing it upon them. Engage not all the novices indifferently to those trials which their nature most abhors; but examine well the strength of each, and suit their mortification to their temper, to their education, to the advance they make in spirituals, in such sort, that the trial may not be unprofitable, but that it may produce its effect according to that measure of grace which is given them. If he who directs the novices has not all these considerations, it will fall out, that they who were capable of making a great proficiency in virtue, with good management, will lose their courage, and go backward; and besides, those indiscreet trials, too difficult for beginners, take off the love of the master from his novices, and cause his disciples to lessen their confidence in his directions. In the mean time, whoever forms young people to a religious life, ought to leave nothing untried to bring them to a candid and free discovery of their evil inclinations, and the suggestions of the devil, at the same moment when they are tempted: for without this they will never be able to disentangle themselves from the snares of the tempter; never will they arrive to a religious perfection. On the contrary, those first seeds of evil being brooded over, and nourished, as I may say, by silence, will insensibly produce most lamentable effects; even so far, until the novices come to grow weary of regular discipline, to nauseate it, and at length throw off the yoke of Jesus Christ, and replunge themselves in the pollutions of the world.

"They amongst those young men whom you shall observe to be most subject to vain-glory, and delighted with sensual pleasures, and other vices, ought to be cured in this following manner: Make them search for reasons, and for proofs, against those vices to which they are inclined; and when they have found many, help them to compose some short discourses on them. Cause them afterwards to pronounce those discourses, either to the people in the church, or in the hospitals, to those who are in a way of recovery, so as to be present at them, or in other places;--there is reason to hope, that the things which they have fixed in their minds, by constant study and strong application, will be at least as profitable to themselves as to their audience. Doubtless they will be ashamed not to profit by those remedies which they propose to others, and to continue in those vices from which they endeavour to dissuade their hearers. You shall use proportionally the same industry towards those sinners who cannot conquer themselves so far, as, they commonly say, to put away the occasions of their sin, or to make restitution of those goods which they have gotten unlawfully, and detain unjustly from other men. After you have endeared yourself to them by a familiar acquaintance, advise them to say that to their own hearts which they would say to a friend on the like occasion, and engage, as it were for the exercise of their parts, to devise such arguments as condemn their actions in the person of another.

"Sometimes you will see before you, when you are seated in the tribunal of penance, men who are enslaved to their pleasures and their avarice, whom no motive of God's love, nor thought of death, nor fear of hell, can oblige to put away a mistress, or to restore ill-gotten goods. The only means of reducing such people, is to threaten them with the misfortunes of this present life, which are the only ills they apprehend. Declare then to them, that if they hasten not to appease Divine Justice, they shall suddenly suffer considerable losses at sea, and be ill treated by the governors; that they shall lose their law-suits; that they shall languish many years in prison; that they shall be seized with incurable diseases, and reduced to extreme poverty, without any to relieve them; in fine, that they and their posterity, becoming infamous, shall be the objects of the public hate and curses. Tell them, by way of reason for those accidents, that no man who sets God at nought remains unpunished; and that his vengeance is so much the more terrible, by how much longer his patience has been abused. The images of these temporal punishments will affright those carnal men who are not to be wrought on but by their senses, and will bring forth in their insensible souls the first motions of the fear of God,--of that saving fear which is the beginning of wisdom.

"Before you treat with any one concerning his spiritual affairs, endeavour to understand how his soul stands affected. Whether it be calm, or tossed with any violent passion; whether he be ready to follow the right way when it shall be shewn to him, or whether he wanders from it of set purpose; whether it be the tempter, or the bias of his own inclination, which seduces him to evil; whether he be docile, and disposed to hear good counsel, or of that untractable humour on which no hold is to be fastened,--it will behove you to vary your discourse according to these several dispositions: But though more circumspection is to be taken with hardened souls, and difficult of access, you are never to flatter the disease, nor say any thing to him which may weaken the virtue of the remedy, and hinder its effect.

"Wheresoever you shall be, even though you only pass through a place, and stay but little in it, endeavour to make some acquaintance; and inquire of those who have the name of honest and experienced men, not only what crimes are most frequently committed in that town, and what deceits most used in traffic, as I have already taught you in relation to Ormuz; but farther, learn the inclinations of the people, the customs of the country, the form of government, the received opinions, and all things respecting the commerce of human life: for, believe me, the knowledge of those things is very profitable to a missioner, for the speedy curing of spiritual diseases, and to have always at hand wherewithal to give ease to such as come before you.

"You will understand from thence, on what point you are most to insist in preaching, and what chiefly to recommend in confessions. This knowledge will make, that nothing shall be new to you, nothing shall surprise or amaze you; it will furnish you with the address of conducting souls, and even with authority over them. The men of the world are accustomed to despise the religious as people who understand it not: But if they find one who knows how to behave himself in conversation, and has practised men, they will esteem him as an extraordinary person; they will give themselves up to him; they will find no difficulty, even in doing violence to their own inclinations, under his direction, and will freely execute what he enjoins, though never so repugnant to their corrupt nature. Behold the wonderful fruit of knowing well the world:--so that you are not, at this present, to take less pains in acquiring this knowledge, than formerly you have done in learning philosophy and divinity. For what remains, this science is neither to be learned from ancient manuscripts nor printed books; it is in living books, and the conversation of knowing men, that you must study it: with it, you shall do more good, than if you dealt amongst the people, all the arguments of the doctors, and all the subtilties of the schools.

"You shall set apart one day of the week, to reconcile differences, and regulate the interests of such as are at variance, and are preparing to go to law. Hear them one after the other, and propose terms of accommodation to them. Above all things, give them to understand, that they shall find their account in a friendly reconciliation, sooner than in casting themselves into eternal suits, which, without speaking of their conscience, and their credit, ever cost much money, and more trouble. I know well, that this will not be pleasing to the advocates and proctors, whom the spinning out a process, and tricks of wrangling, still enrich. But trouble not yourself with what those bawlers say; and make even them comprehend, if it be possible, that by perpetuating suits, by these numberless formalities, they expose themselves to the danger of eternal damnation. Endeavour also to engage them into a retirement of some few days, to the end their spiritual exercises may work them off to other courses.

"Stay not till your arrival at Ormuz before you preach. Begin on shipboard, and as soon as you come there. In your sermons, affect not to make a show of much learning, or of a happy memory, by citing many passages of ancient authors; some few are necessary, but let them be chosen and fitted to the purpose. Employ the best part of your sermon, in a lively description of the interior estate of worldly souls. Set before their eyes, in your discourse, and let them see, as in a glass, their own disquiets, their little cunnings, their trifling projects, and their vain hopes. You shall also show them, the unhappy issue of all their designs. You shall discover to them, the snares which are laid for them by the evil spirit, and teach them the means of shunning them. But, moreover, you shall tell them, that if they suffer themselves to be surprised by them, they are to expect the worst that can happen to them; and by this you shall gain their attention; for a man never fails of attentive audience, when the interest of the hearer is the subject of the discourse. Stuff not out your sermons with sublime speculations, knotty questions, and scholastical controversies. Those things which are above the level of men of the world, only make a noise, and signify nothing. It is necessary to represent men to themselves, if you will gain them. But well to express what passes in the bottom of their hearts, you must first understand them well; and in order to that, you must practise their conversation, you must watch them narrowly, and fathom all their depths. Study then those living books; and assure yourself, you shall draw out of them the means of turning sinners on what side you please.

"I do not forbid you, nevertheless, to consult the holy scriptures on requisite occasions, nor the fathers of the church, nor the canons, nor books of piety, nor treatises of morality; they may furnish you with solid proofs for the establishment of Christian truths, with sovereign remedies against temptations, and heroical examples of virtue. But all this will appear too cold, and be to no purpose, if souls be not disposed to profit by them; and they cannot profit but by the ways I have prescribed. So that the duty of a preacher is to sound the bottom of human hearts, to have an exact knowledge of the world, to make a faithful picture of man, and set it in so true a light, that every one may know it for his own.

"Since the king of Portugal has ordered, that you shall be allowed from the treasury what is needful for your subsistence, make use of the favour of so charitable a prince, and receive nothing but from his ministers. If other persons will give you any thing, refuse it, though they should offer it of their own mere motion. For as much, as it is of great consequence to the liberty of an apostolical man, not to owe his subsistence to those whom he ought to conduct in the way of salvation, and whom he is bound to reprove, when they go astray from it; one may truly say of those presents, that he who takes, is taken. And it is for this, that when we are to make a charitable reprehension, to such of whom we receive alms, we know not well how to begin it, or in what words to dress it. Or if our zeal emboldens us to speak freely, our words have less effect upon them, because they treat us with an assuming air of loftiness, as if that which we received from them had made them our masters, and put them in possession of despising us. What I say, relates chiefly to a sort of persons, who are plunged in vice, who would willingly be credited with your friendship, and will endeavour by all good offices to make way to your good will. Their design is not to profit by your conversation, for the amendment of their lives; all they pretend to, is to stop your mouth, and to escape a censure, which they know they have deserved. Be upon your guard against such people: yet I am not of opinion, that you should wholly reject them, or altogether despise their courtesy. If they should invite you to their table, refuse it not; and yet less refuse their presents of small value, such as are usually made in the Indies by the Portuguese to each other, and which one cannot refuse without giving an affront; as, for example, fruits and drinks. At the same time, declare to them, that you only receive those little gifts, in hope they will also receive your good advice; and that you go to eat with them, only that you may dispose them, by a good confession, to approach the holy table. For such presents as I have named, such I mean as are not to be refused, when you have received them, send them to the sick, to the prisoners, or to the poor. The people will be edified with this procedure, and no occasion left of suspecting you, either of niceness or covetousness.

"For what relates to your abode, you will see at your arrival; and having prudently considered the state of things, you may judge where it will be most convenient for you to dwell, either in the hospital, or the house of mercy, or any little lodging, in the neighbourhood. If I think fit to call you to Japan, you shall immediately give notice of it, by writing to the rector of this college by two or three different conveyances, to the end, he may supply your place with one of our fathers, a man capable of assisting and comforting the city of Ormuz. In fine, I recommend you to yourself; and that in particular, you never forget, that you are a member of the Society of Jesus.

"In the conjunctures of affairs, experience will best instruct you what will be most for God's service; for there is no better master than practice, and observation, in matters of prudence. Remember me always in your prayers; and take care, that they who are under your direction, recommend me in theirs to the common Master whom we serve. To conclude this long instruction, the last advice I give you, is to read over this paper carefully once a week, that you may never forget any one of the articles contained in it. May it please the Lord to go along with you, to conduct you in your voyage, and at the same time to continue here with us!"--

Eight days after Gasper Barzæus was gone for Ormus, with his companion Raymond Pereyra, Father Xavier went himself for Japan; it was in April 1549. He embarked in a galley bound no farther than

Cochin, where waited for him a ship, which was to go towards Malacca. He took for companions Father Cozmo de Torrez, and John Fernandez, besides the three Japonese, Paul de Sainte Foy, and his two servants, John and Anthony.

It is true, there embarked with him in the same galley, Emanuel Moralez, and Alphonso de Castro; but it was only that the Father might carry them to Malacca, from whence both of them were to be transported to the Moluccas. The ship, which attended the Father at Cochin, being just ready to set sail they made but a short stay in that place, but it was not unprofitable. The saint walking one day through the streets, happened to meet a Portuguese of his acquaintance; and immediately asked him, "how he was in health?" The Portuguese answered, "he was very well." "Yes," replied Xavier, "in relation to your body, but, in regard of your soul, no man can be in a worse condition." This man, who was then designing in his heart a wicked action, knew immediately that the Father saw into the bottom of it; and seriously reflecting on it, followed Xavier, confessed himself, and changed his evil life. The preaching of Castro so charmed the people, that they desired to have retained him at Cochin, there to have established the college of the Society; but Xavier who had designed him for the Moluccas opposed it. And Providence, which destined the crown of martyrdom to that missioner, suffered him not to continue in a place, where they had nothing but veneration for him.

They left Cochin on the 25th of April, and arrived at Malacca on the last of May. All the town came to meet Father Xavier, and every particular person was overjoyed at his return. Alphonso Martinez, grand vicar to the bishop, at that time lay dangerously sick, and in such an agony of soul, as moved compassion. For, having been advertised to put himself in condition of giving up his accounts to God of that ministry which he had exercised for thirty years, and of all the actions of his life, he was so struck with the horror of immediate death, and the disorders of his life, which was not very regular for a man of his profession, that he fell into a deep melancholy, and totally despaired of his salvation. He cast out lamentable cries, which affrighted the hearers; they heard him name his sins aloud, and detest them with a furious regret, not that he might ask pardon for them, but only to declare their enormity. When they would have spoken to him of God's infinite mercy, he broke out into a rage, and cried out as loud as he was able, "that there was no forgiveness for the damned, and no mercy in the bottomless pit." The sick man was told, that Father Francis was just arrived; and was asked if he should not be glad to see him? Martinez, who formerly had been very nearly acquainted with him, seemed to breathe anew at the hearing of that name, and suddenly began to raise himself, to go see, said he, the man of God. But the attempt he made, served only to put him into a fainting fit. The Father, entering at the same moment, found him in it. It had always been his custom, to make his first visit to the ecclesiastical superiors; but besides this, the sickness of the vicar hastened the visit. When the sick man was come, by little and little, to himself, Xavier began to speak to him of eternity, and of the conditions requisite to a Christian death. This discourse threw Martinez back again into his former terrors; and the servant of God, in this occasion, found that to be true, which he had often said, that nothing is more difficult than to persuade a dying man to hope well of his salvation, who in the course of his life had flattered himself with the hopes of it, that he might sin with the greater boldness.

Seeing the evil to be almost past remedy, he undertook to do violence to heaven, that he might obtain for the sick man the thoughts of true repentance, and the grace of a religious death. For he made a vow upon the place, to say a great number of masses, in honour of the most Holy Trinity, of the Blessed Virgin, of the angels, and some of the saints, to whom he had a particular devotion. His vows were scarcely made, when Martinez became calm; began to have reasonable thoughts, and received the last sacraments, with a lively sorrow for his sins, and a tender reliance on God's mercies; after which, he died gently in the arms of Xavier, calling on the name of Jesus Christ.

His happy death gave great consolation to the holy man; but the apostolic labours of Francis Perez and Roch Oliveira increased his joy. He had sent them the year before to Malacca, there to found a college of the Society, according to the desire of the people, and they had been very well received. Perez had begun to open a public school, for the instruction of the youth in learning and piety, according to the spirit of their institute. Oliveira had wholly given himself to the ministry of preaching, and the conduct of souls; but tying himself more especially to the care of Turks and Jews, of which there was always a vast concourse in the town. For the first came expressly from Mecca, and the last from Malabar, to endeavour there to plant Mahometanism and Judaism, where Christianity then flourished.

The example of the two missioners drew many Portuguese to that kind of life, of which they both made profession. The most considerable of all, was a young gentleman, whose name was Juan Bravo; who, by his noble birth and valour, might justly hope to raise his fortunes in the world. But he preferring evangelical poverty, and religious humility, before all those earthly expectations and establishments, was just then ready to have taken ship for Goa, there to execute those thoughts with which heaven had inspired him, when he was informed, that Xavier would take Malacca in his way. He therefore waited for him, and in the mean time lived with Perez and Oliveira as if he had been already of the Society. At least he conformed himself as much as he was able to their manners, and habited himself like them; that is to say, instead of rich garments, he put on an old threadbare cassock, with which he looked the world in the face without having yet forsaken it. He performed the spiritual exercises for a month together, and never came out of his retirement, but to employ himself in works of charity in the hospital. There, for three months, he attended the sick, living in poverty, and begging his bread from door to door, even in the sight of James Sosa his kinsman, admiral of the fleet, which was rigging out for the Moluccas.

These trials obliged the Father to receive Bravo into the Society. He admitted him almost immediately to take the first vows; and finding in him an excellent foundation for all the apostolical virtues, he took care to cultivate him, even so far, as to leave him in writing these following rules, before his departure to Japan.

"See here, my dear brother, the form of life which you are constantly to practise every day. In the morning, as soon as you are awakened, prepare yourself to meditate on some mystery of our Lord; beginning from his holy nativity, and continuing to his glorious ascension: the subjects of the meditations are marked, and put in order, in the book of Exercises. Employ, at the least, half-an-hour in prayers; and apply yourself to it with all those interior dispositions, which you may remember you practised in your retirement of a month. Consider every day one mystery, in such manner, that if, for example, on Monday, the birth of our Saviour was the subject of your meditation, that of his circumcision shall be for Tuesday, and so in course, till in a month's time, having run through all the actions of Jesus Christ, you come to contemplate him ascending into heaven in triumph. You are every month to begin these meditations again in the same order.

"At the end of every meditation, you shall renew your vows of poverty, chastity, and obedience, to which you have obliged yourself. You shall make them, I say, anew, and offer them to God with the same fervency wherewith you first made them. This renewing of your vows will weaken in you the motions of concupiscence, and render all the powers of hell less capable of hurting you; for which reason, I am of opinion that you ought never to omit them.

"After dinner, you shall resume your morning's prayer, and reflect on the same mystery half an hour; you shall also renew your vows, at the end of your meditation. You are to employ yourself in this manner interiorly through all the variety of your outward business; giving an hour in every day to the consideration of the most holy life of our Lord Jesus, in whatsoever affair, or in whatsoever incumbrance, you are engaged. You may practise this with most convenience, by allowing half-an-hour in the morning, and another half in the afternoon, according to my direction.

"Before you lie down at night, examine well your conscience, in calling over your thoughts, words, and actions, of all the day; and even observing, if you have not failed of doing something, which it was your duty to have done: let this discussion be as exact, as if you were just ready to confess yourself. After you have conceived a most lively sorrow for your faults, by the motive of God's love, you shall humbly ask pardon of Jesus Christ, and vow amendment to him. In fine, you shall so dispose yourself to rest, that your sleep may come upon you, in thoughts of piety, and in resolutions of passing the next day with greater holiness.

"On the morrow, at your waking, think on the sins which you observed in the examen of the night before; and while you are putting on your clothes, ask the assistance of God's grace, that you may not that day relapse into your yesterday's offences. Then perform your morning's meditation, and proceed through your whole day's work, as I have ordered you. But be so punctual, and so constant in all these spiritual practices, that nothing but sickness cause you to forbear them. For if, when you are in health, you should defer, or leave them off, under some pretence of business, be sure you make a scruple of it, and let not the day pass over you, till, in the presence of your brethren, you confess your fault, and of your own free motion demand penance for having omitted or neglected that which was so strictly commanded by your superior.

"For what remains, whatsoever you do, or in whatsoever condition of spirit you may be, labour with all your power still to overcome yourself. Subdue your passions, embrace what is most abhorring to your sense, repress all natural desire of glory most especially; and spare not yourself in that particular, till you have torn out of your heart the very roots of pride; not only suffering yourself to be debased beneath all men, but being glad to be despised. For hold this for certain, that, without this humility and mortification, you can neither advance in virtue, nor serve your neighbour as you ought, nor be acceptable to God, nor, to conclude all, persevere in the Society of Jesus.

"Obey in all things the Father with whom you live; and however displeasing or difficult the things may be which he commands you, perform them with much cheerfulness, never opposing his orders, nor making any exceptions on your part, on any account whatsoever. In fine, hearken to him, and suffer yourself to be directed in all things by him, as if Father Ignatius were personally present, speaking to you, and directing you.

"With whatsoever temptations you shall find yourself assaulted, discover them all sincerely to him who governs you; and remain persuaded, that this is the only means of subduing them. Besides this advantage, there accrue other spiritual profits, in making known the secret motions of your heart; for the violence which you do to yourself, to surmount, that natural shamefacedness which hinders you from acknowledging your imperfections and frailties, draws down the grace of God upon you; and on the other side, this overture, and frankness of your heart, ruins the designs of the evil spirit, who can never do mischief but when he is in disguise; but when once discovered, is so far disarmed, and despicably weak, that they, for whom he lies in ambush, laugh at him."--

It was in this manner, that the holy apostle, Francis Xavier, instructed the young men of the Society; and nothing, perhaps, could better explain to us the great resemblance that was betwixt the souls of Xavier and Ignatius.

At this time, there came news from Japan; and some letters reported, that one of the kings of that island had desired some preachers to be sent to him, by an express embassy to the viceroy of the Indies. That this king had learnt somewhat of the Christian law, and that a strange accident had made him desirous of knowing more. This accident was related in those letters, after the following manner.

"Some Portuguese merchants, being landing at the port, belonging to the capital city of one of those kingdoms of Japan, were lodged by the king's order in a forsaken house, which was thought to be haunted by evil spirits: the common opinion was not ill grounded, and the Portuguese soon perceived, that their lodging was disturbed. They heard a horrible rumbling all the night; they felt themselves pulled out of their beds, and beaten in their sleep, without seeing any one. One night being awakened, at the cry of one of their servants, and running with their arms towards the place from whence the noise was heard, they found the servant on the ground, trembling for fear. They asked him the occasion of his outcry, and why he shook in that manner? He answered, 'That he had seen a frightful apparition, such a one as painters use to draw for the picture of the devil.' As this servant was not thought either faint-hearted, or a liar, the Portuguese no longer doubted, what was the meaning of all that rattling and clutter, which they heard every night; to put an end to it, they set crosses in all the rooms, after which they heard no more of it."

The Japonese were much surprised to hear the house was now at quiet: the king himself, to whom the Portuguese had said, "That the Christian cross had driven away the evil spirits," admired that wonderful effect, and commanded crosses to be set up in all places, even in his own palaces, and in the highways. In consequence of this, he desired to be informed from whence the cross derived that virtue, and for what cause the devils so much feared it. Thus, by little and little, he entered into the mysteries of faith. But as the Japonese are extremely curious, not content to be instructed by soldiers and merchants, he thought of sending for preachers, and in that prospect sent an ambassador to the Indies.

This news gave infinite satisfaction to Father Xavier; and so much the more hastened his voyage, by how much he now perceived the Japonians were disposed to receive the gospel. There were in the port of Malacca many Portuguese vessels, in readiness to set sail for Japan; but all of them were to make many other voyages by the way, which was not the saint's business. His only means was to have recourse to a junk of China, (so they call those little vessels,) which was bound directly for Japan. The master of the vessel, called Neceda, was a famous pirate; a friend to the Portuguese, notwithstanding the war which was newly declared against them; so well known by his robberies at sea, that his ship was commonly called, The Robber's Vessel. Don Pedro de Sylva, governor of Malacca, got a promise from the Chinese captain, that he would carry the Father, safely, and without injury, and took hostages to engage him inviolably to keep his faith; but what can be built on the word of a pirate, and a wicked man?

Xavier, and his companions, embarked on the twenty-fourth of June, in the dusk of the evening; and set sail the next morning, at break of day, with a favourable wind. When they were out at sea, the captain and ship's crew, who were all idolaters, set up a pagod on the poop; sacrificed to it in spite of Xavier, and all his remonstrances to the contrary; and consulted him by magical ceremonies, concerning the success of their voyage. The answers were sometimes good, and sometimes ill: in the meantime they cast anchor at an isle, and there furnished themselves with timber, against the furious gusts of those uncertain seas. At the same time they renewed their interrogatories to their idol; and cast lots, to know whether they should have good winds. The lots promised them a good passage, whereupon the Pagans pursued their course merrily. But they were no sooner got out to sea again, when they drew lots the third time, to know, whether the junk should return safely from Japan to Malacca. The answer was, that they should arrive happily at Japan, but were never more to see Malacca. The pirate, who was extremely superstitious, resolved at the same instant to change his course; and in effect tacked about, and passed his time in going to every isle which was in view. Father Xavier was sensibly displeased, that the devil should be master of their destiny, and that all things should be ordered, according to the answers of the enemy of God and man.

In cruising thus leisurely, they made the coast of Cochin China; and the tempests, which rose at the same time, threatened them more than once with shipwreck. The idolaters had recourse to their ordinary superstitions. The lot declared, that the wind should fall, and that there was no danger. But an impetuous gust so raised the waves, that the mariners were forced to lower their sails, and cast anchor. The shog of the vessel threw a young Chinese (whom Xavier had christened, and carried along with him) into the sink, which was then open. They drew him out half dead, much bruised, and hurt in the head very dangerously. While they were dressing him, the captain's daughter fell into the sea, and was swallowed by the waves, notwithstanding all they could do to save her.

This dismal accident drove Neceda to despair; "and it was a lamentable sight," says Xavier himself, in one of his letters, "to behold the disorder in the vessel. The loss of the daughter, and the fear of shipwreck, filled all with tears, and howlings, and confusion."

Nevertheless, the idolaters, instead of acknowledging that their idol had deceived them with a lie, took pains to appease him, as if the death of the Chinese woman had been an effect of their god's displeasure. They sacrificed birds to him, and burnt incense in honour of him; after which they cast lots again to know the cause of this disaster which had befallen them. They were answered, "That if the young Christian, who had fell into the sink, had died, the captain's daughter had been preserved." Then Neceda, transported with fury, thought to throw Xavier and his companions overboard. But the storm ceasing in an instant, his mind grew calmer by degrees, he weighed anchor, and set sail again, and took the way of Canton, with intention there to pass the winter. But the designs of men, and power of devils, can do nothing against the decrees of Providence. A contrary wind broke all the projects of the captain, constraining him, in his own despite, to enter with full sails into the ocean of Japan. And the same wind carried the junk of the pirate toward Cangoxima, the birth-place of Anger, sirnamed Paul de Sainte Foy. They arrived there on the fifteenth of August, in the year 1549.

BOOK V.

The situation of Japan, and the nature of the country. The estate of the government of Japan. The religion of the Japonese when the Father arrived in that country. The six jesuits who were sent to Siam in 1685, _in their relation of the religion of the Siamois, which much resembles this of Japan, guess, with more probability, that these opinions were the corruptions of the doctrine preached in the Indies by St Thomas. Paul de Sainte Foy goes to wait on the king of Saxuma. That which passed at the court of Saxuma. The saint applies himself to the study of the Japonian tongue. He baptizes the whole family of Paul de Sainte Foy. He goes to the court of Saxuma, and is well received. He begins to preach at Cangorima, and converts many. He visits the Bonzas, and endeavours to gain them. He proves the soul's immortality to the chief of the Bonzas. The Bonzas rise against him. The Bonzas succeed not in their undertaking. He leads a most austere life. He works divers miracles. He raises a maid from death. God avenges the saint. A new persecution raised against Xavier by the Bonzas. The king of Saxuma is turned against Xavier and the Christians. The saint fortifies the Christians before he leaves them. He causes his catechism to be printed before his departure. He departs from Cangoxima. He goes to the castle of Ekandono. He declares the gospel before Ekandono, and the fruits of his preaching. What he does for the preservation of the faith in the new Christians of the castle. Thoughts of a Christian of Ekandono. He leaves a disciple with the steward of Ekandono, and the use he makes of it. He leaves a little book with the wife of Ekandono, and for what it served. He arrives at Firando; and what reception he had there. He preaches at Firando with great success. He takes Amanguchi in his way to Meaco. He stays at Amanguchi; his actions there. What hindered the fruit of his preaching at Amanguchi. He appears before the king of Amanguchi, and expounds to him the doctrine of Christianity. He preaches before the king in Amanguchi without success. He pursues his voyage for Meaco. His sufferings in the voyage of Meaco. He follows a horseman with great difficulty. He instructs the people in passing through the towns. He arrives at Meaco, and labours there unprofitably. He departs from Meaco to return to Amanguchi. Being returned to Amanguchi, he gains an audience of the king. He obtains permission to preach. He is visited by great multitudes. The qualities which he thinks requisite in a missioner to Japan. He answers many men with one only word. He preaches in Amanguchi. He speaks the Chinese language without learning it. The fruit of his preaching. His joy in observing the fervour of the faithful. His occasions of sorrow amongst his spiritual joys. The faith is embraced, notwithstanding the prince's example; and by what means. Divers conversions. He declares against the Bonzas. The Bonzas oppose the Christian religion. He answers the arguments of the Bonzas. The Bonzas provoke the king against the Christians. The number of Christians is augmented together with the reputation of the saint. He sends a Japonian Christian to the kingdom of Bungo; and for what reason. He departs from Amanguchi, and goes for Bungo. He falls sick with overtravelling himself; and after a little rest, pursues his journey. He is received with honour by the Portuguese, and complimented from the king of Bungo. He is much esteemed by the king of Bungo. The letter of the king of Bungo to Father Xavier. In what equipage he goes to the court of Bungo. His entry into the palace of the king of Bungo. He receives the compliments of several persons in the court. He is introduced to an audience of the king of Bungo, and what passes in it. What passes betwixt the king of Bungo and Xavier. The honour of Xavier in the kingdom of Bungo, and the success of his labours there. He converts a famous Bonza. In what manner he prepares the Gentiles for baptism. What happens to the companions of Xavier at Amanguchi. The death of the king of Amanguchi, and the desolation of the town. The brother of the king of Bungo is chosen king of Amanguchi: the saint rejoices at it. He prepares to leave Japan, and takes leave of the king of Bungo. The advice which he gives to the king of Bungo. The Bonzas rise anew against Xavier. A new artifice of the Bonzas against the saint. The beginning of the conference betwixt Xavier and Fucarandono. The advantage of the dispute on the side of Xavier. The fury of the Bonzas forces the Portuguese to retire to their ship. The captain of the ship endeavours to persuade Xavier to return, but in vain. The captain takes up a resolution to stay with Xavier. A new enterprize of the Bonzas against him. He returns to the palace, to renew the conference with Fucarandono. The dispute renewed. The answer of Xavier to the first question of Fucarandono. The second question of Fucarandono, to which the Father answers with the same success as to the former. The sequel of the dispute betwixt Xavier and Fucarandono. The honour which the king of Bungo does to Xavier. The Bonzas present a writing to the king, but without effect. They wrangle about the signification of words. They dispute in the nature of school-divines. He answers the objections of the Bonzas, and their replies. The fruit of his disputation with the Bonzas. He leaves Japan, and returns to the Indies. God reveals to him the siege of Malacca. What happens to him in his return from Japan to the Indies. How Xavier behaves himself during the tempest. What happens to the chalop belonging to the ship. He expects the return of the chalop, or cockboat, notwithstanding all appearances to the contrary. He renews his prayers for the return of the chalop. He prays once more for the return of the chalop. The chalop appears, and comes up with the ship. He arrives at the isle of Sancian; and goes off after a little time. His prediction to the pilot. A marvellous effect of the saint's prophecy. He forms the design of carrying the faith to China. He takes his measures with Pereyra, for the voyage of China. He dissipates a tempest; his prophecy concerning the ship of James Pereyra. His reception at Malacca. The history of the ship called Santa Cruz. He arrives at Cochin; and finishes the conversion of the king of the Maldivias. He writes into Europe, and comes to Goa. He cures a dying man immediately upon his arrival. He hears joyful news of the progress of Christianity in the Indies. The conversion of the king of Tanor. The conversion of the king of Trichenamalo. The letter from the bishop of the Indies to Father Ignatius. He hears other comfortable news. He is afflicted with the misdemeanors of Father Antonio Gomez. How Gomez attacks the authority of Paul de Camerine. The extravagances of Gomez in matters of religion. The violence and injustice of Gomez. Xavier repairs the faults committed by Gomez. He expels Gomez from the Society._

I undertake not to make an exact description of Japan, after those which have been made of it by geographers and travellers: by an ordinary view of the charts, and common reading of the relations of the Indies, it is easy to understand, that Japan is situate at the extremity of Asia, over against China; that it is a concourse of islands which compose as it were one body, and that the chiefest of them gives the name to all the rest; that this world of islands, as it is called by a great geographer, is filled with mountains, some of which are inaccessible, and almost above the clouds; that the colds there are excessive, and that the soil, which is fruitful in mines of gold and silver, is not productive of much grain of any sort necessary to life, for want of cultivation. Without dwelling longer either on the situation or nature of the country, or so much as on the customs and manners of the inhabitants, of which I have already said somewhat, and shall speak yet farther, as my subject requires it, I shall here only touch a little on the government and religion, which of necessity are to be known at the beginning, for the understanding of the history which I write.

Japan was anciently one monarchy. The emperor, whom all those isles obeyed, was called the Dairy; and was descended from the Camis, who, according to the popular opinion, came in a direct line from the Sun. The first office of the empire was that of the Cubo, that is to say, captain-general of the army. For the raising of this dignity, which in itself was so conspicuous, in process of time, the name of Sama was added to that of Cubo; for Sama in their language signifies Lord. Thus the general of Japan came to be called Cubo Sama.

Above three hundred years ago, the Cubo Sama then being, beholding the sceptre of Japan in the hands of a Dairy, who was cowardly and effeminate, revolted from him, and got possession of the regal dignity. His design was to have reduced the whole estate under his own dominion; but he was only able to make himself master of Meaco, where the emperor kept his court, and of the provinces depending on it. The governors of other provinces maintained themselves in their respective jurisdictions by force of arms, and shook of the yoke as well as he; insomuch, that the monarchy came to be suddenly divided into sixty-six cantons, which all assumed the names of kingdoms.

Since these revolutions, the king of Meaco took the title of Cubo Sama, and he who had been deprived of it still retained the name of Dairy; and, excepting only the power, there was still left him all the privilege of royalty, in consideration of the blood of the Camis. His descendants have had always the same title, and enjoyed the same advantages. This, in general, was the face of the government, in the time of St Francis Xavier. For some years afterwards, Nabunanga, one of the neighbour kings to him of Meaco, defeated the Cubo Sama in a pitched battle, and followed his blow with so much success, that, having destroyed all those petty princes, he re-united the whole empire of Japan under his sole obedience.

As to what concerns religion, all the Japonians, excepting some few who make profession of atheism, and believe the soul mortal, are idolaters, and hold the transmigration of souls, after the doctrine of Pythagoras. Some of them pay divine worship to the sun and moon; others to the Camis, those ancient kings of whom we have made mention; and to the Potoques, the gods of China. There are divers of them who adore some kinds of beasts, and many who adore the devil under dreadful figures. Besides these, they have a certain mysterious deity, whom they call Amida; and say, this god has built a paradise of such distance from the earth, that the souls cannot reach it under a voyage of three years. But the god Xaca is he of whom they report the greatest wonders, who seems to be a counterfeit of the true Messiah, set up by the devil himself, or by his ministers. For if one would give credit to them, Xaca being born of a queen, who never had the carnal knowledge of man, retired into the deserts of Siam, and there underwent severe penances, to expiate the sins of men: that coming out of his wilderness, he assembled some disciples, and preached an heavenly doctrine in divers countries.

It is incredible how many temples have been built to the honour of Amida and Xaca; all the cities are full of them, and their magnificence is equal to their number. Nor is it easy to imagine how far their superstition carries the worshippers of these two deities. They throw themselves headlong down from rocks, or bury themselves alive in caves; and it is ordinary to see barques, full of men and women, with stones hanging at their necks, and singing the praises of their gods, after which they cast themselves into the sea.

For what remains, the spirit of lies has established in Japan a kind of hierarchy, not unlike that of the Catholic church. For these people have a chief of their religion, and a kind of sovereign priest, whom they call Saco. He keeps his court in the capital city of the empire; and it is he who approves the sects, who institutes the ceremonies, who consecrates, if I may be allowed to say so, the Tundi, who resemble our bishops, and whose principal function is to ordain the priests of idols, by conferring on them the power of offering sacrifice. These priests, who are called Bonzas, part of them living in desarts, the rest in towns, all affect a rigid austerity of manners, and are amongst the Japonese what the Brachmans are amongst the Indians, unless that they are yet more impious, and greater hypocrites.

To resume our history: immediately after the arrival of Xavier and his companions, Paul de Sainte Foy, whom formerly we called Anger, went to pay his duty to the king of Saxuma; on which Cangoxima is depending, and whose palace is about the distance of six leagues from it. That prince, who had heretofore shewn great favour to him, received him with much humanity, and with so much the greater joy, because he had believed him dead. This kind reception gave Paul de Sainte Foy the confidence to petition the king for the pardon of that action, which had occasioned his departure, and it was not difficult for him to obtain it.

The king, naturally curious, as the Japonians generally are, enquired much of him concerning the Indies; as, what was the nature of the country, and the humour of the people, and whether the Portuguese were as brave and as powerful as they were represented by common fame. When Paul had satisfied him on these and the like particulars, the discourse fell on the different religions in the Indies, and finally on Christianity, which was introduced by the Portuguese in India.

Paul unfolded at large the mysteries of our faith; and seeing with what pleasure he was heard, produced a tablet of the Virgin, holding the little Jesus in her arms. The tablet was very curious, and Xavier had given it to this Japonese, that he might shew it as occasion offered. The sight alone of this excellent painting wrought so much upon the king, that, being touched with thoughts of piety and reverence, he fell on his knees, with all his courtiers, to honour the persons therein represented, which seemed to him to have an air that was more than human.

He commanded it should be carried to the queen, his mother. She was also charmed with it, and prostrated herself by the same instinct, with all the ladies of her train, to salute the Mother and the Son. But as the Japonian women are yet more inquisitive than the men, she asked a thousand questions concerning the Blessed Virgin and our Saviour, which gave Paul the desired opportunity of relating all the life of Jesus Christ; and this relation so much pleased the queen, that some few days after, when he was upon his return to Cangoxima, she sent one of her officers to have a copy of the tablet which she had seen; but a painter was not to be found to satisfy her curiosity. She required, that at least she might have an abridgment in writing of the chief points of Christianity, and was satisfied therein by Paul.

The Father, overjoyed at these good inclinations of the court, thought earnestly of making himself capable to preach in the language of the country. There is but one language spoken through all Japan; but that so ample, and so full of variety, that, in effect, it may be said to contain many tongues. They make use of certain words and phrases, in familiar discourse; and of others in studied compositions. The men of quality have a language quite differing from the vulgar. Merchants and soldiers have a speech proper to their several professions, and the women speak a dialect distinct from any of the rest. When they treat on a sublime subject, (for example, of religion, or affairs of state,) they serve themselves of particular terms; and nothing appears more incongruous amongst them, than to confound these different manners of expression.

The holy man had already some light notions of all these languages, by the communication he had with the three Japonian Christians; but he knew not enough to express him with ease and readiness, as himself acknowledges in his epistles, where he says, "that he and his companions, at their first arrival, stood like statues, mute and motionless." He therefore applied himself, with all diligence, to the study of the tongue, which he relates in these following words: "We are returned to our infancy," says he, "and all our business at present is to learn the first elements of the Japonian grammar. God give us the grace to imitate the simplicity and innocence of children, as well as to practise the exercises of children."

We ought not to be astonished in this passage last quoted, that a man to whom God had many times communicated the gift of tongues, should not speak that of Japan, and that he should be put to the pains of studying it. Those favours were transient, and Xavier never expected them; insomuch, that being to make abode in a country, he studied the language of it as if he could not have arrived to the knowledge of it but by his own industry. But the Holy Spirit assisted him after an extraordinary manner, on those occasions, as we have formerly observed. And we may say, that the easiness wherewith he learnt so many tongues, was almost equivalent to the lasting gift of them.

While Xavier and his companions were labouring to acquire that knowledge which was necessary for their preaching the word of Jesus Christ to the people of Cangoxima, Paul de Sainte Foy, with whom they lodged, himself instructed his own family. God gave that blessing to his zeal, that, besides his mother, his wife and daughter, many of his relations were converted and baptized by Xavier. Within the compass of forty days, the saint understood enough of the language to undertake the translation of the apostles' creed, and the exposition of it, which he had composed in India. As fast as he translated, he got every parcel of it by heart; and with that help, was of opinion, that he might begin to declare the gospel. But seeing that in Japan all the measures of the laws and customs are to be taken, and observed with great exactness, and nothing to be attempted in public without permission from the government, he would first visit the king of Saxuma, and chose the time on the day of St Michael the archangel He had put the whole empire under the protection of that glorious general of the celestial host, who chased the rebellious angels out of heaven, and recommended in his daily prayers to him, that he would exterminate those devils from Japan, who had usurped the dominion of it for so many ages.

The apostle of the Indies was not unknown at the court of Saxuma. Paul de Sainte Foy had spoken of him there, in such a manner, as infused the desire of seeing him into all hearts, and caused him to be looked on with admiration when he first appeared. The king and queen treated him with honour, testified great affection to him, and discoursed with him the better part of the night. They could not but be astonished, that he and his companions were come from another world, and had passed through so many stormy seas, not out of an avaricious design of enriching themselves with the gold of Japan, but only to teach the Japonese the true way of eternal life. From the very first meeting, the king cautioned Xavier to keep safely all the books and writings which contained the Christian doctrine; "for," said he, "if your faith be true, the demons will be sure to fly furiously upon you, and all manner of mischief is to be expected from their malice." Afterwards he granted permission to the saint to preach the Christian law within the whole extent of his dominions; and farther, caused his letters patent to be expedited, by virtue of which, all his subjects had free liberty of being made Christians, if they so desired.

Xavier took advantage of this happy conjuncture, and deferred no longer his preaching in Cangoxima. He began by explaining the first articles of the creed. That of the existence of one God, all powerful, the Creator of heaven and earth, was a strange surprise to his auditors, who knew nothing of a first Being, on whom the universe depended, as on its cause and principle. The other articles, which respect the Trinity and Incarnation, appeared to them yet more incredible; insomuch, that some of them held the preacher for a madman, and laughed him to scorn. Notwithstanding which, the wiser sort could not let it sink into their belief, that a stranger, who had no interest to deceive them, should undergo so many hardships and dangers, and come so far, on set purpose to cheat them with a fable. In these considerations, they were desirous of clearing those doubts, which possessed them, in relation to those mysteries which they had heard. Xavier answered them so distinctly, and withal so reasonably, with the assistance of Paul de Sainte Foy, who served him for interpreter in case of need, that the greatest part, satisfied with his solutions, came over to the faith.

The first who desired baptism, and received it, was a man of mean condition, destitute of the goods of fortune; as if God willed, that the church of Japan should have the same foundations of meanness and poverty with the universal church: The name of Bernard was given him, and, by his virtue, he became in process of time illustrious.

In the mean time, Xavier visited the Bonzas, and endeavoured to gain their good will; being persuaded that Christianity would make but little progress amongst the people, if they opposed the preaching of the gospel: And, on the other side, judging that all the world would embrace the law of the true God, in case they should not openly resist it. His good behaviour and frankness immediately gained him the favour of their chief: he was a man of four-score years of age, and, for a Bonza, a good honest man; in that estimation of wisdom, that the king of Saxuma entrusted him with his most important affairs; and so well versed in his religion, that he was sirnamed Ningit, which is to say, the Heart of Truth. But this name was not altogether proper to him; and Xavier presently perceived, that the Veillard knew not what to believe concerning the immortality of the soul; saying sometimes, "That our souls were nothing different from those of beasts;" at other times, "That they came from heaven, and that they had in them somewhat of divine."

These uncertainties of a mind floating betwixt truth and falsehood, gave Xavier the occasion of proving the immortality of the soul, in the conversations they had together; and he reasoned strongly thereupon, according to natural principles alone. Yet his arguments had no other effect, than the praises which were given them. Ningit commended the knowledge of the European Bonza, (so they called the Father,) and was satisfied that no man had a deeper insight into nature. But he still remained doubtful on the business of religion, either out of shame to change his opinion at that age, or perhaps because those who have doubted all their life, are more hard to be convinced, than those who have never believed at all.

The esteem which Ningit had for Xavier, caused him to be had in great repute with the rest of the Bonzas. They heard him with applause, when he spoke of the divine law; and confessed openly, that a man who was come from the other end of the 'world, through the midst of so many dangers, to preach a new religion, could only be inspired by the spirit of truth, and could propose nothing but what was worthy of belief.

The testimony of the Bonzas authorised the preaching of the gospel; but their scandalous way of living, hindered them from following our holy law. Notwithstanding, before the conclusion of the year, two of them of less corrupt manners than the rest, or more faithful to the grace of Jesus Christ, embraced Christianity; and their example wrought so far upon the inhabitants of Cangoxima, that many of them desired to be baptized.

These first fruits of preaching promised greater, and the faith flourished daily more and more in Cangoxima, when a persecution, raised on a sudden, ruined these fair expectations, and stopt the progress of the gospel The Bonzas, surprised to see the people ready to forsake the religion of the country, opened their eyes to their own interest, and manifestly saw, that if this new religion were once received, as they only lived on the alms and offerings which were made to their deities, they should be wholly deprived of their subsistence. They judged, in consequence, that this evil was to be remedied, before it grew incurable; and nothing was to be spared for the rooting out these Portuguese preachers. It was then manifest, that those religious idolaters, who at first had been so favourable to Xavier, now made open war against him. They decried him in all places, and publicly treated him as an impostor. Even so far they proceeded, that one day as he was preaching, in one of the public places of the city, a Bonza interrupted him in the midst of his discourse, and warned the people not to trust him; saying, "That it was a devil, who spoke to them in the likeness of a man."

This outrageousness of the Bonzas failed of the effect which they desired; the Japonians, who are naturally men of wit, and plain dealers, came easily to understand the motives of their priests, to change their manner of behaviour, and finding interest in all they said or did, grew more and more attentive to the doctrine of the Father.

Some of them upbraided the Bonzas, that their proper concernments had kindled their zeal to such an height: that religion was not to be defended by calumnies and affronts, but by solid arguments: that if the doctrine of the European was false, why did they not demonstrate clearly the falsehood of it: that, for the rest, it was of little consequence whether this new preacher was a demon or a man; and that truth was to be received, whosoever brought it: that, after all, he lived with great austerity, and was more to be credited than any of them.

In effect, Xavier, for the edification of the people, who commonly judge by appearances of things, abstained entirely both from flesh and fish. Some bitter roots, and pulse boiled in water, were all his nourishment, in the midst of his continual labours. So that he practised, rigorously and literally, that abstinence of which the Bonzas make profession, or rather that which they pretend to practise. And he accustomed himself to this immediately, upon what Paul de Sainte Foy had told him, that it would look ill if a religious Christian should live with less austerity than the priests of idols should in their course of life.

The wonders which God wrought, by the ministration of his servant, gave farther confirmation to the Christian law. The saint walking out one day upon the sea-shore, met certain fishers, who were spreading their empty nets, and complained of their bad fortune. He had pity on them, and, after making some short prayers, he advised them to fish once more. They did so on his word, and took so many fish, and of such several sorts, that they could hardly draw their nets. They continued their fishing for some days after with the same success; and what appears more wonderful, the sea of Cangoxima, which was scarce of fish, from that time forward had great plenty.

A woman, who had heard reports of the cures which the apostle had made in the Indies, brought him her little child, who was swelled over all the body, even to deformity. Xavier took the infant in his arms, looked on him with eyes of pity, and pronounced thrice over him these words, "God bless thee;" after which, he gave the child back to his mother, so well and beautiful, that she was transported with joy and admiration.

This miracle made a noise about the town; and gave occasion to a leper to hope a cure for his disease, which he had sought in vain for many years. Not daring to appear in public, because his uncleanness had excluded him from the society of men, and made him loathsome to all companies; he sent for Xavier, who at that time happened to be engaged in business, and could not come; but deputed one of his companions to visit him; giving orders to ask him thrice, if he was content to believe in Christ, in case he should be healed of his leprosy; and thrice to make the sign of the cross over him, if he promised constantly to embrace the faith. All things passed according to the commission of the Father: the leper obliged himself to become a Christian, upon the recovery of his health; and the sign of the cross was no sooner made over him, but his whole body became as clean as if he had never been infected with leprosy. The suddenness of the cure wrought in him to believe in Christ without farther difficulty, and his lively faith brought him hastily to baptism.

But the most celebrated miracle which Xavier wrought in Cangoxima, was the resurrection of a young maid of quality. She died in the flower of her youth, and her father, who loved her tenderly, was ready to go distracted with his loss. Being an idolater, he had no source of comfort remaining for his affliction; and his friends, who came to condole with him, instead of easing, did but aggravate his grief. Two new Christians, who came to see him before the burial of his daughter, advised him to seek his remedy from the holy man, who wrought such wonders, and beg her life of him, with strong assurance of success.

The heathen, persuaded by these new believers, that nothing was impossible to this European Bonza, and beginning to hope against all human appearances, after the custom of the distressed, who easily believe what they infinitely desire, goes to find Father Xavier, throws himself at his feet, and, with tears in his eyes, beseeches him to raise up from death his only daughter; adding, that the favour would be to give a resurrection to himself. Xavier moved at the faith and affliction of the father, withdraws, with Fernandez, his companion, to recommend his desire to Almighty God; and having ended his prayer, returns a little time after: "Go," says he to the sorrowful father, "your daughter is alive."

The idolater, who expected that the saint would have accompanied him to his house, and there called upon the name of his God, over the body of his daughter, thought himself ill used and cheated, and Trent away dissatisfied. But before he had walked many steps homeward, he saw one of his servants, who, transported with joy, cried out aloud to him, at a distance, that his daughter lived. Soon after this, his daughter came herself to meet him, and related to her father, that her soul was no sooner departed from her body, but it was seized by two ugly fiends, who would have thrown her headlong into a lake of fire; but that two unknown persons, whose countenances were venerably modest, snatched her out of the gripe of her two executioners, and restored her to life, but in what manner she could not tell.

The Japonian suddenly apprehended who were the two persons concerned in her relation, and brought her straight to Xavier, to acknowledge the miraculous favour she had received. She no sooner cast her eyes on him, and on Fernandez, than she cried out, "Behold my two redeemers!" and at the same time both she and her father desired baptism. Nothing of this nature had ever been seen in that country: no history ever made mention, that the gods of Japan had the power of reviving the dead. So that this resurrection gave the people a high conception of Christianity, and made famous the name of Father Xavier.

But nothing will make more evident how much a favourite he was of heaven, and how prevalent with that God, whom he declared, than that exemplary judgment with which Divine Justice punished the bold impiety of a man, who, either carried on by his own madness, or exasperated by that of the Bonzas, one day railed at him, with foul injurious language. The saint suffered it with his accustomed mildness; and only said these words to him, with somewhat a melancholy countenance, "God preserve your mouth." Immediately the miscreant felt his tongue eaten with a cancer, and there issued out of his mouth a purulent matter, mixed with worms, and a stench that was not to be endured. This vengeance, so visible, and so sudden, ought to have struck the Bonzas with terror; but their great numbers assured them in some measure; and all of them acting in a body against the saint, each of them had the less fear for his own particular. What raised their indignation to the height, was, that a lady of great birth and riches, wife to one of the most considerable lords of all the court, and very liberal to the pagods, was solemnly baptized with all the family.

Seeing they prevailed nothing by the ways they had attempted, and that persons of quality were not less enamoured of the Christian doctrine than the vulgar; and, on the other side, not daring to use violence, in respect of the king's edicts, which permitted the profession of Christianity, they contrived a new artifice, which was to address a complaint to the king, of the king himself, on the part of their country deities. The most considerable of the Bonzas having been elected, in a general assembly for this embassy, went to the prince, and told him, with an air rather threatening than submissive, that they came, in the name of Xaca and Amida, and the other deities of Japan, to demand of him, into what country he would banish them; that the gods were looking out for new habitations, and other temples, since he drove them shamefully out of his dominions, or rather out of theirs, to receive in their stead a stranger God, who usurps to himself divine honours, and will neither admit of a superior nor an equal. They added haughtily, that it is true he was a king; but what a kind of king was a profane man? Was it for him to be the arbiter of religion, and to judge the gods? What probability was there too, that all the religions of Japan should err, and the most prudent of the nation be deceived after the run of so many ages? What would posterity say, when they should hear, that the king of Saxuma, who held his crown from Amida and Xaca, overthrew their altars, and deprived them of the honours which they had so long enjoyed? But what would not the neighbouring provinces attempt, to revenge the injury done to their divinities? that all things seemed lawful to be done on such occasions; and the least he had to fear was a civil war, and that, so much the more bloody, because it was founded on religion.

The conjuncture in which the Bonzas found the king, was favourable to them. It was newly told him, that the ships of Portugal, which usually landed at Cangoxima, had now bent their course to Firando, and he was extremely troubled at it; not only because his estates should receive no more advantage by their trade, but also because the king of Firando, his enemy, would be the only gainer by his loss. As the good-will which he shewed in the beginning to Father Xavier had scarce any other principle but interest, he grew cold to him immediately after this ill news; and this coldness made him incline to hearken to the Bonzas. He granted all they demanded of him, and forbade his subjects, on pain of death, to become Christians, or to forsake the old religion of their country.

Whatsoever good inclinations there were in the people to receive the gospel, these new edicts hindered those of Cangoxima from any farther commerce with the three religious Christians; so easily the favour or displeasure of the prince can turn the people.

They, notwithstanding, whose heart the Almighty had already touched, and who were baptized, far from being wanting to the grace of their vocation, were more increased in faith, not exceeding the number of an hundred; they found themselves infinitely acknowledging to the Divine Mercy, which had elected them to compose this little flock. Persecution itself augmented their fervour; and all of them declared to Father Xavier, that they were ready to suffer banishment or death, for the honour of our Saviour.

Though the Father was nothing doubtful of their constancy, yet he would fortify them by good discourses, before he left a town and kingdom where there was no farther hope of extending the Christian faith. For which reason he daily assembled them; where, having read some passages of scripture, translated into their own language, and suitable to the present condition of that infant church, he explained to them some one of the mysteries of our Saviour's life; and his auditors were so filled with the interior unctions of the Holy Spirit, that they interrupted his speech at every moment with their sighs and tears,

He had caused divers copies of his catechism to be taken for the use of the faithful Having augmented it by a more ample exposition of the creed, and added sundry spiritual instructions, with the life of our Saviour, which he entirely translated, he caused it to be printed in Japonese characters, that it might be spread through all the nation. At this time the two converted Bonzas, and two other baptized Japonians, undertook a voyage to the Indies, to behold with their own eyes, what the Father had told them, concerning the splendour of Christianity at Goa; I mean the multitude of Christians, the magnificence of the churches, and the beauty of the ecclesiastic ceremonies.

At length he departed from Cangoxima, at the beginning of September, in the year 1550, with Cozmo de Torrez, and John Fernandez, carrying on his back, according to his custom, all the necessary utensils for the sacrifice of the mass. Before his departure, he recommended the faithful to Paul de Sainte Foy. It is wonderful, that these new Christians, bereft of their pastors, should maintain themselves in the midst of Paganism, and amongst the persecuting Bonzas, and not one single man of them should be perverted from the faith. It happened, that even their exemplary lives so edified their countrymen, that they gained over many of the idolaters; insomuch, that in the process of some few years, the number of Christians was encreased to five hundred persons; and the king of Saxuma wrote to the viceroy of the Indies, to have some of the fathers of the Society, who should publish through all his territories a law so holy and so pure. The news which came, that the Portuguese vessels, which came lately to Japan, had taken their way to Firando, caused Xavier to go thither; and the ill intelligence betwixt the two princes, gave him hopes that the king of Firando would give him and his two companions a good reception.

They happened upon a fortress on their way, belonging to a prince called Ekandono, who was vassal to the king of Saxuma. It was situate on the height of a rock, and defended by ten great bastions. A solid wall encompassed it, with a wide and deep ditch cut through the middle of the rock. Nothing but fearful precipices on every side; and the fortress approachable by one only way, where a guard was placed both day and night. The inside of it was as pleasing as the outside was full of horror. A stately palace composed the body of the place, and in that palace were porticoes, galleries, halls, and chambers, of an admirable beauty; all was cut in the living stone, and wrought so curiously, that the works seemed to be cast within a mould, and not cut by the chizzel.

Some people of the castle, who were returning from Cangoxima, and who had there seen Xavier, invited him, by the way, to come and visit their lord; not doubting but Ekandono would be glad to see so famous a person.

Xavier, who sought all occasions of publishing the gospel, lost not that opportunity. The good reception which was made him, gave him the means of teaching immediately the true religion, and the ways of eternal life. The attendants of the prince, and soldiers of the garrison, who were present, were so moved, both by the sanctity which shone in the apostle's countenance, and by the truth which beamed out in all his words, that, after the clearing of their doubts, seventeen of them at once demanded baptism; and the Father christened them in presence of the Tono, (so the Japonese call the lord or prince of any particular place) The rest of them were possessed with the same desire, and had received the same favour, if Ekandono had not opposed it by reason of state, and contrary to his own inclinations, for fear of some ill consequences from the king of Saxuma; for in his heart he acknowledged Jesus Christ, and permitted Xavier privately to baptize his wife and his eldest son. For the rest, he promised to receive baptism, and to declare himself a Christian, when his sovereign should be favourable to the law of God.

The steward of Ekandono's household was one who embraced the faith. He was a man stepped into years, and of great prudence. Xavier committed the new Christians to his care, and put into his hands the form of baptism in writing, the exposition of the creed, the epitome of our Saviour's life, the seven penitential psalms, the litanies of the saints, and a table of saints' days as they are celebrated in the church. He himself set apart a place in the palace proper for the assemblies of the faithful; and appointed the steward to call together as many of the Pagans as he could, to read both to the one and the other sort some part of the Christian doctrine every Sunday, to cause the penitential psalms to be sung on every Friday, and the litanies every day The steward punctually performed his orders; and those seeds of piety grew up so fast, that some few years after, Louis Almeyda found above an hundred Christians in the fortress of Ekandono. all of an orderly and innocent conversation; modest in their behaviour, assiduous in prayer, charitable to each other, severe to themselves, and enemies to their bodies; insomuch that the place had more resemblance to a religious house, than to a garrison. The Tono, though still an idolater, was present at the assemblies of the Christians, and permitted two little children of his to be baptized.

One of these new converts composed elegantly, in his tongue, the history of the redemption of mankind, from the fall of Adam to the coming down of the Holy Ghost The same man being once interrogated, what answer he would return the king, in case he should command him to renounce his faith? "I would boldly answer him," said he, "in this manner: 'Sir, you are desirous, I am certain, that, being born your subject, I should be faithful to you; you would have me ready to hazard my life in your interests, and to die for your service; yet, farther, you would have me moderate with my equals, gentle to my inferiors, obedient to my superiors, equitable towards all; and, for these reasons, command me still to be a Christian, for a Christian is obliged to be all this. But if you forbid me the profession of Christianity, I shall become, at the same time, violent, hard-hearted, insolent, rebellious, unjust, wicked; and I camiot answer for myself, that I shall be other."

As to what remains, Xavier, when he took leave of the old steward, whom he constituted superior of the rest, left him a discipline, which himself had used formerly. The old man kept it religiously as a relique, and would not that the Christians in the assemblies, where they chastised themselves, should make a common use of it. At the most, he suffered not any of them to give themselves above two or three strokes with it, so fearful he was of wearing it out; and he told them, that they ought to make use of it the less in chastising their flesh, that it might remain for the preservation of their health. And indeed it was that instrument which God commonly employed for the cures of sick persons in the castle. The wife of Ekandono being in the convulsions of death, was instantly restored to health, after they had made the sign of the cross over her, with the discipline of the saint.

Xavier, at his departure, made a present to the same lady of a little book, wherein the litanies of the saints, and some catholic prayers, were written with his own hand. This also in following times was a fountain of miraculous cures, not only to the Christians, but also the idolaters; and the Tono himself, in the height of a mortal sickness, recovered his health on the instant that the book was applied to him by his wife. So that the people of the fortress said, that their prince was raised to life, and that it could not be performed by human means.

The saint and his companions being gone from thence, pursued their voyage, sometimes by sea, and sometimes travelled by land. After many labours cheerfully undergone by them, and many dangers which they passed, they arrived at the port of Firando, which was the end of their undertaking. The Portuguese did all they were able for the honourable reception of Father Xavier. All the artillery was discharged at his arrival; all the ensigns and streamers were djsplayed, with sound of trumpets; and, in fine, all the ships gave shouts of joy when they beheld the man of God. He was conducted, in spite of his repugnance, with the same pomp to the royal palace; and that magnificence was of no small importance, to make him considered in a heathen court, who without it might have been despised, since nothing was to be seen in him but simplicity and poverty. The king of Firando, whom the Portuguese gave to understand, how much the man whom they presented to him was valued by their master, and what credit he had with him, received him with so much the greater favour, because he knew the king of Carigoxima had forced him to go out of his estates: for, to oblige the crown of Portugal, and do a despite to that of Cangoxima, he presently empowered the three religious Christians to publish the law of Jesus Christ through all the extent of his dominions.

Immediately they fell on preaching in the town, and all the people ran to hear the European Bonzas. The first sermons of Xavier made a great impression on their souls; and in less than twenty days, he baptized more infidels at Firando, than he had done in a whole year at Cangoxima. The facility which he found of reducing those people under the obedience of the faith, made him resolve to leave with them Cosmo de Torrez, to put the finishing hand to their conversion, and in the mean time to go himself to Meaco, which he had designed from the beginning; that town being the capital of the empire, from whence the knowledge of Christ Jesus might easily be spread through all Japan.

Departing with Fernandez, and the two Japonian Christians, Matthew and Bernard, for this great voyage at the end of October, in the year 1550, they arrived at Facata by sea, which is twenty leagues distant from Firando; and from thence embarked for Amanguchi, which is an hundred leagues from it. Amanguchi is the capital of the kingdom of Naugato, and one of the richest towns of all Japan, not only by the traffic of strangers, who come thither from all parts, but also by reason of silver mines, which are there in great abundance, and by the fertility of the soil; but as vices are the inseparable companions of wealth, it was a place totally corrupted, and full of the most monstrous debaucheries.

Xavier took that place only as his passage to Meaco; but the strange corruption of manners gave him so much horror, and withal so great compassion, that he could not resolve to pass farther without publishing Christ Jesus to those blind and execrable men, nor without making known to them the purity of the Christian law. The zeal which transported him, when he heard the abominable crimes of the town, suffered him not to ask permission from the king, as it had been his custom in other places. He appeared in public on the sudden, burning with an inward fire, which mounted up into his face, and boldly declared to the people the eternal truths of faith. His companion Fernandez did the same in another part of the town. People heard them out of curiosity; and many after having inquired who they were, what dangers they had run, and for what end, admired their courage, and their procedure, void of interest, according to the humour of the Japonians, whose inclinations are naturally noble, and full of esteem for actions of generosity. From public places they were invited into houses, and there desired to expound their doctrine more at large, and at greater leisure. "For if your law appear more reasonable to us than our own," said the principal of the town, "we engage ourselves to follow it."

But when once a man becomes a slave to shameful passions, it is difficult to follow what he thinks the best, and even to judge reasonably what is the best. Not a man amongst them kept his word. Having compared together the two laws, almost all of them agreed, that the Christian doctrine was most conformable to good sense, if things were only to be taken in the speculation; but when they came to consider them in the practice, and saw how much the Christian law discouraged vengeance, and forbade polygamy, with all carnal pleasures, that which had appeared just and reasonable to them, now seemed improbable, and the perversity of their wills hoodwinked the light of their understanding; so that, far from believing in Jesus Christ, they said, "That Xavier and his companions were plain mountebanks, and the religion which they preached a mere fable." These reports being spread abroad, exasperated the spirits of men against them, so that as soon as any of them appeared, the people ran after them, not as before, to hear them preach, but to throw stones at them, and revile them: "See," they cried, "the two Bonzas, who would inveigle us to worship only one God, and persuade us to be content with a single wife."

Oxindono, the king of Amanguchi, hearing what had passed, was willing to be judge himself of the Christians' new doctrine. He sent for them before him, and asked them, in the face of all his nobles, of what country they were, and what business brought them to Japan? Xavier answered briefly, "That they were Europeans, and that they came to publish the divine law. For," added he, "no man can be saved who adores not God, and the Saviour of all nations, his Son Christ Jesus, with a pure heart and pious worship." "Expound to me," replied the prince, "this law, which you have called divine." Then Xavier began, by reading a part of the book which he had composed in the Japonian tongue, and which treated of the creation of the world, of which none of the company had ever heard any thing, of the immortality of the soul, of the ultimate end of our being, of Adam's fall, and of eternal rewards and punishments; in fine, of the coming of our Saviour, and the fruits of our redemption. The saint explained what was needful to be cleared, and spoke in all above an hour.

The king heard him with attention, and without interrupting his discourse; but he also dismissed him without answering a word, or making any sign, whether he allowed or disapproved of what he said. This silence, accompanied with much humanity, was taken for a permission, by Father Xavier, to continue his public preaching. He did so with great warmth, but with small success: Most of them laughed at the preacher, and scorned the mysteries of Christianity: Some few, indeed, grew tender at the hearing of our Saviour's sufferings, even so far as to shed tears, and these motions of compassion disposed their hearts to a belief; but the number of the elect was inconsiderable; for the time pre-ordained for the conversion of that people was not yet come, and was therefore to be attended patiently.

Xavier then having made above a month's abode in Amanguchi, and gathered but small fruit of all his labours, besides affronts, continued his voyage towards Meaco with his three companions, Fernandez, Matthew, and Bernard. They continually bemoaned the blindness and obduracy of those wretches, who refused to receive the gospel; yet cheered up themselves with the consideration of God's mercies, and an inward voice was still whispering in their hearts, that the seed of the divine word, though cast into a barren and ungrateful ground, yet would not finally be lost.

They departed toward the end of December, in a season when the rains were continually falling, during a winter which is dreadful in those parts, where the winds are as dangerous by land as tempests are at sea. The colds are pinching, and the snow drives in such abundance, that neither in the towns nor hamlets, people dare adventure to stir abroad, nor have any communication with each other, but by covered walks and galleries: It is yet far worse in the country, where nothing is to be seen but hideous forests, sharp-pointed and ragged mountains, raging torrents across the vallies, which sometimes overflow the plains. Sometimes it is so covered over with ice, that the travellers fall at every step; without mentioning those prodigious icicles hanging over head from the high trees, and threatening the passengers at every moment with their fall.

The four servants of God travelled in the midst of this hard season, and rough ways, commonly on their naked feet, passing the rivers, and ill accommodated with warm clothes, to resist the inclemencies of the air and earth, loaden with their necessary equipage, and without other provisions of life than grains of rice roasted or dried by the fire, which Bernard carried in his wallet. They might have had abundantly for their subsistence, if Xavier would have accepted of the money which the Portuguese merchants of Firando offered him, to defray the charges of his voyage, or would have made use of what the governor of the Indies had supplied him with in the name of the king of Portugal: But he thought he should have affronted Providence, if he should have furnished himself with the provisions needful to a comfortable subsistence; and therefore taking out of the treasury a thousand crowns, he employed it wholly for the relief of the poor who had received baptism. Neither did he rest satisfied with this royal alms, he drew what he could also from his friends at Goa and Malacca; and it was a saying of his, "That the more these new converts were destitute of worldly goods, the more succour they deserved; that their zeal was worthy the primitive ages of the church; and that there was not a Christian in Japan, who would not choose rather to lose his life, than forfeit the love of Jesus Christ."

The journey from Amanguchi to Meaco is not less than fifteen days, when the ways are good, and the season convenient for travelling; but the ill weather lengthened it to our four travellers, who made two months of it; sometimes crossing over rapid torrents, sometimes over plains and forests thick with snow, climbing up the rocks, and rolling down the precipices. These extreme labours put Father Xavier into a fever from the first month, and his sickness forced him to stop a little at Sacay; but he would take no remedies, and soon after put himself upon his way.

That which gave them the greatest trouble was, that Bernard, who was their guide, most commonly misled them. Being one day lost in a forest, and not knowing what path to follow, they met a horseman who was going towards Meaco; Xavier followed him, and offered to carry his mail, if he would help to disengage them from the forest, and shew them how to avoid the dangerous passages. The horseman accepted Xaviers offer, but trotted on at a round rate, so that the saint was constrained to run after him, and the fatigue lasted almost all the day. His companions followed him at a large distance; and when they came up to the place where the horseman had left him, they found him so spent, and over-laboured, that he could scarcely support himself. The flints and thorns had torn his feet, and his legs were swelled so that they broke out in many places. All these inconveniences hindered him not from going forward: He drew his strength from the union he had with God, continually praying from the morning to the evening, and never interrupting his devotions but only to exhort his friends to patience.

In passing through the towns and villages where his way led him, Xavier always read some part of his catechism to the people who gathered about him. For the most part they only laughed at him; and the little children cried after him, "Deos, Deos, Deos," because, speaking of God, he had commonly that Portuguese word in his mouth, which he seldom pronounced without repetition; for, discoursing of God, he would not use the Japonese language till they were well instructed in the essence and perfections of the Divine Majesty: and he gave two reasons for it; the first, because he found not one word in all the language which well expressed that sovereign divinity, of which he desired to give them a distinct notion; the second, because he feared lest those idolaters might confound that first Being with their Camis, and their Potoques, in case he should call it by those names which were common to their idols. From thence he took occasion to tell them, "That as they never had any knowledge of the true God, so they never were able to express his name; that the Portuguese, who knew him, called him Deos:" and he repeated that word with so much action, and such a tone of voice, that he made even the Pagans sensible what veneration was due to that sacred name. Having publicly condemned, in two several towns, the false sects of Japan, and the enormous vices reigning there, he was drawn by the inhabitants without the walls, where they had resolved to stone him. But when they were beginning to take up the stones, they were overtaken by a violent and sudden storm, which constrained them all to betake themselves to flight: The holy man continued in the midst of this rack of heaven, with flashes of lightning darting round about him, without losing his habitual tranquillity, but adoring that Divine Providence which fought so visibly in his favour.

He arrived at length at Meaco with his three companions in February 1551. The name of that celebrated town, so widely spread for being the seat of empire and religion, where the Cubosama, the Dairy, and the Saso kept their court, seemed to promise great matters to Father Xavier; but the effect did not answer the appearances: Meaco, which in the Japonian tongue signifies a thing worth seeing, was no more than the shadow of what formerly it had been, so terribly wars and fires had laid it waste. On every side ruins were to be beheld, and the present condition of affairs threatened it with a total destruction. All the neighbouring princes were combined together against the Cubosama, and nothing was to be heard but the noise of arms.

The man of God endeavoured to have gained an audience from the Cubosama, and the Dairy, but he could not compass it: He could not so much as get admittance to the Saso, or high-priest of the Japonian religion. To procure him those audiences, they demanded no less than an hundred thousand caixes, which amount to six hundred French crowns, and the Father had it not to give. Despairing of doing any good on that side, he preached in the public places by that authority alone which the Almighty gives his missioners. As the town was all in confusion, and the thoughts of every man taken up with the reports of war, none listened to him; or those who casually heard him in passing by, made no reflections on what he said.

Thus, after a fortnight's stay at Meaco to no purpose, seeing no appearance of making converts amidst the disturbance of that place, he had a strong impulse of returning to Amanguchi, without giving for lost all the pains he had taken at Meaco; not only because of his great sufferings, (and sufferings are the gains of God's apostles) but also because at least he had preached Christ Jesus in that place, that is to say, in the most idolatrous town of all the universe, and opened the passage for his brethren, whom God had fore-appointed in the years following, there to establish Christianity, according to the revelations which had been given him concerning it.

He embarked on a river which falls from the adjoining mountains, and washing the foot of the walls of Meaco, disembogues itself afterwards into an arm of the sea, which runs up towards Sacay. Being in the ship, he could not turn off his eyes from the stately town of Meaco; and, as Fernandez tells us, often sung the beginning of the 113th Psalm, _In exitu Israel de Ægypto, domus Jacob de populo Barbaro,_ &c. whether he considered himself as an Israelite departing out of a land of infidels by the command of God, or that he looked on that barbarous people, as one day destined to be the people of God. As for what remains, perceiving that presents are of great force to introduce foreigners to the princes of Japan, he went from Sacay to Firando, where he had left what the viceroy of the Indies and the governor of Malacca had obliged him to carry with him to Japan, that is to say, a little striking clock, an instrument of very harmonious music, and some other trifles, the value of which consisted only in the workmanship and rarity.

Having also observed, that his ragged habit had shocked the Japonese, who judge by the outside of the man, and who hardly vouchsafe to hear a man ill clothed, he made himself a new garment, handsome enough, of those alms which the Portuguese had bestowed on him; being verily persuaded, that an apostolic man ought to make himself all to all, and that, to gain over worldly men, it was sometimes necessary to conform himself a little to their weakness.

Being come to Amanguchi, his presents made his way for an audience from the king, and procured him a favourable reception. Oxindono, who admired the workmanship of Europe, was not satisfied with thanking the Father in a very obliging manner, but the same day sent him a large sum of money, by way of gratification; but Xavier absolutely refused it, and this very denial gave the king a more advantageous opinion of him. "How different," said Oxindono, "is this European Bonza from our covetous priests, who love money with so much greediness, and who mind nothing but their worldly interest!"

On the next morning Xavier presented to the king the letters of the governor and of the bishop of the Indies, in which the Christian faith was much extolled; and desired him, instead of all other favours, to grant him the permission of preaching it, assuring him once again, that it was the only motive of his voyage. The king increasing his admiration at the Father's generosity, granted him, by word of mouth, and also by a public edict, to declare the word of God. The edict was set up at the turnings of streets, and in public places of the town. It contained a free toleration for all persons to profess the European faith, and forbade, on grievous penalties, any hinderance or molestation to the new Bonzas in the exercise of their functions.

Besides this, Oxindono assigned them, for their lodgings, an old monastery of the Bonzas, which was disinhabited. They were no sooner established in it, than great numbers of people resorted to them: Some out of policy, and to please the king; others to observe their carriage, and to pick faults in it; many out of curiosity, and to learn something that was new. All in general proposed their doubts, and disputed with so much vehemence, that most of them were out of breath. The house was never empty, and these perpetual visits took up all the time of the man of God.

He explains himself on this subject, and almost complains, in the letters which he writes to Father Ignatius concerning his voyage to Japan. For after he had marked out to him the qualities which were requisite in a labourer of the Society, proper to be sent thither, "That he ought, in the first place, to be a person of unblameable conversation, and that the Japonese would easily be scandalised, where they could find occasion for the least reproach; that, moreover, he ought to be of no less capacity than virtue, because Japan is also furnished with an infinite number of her own clergymen, profound in science, and not yielding up any point in dispute without being first convinced by demonstrative reasons; that, yet farther, it was necessary, that a missioner should come prepared to endure all manner of wants and hardships; that he must be endued with an heroic fortitude to encounter continual dangers, and death itself in dreadful torments, in case of need," Having, I say, set these things forth, and added these express words in one of his letters, "I write to Father Simon, and, in his absence, to the rector of Coimbra, that he shall send hither only such men as are known and approved by your holy charity," he continues thus:

"These labourers in the gospel must expect to be much more crossed in their undertaking than they imagine. They will be wearied out with visits, and by troublesome questions, every hour of the day, and half the night: They will be sent for incessantly to the houses of the great, and will sometimes want leisure to say their prayers, or to make their recollections. Perhaps, also, they will want time to say their mass or their breviary, or not have enough for their repast, or even for their natural repose, for it is incredible how importunate these Japonians are, especially in reference to strangers, of whom they make no reckoning, but rather make their sport of them. What therefore will become of them, when they rise up against their sects, and reprehend their vices?" Yet these importunities became pleasing to Father Xavier, and afterwards produced a good effect. As the Japonese are of docible and reasonable minds, the more they pressed him in dispute, they understood the truth the more: So that their doubts being satisfied, they comprehended easily, that there were no contradictions in our faith, nothing that would not abide the test of the most severe discussion.

It was in the midst of these interrogations, with which the saint was overburdened, that, by a prodigious manner of speech, the like of which was scarcely ever heard, he satisfied, with one only answer, the questions of many persons, on very different subjects, and often opposite to each other; as suppose, the immortality of the soul; the motions of the heavens; the eclipses of the sun and moon; the colours of the rainbow; sin and grace; hell and heaven. The wonder was, that after he had heard all their several demands, he answered them in few words, and that these words, being multiplied in their ears, by a virtue all divine, gave them to understand what they desired to know, as if he had answered each of them in particular. They frequently took notice of this prodigy; and were so much amazed at it, that they looked on one another like men distracted, and regarded the Father with admiration, as not knowing what to think or say. But as clear-sighted and able as they were, for the most part, they could not conceive that it was above the power of nature. They ascribed it to I know not what secret kind of science, which they imagined him only to possess. For which reason, Father Cozmo de Torrez, being returned from Firando to Amanguchi, the Bonzas said, "This man is not endued with the great knowledge of Father Francis, nor has the art of resolving many doubts with one only answer."

The process of the saint's canonization makes mention of this miracle; and Father Antonio Quadros, who travelled to Japan four years after Father Xavier, writes it to Father Diego Moron, provincial of Portugal,

These are his words: "A Japonese informed me, that he had seen three miracles wrought by Father Xavier in his country. He made a person walk and speak, who was dumb and taken with the palsy; he gave voice to another mute; and hearing to one that was deaf. This Japonian also told me, that Father Xavier was esteemed in Japan for the most knowing man of Europe; and that the other Fathers of the Society were nothing to him, because they could answer but one idolater at a time, but that Father Xavier, by one only word, decided ten or twelve questions. When I told him, that this might probably happen because those questions were alike, he assured me it was not so; but that, on the contrary, they were very different. He added, lastly, that this was no extraordinary thing with him, but a common practice."

When Xavier and his companion Fernandez were a little disengaged from these importunities, they set themselves on preaching twice a day, in the public places of the town, in despite of the Bonzas. There were seven or eight religions in Amanguchi quite opposite to each other, and every one of them had many proselytes, who defended their own as best; insomuch, that these Bonzas, who were heads of parties, had many disputes amongst themselves: But when once the saint began to publish the Christian law, all the sects united against their common enemy; which, notwithstanding, they durst not openly declare, against a man who was favoured by the court, and who seemed, even to themselves, to have somewhat in him that was more than human.

At this time God restored to Father Xavier the gift of tongues, which had been given him in the Indies on divers occasions; for, without having ever learned the Chinese language, he preached every day to the Chinese merchants, who traded at Amanguchi, in their mother-tongue, there being great numbers of them. He preached in the afternoon to the Japonians in their language; but so naturally and with so much ease, that he could not be taken for a foreigner.

The force of truth, against which their doctors could oppose nothing that was reasonable in their disputations; the novelty of three miracles, which we have mentioned, and of many others which Xavier wrought at the same time; his innocent and rigid life; the Divine Spirit which enlivened his discourses;-- all these together made so great an impression on their hearts, that in less than two months time, more than five hundred persons were baptized; the greatest part men of quality and learning, who had examined Christianity to the bottom, and who did not render up themselves for any other reason, than for that they had nothing farther to oppose.

It was wonderful, according to the report of the saint himself, to observe, that there was no other speech but of Jesus Christ through all the town; and that those who had most eagerly fought against the Christian law in their disputes, were now the most ardent to defend it, and to practise it with most exactness. All of them were tenderly affectionate to the Father, and were ever loath to leave his company They took delight in making daily questions to him, concerning the mysteries of faith; and it is unspeakable what inward refreshments they found, in seeing that all was mysterious even, in the most ordinary ceremonies,--as, for example, in the manner wherewith the faithful sign themselves with the cross.

The Father, on his side, had as ample a satisfaction; and he confesses it himself, in a letter which he directed some time after to the Jesuits in Europe: "Though my hairs are already become all hoary," says he to them, "I am more vigorous and robust than I ever was; for the pains which are taken to cultivate a reasonable nation, which loves the truth, and which covets to be saved, afford me matter of great joy. I have not, in the course of all my life, received a greater satisfaction than at Amanguchi, where multitudes of people came to hear me, by the king's permission. I saw the pride of their Bonzas overthrown, and the most inflamed enemies of the Christian name subjected to the humility of the gospel. I saw the transports of joy in those new Christians, when, after having vanquished the Bonzas in dispute, they returned in triumph. I was not less satisfied, to see their diligence in labouring to convince the Gentiles, and vying with each other in that undertaking; with the delight they took in the relation of their conquests, and by what arguments and means they brought them over, and how they rooted out the heathen superstitions; all these particulars gave me such abundant joy, that I lost the sense of my own afflictions. Ah, might it please Almighty God, that, as I call to my remembrance those consolations which I have received from the fountain of all mercies in the midst of my labours, I might not only make a recital of them, but give the experience also, and cause them to be felt and considered as they ought, by our universities of Europe, I am assured, that many young men, who study there, would come hither to employ all the strength of their parts, and vigour of their minds, in the conversion of an idolatrous people, had they once tasted those heavenly refreshments which accompany our labours."

These inward delights of God's servant were not yet so pure, but that some bitterness was intermixed. He was not without sorrow for Oxindono king of Amanguchi; who, though persuaded of the excellence of Christianity, was retained in idolatry by carnal pleasures: and for Neatondono, first prince of the kingdom, who, having noble and virtuous inclinations, might have proved the apostle of the court, if some trivial reasons had not hindered him from becoming a Christian. He, and the princess his wife, respected Xavier as their father, and even honoured him as a saint. They also loved the faithful, and succoured them in all their needs. They spoke of our faith in terms of great veneration; but, having founded many monasteries of Bonzas, it troubled them, as they said, to lose the fruit of charity: and thus the fear of being frustrated of I know not what rewards, which the Bonzas promised them, caused them to neglect that eternal recompence of which the holy man assured them.

But how powerful soever the example of princes is usually in matters of religion, yet on all sides Christianity was embraced; and an action of Xavier's companion did not a little contribute to the gaining over of the most stubborn. Fernandez preached in one of the most frequented places of the town; and amongst his crowd of auditors were some persons of great wit, strongly opinioned of their sect, who could not conceive the maxims of the gospel, and who heard the preacher with no other intention than to make a sport of him. In the midst of the sermon, a man, who was of the scum of the rabble, drew near to Fernandez, as if it were to whisper something to him, and hawking up a mass of nastiness, spit it full upon his face. Fernandez, without a word speaking, or making the least sign that he was concerned, took his hand-kerchief, wiped his face, and continued his discourse.

Every one was suprised at the moderation of the preacher:--the more debauched, who had set up a laughter at this affront, turned all their scorn into admiration, and sincerely acknowledged, that a man who was so much master of his passions, as to command them on such an occasion, must needs be endued with greatness of soul and heroic courage. One of the chief of the assembly discovered somewhat else in this unshaken patience: He was the most learned amongst all the doctors of Amanguchi, and the most violent against the gospel He considered, that a law which taught such patience, and such insensibility of affronts, could only come from heaven; and argued thus within himself: "These preachers, who with so much constancy endure the vilest of all injuries, cannot pretend to cozen us. It would cost them too dear a price; and no man will deceive another at his own expence. He only, who made the heart of man, can place it in so great tranquillity. The force of nature cannot reach so far; and this Christian patience must proceed alone from some divine principle. These people cannot but have some infallible assurance of the doctrine they believe, and of the recompence which they expect; for, in line, they are ready to suffer all things for their God, and have no human expectations. After all, what inconvenience or danger can it be to embrace their law? If what they tell us of eternity be true, I shall be eternally miserable in not believing it; and supposing there be no other life but this, is it not better to follow a religion which elevates a man above himself, and which gives him an unalterable peace, than to profess our sects, which continue us in all our weakness, and which want power to appease the disorders of our hearts?" He made his inward reflections on all these things, as he afterwards declared; and these considerations being accompanied with the motions of grace, touched him so to the quick, that, as soon as the sermon was ended, he confessed that the virtue of the preacher had convinced him; he desired baptism, and received it with great solemnity.

This illustrious conversion was followed with answerable success. Many who had a glimmering of the truth, and feared to know it yet more plainly, now opened their eyes, and admitted the gospel light; amongst the rest, a young man of five-and-twenty years of age, much esteemed for the subtlety of his understanding, and educated in the most famous universities of Japan. He was come to Amanguchi, on purpose to be made a Bonza; but being informed that the sect of Bonzas, of which he desired to be a member, did not acknowledge a first Principle, and that their books had made no mention of him, he changed his thoughts, and was unresolved on what course of living he should fix; until being finally convinced, by the example of the doctor, and the arguments of Xavier, he became a Christian. The name of Laurence was given him; and it was he, who, being received by Xavier himself into the Society of Jesus, exercised immediately the ministry of preaching with so much fame, and so great success, that he converted an innumerable multitude of noble and valiant men, who were afterwards the pillars of the Japonian church.

As to what remains, the monasteries of the Bonzas were daily thinned, and grew insensibly to be dispeopled by the desertion of young men, who had some remainders of modesty and morality. Being ashamed of leading a brutal life, and of deceiving the simple, they laid by their habits of Bonzas, together with the profession, that, coming back into the world, they might more easily be converted. These young Bonzas discovered to Xavier the mysteries of their sects, and revealed to him their hidden abominations, which were covered with an outside of austerity.

The Father, who was at open defiance with those men, who were the mortal enemies of all the faithful, and whose only interest it was to hinder the establishment of the faith, published whatsoever was told him in relation to them, and represented them in their proper colours. These unmasked hypocrites became the laughter of the people; but what mortified them more, was, that they, who heard them like oracles before this, now upbraided them openly with their ignorance. A woman would sometimes challenge them to a disputation; and urge them with such home and pressing arguments, that the more they endeavoured to get loose, the more they were entangled: For the Father, being made privy to the secrets of every sect, furnished the new proselytes with weapons to vanquish the Bonzas, by reducing them to manifest contradictions; which, among the Japonese, is the greatest infamy that can happen to a man of letters. But the Bonzas got not off so cheap, as only to be made the derision of the people; together with their credit and their reputation they lost the comfortable alms, which was their whole subsistence: So that the greater part of them, without finding in themselves the least inclinations to Christianity, bolted out of their convents, that they might not die of hunger in them; and changed their profession of Bonzas, to become either soldiers or tradesmen; which gave the Christians occasion to say, with joy unspeakable, "That, in a little time, there would remain no more idolaters in Amanguchi, of those religious cheats, than were barely sufficient to keep possession of their monasteries."

The elder Bonzas, in the mean time, more hardened in their sect, and more obstinate than the young, spared for nothing to maintain their possession. They threatened the people with the wrath of their gods, and denounced the total destruction of the town and kingdom; they said, "The God whom the

Europeans believed, was not Deos, or Deus, as the Portuguese called him, but Dajus, that is to say, in the Japonian tongue, a lie, or forgery." They added, "That this God imposed on men a heavy yoke. What justice was it to punish those who transgressed a law, which it was impossible to keep? But where was Providence, if the law of Jesus was necessary to salvation, which suffered fifteen ages to slide away without declaring it to the most noble part of all the world? Surely a religion, whose God was partial in the dispensation of his favours, could not possibly be true; and if the European doctrine had but a shadow of truth in it, China could never have been so long without the knowledge of it." These were the principal heads of their accusation, and Xavier reports them in his letters; but he gives not an account of what answers he returned, and they are not made known to us by any other hand. Thus, without following two or three historians, who make him speak according to their own ideas on all these articles, I shall content myself with what the saint himself had left in writing. The idolaters, instead of congratulating their own happiness, that they were enlightened by the beams of faith, bemoaned the blindness of their ancestors, and cried out in a lamentable tone, "What! are our forefathers burning in hellfire, because they did not adore a God who was unknown to them, and observed not a law which never was declared?" The Bouzas added fuel to their zeal, by telling them,

"The Portuguese priests were good for nothing, because they could not redeem a soul from hell; whereas they could do it at their pleasure, by their fasts and prayers: that eternal punishments either proved the cruelty or the weakness of the Christian God; his cruelty, if he did not deliver them, when he had it in his power; his weakness, if he could not execute what he desired; lastly, that Amida and Xaca were far more merciful, and of greater power; but that they were only pleased to redeem from hell those who, during their mortal life, had bestowed magnificent alms upon the Bonzas."

We are ignorant of all those particular answers of the saint, as I said above: we only know from his relation, that, concerning the sorrow of the Japonians for having been bereft for so many ages of Christian knowledge, he had the good fortune to give them comfort, and put them in a way of more reasonable thoughts; for he shewed them in general, that the most ancient of all laws is the law of God, not that which is published by the sound of words, but that which is written in hearts by the hand of nature; so that every one who comes into the world, brings along with him certain precepts, which his own instinct and reason teach him. "Before Japan received its laws from the wise men of China," said Xavier, "it was known amongst you, that theft and adultery were to be avoided; and from thence it was that thieves and palliards sought out secret places, wherein to commit those crimes. After they had committed them, they felt the private stings of their own consciences, which cease not to reproach the guilty to themselves, though their wickedness be not known to others, nor even so much as prohibited by human laws. Suppose an infant bred up in forests amongst the beasts, far from the society of mankind, and remote from the civilized inhabitants of towns, yet he is not without an inward knowledge of the rules of civil life; for ask him, whether it be not an evil action to murder a man, to despoil him of his goods, to violate his bed, to surprise him by force, or circumvent him by treachery, he will answer without question, 'That nothing of this is to be done.' Now if this be manifest in a savage, without the benefit of education, how much more way it be concluded of men well educated, and living in mutual conversation? Then," added the holy man, "it follows, that God has not left so many ages destitute of knowledge, as your Bonzas have pretended" By this he gave them to understand, that the law of nature was a step which led them insensibly to the Christian law; and that a man who lived morally well, should never fad of arriving to the knowledge of the faith, by ways best known to Almighty God; that is to say, before his eath, God would either send some preacher to him, or illuminate his mind by some immediate revelation. These reasons, which the fathers of the church have often used on like occasions, gave such satisfaction to the Pagans, that they found no farther difficulty in that point, which had given them so much trouble.

The Bonzas perceiving that the people preferred the authority of Xavier above theirs, and not knowing how to refute their adversary, made a cabal at court, to lessen the Christians in the good opinion of the king. They gave him jealousies of them, by decrying their behaviour, and saying, "They were men of intrigue, plotters, enemies of the public safety, and dangerous to the person of the king;" insomuch, that Oxindono, who had been so favourable to them, all on the sudden was turned against them. It is true, that as the Japonese value themselves above all things, in the inviolable observation of their word, when they have once engaged it, he durst not revoke that solemn edict, which he had published in favour of the Christians; but to make it of no effect, he used the faithful with great severity, even so far as to seize upon their goods, and began with men of the first rank in his dominions. At the same time, the Bonzas, grown insolent, and swelled with this new turn of tide, wrote letters and libels full of invectives against Xavier. They said, he was a vagabond beggar, who, not knowing how to maintain himself in India, was come to Japan to live on charity. They endeavoured above all things to make him pass for a notorious magician, who, through the power of his charms, had forced the devil to obey him, and one who, by the assistance of his familiars, performed all sorts of prodigies to seduce the people.

But neither this alteration in the king, nor these calumnies of the Bonzas, hindered the progress of the gospel. The number of Christians amounted in few days to three thousand in Amanguchi, and they were all so fervent, that not one of them but was ready, not only to forego his fortunes, but also to shed his blood for the defence of his faith, if the king should be carried on to persecute the growing church with fire and sword, as it was believed he would. The reputation of the apostle was also encreased, in spite of the false reports which were spread concerning him; and his name became so famous in the neighbouring kingdoms, that all the people round about were desirous to see the European Bonza.

Xavier had of late some thoughts of returning to the Indies, there to make a choice himself of such labourers as were proper for Japan; and his design was to come back by China, the conversion of which country had already inflamed his heart. For discoursing daily with such Chinese merchants as were resident at Amanguehi, he had entertained a strong opinion, that a nation so polite, and knowing, would easily be reduced to Christianity; and on the other side, he had great hopes, that when China should be once converted, Japan would not be long after it; at least the more unbelieving sort of Japonese often said, "That they would not alter their religion till the Chinese had led the way. Let him carry his gospel to that flourishing and vast empire; and when he had subdued it to Jesus Christ, then they would also think of turning Christians."

In the meantime, a Portuguese vessel, commanded by Edward de Gama, arrived at the kingdom of Bungo, and news came to Amanguchi, that this ship, which was sailed thither from the Indies, would be on its way back again in a month or two. Xavier, to learn what truth there was in this report, sent Matthew to those parts, who was one of the Japonian converts, which accompanied him, and gave him a letter, directed to the captain and merchants of the vessel. The saint desired them to send him word, who they were, from whence bound, and how soon they intended to return; after which he told them, "That his intentions were to return to the Indies, and that he should be glad to meet them, in case they were disposed to repass thither." In conclusion, he desired them earnestly, that they would borrow so much time from their affairs of merchandize as to think a little on their souls; and declared to them, that all the silks of China, whatever gain they might afford them, could not countervail the least spiritual profit which they might make, by a daily examination of their consciences. The ship was at the port of Figen, about fifty leagues from Amanguchi, and within a league of Fucheo, which some call Funay, the metropolis of Bungo. The Portuguese were overjoyed to hear news of Father Xavier. They sent him an account of theirs, and withal advertised him, that, in the compass of a month at farthest, they should set sail for China, where they had left three vessels laden for the Indies, which were to return in January, and that James Pereyra, his familiar friend, was on board of one of them. Matthew came back in five days time; and, besides the letters which he brought the Father from the captain, and the principal merchants, he gave him some from Goa; by which the Fathers of the college of St Paul gave him to understand, that his presence in that place was of absolute necessity, for the regulation of affairs belonging to the Society.

Then Xavier, without losing time, after he had recommended the new Christians to the care of Cosmo de Torrez, and John Fernandez, whom he left at Amanguchi, put himself upon his way towards Mid-September, in the year 1551. He might have made this voyage easily by sea, but he loved rather to go by land, and that on foot, according to his custom. He took for his companions, Matthew and Bernard; two Christian lords would be also of the party. Their goods had lately been confiscated, as a punishment for changing their religion; but the grace of Jesus Christ, which was to them instead of all, rendered their poverty so precious, that they esteemed themselves richer than they had been formerly. Another Christian bore them company; that Laurence sirnamed the Squint-eyed, because of that imperfection in his sight.

The Father walked cheerfully with his five companions, as far as Pinlaschau, a village distant a league or two from Figen. Arriving there he found himself so spent with travelling, that his feet were swollen, and he was seized with a violent headach, so that he could go no farther. Matthew, Laurence, and Bernard, went on to carry news of him to the vessel. When Edward de Gama understood that the holy man was so near, he called together all the Portuguese who resided at Fucheo; and having chosen out the principal amongst them, got on horseback with them, to pay him their respects in ceremony. Xavier, whom a little rest had now recruited, and who was suspicious of the honour which they intended him, was already on his journey, but fell into that ambush of civility, which he would willingly have shunned. The cavalcade came up to him within a league's distance of Figen; and found him walking betwixt the two lords of Amanguchi, who had never left him, and himself carrying his own equipage. Gama was surprised to see a person so considerable in the world in such a posture, and alighting from his horse, with all his company, saluted him with all manner of respect. After the first compliments were over, they invited the Father to mount on horseback, but he could not be persuaded; so that the Portuguese giving their horses to be led after them, bore him company on foot even to the port.

The ship was equipped in all its flourish, with flags hung out, and streamers waving, according to the orders of the captain. They who were remaining in her appeared on the decks, and stood glittering in their armour. They gave him a volley at his first approach, and then discharged all their cannon. Four rounds of the artillery being made, the noise of it was heard so distinctly at Fucheo, that the city was in a fright, and the king imagined that the Portuguese were attacked by certain pirates, who lately had pillaged all the coasts. To clear his doubts, he dispatched away a gentleman of his court to the ship's captain. Gama shewing Father Francis to the messenger, told him, that the noise which had alarmed the court, was only a small testimony of the honour which was owing to so great a person, one so dear to heaven, and so much esteemed in the court of Portugal.

The Japanner, who saw nothing but poverty in the person of the Father, and remembered what had been written of him from Amanguchi, stopped a little without speaking; then, with amazement in his face, "I am in pain," said he, "what answer I shall return my prince; for what you tell me has no correspondence either with that which I behold, or with the account we have received from the Bonzas of Amanguchi; who have seen your Father Bonza entertain a familiar spirit, who taught him to cast lots, and perform certain magical operations to delude the ignorant. They report him to be a wretch forsaken, and accurst by all the world; that the vermin which are swarming all over him, are too nice to feed on his infectious flesh; besides which, I fear, that if I should relate what you say concerning him, our priests would be taken either for idiots, or men of false understanding, or for envious persons, and impostors." Then Gama replying, told the Japonian all that was necessary to give him a good impression of the saint, and to hinder him from contempt of his mean appearance. On this last article he declared to him, that he, who had so despicable an outside, was of noble blood; that fortune had provided him with wealth, but that his virtue had made him poor; and that his wilfull want of all things was the effect of a great spirit, which despised those empty pomps that are so eagerly desired by mankind. This discourse ravished the Japanner with admiration; he made a faithful relation of it to his king; and added of himself, that the Portuguese were more happy in the possession of this holy man, than if their vessel were laden with ingots of gold.

The king of Bungo had already heard speak of Father Francis; and gave no credit to what the Bonzas of Amanguchi had written of him. He was a prince of five-and-twenty years of age, very judicious, generous, and civil; but too much engaged in carnal pleasures, after the manner of the Japonian princes. What he had heard from the relation of the messenger, increased his longing to behold Xavier; and the same day he writ to him, in these very terms:--

"Father Bonza of Chimahicoghin, (for by that name they call Portugal,) may your happy arrival in my estates be as pleasing to your God, as are the praises wherewith he is honoured by his saints. Quansyonofama, my domestic servant, whom I sent to the port of Figen, tells me, that you are arrived from Amanguchi; and all my court will bear me witness, with what pleasure I received the news. As God has not made me worthy to command you, I earnestly request you to come before the rising of the sun to-morrow, and to knock at my palace gate, where I shall impatiently attend you. And permit me to demand this favour of you without being thought a troublesome beggar. In the meantime, prostrate on the ground, and on my knees before your God, whom I acknowledge for the God of all the gods, the Sovereign of the best and greatest which inhabit in the heavens, I desire of him, I say, to make known to the haughty of the world, how much your poor and holy life is pleasing to him; to the end, that the children of our flesh may not be deceived by the false promises of the earth. Send me news of your holiness, the joy of which may give me a good night's repose, till the cocks awaken me with the welcome declaration of your visit."

This letter was carried by a young prince of the blood royal, attended by thirty young lords belonging to the court; and accompanied by a venerable old man, who was his governor, called Poomendono, one of the wisest and most qualified of all the kingdom, and natural brother to the king of Minato. The honour which was paid by the Portuguese to Father Xavier, so surprised the prince, that, turning to his governor, he said aloud, "the God of these people must be truly great, and his counsels hidden from mankind, since it is his pleasure, that these wealthy ships should be obedient to so poor a man as is this Bonza of the Portuguese; and that the roaring of their cannon should declare, that poverty has wherewithal to be pleasing to the Lord of all the world; even that poverty which is so despicable of itself, and so disgraceful in the general opinion, that it seems even a crime to think of it."

"Though we have a horror for poverty," replied Poomendono, "and that we believe the poor incapable of happiness, it may be this poor man is so much enamoured of his wants, and so esteems them, that he is pleasing to the God whom he adores, and that practising it with all imaginable rigour for his sake, he may be richer than the greatest monarch of the world."

The young ambassador being returned to court, reported to the king with what respect his letter had been received; and took upon him to persuade that prince, that this European Bonza was to be treated with greater honour, and far otherwise than their ordinary Bonzas; even so far as to say, that it would be an enormous sin to level him with them; that for the rest, he was not so poor as his enemies had suggested; that the captains and Portuguese merchants would bestow on him both their ship and all their treasure, in case he would accept of them; and that, properly speaking, he was not to be accounted poor, who possessed as much as he desired. In the mean time, the Portuguese being assembled, to consult how Father Xavier should appear in court the next morning, all of them were of opinion, that he should present himself with all the pomp and magnificence they could devise. At first he opposed it, out of the aversion he had for this pageant show, so unsuitable to the condition of a religious man; but afterwards he yielded to the request, and withal to the reasons of the assembly. Those reasons were, that the Bonzas of Amanguchi, having written all they could imagine, to render Xavier contemptible, it was convenient to remove those false conceptions from the people; and at the same time, to let them see how much the Christians honour their ministers of the gospel, that thereby the Heathens might be the more easily induced to give credit to them; so that the honour would reflect on Jesus Christ, and the preaching would be raised in value, according to the esteem which was given to the preacher.

They prepared therefore, with all diligence, for the entry of the saint, and set out the next morning before day-light, in a handsome equipage. There were thirty Portuguese, of the most considerable amongst them, richly habited; with their chains of gold, and adorned with jewels. Their servants and slaves, well clothed likewise, were attending on their masters. Father Xavier wore a cassock of black chainlet, and over it a surplice, with a stole of green velvet, garnished with a gold brocard. The chalop and the two barques, wherein they made their passage from the ship to the town, were covered on the sides with the fairest China tapestry, and hung round with silken banners of all colours. Both in the sloop, and in the barques, there were trumpets, flutes, and hautboys, and other instruments of music, which, playing together, made a most harmonious concert: the news which was spread about Fucheo, that the great European Bonza was to enter into the town that morning, drew many persons of quality to the sea-side; and such a multitude of people ran crowding together, at the sounding of the trumpets, that the Portuguese could hardly find footing to come on shore.

Quansyandono, captain of Canafama, and one of the principal of the court, was there attending them, by order from the king. He received the saint with great civility, and offered him a litter to carry him to the palace; but Xavier refused it, and walked on foot, with all his train, in this order: Edward de Gama went foremost bare-headed, with a cane in his hand, as the gentleman of the horse, or Major Domo to the Father. Five other Portuguese followed him, who were the most considerable persons of the ship. One of them carried a book in a bag of white satin; another a cane of Bengal, headed with gold; a third his slippers, which were of a fine black velvet, such as are worn only by persons of the first quality, a fourth carried a fair tablet of Our Lady, wrapt in a scarf of violet damask; and the fifth a magnificent parasol. The Father came next after them, in the habit which I have described; with an air composed betwixt majesty and modesty. The rest of the Portuguese followed; and to behold their countenance, their dress, and the beauty of their train, they resembled rather cavaliers and lords, than a company of merchants. They passed in this manner through the chief streets of the city, with sound of trumpets, flutes, and hautboys, followed by an infinite multitude of people, without reckoning into the number those who filled the windows, the balconies, and the tops of houses. Being arrived at the great place, which fronts the royal palace, they found there six hundred of the king's guards, drawn up, some armed with lances, others with darts, all of them with rich scymiters hanging by their sides, and costly vests upon their backs. These guards, at the sign given them by their captain, called Fingeiridono, advanced in good order towards the saint, after which they divided into two ranks, and opened a passage for the Father through the midst of them.

Being come to the palace, the Portuguese, who walked immediately before the Father, turned towards him, and saluted him with great respect. One presented him the cane, and another the velvet slippers; he, who held the parasol, spread it over his head; and the two others, who carried the book and picture, placed themselves on each side of him. All this was so gracefully performed, and with so much honour to the Father, that the lords who were present much admired the manner of it: and they were heard to say amongst themselves, that Xavier had been falsely represented to them by the Bonzas; that questionless he was a man descended from above, to confound their envy, and abate their pride.

After they had gone through a long gallery, they entered into a large hall full of people; who, by their habit, which was of damask, heightened with gold, and diversified with fair figures, seemed to be persons of the highest quality. There a little child, whom a reverend old man held by the hand, coming up to the Father, saluted him with these words: "May your arrival in the palace of my lord the king, be as welcome to him, as the rain of heaven to the labourers, in a long and parching drought: Enter without fear," continued he, "for I assure you of the love of all good men, though the wicked cannot behold you without melancholy in their faces, which will make them appear like a black and stormy night." Xavier returned an answer suitable to his age who had made the compliment; but the child replied in a manner which was far above his age. "Certainly," said he, "you must be endued with an extraordinary courage, to come from the end of all the world into a strange country, liable to contempt, in regard of your poverty; and the goodness of your God must needs be infinite, to be pleased with that poverty against the general opinion of mankind. The Bonzas are far from doing any thing of this nature; they who publicly affirm, and swear, that the poor are no more in a possibility of salvation than the women." "May it please the divine goodness of our Lord," replied Xavier, "to enlighten those dark and wretched souls with the beams of his celestial truth, to the end they may confess their error, both as to that particular, and to the rest of their belief."

The child discoursed on other subjects, and spoke with so much reason, and with that sublimity of thought, that the Father doubted not but he was inspired by the Holy Spirit, who, when he pleases, can replenish the souls of infants with wisdom, and give eloquence to their tongues, before nature has ripened in them the use of reason.

In these entertainments, which were surprising to all the assistants, they passed into another hall, where there were many gentlemen richly habited, and of good mein. At the moment when the Father entered, all of them bowed with reverence; which action they repeated thrice, and so very low, that they touched the ground with their foreheads, as the Japonese are very dextrous at that exercise. And this reverence, which they call Gromenare, is only performed by the son to the father, and by the vassal to his lord. After this, two of them separating from the company, to testify their general joy at the sight of him, one of them spoke in this manner: "May your arrival, holy Father Bonza, be as pleasing to our king as the smiles of a babe are to his mother, who holds him in her arms; which certainly will be, for we swear to you by the hairs of our heads, that every thing, even to the very walls, which seem to dance for joy at your desired presence, conspires to your good reception, and excites us to rejoice at your arrival; we doubt not but it will turn to the glory of that God. of whom you have spoken so greatly at Amanguchi." This compliment being ended, these young lords were following the Father; but the child of whom we made mention, and whom Xavier led by the hand, made a sign to them, that they should go no farther. They mounted on a terrace bordered with orange trees, and from thence entered into another hall, more spacious than either of the former. Facharandono, the king's brother, was there, with a magnificent retinue. Having done to the saint all the civilities which are practised to the greatest of Japan, he told him, "that this day was the most solemn and auspicious of all the year for the court of Bungo; and that his lord the king esteemed himself more rich and happy to have him in his palace, than if he were master of all the silver contained in the two-and-thirty treasuries of China. In the mean time," added the prince, "I wish you an increase of glory, and an entire accomplishment of that design, which brought you hither from the extremities of the earth."

Then the child, who had hitherto been the master of the ceremonies to the Father, left him in the hands of Facharandono, and retired apart. They entered into the king's antichamber, where the principal lords of the kingdom were attending him. After he had been received by them with all possible civilities, he was at last introduced to his audience in a chamber which glittered with gold on every side. The king, who was standing, advanced five or six paces at the first appearance of the Father, and bowed himself even to the ground thrice successively, at which action all the company were in great amazement. Xavier, on his side, prostrated himself before that prince, and would have touched his foot, according to the custom of the country, but the king would not permit him, and himself raised up the saint; then taking him by the hand, he caused him to sit down by him on the same estrade. The prince, his brother, was seated somewhat lower; and the Portuguese were placed over against them, accompanied by the most qualified persons of the court. The king immediately said all the obliging things to the Father which could be expected from a well-bred man; and, laying aside all the pomp of majesty, which the kings of Japan are never used to quit in public, treated him with the kindness and familiarity of a friend. The Father answered all these civilities of the prince with a most profound respect, and words full of deference and submission; after which, taking occasion to declare Jesus Christ to him, he explained, in few words, the principal maxims of Christian morality; but he did it after so plausible a manner, that at the conclusion of his discourse, the king cried out in a transport of admiration, "How can any man learn from God these profound secrets? Why has he suffered us to live in blindness, and this Bonza of Portugal to receive these wonderful illuminations? For, in fine, we ourselves are witnesses of what we had formerly by report; and all we hear is maintained by proofs so strong and evident, and withal so conformable to the light of nature, that whoever would examine these doctrines, according to the rules of reason, will find that truth will issue out, and meet him on every side, and that no one proposition destroys another. It is far otherwise with our Bonzas; they cannot make any discourse without the clashing of their own principles; and from thence it happens, that the more they speak, the more they entangle themselves. Confused in their knowledge, and yet more confused in the explication of what they teach, rejecting to day as false what yesterday they approved for true; contradicting themselves, and recanting their opinions every moment, insomuch, that the clearest head, and the most ready understanding, can comprehend nothing of their doctrine; and in relation to eternal happiness, we are always left in doubt what we should believe; a most manifest token that they only follow the extravagancies of their own fancies, and have not, for the rule and foundation of their faith, any permanent and solid truth."

In this manner spoke the king; and it was easy to judge by the vehemence of his action, that he spoke from the abundance of his heart. There was present a Bonza, very considerable in his sect, and of good knowledge, but too presuming of his understanding, and as much conceited of his own abilities as any pedant in the world. This Bonza, whose name was Faxiondono, either jealous of the honour of his profession, or taking to himself in particular what the king had said of all in general, was often tempted to have interrupted him, yet he mastered his passion till the king had done; but then losing all manner of respect, and not keeping any measures of decency, "How dare you," said he, "decide matters relating to religion; you who have never studied in the university of Fianzima, the only place where the sacred mysteries of the gods are explicated? If you know nothing of yourself, consult the learned. I am here in person to instruct you."

The insolence of the Bonza raised the indignation of all the company, the king excepted, who, smiling, commanded him to proceed, if he had more to say. Faxiondono growing more arrogant by this moderation of his prince, began raising his note by extolling the profession of a Bonza: "That nothing was more certain than that the Bonzas were the favourites of heaven, both observing the law themselves, and causing it to be observed by others; that they passed the longest nights, and the severest colds, in praying for their benefactors; that they abstained from all sensual pleasures; that fresh fish never came upon their tables; that they administered to the sick, instructed the children, comforted the distressed, reconciled enemies, appeased seditions, and pacified kingdoms; that, which was first and chiefest, they gave letters of exchange for another life, by which the dead became rich in heaven; that, in fine, the Bonzas were the familiar friends of the stars, and the confidents of the saints; that they were privileged to converse with them by night, to cause them to descend from heaven, to embrace them in their arms, and enjoy them as long as they desired." These extravagancies set all the company in a laughter; at which the Bonza was so enraged, that he flew out into greater passion, till the king commanded his brother to impose silence on him; after which, he caused his seat to be taken from under him, and commanded him to withdraw, telling him, by way of raillery, "That his choler was a convincing proof of a Bonza's holiness;" and then seriously adding, "That a man of his character had more commerce with hell than heaven." At these words, the Bonza cried out with excess of rage, "The time will come, when no man of this world shall be worthy enough to serve me; there is not that monarch now breathing on the face of the earth, but shall be judged too vile to touch the hem of my garment." He meant, when he was to be transformed into one of their deities, and that God and he should be mixed into one divinity, which is the reward of a Bonza after death. Though the king could not hear his madness without smiling, yet he had so much compassion on his folly, that he took upon him to confute those extravagant propositions; but Xavier desired him to defer it to a fitter time, till he had digested his fury, and was more capable of hearing reason. Then the king said only to Faxiondono, "That he should go and do penance for the pride and insolence of his speech, wherein he had made himself a companion of the gods." Faxiondono did not reply, but he was heard to mutter, and grind his teeth, as he withdrew. Being at the chamber door, and ready to go out, "May the gods," said he aloud, "dart their fire from heaven to consume thee, and burn to ashes all those kings who shall presume to speak like thee!"

The king and Xavier prosecuted their discourse on several articles of religion till dinner time; when the meat was on the table, the king invited the Father to eat with him. Xavier excused himself with all possible respect, but that prince would absolutely have it so. "I know well," said he, "my friend and father, that you are not in want of my table; but, if you were a Japanner, as we are, you would understand, that a king cannot give those he favours a greater sign of his good will, than in permitting them to eat with him; for which reason, as I love you, and am desirous of shewing it, you must needs dine with me; and farther, I assure you, that I shall receive a greater honour by it, than I bestow." Then Xavier, with a low reverence, kissing his scymitar, which is a mark of most profound respect, much practised in Japan, said thus to him: "I petition the God of heaven, from the bottom of my heart, to reward your majesty for all the favours you have heaped on me, by bestowing on you the light of faith, and the virtues of Christianity, to the end you may serve God faithfully during your life, and enjoy him eternally after death." The king embraced him, and desired of God, on his side, that he would graciously hear the saint's request, yet on this condition, that they might remain together in heaven, and never be divided from each other, that they might have the opportunity of long conversations, and of discoursing to the full of divine matters. At length they sat to dinner: while they were eating, the Portuguese, and all the lords of the court, were on their knees, together with the chief inhabitants of the town, amongst whom were also some Bonzas, who were enraged in their hearts; but the late example of Faxiondono hindered them from breaking into passion.

These honours which Xavier received from the king of Bungo, made him so considerable, and gave him so great a reputation with the people, that being at his lodgings with the Portuguese, they came thronging from all quarters to hear him speak of God. His public sermons, and his private conversations, had their due effect. Vast multitudes of people, from the very first, renounced their idols, and believed in Jesus Christ. The saint employed whole days together in baptising of idolaters, or in teaching new believers; so that the Portuguese could not enjoy him to themselves for their own spiritual consolation, unless at some certain hours of the night, while he was giving himself some breathing time after his long labours. Loving him so tenderly as they did, and fearing that his continual pains might endanger his health, they desired him to manage it with more caution, and to take at least those refreshments which human nature exacted from him, before he sunk at once under some distemper. But he answered them, "That if they truly loved him, they would trouble themselves no more concerning him; that they ought to look on him as one who was dead to all outward refreshments; that his nourishment, his sleep, and his life itself, consisted in delivering from the tyranny of the devil those precious souls, for whose sake chiefly God had called him from the utmost limits of the earth."

Amongst the conversions which were made at Fucheo, one of the most considerable was that of a famous Bonza, of Canafama, called Sacay Ecran. This Bonza, who was very learned, and a great pillar of his sect, seeing that none of his brethren durst attempt Xavier on the matter of religion, undertook a public disputation with him. The conference Avas made in a principal place of the town, in presence of a great multitude. Scarcely had Xavier made an end of explaining the Christian doctrine, when the Bonza grew sensible of his errors. The infidel, notwithstanding, went on to oppose those truths, of which he had already some imperfect glimpse; but being at length convinced, by the powerful reasons of his adversary, and inwardly moved by God's good spirit, he fell on his knees, and lifting up his hands towards heaven, he pronounced aloud these words, Math tears trickling from his eyes; "O Jesus Christ, thou true and only son of God, I submit to thee. I confess from my heart, and with my mouth, that thou art God eternal and omnipotent; and I earnestly desire the pardon of all my auditors, that I have so often taught them things for truth, which I acknowledge, and at this present declare before them, were only forgeries and fables."

An action which was so surprising, moved the minds of all the assistants; and it was in the power of Father Xavier to have baptized that very day five hundred persons, who, being led by the example of the Bonza of Canafama, all of them earnestly desired baptism. He might perhaps have done this in the Indies, where there were no learned men to oppose the mysteries of our faith, and to tempt the fidelity of the new converts by captious queries. But he judged this not to be practicable in Japan, where the Bonzas, not being able to hinder the conversion of idolaters, endeavoured afterwards to regain them by a thousand lying artifices and sophistications; and it appeared necessary to him, before he baptized those who were grown up to manhood, to fortify them well against the tricks of those seducers.

Accordingly, the saint disposed the souls of those Gentiles by degrees to this first sacrament, and began with the reformation of their manners, chusing rather not to baptize the king of Bungo, than to precipitate his baptism; or rather he thought, that his conversion would be always speedy enough, provided it were sincere and constant. Thus, the great care of Father Xavier, in relation to the prince, was to give him an aversion to those infamous vices which had been taught him by the Bonzas, and in which he lived without scruple, upon the faith of those his masters. Now the king, attending with great application to the man of God, and having long conversations with him, began immediately to change his life, and to give the demonstrations of that change. From the very fist, he banished out of his chamber a beautiful youth, who was his minion, and also forbade him the entry of his palace. He gave bountifully to the poor, to whom he had formerly been hard-hearted, as thinking it was a crime to pity them, and an act of justice to be cruel to them, according to the doctrine of his Bonzas, who maintained, that poverty not only made men despicable and ridiculous, but also criminal, and worthy of the severest punishments. According to the principles of the same doctors, women with child were allowed to make themselves miscarry by certain potions, and even to murder those children whom they brought into the world against their will; insomuch, that such unnatural cruelties were daily committed, and nothing was more common in the kingdom of Bungo, than those inhuman mothers: Some of them, to save the charges of their food and education, others to avoid the miseries attending poverty, and many to preserve the reputation of chastity, however debauched and infamous they were. The king, by the admonition of the Father, forbade those cruelties on pain of death. He made other edicts against divers Pagan ceremonies, which were lascivious or dishonest, and suffered not the Bonzas to set a foot within his palace. As to what remains, he was wrapt in admiration at the virtue of the holy man; and confessed often to his courtiers, that when he saw him appear at any time, he trembled even to the bottom of his heart, because he seemed to see the countenance of the man of God, as a clear mirror, representing to him the abominations of his life.

While Xavier had this success at the court of Bungo, Cosmo de Torrez, and John Fernandez, suffered for the faith at Amanguchi. After the departure of the saint, the whole nation of the Bonzas rose against them, and endeavoured to confound them in regular disputes; flattering themselves with this opinion, that the companions of Xavier were not so learned as himself, and judging on the other side, that the least advantage which they should obtain against them, would re-establish the declining affairs of Paganism.

It happened quite contrary to their expectations: Torrez, to whom Fernandez served instead of an interpreter, answered their questions with such force of reason, that they were wholly vanquished; not being able to withstand his arguments, they endeavoured to decry him by their calumnies, spreading a report, that the companions of the great European Bonza cut the throats of little children by night, sucked their blood, and eat their flesh; that the devil had declared, by the mouth of an idol, that these two Europeans were his disciples; and that it was himself who had instructed them in those subtle answers which one of them had returned in their public disputations. Besides this, some of the Bonzas made oath, that they had seen a devil darting flakes of fire like thunder and lightning against the palace of the king, as a judgment, so they called it, against those who had received into the town these preachers of an upstart faith. But perceiving that none of these inventions took place according to their desires, and that the people, instead of giving credit to their projects, made their sport at them, partly in revenge, and partly to verify their visions, they engaged in their interests a lord of the kingdom, who was a great soldier, and a malecontent; him they wrought to take up arms against the king. This nobleman, provoked with the sense of his ill usage at court, and farther heightened by motives of religion and interest, raised an army in less than three weeks time, by the assistance of the Bonzas, and came pouring down like a deluge upon Amanguchi.

The king, who was neither in condition to give him battle, nor provided to sustain a siege, and who feared all things from his subjects, of whom he was extremely hated, lost his courage to that degree, that lie looked on death as his only remedy; for, apprehending above all things the ignominy of falling alive into the power of rebels, pushed on by a barbarous despair, he first murdered his son, and then ript up his own belly with a knife, having beforehand left order with one of his faithful servants to burn their bodies so soon as they were dead, and not to leave so much as their ashes at the disposal of the enemy.

All was put to fire and sword within the city. During this confusion, the soldiers, animated by the Bonzas, searched for Torrez and Fernandez, to have massacred them: And both of them had perished without mercy, if the wife of Neatondono, of whom formerly we have made mention, and who, though continuing a Pagan, yet had so great a kindness for Xavier, that, for his sake, she kept them hidden in her palace till the public tranquillity was restored; for, as these popular commotions are of the nature of storms, which pass away, and that so much the more speedily, as they had been more violent, the town resumed her former countenance in the space of some few days.

The heads of the people being assembled for the election of a new king, by common consent pitched on the brother of the king of Bungo, a young prince, valiant of his person, and born for great atchievements. Immediately they sent a solemn embassy to that prince, and presented to him the crown of Amanguchi. The court of Bungo celebrated the election of the new king with great magnificence, while Xavier was yet residing at Fucheo. The saint himself rejoiced the more at this promotion, because he looked, on this wonderful revolution, which was projected by the Bonzas for the ruin of Christianity, as that which most probably would confirm it. He was not deceived in his conjectures; and, from the beginning, had a kind of assurance, that this turn of state would conduce to the advantage of the faith: for having desired the king of Bungo, that he would recommend to the prince his brother the estate of Christianity in Amanguchi, the king performed so fully that request, that the new monarch promised, on his royal word, to be altogether as favourable to the Christians as the king his brother.

Xavier had been forty days at Fucheo when the Portuguese merchants were in a readiness to set sail for China, according to the measures which they had taken. All necessary preparations being made, he accompanied them to take his leave of the king of Bungo. That prince told the merchants, that he envied them the company of the saint; that, in losing him, he seemed to have lost his father; and that the thought of never seeing him again, most sensibly afflicted him.

Xavier kissed his hand with a profound reverence, and told him, that he would return to wait on his majesty as soon as possibly he could; that he would keep him inviolably in his heart; and that in acknowledgement of all his favours, he should continually send up his prayers to heaven, that God would shower on him his celestial blessings.

The king having taken him aside, as to say something in private to him, Xavier laid hold on that opportunity, and gave him most important counsel for the salvation of his soul. He advised him above all things to bear in mind how soon the greatness and pomp of this present life will vanish away; that life is but short in its own nature; that we scarcely have begun to live, before death comes on; and if he should not die a Christian, nothing less was to be expected than eternal misery; that, on the contrary, whoever, being truly faithful, should persevere in the grace of baptism, should have right to an everlasting inheritance with the Son of God, as one of his beloved children. He desired him also to consider what was become of so many kings and emperors of Japan; what advantage was it to them to have sat upon the throne, and wallowed in pleasures for so many years, being now burning in an abyss of fire, which was to last to all eternity. What madness was it for a man to condemn his own soul to endless punishments, that his body might enjoy a momentary satisfaction; that there was no kingdom, nor empire, though the universal monarchy of the world should be put into the balance, whose loss was not to be accounted gain, if losing them, we acquired an immortal crown in heaven; that these truths, which were indisputable, had been concealed from his forefathers, and even from all the Japonians, by the secret judgment of Almighty God, and for the punishment of their offences; that, for his own particular, he ought to provide for that account, which he was to render of himself, how much more guilty would he appear in God's presence, if the Divine Providence having conducted from the ends of the earth, even into his own palace, a minister of the gospel, to discover to him the paths of happiness, he should yet continue wildered and wandering in the disorders of his life. "Which the Lord avert," continued Xavier; "and may it please him to hear the prayers which day and night I shall pour out for your conversion. I wish it with an unimaginable ardour, and assure you, that wheresoever I shall be, the most pleasing news which can be told me, shall be to hear that the king of Bungo is become a Christian, and that he lives according to the maxims of Christianity."

This discourse made such impressions on the king, and so melted into his heart, that the tears came thrice into his eyes; but those tears were the only product of it at that time, so much that prince, who had renounced those impurities, which are abhorred by nature, was still fastened to some other sensual pleasures. And it was not till after some succeeding years, that, having made more serious reflections on the wholesome admonitions of the saint, he reformed his life for altogether, and in the end received baptism.

Xavier having taken leave of the king, returned to the port of Figen, accompanied by the merchants, who were to set sail within few days after. The departure of the saint was joyful to the Bonzas, but the glory of it was a great abatement to their pleasure. It appeared to them, that all the honours he had received redounded to their shame; and that after such an affront, they should remain eternally blasted in the opinion of the people, if they did not wipe it out with some memorable vengeance. Being met together, to consult on a business which so nearly touched them, they concluded, that their best expedient was to raise a rebellion in Fucheo, as they had done at Amanguchi, and flesh the people by giving up to them the ship of the Portuguese merchants, first to be plundered, then burned, and the proprietors themselves to be destroyed. In consequence of this, if fortune favoured them, to attempt the person of the king, and having dispatched him, to conclude their work by extinguishing the royal line. As Xavier was held in veneration in the town, even amongst the most dissolute idolaters, they were of opinion they did nothing, if they did not ruin his reputation, and make him odious to the people. Thereupon, they set themselves at work to publish, not only what the Bonzas of Amanguchi had written of him, but what they themselves had newly invented; "That he was the most wicked of mankind; an enemy of the living and the dead; his practice being to dig up the carcases of the buried, for the use of his enchantments; and that he had a devil in his mouth, by whose assistance he charmed his audience." They added, "That he had spelled the king, and from thence proceeded these new vagaries in his understanding and all his inclinations; but that, in case he came not out of that fit of madness, it should cost him no less than his crown and life: That Amida and Xaca, two powerful and formidable gods, had sworn to make an example of him and of his subjects; that therefore the people, if they were wise, should prevent betimes the wrath of those offended deities, by revenging their honour on that impostor of a Bonza, and these European pirates who made their idol of him." The people were too well persuaded of the holiness of Xavier, to give credence to such improbable stories as were raised of him; and all the Bonzas could say against him, served only to increase the public hatred against themselves. Thus despairing of success amongst the multitude, they were forced to take another course, to destroy him in the good opinion of the king.

About twelve leagues distant from the town there was a famous monastery of the Bonzas, the superior of which was one Fucarandono, esteemed the greatest scholar and most accomplished in all the learning of Japan: he had read lectures of the mysteries of their divinity for the space of thirty years, in the most renowned university of the kingdom. But however skilled he was in all sciences, his authority was yet greater than his knowledge: men listened to him as to the oracle of Japan, and an implicit faith was given to all he said. The Bonzas of Fucheo were persuaded, that if they could bring him to the town, and set him up against Xavier, in presence of the court, they should soon recover their lost honour; such confidence they had of a certain victory over the European doctor. On this account they writ to Fucarandono, with all the warmness of an earnest invitation, and sent him word. "That if he would give himself the trouble of this little journey, to revenge the injury they had received, they would carry him back in triumph, on their shoulders, to his monastery."

The Bonza, who was full as vain as he was learned, came speedily, attended by six Bonzas, all men of science, but his inferiors and scholars. He entered the palace at that point of time when Xavier, and the Portuguese, had audience of the king, for their last farewell, being to embark the next morning. Before the king had dismissed them, he was informed that Fucarandono desired to kiss his hand, in presence of the Portuguese Bonza. At the name of Fucarandono the king was a little nonplused, and stood silent for some time, suspecting that he came to challenge Father Xavier to a disputation, and devising in himself some means of breaking off this troublesome affair, as he afterwards acknowledged. For whatever good opinion he had of the saint's abilities, yet he could not think him strong enough to encounter so formidable an adversary; and therefore, out of his kindness to him, was not willing to expose him to a disgrace in public. Xavier, who perceived the king's perplexity, and imagined from whence it might proceed, begged earnestly of his majesty to give the Bonza leave of entrance, and also free permission of speaking: "for, as to what concerns me," said the Father, "you need not give yourself the least disquiet: the law I preach is no earthly science, taught in any of our universities, nor a human invention; it is a doctrine altogether heavenly, of which God himself is the only teacher. Neither all the Bonzas of Japan, nor yet all the scholars extant in the world, can prevail against it, any more than the shadows of the night against the beams of the rising sun."

The king, at the request of Xavier, gave entrance to the Bonza. Fucarandono, after the three usual reverences to the king, seated himself by Xavier; and after he had fixed his eyes earnestly upon him, "I know not," said he, with an overweaning look, "if thou knowest me; or, to speak more properly, if thou rememberest me." "I remember not," said Xavier, "that I have ever seen you." Then the Bonza, breaking out into a forced laughter, and turning to his fellows, "I shall have but little difficulty in overcoming this companion, who has conversed with me a hundred times, and yet would make us believe he had never seen me." Then looking on Xavier, with a scornful smile, "Hast thou none of those goods yet remaining," continued he, "which thou soldest me at the port of Frenajoma?" "In truth," replied Xavier, with a sedate and modest countenance, "I have never been a merchant in all my life, neither have I ever been at the port of Frenajoma." "What a beastly forgetfulness is this of thine," pursued the Bonza, with an affected wonder, and keeping up his bold laughter, "how canst thou possibly forget it?" "Bring it back to my remembrance," said Xavier mildly, "you, who have so much more wit, and a memory happier than mine." "That shall be done," rejoined the Bonza, proud of the commendations which the saint had given him; "it is now just fifteen hundred years since thou and I, who were then merchants, traded at Frenajoma, and where I bought of thee a hundred bales of silk, at an easy pennyworth: dost thou yet remember it?" The saint, who perceived whither the discourse tended, asked him, very civilly, "of what age he might be?" "I am now two-and-fifty," said Fucarandono. "How can it then be," replied Xavier, "that you were a merchant fifteen hundred years ago, that is fifteen ages, when yet you have been in the world, by your own confession, but half an age? and how comes it that you and I then trafficked together at Frenajoma, since the greatest part of you Bonzas maintain, that Japan was a desart, and uninhabited at that time?" "Hear me," said the Bonza, "and listen to me as an oracle; I will make thee confess that we have a greater knowledge of things past, than thou and thy fellows have of the present.

Thou art then to understand, that the world had no beginning, and that men, properly speaking, never die: the soul only breaks loose from the body in which it was confined, and while that body is rotting under ground, is looking out for another fresh and vigorous habitation, wherein we are born again, sometimes in the nobler, sometimes in the more imperfect sex, according to the various constellations of the heavens, and the different aspects of the moon. These alterations in our birth produce the like changes in our fortune. Now, it is the recompence of those who have lived virtuously, to preserve a constant memory of all the lives which they have passed through, in so many ages; and to represent themselves, entirely, such as they have been from all eternity, under the figure of a prince, of a merchant, of a scholar, of a soldier, and so many other various forms: on the contrary, they who, like thee, are so ignorant of their own affairs, as not to understand who, or what they have been formerly, during those infinite revolutions of ages, shew that their crimes have deserved death, as often as they have lost the remembrance of their lives in every change."

The Portuguese, from whose relation we have the knowledge of what is above written, and who was present at the dispute, as he himself informs us, in his book of Travels, gives us no account of the answers which were made by Xavier. "I have neither knowledge nor presumption enough," says he, "to relate those subtile and solid reasons, with which he confuted the mad imaginations of the Bonza." We only have learnt from this Portuguese, that Fucarandono was put to silence upon the point in question, and that, a little to save his reputation, he changed the subject, but to no purpose, for even there too he was confounded; for, forgetting those decencies which even nature prescribes to men, and common custom has taught us in civil conversation, he advanced infamous propositions, which cannot be related without offending modesty; and these he maintained with a strange impudence, against the reasons of the Father, though the king and the noble auditory thought the Christian arguments convincing. But the Bonza still flying out into passion, and continuing to rail and bawl aloud, as if he were rather in a bear-garden than at a solemn disputation, one of the lords there present said, smiling, to him, "If your business be fighting, why did not you go to the kingdom of Amanguchi, when they were in civil wars? there you might have found some one or other with whom you might have gone to hard-heads. What make you here, where all things are at quiet? But, if you came hither to dispute, why do you not carry on your argument with mildness and good manners, according to the copy which is set you by the European Bonza?"

This sharp raillery had no effect upon Fucarandono: he replied to the lord with so much impudence and haughtiness, that the king, whose patience was tired with so much insolence, caused him to be put out of the hall, saying, "That his coat of a Bonza was the only protection of his life." The affront which Fucarandono had received, was interpreted by the Bonzas as an injury done to the gods, and as such they declared it to the people, saying, "That religion was profaned, and that the king, the court, and the whole nation, had incurred the wrath of heaven." Upon which pretence they shut up the temples, and would neither offer sacrifice nor accept of alms. The multitude, which had already been disposed to rise, began to get together, and had certainly taken arms, if the king, by good management, had not somewhat calmed their spirits.

In the mean time the Portuguese, not believing themselves to be secure against the rage of a superstitious people, and having just grounds of apprehending that the affront which Fucarandono had received might be revenged on their persons, returned with all expedition to their ship, designing to set sail with the benefit of the first fair wind. At their departure from the town, they intreated Father Xavier to follow them; but he could not resolve to run off like a fugitive, or to forsake those new Christians whose ruin had been sworn by the Heathen priests. How eager soever those merchants were to get out of a country where their lives were in so little safety, yet their fear for Father Xavier kept them lingering there some days longer; they deputed the captain of the vessel to him, who was to desire him, in their name, to make haste to them. Edward de Gama, after a long inquiry, found him at last in a poor cabin, with eight Christians, who, having been the most zealous in opposition of the Bonzas, were in reason to expect the more cruel usage at their hands, and were content to offer up their lives, provided they might die in the arms of the man of God.

The captain urged him with the strongest reasons which he could invent, and set before him all the dangers which attended him; that, being at the mercy of the Bonzas, his death was inevitable; and that the means of escaping would be lost when once the tempest should begin to rise. The Father, far from yielding to these arguments, was offended at the captain and the merchants for desiring to hinder him from the crown of martyrdom which he had taken so long a journey to obtain. "My brother," said he to Gama, with a fervour which expressed the holy ambition of his soul, "how happy should I be, if I could receive what you reckon a disgrace, but what I account a sovereign felicity! but I am unworthy of that favour from Almighty God; yet I will not render myself more unworthy of it, which assuredly I should if I embarked with you: For what scandal should I give, by flying hence, to my new converts? Might they not take occasion from it to violate their promises to God, when they should find me wanting to the duty of my ministry? If, in consideration of that money which you have received from your passengers, you think yourself obliged to secure them from the clanger which threatens them, and, for that reason, have summoned them on board, ought not I, by a stronger motive, to guard my flock, and die with them for the sake of a God who is infinitely good, and who has redeemed me at the price of his own life, by suffering for me on the cross? Ought not I to seal it with my blood, and to publish it by my death, that all men are bound to sacrifice their blood and lives to this God of mercies?"

This generous answer wrought so much upon the captain, that, instead of doubling his solicitations on Father Xavier, he resolved to partake his fortune, and not to leave him. Having taken up this resolution, without farther care of what might happen to his ship, or what became of his own person, and accounting all his losses for a trifle while he enjoyed the company of Xavier, he returned indeed to his merchants, but it was only to declare to them the determination of the Father, and his own also; that in case they would not stay, he gave up his vessel to them. They were supplied with mariners and soldiers, and had plentiful provisions laid in, both of food and ammunition for war. They might go at their pleasure wheresoever they designed; but, for his own particular, he was resolved to live and die with the man of God.

Not a man of them but subscribed to the opinion of the captain; and they were one and all for following his example, and the fortune of the saint. Suddenly they put into the port again, for the ship had lain off at a good distance, for fear of some attempt which might be made upon it from the town; soldiers were left for its defence, and the captain and merchants came in company to Fucheo. Their return gave new vigour to the Christians, and amazed the people, who could not but wonder that so poor a man should be had in such esteem by his countrymen, that they chose rather to run the hazard of their wealth, and of their lives, than to lose the sight of him.

This prompt return broke all the measures of the Bonzas, whose courage had been swelled by the flight of Gama, which had given them the opportunity of making their cabals against the Christians; but when they found that those designs might possibly miscarry, and that, on the other side, they were again defied to a new conference on the subject of religion, they thought good to accommodate themselves a little to the times, and to renew the dispute betwixt Xavier and Fucarandono before the court. To seem beforehand with the Christians, they made it their own petition to the king, who freely-granted it, but on some conditions, which were to be observed on either side. These articles were,--"That noise was to be banished in dispute; no flying out to be permitted, nor any provocation by sharp language: That the arguments and answers were to be couched in precise terms, and drawn up in form of a just dispute, as it should be agreed by the judges, who were to moderate: That the approbation of the audience was to decide the victory: That if the point were doubtful betwixt them, the suffrages should be taken, and that he should be judged to have reason on his side who had the majority of voices: Lastly, That whoever was willing to enter himself a Christian, might profess his faith without hinderance or molestation from any man." These conditions were too reasonable to be accepted by the Bonzas. They appealed from the king to the king better informed, and told him boldly, that, in matters of religion, it was not just that the profane (that is the laity) should be umpires; but when they found the king resolved to maintain his point, they quitted theirs. The next morning was agreed on for the conference, and some of the most understanding persons of the court were appointed judges. Fucarandono made his appearance at the time, attended by three thousand Bonzas. The king, who was either apprehensive of his own safety amongst that religious rabble, or feared, at least, that some disorder might ensue, permitted hut four of all the squadron to enter; and sent word to the others, for their satisfaction, that it was not honourable for so many to appear against a single man.

Xavier, who had notice sent him from the king, that his adversary was on the place of combat, came, accompanied with the chiefest of the Portuguese, all richly habited, who appeared as his officers, and paid him all possible respect, attending him bare-headed, and never speaking to him but on the knee. The Bonzas were ready to burst with envy, beholding the pompous entry of their antagonist; and that which doubled their despite was, that they overheard the lords saying to one another,--"Observe this poor man, of whom so many ridiculous pictures have been made to us; would to God our children might be like him, on condition the Bonzas might say as bad of them as they speak of him! Our own eyes are witnesses of the truth; and the palpable lies which they have invented, show what credit is to be given to them." The king took pleasure in those discourses, and told those lords, that the Bonzas had assured him that he should be sick at heart at the first appearance of Father Francis. He acknowledged he was almost ready to have believed them; but being now convinced, by his own experience, he found that the character of an ambassador from heaven, and interpreter of the gods, was not inconsistent with a liar. Fucarandono, who heard all these passages from his place, took them for so many ill omens; and, turning to his four associates, told them, "that he suspected this day would be yet more unsuccessful to them than the last."

The king received Father Xavier with great civility; and, after he had talked with him sometime in private, very obligingly ordered him to begin the disputation. When they had all taken their places, the saint demanded of the Bonza, as the king had desired him, "For what reason the Christian religion ought not to be received in Japan?" The Bonza, whose haughtiness was much abated, replied modestly, "Because it is a new law, in all things opposite to the ancient established laws of the empire; and that it seems made on purpose to render the faithful servants of the gods contemptible,[1] as annulling the privileges which the Cubosamas of former ages had conferred on the Bonzas, and teaches that out of the society of Christians there is no salvation: but especially," added he, a little kindling in the face, "because it presumes to maintain, that the holy Amida and Xaca, Gizon and Canon, are in the bottomless pit of smoke, condemned to everlasting punishment, and delivered up in prey to the dragon of the house of night." After he had thus spoken, the Bonza held his peace; and Xavier, who had received a sign from the king to make reply, said, at the beginning of his discourse, "that seeing Fucarandono had mingled many things together, it was reasonable, for the better clearing of the difficulties, to tie him up to one single proposition, which was not to be left until it was evacuated, and plainly found to be either true or false." All agreed this was fair; and Fucarandono himself desired Xavier to shew cause, why he and his companions spoke evil of the deities of the country.

The saint replied, "That he gave not to idols the name of gods, because they were unworthy of it; and that so sacred a title was only proper to the Sovereign Lord, who had created heaven and earth. Then he proceeded to discourse of the Divine Being, and described those properties which are known to us by the light of nature; that is to say, his independence, his eternity, his omnipotence, his wisdom, goodness, and justice, without circumscription. He made out, that those infinite perfections could not be comprehended by any created understanding, how refined soever. And thus having filled his auditors with a vast idea of the Deity, he demonstrated, that the idols of Japan, who, according to the Japonians themselves, had been men, subject to the common laws of time and nature, were not to be accounted gods; and, at the most, were only to be reverenced as philosophers, lawgivers, and princes, but not in the least as immortal powers, since the date both of their birth and death was registered in the public monuments: That, if their works were duly considered, they were yet less to be accounted for omnipotent: That having not been able, after their decease, to preserve their stately palaces and magnificent sepulchres from decay, there was no appearance that they had built the fabric of the universe, or could maintain it in its present state. Lastly, that this appertained alone to the true God, who is worshipped by the Christians; and that, considering the beauty of the heavens, the fruitfulness of the earth, and the order of the seasons, we might conclude, that he only, who is a spirit, eternal, all-powerful, and all-wise, could be the creator and absolute commander of the world." As soon as Xavier had concluded, the whole assembly cried out, that he spoke reason; and the judges immediately pronounced, as a manifest truth, that the pagods were not gods. Fucarandono would have replied, but the general cry gave it for a cause decided; and the king imposed silence on the Bonza, according to the articles of agreement.

Thus the Bonza passed on to another question in his own despite; and asked Father Xavier, "Why he allowed not of those bills of exchange which they gave in favour of the dead, since the rich found their account in them, and that they had their return of their money, with usury, in heaven?" The Father answered, "That the right we had to a better world was founded not on those deceitful letters, but on the good works which are practised with the faith and doctrine which he preached: That he who inspired it into our souls was Jesus Christ, the true and only Son of God, who was crucified for the salvation of sinners; and that they who preserved that living faith till death should certainly obtain eternal happiness: That for what remained, this holy law was free from worldly interest, and that it excluded not from heaven either the poor or women; that even poverty, which is patiently endured, was a means of gaining the kingdom of heaven; and that the weaker sex had greater advantages than ours, by reason of that modesty and piety which is almost inherent in their nature." The applause which followed this discourse was general; only Fucarandono and his companions, who had not wherewith to reply, and yet were too obstinate to recant, kept a discontented silence. It was judged that Xavier's opinion was the more reasonable, and the dispute adjourned to the day following.

These ill successes would have driven the Bonza to despair, if his presumption had not kept up his spirits. He returned at the time appointed; but, as if he distrusted his own strength, as presuming as he was, he brought with him six other Bonzas, the most learned amongst them, and chosen out of all their sects, not to be bare spectators of the combat, but to relieve each other, and to charge every one in his turn. At the first they propounded very subtile questions concerning the mysteries of our faith. Father Xavier was surprised at the hearing of them; and as those questions, which are not reported by the Portuguese particularly, were in all likelihood above the knowledge of the Pagans, he was almost induced to think the devil had suggested them; at the least he acknowledged, that to solve them he needed an extraordinary assistance from above, and desired the Portuguese to second him with their prayers during the disputation. Whether he received that supernatural assistance, or that those difficulties did not so much surpass his knowledge as he had thought, he answered to the satisfaction of the whole assembly. When judgment was passed that those questions were fully decided, one of the Bonzas, whose heart was wholly set on riches, and who believed that there was nothing more charming in the world than gold and silver, undertook to prove, that God was an enemy to the poor: "For," said the Bonza, "since he denies them those blessings which he bountifully gives the rich, and, in causing them to be born in a mean condition, exposes them to all the miseries and ignominy of life, is it not a sign, that he has neither kindness nor value for them?"

Xavier denied the consequence of that proposition; and argued both from the principles of morality, which look on riches as false goods, and out of the grounds of Christianity, which, in respect of salvation, count them true evils. He reasoned thereupon so justly, and withal so clearly, that his adversaries were forced to give up the cause, according to the relation of the Portuguese, who were witness of it. After this they advanced such extravagant and mad propositions, that they cost the Father no trouble to confute, for they destroyed themselves. But the most pleasant part of this day's work was, that the seven Bonzas not being able to agree on some points of doctrine, fell foul on each other, and wrangled with so much heat and violence, that at last they came to downright railing, and had proceeded to blows, if the king had not interposed his authority, which frightened them into quiet. This was the end of that day's disputation; and nothing more confirmed the minds of the auditors on the side of Xavier, than to see his adversaries at civil wars amongst themselves.

The king going out of his palace the next morning, with a great attendance, to walk in the town, according to his custom, and passing by the house where the Portuguese lodged, sent a message to the holy man, desiring him to come to his gardens, where he would show him sport, provided he came well armed, for he was to kill, with one blow, two kites or puttocks, at the least, out of those seven which yesterday endeavoured to have pulled out his eyes Xavier, who easily understood his meaning, came out to pay him his respects, and to acknowledge the honour which was done him. The king took him by the hand, and led him to the palace amidst the acclamations of the people. The seven Bonzas, represented by the seven kites, were already in the hall, with a confirmed impudence, and so much the more haughty, as they had the less reason so to be; according to the usual character of vain and self-opinioned men.

The first step they made in order to a new dispute, was to enter a protestation, in writing, against the judgment and proceedings of the former day; wherein they declared void the sentence of the umpires, appealed from them, and set forth new objections and difficulties upon the questions formerly debated. The king answered himself, that those points which had been decided had no need of any farther explanation, and that they were already tied up by the conditions of the conference, which both parties had accepted. He added, that Father Xavier was ready to go on ship-board, and that it was not reasonable to lose time by fruitless repetitions, but if they had any new questions to propose, let them begin, and they should be heard; if not, they had free licence to depart.

This positive answer constrained them to supersede their writing, and to pitch on other matters. Fucarandono affecting an air of devotion and modesty, asked, Why the Christians gave obscene names to the saints in Paradise, whensoever they invoked them in their public prayers; giving him to understand, that _sancte_, in the Japonian language, signified something too dishonest to be spoken. The Father declared, that the word in Latin had only a pure and pious meaning. Nevertheless, that it might not give scandal, nor pollute the imagination of the Japonians by an equivocal sound, he ordered the new Christians, from thenceforward, to use the word _beate_ instead of it; and to say, _Beate Petre, Beate Pauls_, in the room of _Sancte Petre, Sancte Paule_. Concerning the name of God, the Bonzas would also have fastened a quarrel on the Father; because _dajus_, in their tongue, signifies a _lie_. He laughed at this ridiculous exception, which was in effect a mere jingle; and the judges and audience concluded it to be no more.

Three other points, on which the Bonzas more insisted, were thought to be more solid, and of greater consequence. The first was proposed in this manner: "Either God foresaw that Lucifer and his accomplices would revolt, and be damned eternally, or he foresaw it not. If he had no foresight of it, his prescience did not extend so far as you would have us to believe; but if he foresaw it, the consequence is worse, that he did not hinder this revolt, which had prevented their damnation. Your God being, as you say, the fountain of all goodness, must now be acknowledged by you for the original cause of so much evil. Thus you are forced," said the Bonza, "to confess, either ignorance or malice in your God."

Xavier was so much amazed to hear a Bonza reasoning like a schoolman, that turning to Edward de Gama, who was by him, "See," says he softly in Portuguese, that he might not be understood by the Japonians, "see how the devil has sharpened the wit of these his advocates." In the mean time, one of the Bonzas coming up to the charge, said, according to the same principle, "That if God had foreknown that Adam would sin, and cast down, together with himself, his whole progeny into an abyss of miseries, why did he create him? At least, when our first father was ready to eat of the forbidden fruit, why did not that omnipotent hand, which gave him being, annihilate him at the same moment?"

A third Bonza, taking the word, urged him with another argument: "If our evil be as ancient as the world," said he, subtilely, "why did God let so many ages pass away without giving it a remedy? Why did he not descend from heaven, and make himself man, to redeem human kind, by his death and sufferings, as soon as ever man was guilty? To what degree did those first men sin, to become unworthy of such a favour? And what has been the merit of their descendants, that they should be more favourably treated than their predecessors?"

These difficulties did not appear new to Xavier, who was very learned, and who had read whatsoever the fathers and school divines had said concerning them. He answered, without doubt, according to their doctrine; but the Portuguese, who relates the objections, durst not undertake to write the solutions of them, if we will believe himself, because they surpassed the understanding of a merchant. The Bonzas made many replies, to all which the Father gave the proper solutions in few words, and according to the rules of the schools. Whether it were that they comprehended not the solutions, or were it out of their hot-headedness, or that they seemed not to understand them to avoid the shame of being baffled, they yielded not, but cried out louder than before. As they disputed more for victory than truth, they denied all things, even to those principles which are self-evident; pretending thereby to encumber their opponent. Xavier knew what use to make of his advantages; he turned the confusion upon them, by reducing them to manifest contradictions, from whence they could never disengage themselves; so that, instead of answering, they gnashed their teeth, foamed at mouth, and stamped and stared about like madmen. The king, whose indignation was raised by seeing the obstinacy of the Bonzas, said to them, in a kind of passion, "As for myself, as far as I am capable of judging, I find that Father Xavier speaks good sense, and that you know not what you say. You should either understand better, or be less violent than you appear, to judge of these truths without prejudice. But, if the divine law be wanting to you, make use of your reason, which, of itself, will let you see, that you are not to deny things which are evident, nor to bark like dogs." After these words he rose from his seat, and, taking Xavier by the hand, brought him back to his own lodging. The people, who followed in great multitudes, made loud acclamations, and the streets rung with the praises of the holy man: While the Bonzas, mad with rage and envy, cried out aloud, "May the fire of heaven fall down upon a prince, who suffers himself to be so easily seduced by this foreign magician!"

Thus concluded the disputations which he had with Fucarandono and the Bonzas. They were very glorious for him, and for the religion which he preached, but brought not forth the expected fruit amongst the idolaters who were present at them; for neither the Portuguese author, whom we have frequently cited, nor other historians of the Father's life, make mention of any new conversions which were made; and it affords great occasion for our wonder, that the lords of the court, who so much approved the doctrine of Christianity, should still continue in the practice of idolatry, and of their vices, if it were not always to be remembered, that, in conversion, the light of the understanding avails nothing unless the heart be also touched, and that the philosophers, of whom St Paul speaks, "having known God, did not glorify him as God." Nevertheless we may probably believe, that these disputations in progress of time failed not of their due; effect; and it is also probable, that they were the seed of those wonderful conversions which were made in following years.

Father Xavier went the next morning to take his last farewell of the king, who was more kind to him than ever, and parted from Japan the same day, which was Nov. 20th, in the year 1551, having continued in that country two years and four months.

Not long before, Clod had made known to his servant, that the town of Malacca was besieged by sea and land; and that the king of Jentana, a Saracen, was personally before it, with an army of twelve thousand men: That neither the conduct of the governor, Don Pedro de Silva, nor the succours of Don Fernandez Carvalio, had been able to defend it against the attempts of the barbarians; that the Javans, a fierce and warlike people, had mastered that place; that of three hundred Portuguese, who were within it, above an hundred had been put to the sword, and the rest of them had only escaped by retiring into the fortress. In short, that Malacca was now become a place of horror, and that the enemy, wearied with the slaughter, had reserved many thousands of the inhabitants for the chain. The saint informed Gama, and the Portuguese of the ship, of these sad tidings, before they left the port, and declared to them, that the sins of that corrupt city had drawn down the curse of God upon it, as he had foretold and threatened; but he desired them, at the same time, to supplicate the Father of all Mercies, for the appeasing of his divine justice, and he himself prayed earnestly in their behalf. Besides the two Japanners, Matthew and Bernard, who had constantly followed the Father, and would never forsake him, an ambassador from the king of Bungo embarked with him in the same vessel. The business of this embassy was to seek the friendship of the viceroy of the Indies, and to obtain a preacher from him, who might finish the conversion of that kingdom, in the room of Father Xavier.

They sailed along the coasts for the space of six days, and the navigation was prosperous till they made an island belonging to the king of Minaco, called Meleitor; from whence, crossing a strait, they put out into the main ocean. At that time the change of the moon altered the weather, and there blew a furious south wind, so that the pilot, with all his art, could not bear up against it. The tempest carried the ship into a sea unknown to the Portuguese; and the face of heaven was so black with clouds, that, during five days and nights, there was no appearance of sun or stars; insomuch that the mariners-were not able to take the elevation of the pole, and consequently not to know whereabouts they were. One day, towards the evening, the wind redoubled with so much fury, that the vessel had not power to break the waves, so high they went, and came on with so much violence. In this terrible conjuncture they thought fit to cut down the forecastle, that the ship might work the better; after which, they bound the sloop which followed with thick cables to the ship: but night coming on while they were thus employed, and being very dark, abundance of rain also falling at the same time, which increased the tempest, they could not draw out of the sloop five Portuguese and ten Indians, as well as slaves and mariners, which were in her.

Those of the ship had neither comfort nor hope remaining, but in the company and assistance of Father Xavier. He exhorted them to lament their sins, thereby to appease the wrath of God; and he himself poured forth whole showers of tears before the face of the Almighty. When night was now at the darkest, a lamentable cry was heard, as of people just upon the brink of perishing, and calling out for succour. The noise came from the sloop, which the violence of the winds had torn off from the vessel, and which the waves were hurrying away. As soon as the captain had notice of it, he ordered the pilot to turn towards those poor creatures, without considering, that, by his endeavour of saving his nephew, Alphonso Calvo, who was one of the five Portuguese in the sloop, the ship must certainly be lost, and himself with her. In effect, as it was difficult to steer the ship, when they would have turned her towards the sloop, she came across betwixt two mountains of water, which locked her up betwixt them; one of those waves fell upon the poop, and washed over the deck; and then it was that the whole company thought their business was done, and nothing but cries and lamentations were heard on every side. Xavier, who was at his prayers in the captain's cabin, ran out towards the noise, and saw a miserable object,--the vessel ready to bulge, the seamen, the soldiers, and the passengers, all tumbling in confusion on each other, deploring their unhappy destiny, and expecting nothing but present death. Then the holy man, lifting up his eyes and hands to heaven, said thus aloud, in the transport of his fervour, "O Jesus, thou love of my soul, succour us, I beseech thee, by those five wounds, which, for our sakes, thou hast suffered on the cross!" At that instant the ship, which already was sinking under water, raised herself aloft, without any visible assistance, and gained the surface of the waves. The mariners, encouraged by so manifest a miracle, so ordered the sails, that they had the wind in poop, and pursued their course.

In the mean time the sloop was vanished out of sight, and no man doubted but she was swallowed by the Waves. The captain lamented for his nephew, the rest shed tears for their lost companions. As for the Father, his greatest affliction was for two Mahometan slaves, whom he could not convert to Christianity: he sighed in thinking of their deplorable condition, but, in the midst of these anxious thoughts, entering into himself, or rather wholly recollecting himself in God, it came into his mind to intercede with Heaven for the protection of the sloop, in case it were not already lost. In this he followed the inspiration of the Holy Spirit, and his prayer was not yet ended when he perceived that it was heard: insomuch, that turning towards Edward de Gama, who was oppressed with sadness, "Afflict not yourself, my brother," said he with a cheerful countenance; "before three days are ended, the daughter will come back and find the mother." The captain was so buried in his grief, that he saw too little probability in what the Father said, to found any strong belief upon it; which notwithstanding, at break of day, he sent one up to the scuttle, to see if any thing were within ken; but nothing was discovered, saving the sea, which was still troubled and white with foam. The Father, who had been in private at his devotions, came out two hours after, with the same cheerfulness upon, his countenance; and having given the good day to the captain and pilot, and six or seven Portuguese who were in company, he enquired "if they had not yet seen the chalop?" they answered they had not: and, because he desired that some one might again get up to the scuttle, one of the Portuguese, called Pedro Veglio, replied thus bluntly, "Yes, Father, the chalop will return, but not until another be lost:" he meant that it was impossible the same chalop should come again.

Xavier mildly reprehended Veglio for his little faith, and told him nothing was impossible to God. "The confidence which I have in the Divine mercy," said he, "gives me hope, that they whom I have put under the protection of the Holy Virgin, and for whose sake I have vowed to say three masses to our Lady of the Mountain, shall not perish." After this he urged Gama to send up to the scuttle for discovery: Gama, to satisfy the man of God, went 'up himself with a seaman, and after having looked round him for the space of half an hour, neither he nor the other could see any thing. In the mean time Xavier, whose stomach was turned with the tossing of the ship, and who had been two days and three nights without eating, was taken with a violent head-ach, and such a giddiness, that he could scarcely stand. One of the Portuguese merchants, called Ferdinand Mendez Pinto, desired him to repose a little while, and offered him his cabin; Xavier, who, by the spirit of mortification, usually lay upon the deck, accepted his courtesy; and desired this further favour, that the servant of this merchant, who was a Chinese, might watch before the door, that none might interrupt his rest.

The intention of the Father was not to give the least refreshment to his body; he set himself again to prayers, and it was affirmed by the Chinese servant, that from seven in the morning, when he retired, he had been constantly on his knees until the evening, groaning in the agony of his spirit, and shedding tears. He came out from his retirement after sunset, and once more enquired of the pilot, if they had not seen the chalop, which could not possibly be far distant. The pilot replied, that it was in vain to think of her, and that it was impossible for her to resist so furious a tempest; but in case that, by some wonderful accident, or rather by some miracle, she had been preserved, she must of necessity be at fifty leagues distance from the ship. It is the propriety of Christian confidence to remain unshaken and secure, when human reason leaves us destitute of hope. The Saint acknowledged the pilot to have spoken judiciously, and yet doubted not but the chalop would return. He constantly maintained that she could not be far off, and pressed him to send up to the scuttle before the dusk. The pilot, less out of complaisance to the Father, than out of his desire to undeceive him, went up himself, and could discover nothing. Xavier, without any regard to the affirmation of the pilot, instantly desired the captain to lower the sails, that the chalop might more easily come up with the ship. The authority of the holy man carried it, above the reasons of the pilot; the sail-yard was lowered, and a stop was made for almost three hours: but at length the passengers grew weary, as not being able any longer to bear the rolling of the ship, and one and all cried out to sail. The Father upbraided them with their impatience; and himself laid hold on the sail-yard, to hinder the seamen from spreading the sails; and leaning his head over it, broke out into sighs and sobbings, and poured out a deluge of tears.

He raised himself a little after, and keeping his eyes fixed on heaven, yet wet with tears, "O Jesus, my Lord and my God," said he, "I beseech thee, by thy holy passion, to have pity on those poor people, who are coming to us, through the midst of so many dangers." He composed himself, after he had uttered this, and continued leaning on the sail-yard, wholly silent for some time, as if he had been sleeping.

Then a little child, who was sitting at the foot of the mast, cried out on the sudden, "A miracle, a miracle, behold the chalop!" All the company gathered together at the cry, and plainly perceived the chalop within musket-shot. Nothing but shouts and exclamations of joy were heard, while she drew still nearer and nearer to the vessel. In the meantime, the greatest part fell down at the feet of Father Xavier, and, confessing they were sinners, unworthy the company of a man so holy, asked him pardon for their unbelief. But the Father, in great confusion for being treated in this manner, escaped out of their hands as soon as possibly he could, and shut himself up within the cabin, in conclusion, the chalop came up with the ship; and it was observed, that though the waves were in great agitation, she came right forward, without the least tossing, and stopped of herself. It was also taken notice of, that she continued without any motion till the fifteen men which she carried were entered the ship, and that the seamen had fastened her behind the poop. When they had embraced those men, whom so lately they had given for lost, every one was desirous of knowing their adventures; and were much surprised to understand, that they were come through the midst of the most horrible tempest which was ever seen, without any apprehension either of drowning or losing of their way; because, said they, Father Francis was our pilot, and his presence freed us even from the shadow of any fear. When the ship's company assured them, that the Father had been always with themselves, those of the chalop, who had beheld him constantly steering it, could not believe what had been told them. After some little dispute on the matter of fact, both sides concluded, that the saint had been at the same time in two places; and this evident miracle made such an impression on the minus of the two Saracen slaves who had been in the chalop, that they abjured their Mahometanism. The impatience of these fifteen men to behold their miraculous steersman, who had so happily brought them to the ship, and who vanished from their eyes at the same moment when they joined her, obliged Xavier to come out and shew himself. They would have saluted him as their protector, by prostrating themselves before him, but he would not suffer it: declaring to them, that it was the hand of the Lord, and not his, which had delivered them from shipwreck. At the same time, he rendered public thanks to God for so eminent a favour, and ordered the pilot to pursue his voyage, assuring him that he should have a good wind immediately. The pilot's experience of the sea did not promise him this sudden change; but this late deliverance of the chalop quickened his belief in the Father's words; and it was not long before he understood, that He, who commands the winds and seas, had authorised the holy man to make that prediction.

The sails were scarcely spread, when a north wind arising, the air cleared up, and the sea was immediately calmed. So that in thirteen days sailing, they arrived at the port of Sancian, where the Portuguese merchants of the ship had traffic. As the season of sailing in those seas was already almost past, there were remaining but two ships of the Indies in port, one of which belonged to James de Pereyra. The ship of Edward de Gama not being in condition to go on directly for Malacca without stopping by the way, and having need of refreshment at Sian, the saint went into the ship of his friend Pereyra. It was wonderful, that at the same moment when he passed into that vessel, the wind, which for the space of fifteen days had blown at north, which was full in their faces who were going for the Indies, came about on the sudden; so that the day following, which was the last of the year 1551, they set sail again. Another ship, which was waiting also for a wind, set out in their company; but that vessel found afterwards to her cost, that she carried not the apostle of the Indies.

Before they put to sea, Xavier discoursing with the pilot concerning the dangers of the ocean, (it was the same pilot who had brought him from Japan, whose name was Francis D'Aghiar,) foretold him, that he should not end his days upon the water; and that no vessel wherein he should be should suffer shipwreck, were the tempest never so outrageous. D'Aghiar was possessed with so firm a belief of what the Father told him, and afterwards found the effect of it so manifest on various occasions, that, without observing either winds or seasons, he often put to sea in an old crazy vessel, ill provided; insomuch, that they who were ignorant of the secret cause of this his confidence, took him for a rash presuming man, and of little understanding in sea affairs.

Once, amongst many other times, he gave a demonstration how much he relied on the promise of the saint, and that was, in going from Tenasserim to the kingdom of Pegu, in a light barque, which was quite decayed, and out of order. A tempest rising in the midst of his voyage, dashed against the rocks, and split in pieces some great vessels, which were following the barque of D'Aghiar. She alone seemed to defy the rocks; and while the sea was in this horrible confusion, the pilot sat singing at his ease, as if the waters had been hushed beneath him. A passenger, who shook with fear, demanded of him, "With what courage he could sing, when he was just upon the brink of death?" "It is because I fear nothing," replied Aghiar: "And I should fear nothing," added he, "though the waves should mount as high again as now we see them, and my barque were also made of glass; for the Father Master Francis has assured me, that I should not die upon the seas, in whatsoever vessel I should go." Some Saracens who were in the barque, and who heard these sayings of the pilot, were so moved with this continued miracle, that they vowed to become Christians so soon as ever they should come on shore; and they complied religiously with their promise. The barque casting anchor at Tanar, they received baptism at that place; so much the more persuaded both of the truth of the miracle, and of the Christian faith, because they saw before their eyes, upon the coast, the wrecks of other vessels, which were floating round about it.

The conversations which Xavier had with Pereyra during all the navigation, were almost wholly relating to Japan and China. The Father told his friend what progress the faith had made in little time in the kingdoms of Saxuma, of Amanguchi, and of Bungo; and what hopes he had conceived, to convert all those islands with great ease, when once the Chinese should be brought to acknowledge Jesus Christ. And on that motive, he had fixed his resolution to go to China; that his return to the Indies was only in order to this intended voyage, after he had regulated the affairs of the Society at Goa; that, on this account, he had brought with him from Japan the translation of his catechism into the Chinese language, by the benefit of which he hoped to overcome the first difficulties, which in matters of conversion are still the greatest. Some Portuguese who were in the same vessel, and were well acquainted with the government of China, thought this proposition of the Father not a little extravagant. They told him, that, besides the ill understanding which was betwixt China and Portugal, it was forbidden to strangers on pain of death, or of perpetual imprisonment, to set a foot upon that kingdom; and that the merchants of their nation, who had stolen thither for the benefit of trade, having been discovered, some of them had lost their heads, others had been put in irons, and cast into dungeons, there to lie and rot for the remainder of their lives. They added, notwithstanding, that there was a safe and certain way of entering into China, provided there was a solemn embassy sent to the emperor of that country from the king of Portugal. But since that could not be compassed without a prodigious expence, if nothing else were to be considered but only the presents for the emperor and his ministers of state, in all probability the viceroy of the Indies would not burden himself with the cost of such an enterprize, at a time when he had enough to do to defray more necessary expences.

These difficulties began to startle Father Xavier, when James Pereyra, who, under the habit of a merchant, had the heart of an emperor, and the zeal of an apostle, made offer of his ship, and all his goods, for the promoting of the expedient which had been mentioned. The Father accepted of his generous proffer with transports of joy, and engaged, on his side, to procure the embassy of China for his friend. Pereyra, who had received intelligence of the siege of Malacca, told the saint, "He apprehended lest an embargo might be put upon his ship, for the immediate service of the town." Xavier, to whom God had revealed the deliverance of Malacca, and to whose prayers that deliverance had perhaps been granted, cheered up his friend, with this assurance, "That when the fortress was just upon the point of yielding, the infidels had been struck with a panic fear, and fled away, so that the town was wholly free."

Percyra had yet another thing which troubled him, concerning the voyage which Father Xavier had to make before that of China. The season being already far spent, he feared there were no vessels at Malacca, which were bound for Goa. He could not carry the Father to Cochin himself, because he was obliged to go on to Sunda, there to unlade his merchandize; but that apprehension was soon at an end, for Xavier, illuminated from heaven, told him positively, "That the ship of Antonio Pereyra was in the port of Malacca, and that they should find it just ready to weigh anchor, and set sail for Cochin."

Xavier discovered these things to his friend during a great calm, which made the navigation pleasing; when suddenly they perceived one of those terrible hurricanes arising, which in a moment sink a vessel. All the company gave themselves for lost; or if they had any hope remaining, it was only in consideration of the saint; and therefore they earnestly desired him to intercede with God in their behalf. The holy man, without replying, retired to his devotions; he returned to them not long after, with his countenance all on fire, and gave his blessing to the ship, pronouncing these following words aloud: "This vessel of the Santa Cruz[1] (for so she was named) shall never perish on the seas; the place where she was built, shall behold her fall in pieces of herself. Might it please Almighty God," continued he, "that the same could be said concerning that vessel which put to sea with us! But we shall be witnesses too soon of her unhappy destiny." At that very instant appeared the signs, which were to begin the verification of the prophecy; the whirlwind was dissipated, and the sea grew calm. Not long afterwards, they beheld the merchandize and dead bodies floating on the waters, and from thence concluded, that the hurricane had destroyed the ship which followed them. Immediately their opinion was confirmed by two mariners, who had gotten on a plank when the ship was foundering; and who, having afterwards struggled with the waves, were driven by them to the board of Pereyra's vessel. The rest of the navigation was prosperous; a calmer season was never known. The ship being landed at the port of Sincapour, Xavier (who knew certainly that Antonio Pereyra was at Malacca, ready to hoist sail towards Cochin, as we have said,) wrote to him by a frigate which went off, to desire that he would wait for him three days longer. He wrote also, by the same conveyance, to Father Francis Perez, superior of the Jesuits at Malacca, and commanded all of them to provide refreshments for the Japonese, who came along with him.

[1: The Holy Cross.]

When it was known in the city that Xavier was coming, the joy was so general, that it almost blotted out the remembrance of all they had suffered in the war. The inhabitants ran crowding to the shore; and at the first appearance of the saint, nothing was to be heard, but acclamations and shouts of rejoicing on every side. They received him at his landing with all the tenderness of affection, and all the reverence imaginable. In conducting him to the house of the Society, they shewed him, as he passed along, the ruins of their houses; and told him, sighing, "that if he had not left them, they had been preserved from the fury of the Javans, as they had formerly been protected from the barbarians of Achen." But the Father answered them, "That their crying sins had called down the wrath of heaven upon them; that nothing could divert it but a speedy change of life; and that the only means of reconciling themselves to God, was to receive those chastisements at his hands, with the spirit of humiliation and of penitence." He visited the old governor Don Pedro de Silva, and the new one who succeeded him, Don Alvarez de Atavda, and communicated to them his design concerning an embassy to China Both of them concurred in the opinion, that it would be advantageous to the crown of Portugal, and to the interests of Christianity. James Pereyra not being capable of accompanying the Father to Goa, for the reason above mentioned, furnished him at present with thirty thousand crowns, for the preparatives of that intended voyage; and sent a servant with the Father, with commission to dispose of all things. Xavier having often embraced this faithful friend, entered with his Japonians into the vessel of Antonio Pereyra, who attended but their company to set sail.

The prediction which the man of God had made in favour of the ship called Santa Cruz, gave it the new name of the "Saint's Vessel;" and from Malacca, from whence she departed at the same time when Xavier went on board of Antonio, her reputation was extended over all the East. Wheresoever she arrived, she was received with ceremony, and saluted by all other ships with the honour of their cannon. All merchants were desirous of stowing their goods in her, and willingly paid the carriage of their wares, and the dues of custom, beyond the common price of other vessels. The weight of lading was never considered, but her freight was always as much as they could crowd into her. As she lasted very long, and that thirty years after the decease of the Father she was in being, and was used for the traffic of the

Indies, they never failed of lading her with an extraordinary cargo, all worn and worm-eaten as she was. The owners into whose hands she came, during the space of those thirty years, took only this one precaution, which was to keep her off from shore; so that when she was to be refitted, that work was constantly done upon the sea. As to what remains, it is true she met with many ill accidents and hardships: she was often engaged with pirates, and combated by tempests; but she escaped clear of all those dangers, and never any one repented of embarking in her. One time it is acknowledged, sailing from Malacca to Cochin, with an extraordinary lading, she sprung a leak, and took in so much water at the beginning of the voyage, that the passengers, who were very numerous, were of opinion to unlade her of half her burden, and half her men, and to put them upon other ships which were in their company. But those vessels, which had already their whole lading, would not consent to ease the Santa Cruz; so that, fear overpowering the ship's company, they returned speedily into the port. The whole town was surprised to see the ship so suddenly come back; and they were laughed to shame for apprehending shipwreck in the vessel of the saint. Being thus publicly upbraided with their want of faith, to mend their error, they took out nothing of the lading, but put again to sea. And what every one said to them, concerning the good fortune which perpetually attended that ship, for two-and-twenty years together, so much renewed their confidence, that they performed their voyage without farther fear. The Santa Cruz continued in this manner, sailing over all the seas, and to every port of Asia, till she came into the possession of the captain who commanded the port of Diu; who perceiving her to be half-rotten, and opened in divers parts, concluded she could serve no longer, unless she were brought into harbour, and set upon the stocks. For which purpose she was sent to Cochin, and hauled ashore on the same dock where she had been built; but she was no sooner there, than she fell in pieces of herself; nothing remaining of that great bulk, besides planks and beams of timber, unprofitable for any thing but for the fire. The inhabitants of Cochin, who knew the prediction of the saint to every circumstance, came out to behold its accomplishment. An inconsiderable merchant, called George Nugnez, who happened to be there present, began to think within himself, that, there might be yet remaining in those planks somewhat of the virtue, which the blessing of the saint had imprinted in them; and thereupon took one of them, which he caused to be nailed to his own frigate, out of the persuasion he had, that with this assistance he should be secure from shipwreck. Thus being filled with a lively faith, he boldly undertook such long and hazardous voyages, that ships of the greatest burden were afraid to make; and without consideration of the weather, adventured many times to cross the most tempestuous gulphs. When he was told, that it was not the part of a prudent man to endanger himself in that manner, he answered, "That the winds and seas were well acquainted with his frigate, and had a reverence for the plank of the Santa Cruz." In effect, his little vessel was ever fortunate enough to escape the greatest perils; and what was most remarkable, was, that having had the same destiny with the ship in her adventures and deliverances, she ended like her, breaking in pieces of herself, on the shore of Coulan, where she was brought to be refitted.

To return to the navigation of Father Xavier:--he arrived at Cochin, January 24th, in the year 1552. The king of the Maldivias had been there for some months: He was a prince of about twenty years of age, born in the Mahometan religion, and bred up in the hatred of Christians. The revolt of his subjects, who loved him not, or hated the government, forced him, for the safeguard of his life, to abandon his kingdom, and to seek sanctuary amongst the Portuguese, by whom he hoped to be restored. The fathers of the Society received him into their house, and went about to convert him, by letting him see the falsehood of his sect. The ill posture of his affairs made him apt to receive the instructions which were given him by Father Antonio Heredia, who endeavoured his conversion with great zeal. But his fear of farther exasperating his rebellious subjects, in case he changed his religion, caused him to defer that change from time to time; and perhaps he had never forsaken the law of Mahomet, if Father Francis had not arrived to complete that work which Heredia had begun. The holy apostle preached the word with so much efficacy to the king of the Maldivias, that at length he reduced him to the obedience of Christ, notwithstanding all the motives of worldly interest to the contrary. Having instructed him anew in the mysteries of Christianity, he solemnly baptized him. In sequel of which, he excited the Portuguese to replace him on the throne, and nominated some of the fathers to accompany the naval army, which should be sent to the Maldivias. His intention was, that they should labour in the conversion of the whole kingdom, when once the king should be established. But because it was of small importance to the crown of Portugal, that those islands, which produce neither gold, nor spices, nor perfumes, should be made tributary to it, the governors did nothing for that exiled prince; who, despairing to recover his dominions, married a Portuguese, and lived a private life till the day of his death; happy only in this, that the loss of his crown was made up to him, by the gift of faith, and the grace of baptism.

When the holy man was ready to depart, an opportunity was offered him of writing into Europe, which he laid hold on, thereby to render an account of his voyage to Japan, both to the king of Portugal, and to the general of his order. Then embarking for Goa, he had a speedy voyage, and arrived there in the beginning of February.

So soon as he was come on shore, he visited the sick in the town-hospitals; and then went to the college of St Paul, which was the house of the Society. After the ordinary embracements, which were more tender than ever, he enquired if none were sick within the college? He was answered, there was only one, who was lying at the point of death. Immediately Xavier went, and read the gospel over him. At the sight of the Father, the dying man recovered his spirits, and was restored to health. The physicians had given him over, and all things had been ordered for his burial; but he himself had never despaired of his recovery: and the day when Xavier arrived, he said, with a dying voice, "That if God would grant him the favour of beholding their good Father, he should infallibly recover."

The relation which Xavier made to the Fathers of Goa, concerning the church of Japan, was infinitely pleasing to them: and he himself was filled with equal consolation, in learning from them the present condition of Christianity in the Indies. The missioners, whom he had dispersed before his departure, were almost all of them united at his return. Some of them were come by his command, and others of their own motion, concerning urgent business; as if the Holy Spirit had re-assembled them expressly, that the presence of the man of God might redouble in them their apostolic zeal, and religious fervour. God had every where blest their labours. The town of Ormus, which fell to the lot of Father Gaspar Barzaeus, had wholly changed its countenance; idolaters, Saracens, and Jews, ran in multitudes to baptism: the temples of idols were consecrated to Christ; the mosques and synagogues were dispeopled, ill manners were reformed, and ill customs totally abolished. Christianity flourished more than ever in the coast of Fishery, since the death of Father Antonio Criminal, who had cultivated it with care, and in that cultivation was massacred by the Badages. The blood of the martyr seemed to have multiplied the Christians: they were reckoned to be more than five hundred thousand, all zealous, and ready to lay down their lives for their religion. The gospel had not made less progress at Cochin, and at Coulan; at Bazain and at Meliapore, at the Moluccas, and in the Isles del Moro. But it is almost incredible, with what profit the gospel labourers preached at Goa. All the priests of idols have been driven out of the Isle of Goa, by order from the governor, and at the solicitation of one of the Fathers belonging to the college of St Paul. It was also prohibited, under severe penalties, to perform any public action of idolatry within the district of Goa; and those ordinances, by little and little, reduced a multitude of Gentiles. As for the Portuguese, their lives were very regular; amidst the liberty of doing whatsoever pleased them, they refrained from all dishonest actions; and concubines were now as scarce as they had been common. The soldiers lived almost in the nature of men in orders; and even their piety edified the people.

But nothing was more pleasing to Xavier, than the conversion of two princes, who during his absence had been at Goa. The first was king of Tanor, a kingdom situate along the coasts of Malabar, betwixt Cranganor and Calecut. This prince, who was party-per-pale, Mahometan and Idolater, but prudent, a great warrior, of a comely shape, and more polite than was usual for a barbarian, had from his youth a tendency to Christianity, without being well instructed in it. He was enamoured of it, after he had been informed to the full concerning the mysteries of our faith, by a religious of the order of St Francis, who frequented his palace. In the mean time, the wars, which he had with other princes for ten years together, hindered him from receiving baptism. At length he was christened, but very secretly; so that, in appearance, he remained an infidel, to keep the better correspondence with his people. Yet he was not without some scruple concerning the manner of his life; and, in order to satisfy his conscience on so nice a point, he desired the bishop of Goa to send him an apostle; for by that name the Fathers of the Society were called by the Indians, as well as by the Portuguese. Father Gomez, who was sent to the king of Tanor, told him positively, that God would be served in spirit and in truth; that dissembling in religion was worse than, irreligion; and that Jesus would disown before his angels, those who disowned him before me. The king, who preferred his salvation before his crown, believed Gomez, and resolved to declare himself solemnly a Christian, as soon as he had made a treaty with his enemies. Having concluded a peace through the mediation of the Father, who had advised him to it, he came to Goa, in despite of all his subjects, who, not being able to gain upon him, either by their reasons, or their desires, had seized upon his person, and shut him up in one of the strongest citadels of the kingdom. He escaped out of his prison, swam a river, and having found eight foists, or half galleys, belonging to Goa, which were purposely sent to favour his passage, he had the good fortune to arrive safely at the town. The bishop and the viceroy conducted him to the cathedral, amidst the acclamations of the people; and at the foot of the altar, he made a public profession of his faith; with such expressions of true devotion as melted the assistants into tears.

The other prince, whose conversion gave so much joy to Father Xavier, was the king of Trichenamalo, who is one of the sovereigns of Ceylon This king, while he was yet an infant, was set upon the throne, and afterwards dispossessed by an usurper, when he was but eight years old. The tyrant, not content to have taken the crown from him, would also have murdered him, but was prevented by a prince of the blood-royal, who carried him out of his reach, being accompanied by forty lords of the loyal party, and sought sanctuary for him on the coasts of Fishery. The Paravas received him with all the charitable compassion which was due to his illustrious birth, to the tenderness of his years, and to his misfortunes; they also promised his attendants to serve him what was in their power; but, at the same time, advised them, to procure him a more durable and more glorious crown; and withal informed them of what they had been taught, concerning the adoption of the sons of God, the kingdom of heaven, and inheritance of the saints. Whether those considerations prevailed upon the prince of the blood-royal, or that the spirit of God wrought powerfully on his heart, lie consented to what the Paravas desired, and put himself into the hands of Father Henriquez to be instructed. The rest of the lords followed his example, and were all baptised together with the king, who seemed at his baptism to have an understanding much above his years. The rulers of the Christians on the fishing coast having afterwards made up an army, supplied with what ammunitions of war, and other provisions which the country could furnish, passed over into the Isle of Ceylon, under the conduct of the prince and the forty lords; but the usurper was so well established in his possession, that the Paravas were forced to retire with speed into their own country. As for the young king, he was brought to Goa; and the Portuguese, who took the conduct of him into their hands, put him into the college of St Paul, where he was virtuously educated by the Fathers of the Society. Xavier praised Almighty God to see the great men of the earth subjected to the empire of Jesus Christ, by the ministry of the children of Ignatius; and rejoiced with his brethren so much the more, because the bishop of Goa, Don Juan de Albuquerque, was so well satisfied of their conduct.

This wise and holy prelate communicated to the Father a letter, which he had written on that subject during his absence to the general of the Society. The letter was in Portuguese, dated from Cochin, November 28, in the year 1550, and is thus translated into our language: "The great performances of your children and subjects, in all the dominions of the East; the holiness of their lives, the purity of their doctrine, their zeal in labouring the reformation of the Portuguese, by the ministry of God's word, and the sacrament of penance; their unwearied travels through all the kingdoms of India, for the conversion of idolaters and Moors; their continual application to study the tongues of this new world, and to teach the mysteries of faith, and principally at the Cape of Comorin,--all this obliges me to write to your reverence, and to give testimony of what I have beheld with my own eyes. Indeed the fathers of your Society are admirable labourers in our Lord's vineyard; and are so faithfully subservient to the bishops, that their endeavours for the good of those souls with which I am intrusted, give me hope of remaining the fewer years in purgatory. I dare not undertake the relation of all their particular actions; and if I durst adventure it, want time for the performance of it: I will only tell you, that they are here like torches lighted up, to dissipate the thick darkness wherein these barbarous people were benighted; and that already, by their means, many nations of infidels believe one God in three persons: for what remains, I freely grant them all they require of me for the good of souls. Every one of them partakes with me in my power and authority, without appropriating any of it to myself: and I look upon myself as one of the members of that holy body, though my life arises not to their perfection. In one word, I love them all in Jesus Christ, with a fervent and sincere charity."

The rest of the letter is nothing appertaining to our purpose, and therefore is omitted.

The man of God received intelligence, at the same time, that the ministers of Portugal at Goa had sent word to Lisbon of the great progress which the Society had made; and that, in particular, the new viceroy, Don Antonio de Norogna, had written, that the Indies were infinitely satisfied with the Jesuits; that none could look on the good effects of their labours without blessing the name of God for them; and that their lives were correspondent to their calling. The saint also was informed, that the king of Portugal had sent word of all these proceedings to the Pope; especially the conversion of the king of Tanor, and the martyrdom of Father Antonio Criminal: That he had communicated to his Holiness his intentions of founding many colleges for the Society, to the end the East might be filled with apostolical labourers; and that, in the mean time, he had ordained, that all the seminaries established in the Indies, for the education of youth, should be put into the hands of the Society, in case it was not already done: Lastly, it was told to Father Xavier, that the viceroy of the Indies, and the captains of the fortresses, had orders from King John III. to defray the charges of the missioners in all their voyages; and that this most religious prince had discharged his conscience of the care of souls, by imposing it on the Society; obliging the Fathers, in his stead, to provide for the instruction of the infidels, according to the ancient agreement which had been made with the Holy See, when the conquests of the East were granted to the crown of Portugal.

Amidst so many occasions of joy and satisfaction, the ill conduct of Antonio Gomez gave Xavier an exceeding cause of grief. Before his voyage to Japan, he had constituted him rector of the college of St Paul, according to the intention, or rather by the order, of Father Simon Rodriguez, who had sent him to the Indies three years after his noviciate; and who, in relation to these missions, had an absolute authority, as being provincial of Portugal, on which the Indies have their dependence. Gomez was master of many eminent qualities which rarely meet in the same person: He was not only a great philosopher, divine, and canonist, but also an admirable preacher, and as well conversant as any man in the management of affairs; and, besides all this, was kindled with a most fervent zeal for the conversion of souls; always prompt to labour in the most painful employments, and always indefatigable in labour: but wonderfully self-opinioned; never guided by any judgment but his own, and acting rather by the vivacity of his own impetuous fancy, than by the directions of the Holy Spirit, or the rules of right reason. As he was of a confirmed age at his entrance into the Society, so he had not soon enough endeavoured to get the mastery of those headstrong passions which ran away with his understanding. And when he had once taken upon him the charge of rector, he began to govern by the dictates of his own capricious humour, even before the face of Xavier, ere he departed from the Indies for Japan; and the Father, who easily perceived that the government of Gomez was not in the least conformable to the spirit of their Institute, would at that time have withdrawn him from Goa, and sent him to Ormuz: but the viceroy, to whom Gomez had been powerfully recommended by one of the chief ministers of Portugal, would not suffer him to be transplanted, or that his authority should be taken from him: so that all Xavier could do, was to temper and draw off from his jurisdiction, by establishing Father Paul de Camerine superior-general of all the missions of the Indies.

But when once the saint was departed from Goa, Gomez usurped the whole government; alleging, for his own justification, that Father Rodriguez had given him an absolute power; and that Camerine was a poor honest creature, more fit to visit the prisons and hospitals of Goa, than to manage the missions, and govern the colleges, of the Society. He began with prescribing new rules to his inferiors; and declared to them, in express terms, that they must return into their mothers' wombs, that they might be born again into a spiritual life, and transformed into other men. Not that they had any need of reformation, they who were themselves the models of a perfect life; but the business was, that he had brought with him out of Europe, I know not what contrivance of new living, framed according to his own fanciful speculations. He undertook then to change their domestic discipline, and to regulate the studies of the Jesuits by the model of the university of Paris, where he had been a student in his youth. There was nothing but change and innovation every day; and he exercised his power with such haughtiness and magisterial hardness, that it appeared more like the dictates of an absolute monarchy, than the injunction of a religious superior: For, to make himself obeyed and feared, he went so far as to tell them he had received an unlimited power from Father Simon Rodriguez, in virtue of which he could imprison, or remand into Portugal, any person who should presume to oppose his government.

His conduct was not less irregular in respect of the young men who were educated in the seminary, of whom the greatest part were Indians. Though they were yet but novices in the faith, and scarcely to be accounted Christians, he enjoined them the practices of the most perfect interior life, which they could not possibly understand; and as they could not acquit themselves of those exercises, which were too sublime for them, he failed not to punish them severely. From thence arose murmurs and combinations, and even despair began to seize on those young ill-treated Indians; and from thence also it came to pass, that many of them, not able to endure so violent a government, leapt over the walls by night, and fled from out the college. Gomez, who could not bear the least contradiction, upon this became more assuming and fantastical; so that one day he turned out all the remaining scholars of the seminary, as if they had been incapable of discipline, and, receiving into their places seven and-twenty Portuguese, who desired to be of the Society, without having any tincture of human learning, he changed the seminary into a noviciate. As he had gained an absolute ascendant over the mind of George Cabral, at that time viceroy of the Indies, no man durst oppose his mad enterprizes, not so much as the Bishop Don Juan d'Albuquerque, who was unwilling to displease the viceroy, and feared to increase the distemper by endeavouring to cure it. Neither was the rector so confined to Goa, that he made not frequent sallies into the country; whether his natural activity would not suffer him to take repose, or that his zeal required a larger sphere; or that, in fine, he looked upon himself as superior general of the missions, and therefore thought it incumbent on him to have an inspection into all affairs, and to do every thing himself.

The town of Cochin being willing to found a college for the Society, he went thither to receive the offer; but he spoiled a good business by ill management. The captain of the fortress immediately gave him a church, called the Mother of God, against the will of the vicar of Cochin, and in despite of a certain brotherhood to which that church belonged. The donation being disputed in law, Gomez, who had it still about him to make a false step, that is, having much _opiniatreté_, great credit, good intentions, took upon him to stand the suit, and to get the church upon any terms. This violent procedure exasperated the people, who had been hitherto much edified by the charily of the Fathers; and the public indignation went so high, that they wrote letters of complaint concerning it to the King of Portugal and Father Ignatius.

This was the present face of things when Xavier returned from Japan; and it was partly upon this occasion that the letters which he received at Amanguchi so earnestly pressed his coming back. His first endeavours were to repair the faults committed by the rector; and he began with the business of Cochin: for, in his passage by it, at his return, knowing the violence of Gomez, he assembled in the choir of the cathedral the magistrate of the town, with all the fraternity of the mother of God, and, in the presence of the vicar, falling on his knees before them, he desired their pardon for what had passed, presented to them the keys of the church, which was the cause of the dispute, and yielded it entirely to them. But submission sometimes gains that, which haughty carriage goes without: The fraternity restored the keys into the hands of Xavier, and, of their own free motion, made an authentic deed of gift of their church to the college of the Society. As for what relates to Goa, the saint dismissed those Portuguese whom Gomez had received into the Society; and, having gathered up as many as he could find of those young Indians, who had either been expelled, or were gone out of the college of their own accord, he re-established the seminary, whose dissolution was so prejudicial to the Christianity of the Indies.

It was only remaining to chastise the criminal, who had made such evil use of his authority. Xavier would make an example of him; and so much the rather, because, having told him what punishment his faults had merited, he found him standing on his terms, insolent, and with no disposition to submit. He judged, upon the whole, that a man who was neither humble nor obedient, after such scandalous misdemeanours, was unworthy of the Society of Jesus; which notwithstanding, he was not willing to pull off his habit at Goa, for fear his departure might make too great a noise; but having made the viceroy sensible of the justice of his proceeding, he sent him to the fortress of Diu, towards Cambaya, with orders to the Fathers residing there to give him his dismission, and to use all manner of persuasions with him that he would return into Portugal, by the opportunity of the first ship which went away. All was performed according to the intentions of the holy man. But Gomez embarking on a vessel which was wrecked in the midst of the voyage, was unfortunately drowned; giving us to understand, by so tragical an end, that the talents of nature, and even the gifts of grace itself, serve only to the destruction of a man in religious orders, who is not endued with the spirit of humility and obedience.

BOOK VI.

_He sends out missioners to divers places. He endeavours an embassy to China. He appoints Barzæus rector of the college of Goa. The form by which Barzæus was made rector of the college, &c. He himself acknowledges Barzæus for superior. In what manner Barzæus receives the offices of rector and vice-provincial. The new instructions which he gives to Barzæus. He makes choice of his companions for China and Japan. He writes to the king of Portugal concerning his voyage to China. He assembles the fathers of Goa by night, and upon what account. He departs from Goa, and what happens him in the way. Before his arrival at Malacca, he knows the plague is in the town. He employs himself in succouring the sick. He raises a young man to life. The embassy of China is crossed by the governor of Malacca. Xavier endeavours all he can to gain the favour of the governor for the embassy. Endeavours are used in vain to get the governor's consent. The governor flies out into fury against the Father. The Father resolves to excommunicate the governor; and what he does in order to it. The grand vicar excommunicates the governor in the name of Xavier. The saint imputes the overthrow of the embassy to his own sins. In writing to the king of Portugal, he makes no complaint of the governor of Malacca. He takes up the design of going to the isle of Sancian, and from thence into China. He departs from Malacca without seeing the governor; and what he does in going out of the town. He embarks, and what happens afterwards. He changes the salt-water into fresh. He restores to a Mahometan his son, who was fallen into the sea. He appears of an extraordinary height, and muck above his own stature. He reassures the captain of the Santa Cruz, and the mariners. He arrives at the isle of Sandan. What passes betwixt Xavier and Veglio. He foretels to Veglio, that he shall be advertised of the day of his death. The prediction of the saint is accomplished in all its circumstances. Other wonderful illuminations. He raises up a dead man, and drives the tygers out of the island. Endeavours are used in vain, to dissuade him from the voyage of China. He takes his measures for the voyage of China. The Portuguese of Sancian traverse the design of Xavier. He defers his voyage, in consideration of the Portuguese merchants. He writes divers letters to Malacca, and to Goa. He gives orders to Father Francis Perez, and to Father Caspar Barzaeus. He foretels the unhappy death of a merchant. He is reduced to an extreme want of all necessaries. The means fail him for his passage into China. He is still in hope, and the expedient which he finds. He falls sick again, and foreknows the day of his death. The nature of his sickness, and how he was inwardly disposed. He entertains himself with God in the extremity of his sickness. He denounces to a young Indian, the unhappy death which was attending him. The Death of the Saint. His age and person. Of the duties which were paid him immediately after his decease. They inter him without any ceremony. The miraculous crucifix in the chapel of the castle of Xavier. He is disinterred, and his body is found without the least corruption. The body of the saint is put on ship-board, to be transported into India. How the body is received at Malacca. The punishment of the governor of Malacca. The town of Malacca is freed from the pestilence at the arrival of the holy body. In what manner the body of the saint is treated in Malacca. They consider of transporting the holy corpse to Goa. The body is put into a crazed old ship, and what happens to it in the passage. How the body is received at Cochin, and the miracle which is wrought at Baticula. They come from Goa to meet the corpse. How the corpse of the saint is received at Goa. The miracles which are wrought, during the procession. The body is placed in the church of Saint Paul. New miracles are wrought in presence of the body. The informations of the saint's life are gathered in the Indies. The people invoke him, and venerate his images. They build churches in honour of him, in divers parts of the East. The praises which are given him by infidels, and the honour they perform to him. How much he is honoured at Japan. His gift of prayer. His love of God. His charity towards his neighbour. His zeal of souls. The various industry of his zeal. The condescendance of his zeal, and how dear the conversion of people costs him. The extent of his zeal. His intrepidity in dangers, and his confidence in God. His humility. His maxims on humility. His submission to God's good pleasure. His religious obedience. His maxims on obedience, and his love for the Society. His poverty, and his mortification. His purity of soul and body. His devotion to the blessed Virgin. His canonization is solicited, and what is done in order to it, by the king of Bungo. He is had in veneration through all Asia.

Miracles are wrought in all places through his intercession. Three remarkable cures. The perpetual miracle of the saint's body. He is beatified, and in sequel canonized. The contents of the bull of his canonization. The veneration of the saint is much increased since his canonization. New miracles are wrought, and chiefly in Italy. What may be concluded from these testimonies, and from all the Book_.

The affairs of the Society being accommodated in this manner, Xavier thought on nothing more than how to supply the missions of the Indies with good labourers; or rather to increase the number of the missioners, who were not sufficient for the common needs. He therefore sent Melchior Nugnez to Bazain, Gonsalvo Rodriguez to Cochin, John Lopez to Meliapor, and Luys Mendez to the Fishery, where he confirmed Henry Henriquez for superior, whom the missioners of that coast had already chosen instead of Antonio Criminal.

After this, he bent his whole endeavours to procure an embassy to China. The viceroy, Don Alphonso de Norogna, with great willingness, granted to James Pereyra that employment which Xavier had desired for him. He promised even to favour it, in all things depending on him; and gave wherewithal to furnish out presents for the emperor of China. Notwithstanding the most magnificent were made at the charges of the ambassador, he had prepared cloth of gold, ornaments for an altar of brocard pictures of devotion, in rich frames, made by the best hands of Europe, with copes and other magnificent church-stuff, all proper to represent to the Chinese the majesty of the Christian religion. The bishop, Don Juan d'Albuquerque, was not less favourable to the designs of the Father than the viceroy; and being willing to write to the emperor of China, thereby to give an honourable testimony to the holy law of God, he ordered his letter to be written in characters of gold, and bordered about with curious painting. Nothing more was wanting than only to make choice of such missioners as were to accompany Xavier to China, and to provide others for Japan; for, besides that the saint himself had his dear Japonians always in his memory, the ambassador of the king of Bungo, who was come with him to Goa, requested some evangelical preachers in his master's name. The man of God had enough to do, to content all those, who were desirous of that employment. There were at that time thirty of the Society in the college of Goa. Some of them had been in the Indies from the first years of Xavier's arrival in those ports; others were either new comers, or had been lately admitted; all of them were of approved virtue, and well worthy of that vocation, which they so earnestly desired; but there was none amongst them who sought it with more eagerness, nor who more signally deserved it, than Caspar Barzaeus.

Xavier, before his voyage to Japan, had recalled him from Ormuz, with design of sending him to that country, or else of taking him with himself to China. Yet he altered both those intentions; for, after many serious debates within himself, he thought it most convenient to leave Barzaeus at Goa, where, since his return from Ormuz, he had laboured in the ministry with great success; but his principal reason was, the necessity of the college of St Paul, which had not yet shaken off all the ill symptoms of the government of Gomez, and which stood in need of a superior, whose conduct should be regular. On these considerations, he made him rector of the college of Goa, and also vice-provincial of the Indies, by the authority which he had received from the general of the order. For the saint, at his return from Japan, found two patients waiting for him, which had been expedited from Rome in the year 1549, one bearing date the 10th of October, the other the 2nd of December, as the minutes which are kept in the archives of the Society declare. By the first, Ignatius constitutes Father Xavier provincial of the Indies, and of all the kingdoms of the East, of which he made a particular province, distinct from that of Portugal; by the second, he endows him with all the privileges which the popes have granted to the head of the order, and to those members of it to whom the general shall please to impart them. For what remains, see here the form of Barzaeus's establishment, which is preserved in the archives of Goa, and written by the hand of Father Xavier.

"Master Gasper, I command you, in virtue of holy obedience, as superior of the company of Jesus in these countries of the Indies, to take the government of this college of Santa Fe, in quality of rector; persuaded, as I am, of your virtue, your humility, your prudence, and of all those qualities which make you proper for the governing of others.

"I will, that all the fathers and Portuguese brothers of the Society of Jesus, who are spread over this new world from the Cape of Good Hope, as far as Malacca, the Moluccas, and Japan, be subject to you. I will, in like manner, that all those who shall come from Portugal, or from any other country of Europe, into the houses of the Society under my obedience, should acknowledge you for their superior; if it happen not, that our Father Ignatius name some other rector of this college of Goa, as I have already requested him by my letters; informing him at large of the necessity of sending hither some experienced person, in whom he much confides, to govern this college, and all the missions of our Society depending on it. If then any of the Society sent by Father Ignatius, or by any other general of the Society of Jesus, with patents signed in due form, shall arrive at Goa, to take the government of this house, and of those who are subjected to it, I command you, in the same virtue of holy obedience, to resign the government into his hands forthwith, and to be obedient to him in all things."

Xavier having thus declared Barzæus superior in a full assembly of the college, kneeled down, and acknowledged him for such, thereby giving a public example of submission. After which, he commanded all of them, in virtue of holy obedience, to be subject to him, and ordered him to expel from the society, all such as should enterprize ought against his authority, or refuse obedience to his orders. He ordered him, I say, positively to expel them, without consideration of their capacity, their eloquence, or any other gifts of nature; adding, that whatever excellent qualities they had, they wanted those which were essential, namely, humility and obedience.

Barzaeus replied not one word when it was intimated to him, that he should not go to China, how desirous soever he were of that voyage; and it may be said, that, on this occasion, he made a noble sacrifice of all his fervent zeal to his obedience. But when he was nominated both rector and vice-provincial, confounded at the mention of those dignities, he said aloud, "That he was not endued with the spirit of government." He was ready to die of shame, when he saw the saint upon his knees before him; and, with great precipitation, fell also on his knees, and humbly begged of him, with tears in his eyes, that he would consider his infirmities. The saint, who had a perfect insight into his integrity, would not hearken to him, and judged him to be so much the more worthy of those two employments, as he judged himself to be incapable. As Barzaeus was the desire of all in all places, and yet his presence was necessary at Goa, not only for the due regulation of the college, but also for the good of missions, Xavier forbade him, in virtue of holy obedience, to depart out of the isle of Goa during the space of three years ensuing; and for this reason, that Barzaeus having this tie of prohibition upon him, might be privileged to refuse any towns which might desire him amongst them; and that if his refusal should displease them, yet at least the unkindness might not rest on him.

After all these punctual orders, Xavier gave in writing, to the new rector, such instructions as he was to use in the government of his inferiors, and in reference to the conduct of himself; according to what all of them had proposed to themselves, to have no design, save only _ad majorem Dei gloriam;_ to God's greater honour. Those instructions are very ample, and I shall give you only the most material.

"Have before your eyes continually your own nothingness; and endeavour, above all things, to have your mind so possessed with it, that the contempt of yourself may never leave you. Always treat the fathers of the Society with great mildness and respect; as well those who inhabit with you, as those who live in other places at a distance. Let not the least roughness, or haughty carriage, appear in you, if it be not when your moderation and humility are turned into contempt; for on such occasions, having nothing in your intentions but the good of your interiors, and not making the contempt of your authority the object of your vengeance, you are to make the guilty somewhat sensible of your power. But you shall only punish them so far as need requires, and for their amendment, and the edification of our brethren, who were witnesses of their fault. All the offences which shall be committed, either by the fathers or the brothers, against the rule of obedience, ought to be punished by some correction; and in so doing, the character of priesthood must be no privilege to the offender. If any of your inferiors act presumptuously against you, and, full of self-opinion, resist you with stubbornness, raise yourself in opposition to their pride, and speak magisterially to them. Let your behaviour towards them have more of severity than of mildness. Impose some public penance on them; and beware, of all things, that they may not observe in you the least remissness, which they will be sure to interpret fear; for nothing more encourages the untractable and haughty to rebellion, than the softness and fearful spirit of a governor. And it is not credible, how assuming, proud, and peremptory, they will grow, when once they find the reins are slackened, and that their pusillanimous superior is afraid of punishing their want of due respect. Impunity hardens that sort of people in their insolence; or rather, it makes them more and more audacious; which disturbs the peace of religious houses. Execute then my orders, without fearing the opinion or speech of people; and let no consideration, no regard of persons, hinder you from the performance of your duty. Amongst your inferiors, you will find some who are neither obstinate nor disobedient, but who are weak; who are forgetful of what is enjoined them, who indeed despise not the orders of their superiors, but sometimes neglect them, either out of faintheartedness, or want of sense. Reprehend such men with more gentleness and moderation, and temper your reproof with the mildness of your countenance; and if you find it necessary to punish them, impose but an easy penance on them. Never admit into the Society such as are not endued with judgment, and good natural parts; nor those who are of a weak constitution, and proper for no employment, or of whom you may reasonably suspect, that they would enter into religion for secular respects, rather than out of a sincere devotion of serving God. When they shall have ended their exercises, you are to employ them in the service of the sick in the public hospitals, and in the meanest offices of the house. You shall cause them to give you an account of the endeavours they have made, to acquit themselves well of their ordinary meditations, according to the form prescribed. If you are assured, that they are lukewarm and faint at their devotions, you will do well to dismiss them, and turn them out of the Society betimes; or if there be any hope of their amendment, you shall withdraw them for some days from those interior exercises; depriving them, by way of penance, of an honour which their negligence has made them unworthy to enjoy; and such indeed is that of communicating with God in prayer, to the end, that, being ashamed to stand excluded from that celestial commerce, they may desire more ardently to be re-admitted to it. I recommend extremely to you, that you pay an extraordinary respect to my lord the bishop; and that you be obedient to him. Beware of doing any thing which may displease him; endeavour, on the contrary, to serve him in all things according to your power; and acknowledge, by all manner of good offices, those infinite obligations which we have to so charitable a father and benefactor. Command those fathers who are out of Goa, to write to him from time to time, but not too prolixly; and to give him an account of the fruit of their labours. That they mention in their letters, as far as truth will give them leave, the commendation of his vicars; and omit not the other good actions of the religious; and if they can say no good of them, let them be silent of them; for we are not to imagine that our duty obliges us to complain to the bishop, of the ill conduct of his vicars, or of other gospel-labourers; there will never be wanting those who will ease us of that trouble. Beware, not to trouble yourself with the management of worldly business; nor even to encumber your inferiors with it, on any occasion whatsoever. When secular men shall desire to engage you in the employments of civil life, return this answer, 'That the time which remains free to you from preaching, and the administration of the sacraments, is scarce sufficient for your studies and devotions, which are yet necessary to you before you go into the pulpit, or appear in the tribune of penance; that you cannot prefer the care of worldly things, before the cure of souls, without perverting the order and rule of charity.' By this means you shall disengage yourself from all those sorts of encumbrances; and without this circumspection, you will do great prejudice to the Society; for you ought to understand, that the world often enters by this door into religious houses, to the extreme damage both of the religious, and of religion.

"In the visits which are made to you, endeavour to find out the bottom and end of their design, who come to see you. For some there are, the least part of whose business is to be instructed in spirituals; it is only temporal interest which brings them to you: there will even be some, who will come to confession, on no other motive, than to acquaint you with the necessities of their family. The best counsel I can give you, is to stand upon your guard with such; and, to be rid of them, let them know from the very first, that you can neither furnish them with money, nor procure them any favour from other men. Be warned to have as little discourse with this sort of people as possibly you can; for most commonly they are great talkers, and if you trouble yourself with giving them the hearing, you are almost certain to lose your time. For what remains, disquiet not yourself with what they think or say of you; let them murmur on, and do you take up a resolution of standing out so firmly, that they may not find the least concernment in you; for the shew of any natural sensibility would discover that you are not enough disengaged from the world, as if you were wavering what part to take betwixt the world and Christ. Remember, that you cannot covet popular approbation without betraying your ministry, or becoming a deserter of your sacred colours, in going back from that evangelical perfection, which you are obliged to follow, with an unrelenting ardour."

After this, Xavier gave Barzaeus sundry particular orders, relating to the persons and houses of the Society.

And now he chose for his companions, Balthazar Gago, Edward Silva, and Peter Alcaceva, with Francis Gonçalez, and Alvarez Ferreyra de Monte Major; without reckoning into the number a young secular Chinese, named Antonio, who had been brought up in the seminary of Sainte Foy. Some of these were intended for China, and others for Japan. Father Ignatius had written to Father Xavier, that it was of great importance to send from the Indies into Europe one of the Society, well versed in the eastern affairs, who might render an exact account of all things to the king of Portugal, and the Pope; as a means of procuring temporal supplies from the one, and spiritual favours from the other; both which were necessary for the further increase of Christianity in Asia. Father Francis did not receive those letters till after his voyage of Japan. He had thought of these very things formerly, but now seeing that the judgment of Ignatius concurred with his, he deputed into Italy and Portugal, Andrew Fernandez, a man of parts and probity, who was not yet in priest's orders. He not only gave him ample informations concerning the present condition of the Indies, but also wrote large letters on the same subject, to the king of Portugal, to Father Ignatius, and to Simon Rodriguez. Being now ready to go for the voyage of China, he gave notice of his intentions to king John, in this ensuing letter.

"I shall depart from Goa within the compass of five days, intending first for Malacca; from whence I shall take the way of China, in the company of James Pereyra, who is named ambassador. We carry with us the rich presents, which are bought partly at the cost of your majesty, and partly at the proper charges of Pereyra: but we carry also a far more precious present, and such an one as no king, at least to my knowledge, has made the like to another prince, namely, the gospel of Jesus Christ; and if the emperor of China once knew its value, I am confident he would prefer that treasure before all his own, how immense soever they may be. I hope, that at length Almighty God will look with eyes of pity on that vast empire, and that he will make known to those great multitudes, who are all made after his own image, their Creator, and the Saviour of mankind, Christ Jesus.

"We are three in company, who go to China with Pereyra; and our design is, to free from prison those Portuguese who are there languishing in chains; to manage the friendship of the Chinese in favour of the crown of Portugal; and, above all things, to make war with the devils, and their adherents: on which occasion, we shall declare to the emperor, and, in sequel, to all his subjects, from the King of Heaven, the great injury which they have done him, to give the devils that adoration which is only payable to the true God, creator of mankind, and to Jesus Christ, their judge and master. The undertaking may seem bold, to come amongst barbarians, and dare to appear before a mighty monarch, to declare the truth to him, and reprehend his vices: but that which gives us courage is, that God himself has inspired us with these thoughts; that he has filled us with the assurance of his mercy; and that we doubt not of his power, which infinitely surpasses that of the emperor of China. Thus our whole success being in the hands of God, what cause of distrust or fear is it possible for us to have? for certain it is, that our only apprehension ought to be of offending him, and of incurring those punishments which are ordained for wicked men. But my hopes are incomparably greater when I consider, that God has made choice of such weak instruments, and such sinners, as we are, for so high an employment, as to carry the light of the gospel almost, I may say, into another world, to a nation blinded with idolatry, and given up to vice."

While they were fitting out the ship, which was to carry the missioners of China and Japan, Xavier assembled the fathers of the college by night, not being able to do it by day, because they were in continual employment till the evening. He discoursed with them concerning the virtues requisite to the apostolic vocation, and spoke with so much ardency and unction, that the congregation was full of sighs and tears, according to the relation of some who were present, and have left it to us in writing. But the instructions which he gave, in taking his last farewell of them, are very remarkable. And I cannot, in my opinion, report them better, than in the very words of the author, who took them from the mouth of the apostle: "The Father, Master Francis," says he, "embracing his brethren before his departure for China, and weeping over them, recommended constancy in their vocation to them; together with unfeigned humility, which was to have for its foundation, a true knowledge of themselves, and particularly a most prompt obedience. He extended his exhortation on this last point, and enjoined them obedience, as a virtue most pleasing to Almighty God, much commended by the Holy Spirit, and absolutely necessary to the sons of the Society."

The apostle went from Goa on holy Thursday, which fell that year, 1552, on the 14th of April. The sea was calm enough, till they came to the height of the islands of Nicubar, which are somewhat above Sumatra, towards the north. Thereabouts the waves began to swell; and presently after, there arose so furious a tempest, that there scarcely remained any hopes of safety. That which doubled their apprehension, was, that two foists, which bore them company, unable to sustain the fury of the waves, sunk both by one another. The ship, which carried Xavier and his companions, was a royal vessel, very large and deep laden, so that her unwieldy bulk and heavy freight hindered her sailing and her steering. It was thought necessary to ease her, and the merchandizes were ready to be cast overboard, when Father Francis desired the captain not to be too hasty. But the sailors saying, that the tempest increasing, as usually it does towards evening, the vessel could not so conveniently be disburdened in the dark, he bid them not disturb themselves about it, for the storm should cease, and they should make land before sun-set. The captain, who knew how certain the predictions of Xavier were, made not the least scruple of believing him, and the event verified the prophecy. The sea grew calm, and land appeared before the setting of the sun.

But while every one was rejoicing at the nearness of the port, the holy man had sadness in his countenance, and often sighed. Some of them enquired the cause, and he bade them pray to God for the city of Malacca, which was visited with an epidemical disease. Xavier said true; for the sickness was so general, and so contagious, that it seemed the beginning of a pestilence. Malignant fevers raged about the town, which carried off the strongest constitutions in a little space, and the infection was caught almost at sight. In this condition the ship found Malacca; and never was the sight of the holy man more pleasing to the inhabitants. Every one promised himself ease of body, and consolation of mind from him; and they were not deceived in their expectation.

So soon as he was set on shore, he went in search of the sick, and found employment enough amongst them for the exercise of his charity. Not a man of them, but desired to confess to Father Francis, and to expire in his arms; according to the popular opinion, that whoever died in that manner, could not fail of being saved. He ran from street to street with his companions, to gather up the poor, who lay languishing on the ground for want of succour. He carried them to the hospitals, and to the college of the Society, which on this occasion he changed into an hospital. And when both the college and the hospitals were full, he ordered cabins to be built along the shore, out of the remainders of rotten vessels, for lodgings, and necessary uses of those distressed creatures. After which he procured them food and medicines, which he begged from the devouter sort, and himself attended them both day and night. That which appeared most wonderful, was, that though the sick could not be served, nor the dying assisted, nor the dead buried, without taking the infection, and it was death to take it, yet Xavier and his companions enjoyed their perfect health in the midst of such dangerous employments. This indeed was wonderful, but there was also an undoubted miracle, which it pleased Almighty God to work by the ministry of his servant, on a young man, whom at that time he restored to life.

This young man, named Francis Ciavus, the only son of a devout woman, who had long been under the conduct of Xavier, having put into his mouth, without thinking of it, a poisoned arrow, such as are used in those eastern parts, died suddenly, so subtile and so mortal was the venom. They were already burying him, when Xavier came by chance that way. He was so moved with the cries and lamentations of the mother, that, taking the dead by the hand, he revived him with these words: "Francis, in the name of Jesus Christ, arise." The youth thus raised, believed from that moment, that he was no more his own, and that he was obliged to consecrate that life to God, which was so miraculously restored: In effect he did it, and out of acknowledgment to Xavier, took the habit of the Society. When the mortality was almost ceased, the saint pursued his design of the embassy to China, and treated with Don Alvarez d'Atayda, the governor of Malacca, on whom the viceroy had reposed the trust of so important an affair Don Alvarez had much approved this enterprize, when Xavier had first opened it, at his return from Japan, and had even promised to favour it with all his power. But envy and interest are two passions, which stifle the most reasonable thoughts, and make men forget their most solemn protestations.

The governor had a grudging to Pereyra, who, the year before, had refused to lend him ten thousand crowns; and could not endure, that a merchant should be sent ambassador to the greatest monarch in the world. He said, "That certainly that Pereyra, whom the viceroy had empowered by his letters, was some lord of the court of Portugal, and not James Pereyra, who had been domestic servant to Don Gonsalvo de Cotigno," But that which most disturbed him, was, that, besides the honour of such an embassy, the merchant should make so vast a profit of his wares, which he would sell off at an excessive rate in China. The governor said, "That in his own person were to be considered the services of the count his father; and that those hundred thousand crowns, which would be gained at least by Pereyra, were a more suitable reward for the son of Atayda, than for the valet de chambre of Cotigno." With such grating thoughts as these, he sought occasions to break off the voyage; yet he Would not declare himself at first; and the better to cover his design, or not to seem unthankful to Father Xavier, he fed him with fair promises. For the holy man had procured him the command of captain-major of the sea, and himself had brought him the provisions for that place: because when first the Father had opened his purpose of going into China, Atayda seemed to have espoused the project with great affection, and engaged himself to make it succeed, in case the ports and navigations of the Portuguese were once depending on him. To oblige him yet farther, the saint had procured from the viceroy, and brought along with him, certain extraordinary privileges, which had not been comprised in the provisions of the command. And, lastly, that he might wholly gain him at his arrival, finding the governor very sick, he attended him with great diligence, and made himself at once both his nurse and his chaplain, watching by him all the night, and saying mass for him in the morning. But all these offices of friendship wrought nothing on a heart, where jealousy and avarice were predominant.

What care soever Don Alvarez took to conceal his ill intentions, Xavier quickly discovered them; and at the same time wrote to Pereyra, who was yet at Sunda, advising him to come without any equipage, and to affect nothing of magnificence, that he might not farther exasperate an interested and jealous soul. But all the modesty of the ambassador could not hinder the governor from breaking out. At the first noise of his arrival, he sent officers of justice, and soldiers, to the port, with orders to make seizure on the ship called Santa Cruz, to take away the rudder, and give it into his hands. This was the first act of jurisdiction, which was exercised by Don Alvarez, as captain of the sea; employing against Xavier himself, that authority which had been procured him by Xavier, and pushing his ingratitude as far as it could go. In the mean time, to cover his passion with the pretext of public good, according to the common practice of men in power, he protested loudly, that the interests of the crown had constrained him to act in this manner; that he had received information from his spies, that the Javans were making preparations of war, to come upon Malacca once again; that he could not have too many ships in readiness, against such formidable enemies; and that the Santa Cruz was of absolute necessity to the king's service. This fable, which was the product of his own brains, was soon exploded by the arrival of some other Portuguese vessels, who, coming from the isles of Java, made oath, that these barbarians, being engaged amongst themselves in civil wars, had no thoughts of any foreign conquest. Don Alvarez not being able any longer to support the credit of his tale, pulled off the mask, and stood upon no farther ceremonies. Xavier perceiving that the love of lucre was his governing passion, made offers to him, by Pereyra, of thirty thousand crowns in pure gift; but the desire of engrossing all the gain, was the reason which prevailed with Atayda to refuse it.

The treasurer, with the rest of the crown-officers, being come to remonstrate to him, that the king's orders were positive, not to stop the navigation of those merchants, who had paid the duties of the port, he threatened them with his cane, which he held up against them, and drove them out of his chamber with great fury, saying, "That he was too old to be counselled; that, as long as he continued governor of Malacca, and captain of the seas, James Pereyra should not go to China, either as ambassador, or merchant; and if Father Xavier was intoxicated with the zeal of converting heathens, he might go to Brazil, or to the kingdom of Monomotapa."

Francis Pereyra, who was auditor-royal, and who had great credit in the town, not being able, either by his intreaties, or his arguments, to oblige Don Alvarez to restore the rudder of the Santa Cruz, would have forced it from him; but this was opposed by Xavier, who foresaw, that the soldiers, who kept the rudder, would defend it with the hazard of their lives, and that this affair would have ill consequences.

The way which was taken by the holy man, was to send to the governor the grand vicar John Suarez, attended by the most considerable persons of the town, to shew him the letters of King John III., which expressly made out his intentions, that Father Xavier should extend the faith, as far as he was able, through all the kingdoms of the East, and that the governors should favour him on all occasions. Suarez read also to the governor, the letter of the vice-king Don Alphonso de Norogna, in which he declared criminal of state, whosoever should hinder or oppose this particular voyage of the saint. That which ought to have reduced Don Alvarez to reason, or at least to have terrified him, served only to make him more unreasonable, and more audacious. He rose from his seat, with the action of a madman, and stamping with his foot, sent back the grand vicar, with this dutiful expression: "The king's interest, you say, requires this to be performed; and I will not suffer it to be performed: Here I am, and will be master."

These outrageous dealings of the governor were not confined to those, who made these remonstrances to him from the Father; they extended even to the saint himself, whom he looked on as the author and head of the enterprize. It is incredible what injurious words he gave him, and how rudely he treated him on several occasions; insomuch, that it was the common talk of Malacca, that this persecution might pass for the martyrdom of Father Xavier. The servant of God resented nothing which was done to his own person. He blessed God continually, for giving him occasions of suffering; but he was extremely sensible of what religion and the progress of the gospel suffered, and was often seen to weep abundantly.

He ceased not for a month together to solicit the governor; sometimes beseeching him by the wounds of a crucified Saviour, sometimes urging him with the fatal consequences of a miserable eternity, and endeavouring to let him understand, what a crime it was to hinder the publication of the gospel; but these divine reasons prevailed as little with Don Alvarez, as the human had done formerly. This strange obduracy quite overwhelmed the Father, when he saw that all these ways of mildness were unsuccessful, and the season of navigation passed away; after he had well consulted God upon it, he concluded, that it was time to try the last remedies. Ten years were now expired since his coming to the Indies, and hitherto no one person, excepting only the bishop of Goa, was made privy to his being the apostolic Nuncio. He had kept this secret in profound silence, and had not once exercised his power; but now he thought himself obliged to own it, in a business of so great consequence, and to strike with the thunders of the church, if occasion were, the man who made open war against the church.

Which notwithstanding, he would not dart the thunderbolt himself, but used the hand of the grand vicar. Having sent for him, he began with shewing him one of the briefs of Paul III., which constituted him his Nuncio in all the kingdoms of the East. After this, he requested Suarez to shew this brief to Don Alvarez, and to explain to him the censures which were incurred by those, who should oppose the pope's legates in matters of religion, and to exhort him, by what was most holy in the world, to suffer the embassy to proceed. In case of refusal, to threaten him with ecclesiastical punishments from the vicar of Jesus Christ, and to adjure him at the same time, by the death of the Saviour of mankind, to take compassion on himself.

Xavier had always hoped, that the governor would open his eyes; and in that writing which he gave the vicar to engage him in that nice commission, there were these following words: "I cannot believe that Don Alvarez can be so hardened, but that he will be mollified, when he shall know the intentions and orders of the holy see." He desired the grand vicar, in the same writing, to send that very paper back to him, together with the answer of Don Alvarez, that both the one and the other might be an authentic evidence to the bishop of Goa, that he had omitted nothing for advancing the embassy; and that if it succeeded not, the fault lay not at his door. Suarez proceeded with the governor, according to all the directions which had been traced out to him by the Father. But nothing could work upon Alvarez. He laughed at the threatenings, and broke out into railing language against the person of Xavier, saying loudly, "That he was an ambitious hypocrite, and a friend of publicans and sinners."

The grand vicar not being able any longer to endure so outrageous and scandalous an impiety, at length excommunicated the governor, according to the agreement betwixt himself and Father Xavier. He also excommunicated all his people, who basely flattered the passion of their master, and spoke insolently of the holy see. This excommunication signified little to a man, who had no principles, either of honour, or of religion. Without giving himself the least disquiet for the wrath of heaven, or talk of men, he made himself master of the ship Santa Cruz, and placed in her a captain, with 25 mariners, all of them in his interests, to go and trade at Sancian, where the Portuguese had established a wealthy traffic. The ill success of the negociation, betwixt the grand vicar and the governor, was very afflicting to Father Xavier; his heart was pierced with sorrow, and he acknowledged to Father Francis Perez, that he never resented any thing with greater grief. The deplorable condition of Don Alvarez in the sight of God, the ruin of his friend Pereyra, the embassy of China utterly destroyed,--all these made him sigh from the bottom of his soul; and so much the more, because he imputed these so great misfortunes to himself; as he gave Pereyra to understand, who lay hidden at Malacca, and to whom he expressed himself in writing, because he knew not with what face to see him.

"Since the greatness of my sins," says he, "has been the reason why God Almighty would not make use of us two for the enterprize of China, it is upon myself that I ought, in conscience, to lay the fault. They are my offences, which have ruined your fortunes, and have caused you to lose all your expences for the embassy of China. Yet God is my witness, that I love him, and that I love you also; and I confess to you, that if my intentions had not been right, I should be yet more afflicted than I am. The favour which I desire of you, is, that you would not come to see me; for fear, lest the condition to which you are reduced, should give me too much trouble; and that your sorrow might be the occasion of increasing mine. In the mean time, I hope this disgrace of yours may be of advantage to you; for I doubt not but the king will reward your zeal, as I have requested of him by my letters. As for the governor, who has broken our voyage, I have no farther communication with him: God forgive him, I pity him, and lament his condition; for he will soon be punished, and more severely than he thinks."

But though Father Xavier wrote very pressing letters to the king of Portugal in favour of Pereyra, he wrote nothing against Don Alvarez; and Alvarez himself was witness of it, having intercepted the letters of the Father. In effect, he found not the least expression of complaint against him, at which he was wonderfully surprised. The man of God daily offered the sacrifice of the mass for him, and shed many tears at the foot of the altar, to the end he might obtain for him the favour of a sincere repentance. He said one day, he should lose at once, his estate, his honour, and his life; and added, I beseech God that he lose not his soul also.

For what remains, though the door of China seemed to be shut upon him, since all hopes of the embassy were vanished, which had facilitated his entrance into that kingdom, yet the saint despaired not of preaching the gospel to the Chinese; and a thought came into his head, that if he could get to an isle, which was neighbouring to Canton, he might from thence go privately over into the continent; that if he were stopped and put in prison, he should at least preach to the prisoners; that from the prisons, the Christian doctrine might spread into the towns, and possibly might reach the court; that perhaps also the great men of the empire, and even the emperor himself, might have the curiosity to see a man who published so new a faith; and then he might gain an opportunity of declaring the whole law of Jesus Christ.

With these considerations, he took up the design of embarking on the Santa Cruz, which the governor of Malacca was sending out for Sancian. But seeing that the entry of China could not be attempted by that way which he had proposed without great hazard, he would be the only priest who should expose himself to those dangers; and retaining with him only one brother of the Society, the Chinese, Antonio de Sainte Foy, and another young Indian, he sent Balthazar Jago, Edward Silvia, and Peter Alcaceva, to several employments; the first to the kingdom of Bungo, and the two others to Amanguchi.

During these passages, it happening that John Beyro came from the Moluccas, to desire some more assistance, for the farther propagation of the faith in those islands, Xavier received from him the comfortable news of the great spreading of Christianity, and sent him to Barzæus, with orders that more companions should be joined to him; and that he should be remanded thither with all expedition.

The Santa Cruz being now upon the point of setting sail, he retired into the church of our Lady of the Mount, to recommend his voyage to the protection of the blessed Virgin. He continued his devotions till the evening; and had also passed the night in prayer, if they had not come to give him notice that the ship had already weighed anchor.

The grand vicar, John Suarez, who bore him company to the ship, asked him by the way, if he had taken leave of the governor; adding, that if he failed in that point of ceremony, the weaker Christians might be scandalized; that it would be a proof of his resentment, and an occasion of public murmur. The saint, who was willing to shew by his example, how excommunicated persons ought to be treated, replied immediately, "Don Alvarez shall never see me in this life; I expect him at the judgment-seat of God, where he will have a great account to answer." Having walked on a little farther, he stopped at a church door, which was near the sea; and, in a transport of spirit, lifting up his eyes to heaven, he prayed aloud for the salvation of the unhappy Don Alvarez. Then he prostrated himself, and was silent for some time, praying from the bottom of his heart to God, with his face to the ground. Soon after he rose up with a vehement action, which had somewhat of a holy disdain in it; he took off his shoes, beat them one against another, and afterwards against a stone, saying, "that he would not bear away the dust of an accursed place." He then foretold, with circumstances at large, and more than formerly, the punishment which heaven had prepared for the governor of Malacca; and going on board, left the people, who had followed him thus far, astonished at his prophecies, and afflicted at his departure.

Immediately they set sail, and there were in the vessel above five hundred persons, counting in the passengers and servants. They were already forward on their voyage, when the wind fell on the sudden; and in a moment the waves were laid, and the face of the ocean grew so smooth, that the Santa Cruz stood still, and moved no more than if she had been at anchor. During this becalming, which lasted fourteen days together, their water failed them, and some died from the first want of it. They rowed on every side with their chalop, to make discovery of some coast where they might find fresh water. Being far at sea, they could discern nothing, but the island of Formosa, at least they believed it so to be. They endeavoured to gain the shore; but in seven days time, notwithstanding all their attempts, they could not reach it.

In the meantime, the ship was full of sick people, who were burnt up with a deadly thirst; and they had all perished, without hope of succour, if one of them, reflecting within himself, that Father Xavier had been always prevalent with God, had not hinted this notion to the rest; whereupon all of them coming on their knees before him, besought him, with more tears than words, to obtain from heaven either wind or water for them.

Xavier bade them address themselves to God in their own behalf; caused them to recite the litany on their knees, at the foot of a large crucifix; and then ordered them to retire, but to have confidence in Jesus Christ. He himself withdrew also into a chamber; from whence coming out some time after, he went down into the chalop with a little child, and having caused him to taste of the sea water, asked him whether it were fresh or salt? The child answering that it was salt, he commanded him to taste again, and the child told him that it was fresh. Then the Father, returning into the ship, ordered them to fill all their vessels; but some amongst them, being eager to drink, found the water salt. The saint made the sign of the cross over the vessels, and at the same moment the water, losing its natural saltness, became so good, that they all protested it was better than that of Bangar, of which the seamen make their ordinary provision, and which is esteemed the best water in all the Indies.

This miracle so struck some Saracen Arabs, who were transporting their whole families into China, that, throwing themselves at the feet of the holy man, they acknowledged the God of the Christians, and desired baptism. The faithful, on their side, admired Father Francis; and all of them, in a body, owned the preservation of their lives to him. But the Father told them, that it was to God, and not to such a sinner as he was, that they were obliged to pay their thanks. The greatest part of the mariners and passengers kept, out of devotion, some of this water, at the first as a testimony of the miracle, afterwards as a celestial remedy: for the water, being carried to the Indies, cured great numbers of sick people; and infusing some small quantity of it into any sort of drink, was sufficient to restore their health.

During the navigation, a child of five years old happened to fall into the sea; the vessel, which had a fore-wind, pursuing its course. The father of this child was not to be comforted, and his grief so overwhelmed him, that he kept in private for three days. He was a Mahometan, and the miracle of the water had not converted him. At length he appeared in public, but all in tears, and never ceasing to lament the loss of his only son. Xavier, who knew nothing of this misfortune, asked him the reason of his sorrow? Having learnt it, he stood recollected in himself a little time, and then said, "Supposing that God should restore your son to you, would you promise me to believe in Jesus Christ, and to become a sincere Christian?" The infidel promised him; and three days after this, before sun-rising, they saw the child upon the hatches. The child knew not what had become of him for those six days, and only remembered his falling into the sea, not being able to give any account how he returned into the ship. His father was ready to die with joy when he received him; and Xavier had no need of putting him in mind of his engagement: he came of his own accord, accompanied by his wife, his son, and his servant; all of them were baptized, and the child was named Francis.

Those of the vessel having been witnesses of these two miracles, spoke of them to the inhabitants of an isle called Cincheo, by which they passed, and which was a place of great traffic, full of merchants from several parts. The desire of seeing so admirable a man, caused about sixty persons, some Ethiopians, other Indians, all Idolaters or Mahometans, to come into the ship: Xavier took the occasion, and preached the gospel to them; withal, instructing them in the holy practices of Christianity. He had no sooner ended his exhortation, than they acknowledged Jesus Christ, and received baptism.

While he was christening them, he appeared of a stature much higher than his own; insomuch, that those who were upon the shore near the vessel, believed he had been standing on some bench; but seeing him coming and going, and always appearing of the same height, they thought there might possibly be some miracle in the matter, and were desirous to be satisfied concerning it: Stephen Ventura went into the ship on purpose, and approaching Father Xavier, saw that with his feet he touched the hatches, and yet his head was higher than the tallest there, on whom he sprinkled the sacred waters of baptism. Ventura likewise observed, that, after he had baptized the company, he returned to his natural proportion.

From Cincheo the ship pursued her voyage towards Sancian, which is but six leagues distant from the continent, over against Canton, a town of China. They had sailed far beyond Canton, and the mariners believed they were still on this side of it. Xavier endeavoured to undeceive them, but they adhered to their first opinion, and they had gone much further out of their way, if the captain, upon the word of the saint, had not struck sail, and cast anchor till the return of the chalop, which he had sent out to discover the neighbouring coast. She was three days before she came back, and all the ship's company imagined that she had been overtaken by some hurricane; but Xavier assured them that she should suddenly return, with refreshments sent them by the Portuguese of Sancian; and that also she should be followed by some vessels, which should come to meet them on their way, and conduct them into the port. All happened as the Father had foretold; and the Santa Cruz, guided by the vessels of Sancian, arrived at that island, twenty-three days after her departure from Malacca.

There are three islands so little distant from each other, that they appear but one; for which reason the Chinese, in their language, call them Samceu; a word composed of _sam_, which signifies three, and _ceu_, which is to say an island. The chief of these islands, which the Portuguese have named Sancian, has a convenient and safe port, all crowned with mountains, and forming a semicircle on that side, which looks towards Macao. It has few inhabitants who are natives, almost no provisions, and is so barren of itself, so uncultivated and so wild, that it seems rather a place of banishment than of commerce. The Chinese had permitted the Portuguese to trade thither, to buy their commodities, and sell their own to them, without breaking their fundamental law, of suffering no stranger to set foot within their country; so that the Portuguese durst come no nearer the main land, for fear of hazarding their lives, or at least their liberty. Neither was it permitted them to build solid houses in the isle; they were only allowed to set up slight cabins, covered with mats, and dressed about with boughs of trees, that they might not always be shut up within their vessels.

Amongst these merchants there was one who was very rich, and infinitely charitable, but of a gay humour, and pleasant in conversation, addicted to all pleasure which decency permits, and loving not to deny himself any thing which will make life comfortable;--for the rest, most affectionate to Father Xavier: his name was Peter Veglio, the same Veglio who was with the saint at Japan, and who returned in his company. Xavier being very desirous of his friend's salvation, exhorted him, from time to time, to mortify his natural inclinations, even sometimes to chastise his body for the expiation of his sins. Veglio understood not that Latin; whether he was too tender of his own person, or thought his sins were not of a nature to deserve such severities, he could never find in his heart to take up the discipline; but instead of macerations and penances, he gave great alms; and Father Francis received from him very large supplies, for the relief of such as were in want. One day, the Father having need of a certain sum of money, to marry a young orphan virgin, who was poor and handsome, and consequently in danger of being ruined, had recourse to Veglio, according to his custom. He found him engaged in play with another merchant; but the business being urgent, he forbore not to request his charity. Veglio, who loved to be merry, made as if he were angry with him, and answered thus; "Father Francis, when a man is losing, he is in no condition of giving alms; and for a wise man as you are, you have made a very gross mistake in this unseasonable demand." "It is always in season to do good," replied Xavier; "and the best time for giving money, is when a man has it in his hand." The merchant continuing in the same tone, and seeming to be displeased with the Father's company, added, as it were to be rid of him, "Here, take the key of my chest; take all my money if you will, and leave me to play my game in quiet." In the merchant's chest were thirty thousand taes, which amount to forty-five thousand crowns of gold. The Father took out three hundred crowns, which were sufficient to marry the orphan maiden. Some time afterward, Veglio counting over his money, and finding the sum was still entire, believed the Father had not touched it, and reproached him with want of friendship for not making use of him; whereupon Xavier protested to him, that he had taken out three hundred crowns. "I swear to you," said Veglio, "that not one of them is wanting; but God forgive you," added he, "my meaning was to have parted the whole sum betwixt us; and I expected, that of my forty-five thousand crowns, you should at least have taken the one moiety."

Xavier, finding that Veglio had spoken very sincerely to him, and out of a pure principle of charity, said, as a man transported out of himself by the spirit of God; "Peter, the design you had, is a good work before the eyes of Him, who weighs the motions and intentions of the heart; He himself will recompence you for it, and that which you have not given, shall be one day restored to you an hundred-fold. In the meantime, I answer for Him, that temporal goods shall be never wanting to you; and when you shall have misfortunes to put you backwards in the world, your friends shall assist you with their purses. I farther declare to you, that you shall not die without being first advertised of the day of your death." After these predictions, Veglio was quite changed into another man, applying himself wholly to exercises of piety; and in the condition of a merchant, lived almost the life of a religious. What had been foretold him, that he should have warning of his death, came frequently into his remembrance; and he could not hinder himself one day from asking the saint, at what time, and in what manner, it should be? The saint told him, without pausing, "When you shall find the taste of your wine bitter, then prepare yourself for death, and know that you have but one day more to live."

The merchant lived in opulence and splendour, even to an extreme old age. He had several losses in his trade, according to the chance of things which are depending on the sea; but his friends continually relieved him in his necessities, and gave him wherewithal to set up again. At length, being one day at a great entertainment, and more gay than ever, having asked for wine, he found the taste of it was bitter. Immediately remembering the prophecy of Father Xavier, he was seized with an inward horror; which beginning from the soul, spread over his body, as if death had been pronounced against him, or the image of death presented to his eyes. Nevertheless, somewhat recovering his spirits, for his farther satisfaction in the point, he desired his fellow-guests at the table to taste the wine out of his glass. All judged it to be excellent, besides himself, who made divers trials of it on his palate. He called for other wines, and another glass; but always found the same bitterness. Then, no longer doubting but that his last hour was coming, after he had made an interior sacrifice of his life to God, he related to the company that prediction, which was now accomplished; and arose from the table with the thoughts of a Christian, who is disposing himself for death. Having distributed his goods betwixt his children and the poor, he went to see his friends, and to give and take the last farewell;--notwithstanding his great age, he was in perfect health. It was thought he doted, and they endeavoured to persuade him out of his melancholy apprehensions. But their arguments prevailed so little on his mind, that he gave orders for his own funeral, and invited his friends to do him the last kind office, of accompanying his corpse to burial. To content him, and to make themselves merry at his folly, they attended him into the church: in their presence he received the viaticum, and the extreme unction, without being sick; afterwards he laid himself upon the bier, and caused them to sing the mass for the dead. The people gathered in a crowd at the strangeness of the report; some drawn by the novelty of the sight, the rest to be eye-witnesses how the prediction of Father Xavier would succeed. Mass being ended, the priest, attended by his inferiors, performed all the ceremonies of the church about the grave, and, at length, sung the last words belonging to a Christian burial over the old man, who was alive, and bore his part in the responses. There now remaining no more to do, the servant of Veglio coming to help his master off the bier, he found him dead. All the assistants were witnesses of the matter of fact, and every one went home full of admiration of God's mercy towards this merchant, who had been so charitable, and blessing the memory of the holy apostle of the Indies.

This was not the only prophetical light, which Xavier had in the isle of Sancian. A ship, which went from Macao to Japan, appeared in sight of Sancian, to be overtaken by a dreadful hurricane. The Portuguese, who had great concernments in that vessel, being alarmed at so inevitable a danger, came running for comfort to Father Xavier; but the Father assured them, they had no cause of fear, and that the ship was safely arrived at her port. They kept themselves quiet, upon the assurance of his word, till finding that the ship made no return, which was to stay at Japan but some few days, they gave her for lost. Xavier reproved their want of faith, and positively told them, that she should come back before the week were ended. In effect, she returned two days afterwards, laden with rich merchandizes, and proud of her escape from the fury of the hurricane.

At the same time, Xavier was inspired with the knowledge of the quarrel betwixt Don Alvarez de Atayda, governor of Malacca, and Don Bernard de Sosa, who was newly arrived from the Moluccas; and told the circumstances of it to the Portuguese, who, having afterwards the particulars of it from some of Malacca, were astonished to find them the very same which the Father had related.

This miraculous foreknowledge was accompanied by actions as surprising; and without speaking of a dead infant, which Xavier restored to life, but whose resurrection is without circumstances in the acts of the saint's canonization, he cleared the country of the tygers, which laid it waste. These furious beasts came in herds together out of the forests, and devoured not only the children, but the men also, whom they found scattered in the fields, and out of distance from the entrenchments which were made for their defence. One night the servant of God went out to meet the tygers, and when they came near him, he threw holy water upon them, commanding them to go back, and never after to return. The commandment had its full effect, the whole herd betook themselves to flight, and from that time forward no tygers were ever seen upon the island.

The joy which the Portuguese had conceived at the arrival of Father Xavier, was immediately changed to sadness, when they understood that he had only taken Sancian in his way to China. They all endeavoured to dissuade him from it, and set before his eyes the rigorous laws of that government; that the ports were narrowly observed by vigilant and faithful officers, who were neither to be circumvented nor bribed with presents; that the Mandarins were cruel to all strangers; that, the year before, some Portuguese seamen being cast by tempest on the coast of Canton, had been severely whipped, and afterwards inclosed in dark dungeons, where, if they were not already dead, they were still exercised with new punishments; that, for himself, the least he could expect was perpetual imprisonment, which was not the business of an apostle, who designed to run from place to place, and propagate the faith through all the East. These arguments made no impression on the saint; he had fortified his resolution with more potent reasons, and answered the merchants in the same tenor in which he had written to Father Francis Perez, that he could not distrust the Divine Goodness, and that his distrust would be so much the more criminal, because the powerful inspiration of the Holy Spirit pushed him forward to teach the Chinese the gospel of the living God. "I am elected," said he, "for this great enterprize, by the special grace of heaven. If I should demur on the execution, or be terrified with the hardships, and want courage to attempt those difficulties, would it not be incomparably worse than all the evils with which you threaten me? But, what can the demons and their ministers do against me? Surely no more than what is permitted them by the sovereign Lord of all the world; and that in giving up myself in this manner, I shall obey my Lord Jesus, who declares in his gospel, 'That whosoever will save his life shall lose it, and whoever will lose it for my sake, shall find it.' Our Saviour also says, 'That he who, having put his hand to the plough, shall look behind him, is not fit for the kingdom of heaven.' The loss of the body being then without comparison less to be feared than that of the soul, according to the principles of Eternal Wisdom, I am resolved to sacrifice a frail and miserable life for everlasting happiness. In fine, I have set up my rest, I will undertake this voyage, and nothing is capable of altering my resolution. Let all the powers of hell break loose upon me, I despise them, provided God be on my side; for if he be for us, who shall be against us?" The Portuguese being of opinion, that this fixed intention of the man of God was partly grounded on his ignorance of the dangers, which he believed they magnified to him beyond their natural proportion, sent some Chinese merchants, with whom they traded, to discourse the business calmly with him; but the matter went otherwise than they had imagined. Those Chinese, to whom Xavier failed not to speak of Christianity, and who were men of understanding, advised him to the voyage, instead of dissuading him. They counselled him only to carry books which contained the Christian doctrine; and added, that, not long since, the emperor had sent some learned men into the neighbouring kingdoms, to inform themselves of such religions as were different from the received opinions of the Chinese; that they believed the Christian doctrine would be well received at court; and that it seemed probable to them, that the novelty of so reasonable a belief would make his way who was the first bearer of it.

Xavier was overjoyed to find a passage opened for the gospel, to the most polite nation of the world; and doubted not but that the Christian religion, coming to be compared by judicious men with the other opinions of the East, would have the advantage. Being thus encouraged to pursue his purpose, his first business was to provide himself of a good interpreter. For Antonio, the Chinese, whom he had brought from Goa, was wholly ignorant of the language which is spoken at the court, and had almost forgotten the common idiom of the vulgar. He found out another Chinese, who had a perfect knowledge of the language of the Mandarins, and who could also write excellently well, in which consists the principal knowledge of China. For the rest, he was a man well shaped, of a good presence, of great natural parts, of a pleasing conversation, and, which was above all, he seemed entirely devoted to the Christians: he promised all possible good offices,--whether he hoped to make his fortune, by presenting to the emperor one who published a new law, or that God had inspired him with those pious thoughts.

There was more difficulty in finding seamen to transport the Father; for there was no less venture than that of life, for any one who undertook that business. But interest gives him courage to hazard all, who values money more than life itself. A Chinese merchant, called Capoceca, offered himself to carry Xavier into the province of Canton, provided he might be well paid; and asked the value of two hundred pardos[1]in pepper. The Chinese promised to take Xavier into his barque by night, and to land him before day on some part of the coast, where no houses were in view; and if this way was thought uncertain, he engaged to hide the Father in his own house, and four days after to conduct him, early in the morning, to the gates of Canton. But he would have Xavier oblige himself also, on his side, to go immediately to the Mandarin, with the letters which the viceroy of the Indies, and the bishop of Goa, had written to the emperor; for the Father had still reserved by him those letters which related to the embassy, though the design had been ruined by the governor of Malacca. The Chinese also exacted an oath of secrecy from the saint, that no torments, however cruel, should bring him to confess either the name or the house of him who had set him on shore.

[1: A pardo (says Tavernier) is of the value of twenty-seven sous, French money; ten of which make about a shilling English.]

Xavier made as solemn an engagement as he could desire, not without knowledge of the hazard which he ran, as himself related to one of his dearest friends. "I perceive," said he, "two dangers, which are almost inevitable in this affair; on the one side, there is great cause of apprehension, lest the idolatrous merchant, having received the price of my passage, should throw me overboard, or leave me on some desart isle; on the other side, lest the governor of Canton should discharge his fury upon me, and make me an example to all strangers, by putting me to a cruel death, or condemning me to perpetual imprisonment. But in case I follow the voice which calls me, and obey my Lord, I count my life and liberty at nothing."

When the voyage of China was on these terms, and that all things seemed to favour it, the Portuguese of Sancian put an obstacle in the way, of which Xavier had never thought. The appetite of gain made them apprehend, lest his zeal should bring them into trouble; and they said to one another, that the Mandarin governor of Canton would certainly revenge on them the boldness of their countryman: That he would commission his officers to pillage their ships, and confiscate their effects, and that their lives were not in safety. In this general affrightment, which was not ill grounded, and which increased daily, the wealthier sort addressed themselves to Father Xavier, and desired him to take compassion on them, and on their wives and children, if he would have no compassion on himself.

Xavier, who was no less careful for the interests of others, than he was negligent of his own, found an expedient to satisfy them. He engaged his word, that he would not pass over into China, till they had ended all their business, and were gone from Sancian. This gave opportunity to the Chinese merchant, with whom he had treated, to make a short voyage, under promise, notwithstanding, to return at a time which was prefixed. While these things were thus managed, the Father fell sick of a violent fever, which continued on him fifteen days. The Portuguese took occasion from thence to tell him, that heaven had declared against the voyage of China; but being recovered, he followed his design with more warmth than ever. While the merchants were lading their ships, he entertained himself day and night with the prospect of converting China; and all his pleasure was to think, how happy he should be, in dispossessing the devil of the largest empire in the world. "If yet," said he, "it shall please Almighty God to employ so vile an instrument as I am, in so glorious an undertaking." Taken up with these and such-like meditations, he often took his walk along the shore, and turning his eyes towards that desired country, sent out ardent sighs. He said sometimes amongst his friends, that his only wish was to be set down at the gates of Canton, and troubled not himself with what might happen afterwards: happy he, if he could once declare the Son of God to the Chinese, and more happy, if, for his sake, he might suffer martyrdom.

In the mean time, all the Portuguese vessels, excepting only the Santa Cruz, which had not yet her whole lading, set sail from Sancian for the Indies. Xavier gave many letters to the merchants, to be delivered both at Malacca and at Goa. He wrote to his friend James Pereyra, in terms which were full of acknowledgment and charity. "Almighty God," said he in his letter, "abundantly reward you, since I am not able of myself to do it; at least, while I continue in this world, I shall not fail to implore the Divine Goodness to confer on you, during your life, his holy grace, accompanied with perfect health, and after your death eternal happiness. But as I am persuaded, that I cannot acquit myself, by these my prayers, of the great obligements which I have to you, I beg all those of our Society in the Indies, to desire of God the same blessings in your behalf. For what remains, if I compass my entrance into China, and if the gospel enter with me, it is to you, next to Almighty God, to whom both the Chinese and myself shall be owing for it. You shall have the merit of it in the sight of God, and the glory in the sight of men. Thus, both the Chinese, who shall embrace the faith, and those of our Society, who shall go to China, shall be obliged, to offer, without ceasing, their vows to heaven in favour of you. God grant us both the happiness once to meet in the court of China! As for myself, I am of opinion if I get into that kingdom, and that you come thither, you will either find me a prisoner at Canton, or at Pequin, which is the capital city of that empire; and I beseech the Lord, out of his infinite mercy, that we may be joined together either in the kingdom of China, or at least in the kingdom of immortal glory."

He wrote by the same conveyance to Father Francis Perez, superior of Malacca. He commanded him, in virtue of holy obedience, to depart with the soonest out of that unhappy town, and to conduct his inferiors to Cochin, where he established him rector of the college, in the place of Antonio Heredia, whom he sent to Goa. Though Father Xavier deplored anew, the wretched condition of Don Alvarez, it hindered him not from enjoining Father Barzæus, in his letter to him, that he should work the bishop to send his orders to the grand vicar of Malacca, therein declaring the governor to be excommunicated. And he took this way, not only because hardened and scandalous offenders, such as Don Alvarez, ought to incur a public dishonour, by that means to induce them to a serious consideration of their own estate, and that others might take warning by them; but also, that succeeding governors might fear, by the example of his punishment, to set themselves in opposition to any intended voyage of the missioners, who should be sent hereafter to the Moluccas, Japan, or any other places.

He desired Father Barzæus, in the same letter, to receive few persons into the Society, and to make an exact trial of those whom he should receive: "For I fear," said he, "that many of them who have been admitted, and daily are admitted, were better out of our walls than within them.

"You ought to deal with such people, as you have seen me deal with many at Goa; and as I have lately treated my companion, whom I have dismissed from the Society, not having found him proper for our business." He meant Alvarez Pereyra, whom he had brought with him from the Indies, and whom he sent back from Sancian with the Portuguese vessels.

Amongst those merchants who went off from Sancian, there was one who made more haste than any of the rest; without giving notice of his departure to the Father, whom he had lodged in his cabin, or without waiting for a Chinese vessel, which he had bought at the port of Canton. One morning while the Father was saying mass very early, this merchant had put off from shore, and fled with as much precipitation as if the island was ready to be swallowed by the sea. After mass was ended, he looked round him, and not seeing him for whom he searched, "What is become of my host?" said he, with the looks and gesture of a man inspired. Being answered, that he was already in open sea; "What could urge him," continued he, "to so prompt a resolution? why did he not expect the ship which comes from Canton? And whither is he dragged by his unhappy destiny?" That very evening the Chinese vessel was seen to arrive: as for the fugitive merchant, he was no sooner landed at Malacca, when, going into a wood to seek materials for the refitting of his ship, he was poniarded by robbers.

All the Portuguese vessels being gone, saving only that which belonged to the governor of Malacca, or rather of which the governor had possessed himself by violence, Xavier was reduced to so great a want of all necessaries, that he had scarcely wherewithal to sustain nature. It is certainly a matter of amazement, that they, whose lives he had preserved by changing the salt sea-water into fresh; should be so hard-hearted as to abandon him to die of hunger. Some have thought that Don Alvarez had given orders, that all things should be refused him; but I rather think, that Providence would try him in the same manner, as sometimes God is pleased to prove those whom he loves the best, and permitted that dereliction of him for the entire perfection of the saint.

That which most afflicted him, was, that the Chinese interpreter, who had made him such advantageous offers, recalled his word, either of himself for fear of danger, or at the solicitation of those who were devoted to the governor of Malacca. Yet the Father did not lose his courage; he still hoped that God would assist him some other way; and that, at the worst, Antonio de Sainte Foy might serve his turn for an interpreter. But for the last load of his misfortunes, the merchant, who had engaged to land him on the coast of China, returned not at the time appointed, and he in vain expected him for many days.

Despairing of any thing on that side, he still maintained his resolution, and another expedient seemed to promise him success. News was brought him, that the king of Siam, whose dominions are almost bordering on Malacca, and who also was in league with Portugal, was preparing a magnificent embassy to the emperor of China for the year following. Whereupon Xavier resolved on returning to Malacca by the first opportunity, and to use his best endeavours, that he might accompany the ambassador of Siam to China.

But the Eternal Wisdom, which sometimes inspires his servants with great designs, does not always will the performance of them; though he wills that on their side nothing be omitted for the execution. God was pleased to deal with Xavier as formerly he had dealt with Moses, who died in view of that very land whither he was commanded to conduct the Israelites. A fever seized on Father Francis on the 20th of November; and at the same time he was endued with a clear knowledge of the day and hour of his death; as he openly declared to the pilot of the vessel, Francis D'Aghiar, who afterwards made an authentic deposition of it by solemn oath.

From that moment he perceived in himself a strange disgust of all earthly things, and thought on nothing but that celestial country whither God was calling him. Being much weakened by his fever, he retired into the vessel, which was the common hospital of the sick, that there he might die in poverty; and the Captain Lewis Almeyda received him, notwithstanding all the orders of his master Don Alvarez. But the tossing of the ship giving him an extraordinary headach, and hindering him from applying himself to God, as he desired, the day ensuing he requested that he might be set on shore again. He was landed and left upon the sands, exposed to the injury of the air, and the inclemency of the season, especially to the blasts of a piercing north wind, which then arose. He had there died without relief, had not a Portuguese more charitable than the rest, whose name was George Alvarez, caused him to be carried into hiscabin; which yet was little different from the naked shore, as being open on every side.

The indications of his disease being an acute pain in his side, and a great oppression, Alvarez was of opinion that they ought to breathe a vein; and the Father was consenting to it, by a blind submission to the judgment of his host, though he knew beforehand that all manner of remedies were in vain. A chirurgeon of the ship, who was awkward at his work, and of small experience in his art, bled him so unluckily, that he hurt the nerves, and the patient fell immediately into swooning convulsions; yet they drew blood from him a second time; and that operation had all the ill accidents of the former. Besides which, it was attended with a horrible nauseousness; insomuch, that he could take no nourishment, at least the little which he took, consisted only of some few almonds, which the captain of the vessel sent him out of charity. The disease increased hourly, and he grew weaker every day; but his countenance was still serene, and his soul enjoyed a perpetual calmness. Sometimes he lifted up his eyes to heaven, and at other times fixed them on his crucifix, entertaining divine conversation with his God, and not without shedding abundant tears. He remained in this condition till the 28th of November, when the fever mounted into his head. During this delirium he talked of nothing but of God, and of his passage into China, but in terms more tender and ardent than ever formerly.

At length he lost his speech, and recovered not the use of it till three days afterwards: his strength then left him all at once, so that it was expected every moment that he would pass away; which notwithstanding, he once more recovered, and having the free exercise both of his reason and his speech, he renewed his entertainments with his Saviour in an audible manner. Nothing was to be heard from him but devout aspirations, and short ejaculations of prayer, but those full of life and of affection. The assistants understood not all he said, because he continually spoke in Latin; and Antonio de Sainte Foy, who never left him, has only reported, that the man of God made frequent repetition of these words, _Jesu, fili David, miserere mei!_ and these also, which were so familiar to him, _sanctissima Trinitas_! Besides which, invoking the blessed Virgin, he would say, _Monstra te esse Matrem!_ He passed two days without taking any food; and having ordered his priestly habits, and the other church-stuff which he used in saying mass, to be carried aboard the ship, together with those books which he had composed for the instruction of the Eastern people, he disposed himself for his last hour, which was near approaching.

Besides Antonio de Sainte Foy, he had near his person a young Indian, whom he had brought with him from Goa. The saint, dying as he was, cast his eyes on the young man, and appeared discomposed in looking on him; afterwards, with a compassionate regard, he twice pronounced these words, "Ah miserable man!" and afterwards shed tears. God, at that moment, was pleased to reveal to Xavier, the unhappy death of this young Indian, who, five or six months afterwards, falling into most horrible debauches, was killed on the place by the shot of an arquebuse. So that the spirit of prophecy accompanied the holy man, even to his last breath.

At last, on the 2d of December, which fell on Friday, having his eyes all bathed in tears, and fixed with great tenderness of soul upon his crucifix, he pronounced these words, _In te, Domine, speravi, non confundar in aeternum_; and at the same instant, transported with celestial joy, which appeared upon his countenance, he sweetly gave up the ghost, towards two of the clock in the afternoon, and in the year of God 1552.

He was six-and-forty years of age, and had passed ten-and-a-half of them in the Indies. His stature was somewhat above the middle size; his constitution strong; his air had a mixture of pleasingness and majesty; he was fresh-coloured, had a large forehead, a well-proportioned nose; his eyes were blue, but piercing and lively; his hair and beard of a dark chesnut; his continual labours had made him gray betimes; and in the last year of his life, he was grizzled almost to whiteness. This without question gave occasion to his first historians to make him five-and-fifty years old, before the certain proofs of his age came at length to be discovered.

When it was known that Father Francis was expired, many of the ship, and even the most devoted to the governor, ran to the cabin. They found the same fresh colour on his face as he had when living, and at the first sight could hardly persuade themselves that he was dead. When they had looked on him at a nearer distance, piety began to be predominant over all their other thoughts: they kneeled down by him, and kissed his hands with reverence, recommending themselves to him, with tears in their eyes, as nothing doubting but that his happy soul was perfectly enjoying God in heaven.

His corpse was not laid into the ground till Sunday towards noon. His funerals were made without any ceremony; and, besides Antonio de Sainte Foy, Francis d'Aghiar, and two others, there were not any more assistants. An historian of the Indies has written, that the unsupportable coldness of that day, was the occasion of it. But in all probability, the apprehension which the ship's company had of drawing on themselves the displeasure of the governor, Don Alvarez, had at least as great a share in it as the sharpness of the season. They took off his cassock, which was all in tatters; and the four, who had paid him those last duties, divided it amongst them, out of devotion; after which they arrayed him in his sacerdotal habits.

George Alvarez took upon himself the care of bestowing the body in a large chest, made after the Chinese fashion; he caused this chest to be filled up with unslaked lime; to the end that, the flesh being soon consumed, they might carry the bones in the vessel, which within some few months was to return to India.

At the point of the haven there was a little spot of rising ground, and at the foot of this hillock a small piece of meadow, where the Portuguese had set up a cross. Near that cross they interred the saint: they cast up two heaps of stones, the one at his head, the other at his feet, as a mark of the place where he was buried.

In the mean season, God made manifest the holiness of his servant in the kingdom of Navarre, by a miraculous accident, or rather by the ceasing of a miracle. In a little chapel, at the castle of Xavier, there was an ancient crucifix made of plaster, of about the stature of a man. In the last year of the Father's life, this crucifix was seen to sweat blood in great abundance every Friday, but after Xavier was dead the sweating ceased. The crucifix is to be seen even at this day, at the same place, with the blood congealed along the arms and thighs, to the hands and sides. They, who have beheld it, have been informed by the inhabitants of the neighbourhood, that some persons of that country having taken away some of the flakes of that clotted blood, the bishop of Pampeluna had forbidden any one from henceforward to diminish any part of it, under pain of excommunication. They also learnt, that it had been observed, according; to the news which came from the Indies, that at the same time when Xavier laboured extraordinarily, or that he was in some great danger, this crucifix distilled blood on every side; as if then, when the apostle was actually suffering for Jesus Christ, Jesus Christ was suffering for him, notwithstanding that he is wholly impassible. The ship, which was at the port of Sancian, being at the point of setting sail For the Indies, Antonio de Sainte Foy, and George Alvarez, desired the captain, Luys Almeyda, not to leave upon the isle the remainders of Father Francis.

One of the servants of Almeyda opened the coffin, by the order of his master, on the 17th of February, 1553, to see if the flesh were totally consumed, so that the bones might be gathered together; but having taken the lime from off the face, they found it ruddy and fresh-coloured, like that of a man who is in a sweet repose. His curiosity led him farther to view the body; he found it in like manner whole, and the natural moisture uncorrupted. But that he might entirely satisfy all doubts and scruples, he cut a little of the flesh on the right thigh, near the knee, and beheld the blood running from it. Whereupon he made haste to advertise the captain of what he was an eye-witness; and carried with him a little piece of flesh, which he had cut off, and which was about a finger's length. All the company ran immediately to the place of burial, and having made an exact observation of the body, found it to be all entire, and without any putrefaction. The sacerdotal habits, with which he had' been vested after his disease, were nowise damaged by the lime. And what was most amazing to them all, was, that the holy corpse exhaled an odour so delightful, and so fragrant, that, by the relation of many there present, the most exquisite perfumes came nothing near it, and the scent was judged to be celestial.

Then those very people, who, basely to comply with the brutality of Alvarez, had misused Father Xavier in his life, after his decease did honours to him; and many of them asked his pardon with weeping eyes, that they had forsaken him so unworthily in his sickness. Some amongst them exclaimed openly againt Alvarez, without fearing the consequence; and there was one who said aloud, what was said afterwards by the viceroy of the Indies, Don Alphonso de Norogna, "That Alvarez de Atayda had been the death of Father Francis, both by his persecutions at Malacca, and by the cruelties of his servants at Sancian." With these pious meditations, having laid the unslaked lime once more upon the face and body, the sacred remains were carried into the ship; and not long after they set sail, esteeming themselves happy to bear along with them so rich a treasure to the Indies.

They arrived at Malacca, March 22, without meeting in their passage any of those dreadful whirlwinds which infest those seas; as if the presence of this holy corpse was endued with virtue to dispel them. Before they had gained the port, they sent in their chalop to give them notice in the town of the present which they were about to make them: though none of the Society were in Malacca, and that the plague was there violently raging, yet the whole nobility, and all the body of the clergy, came with James Pereyra to the shore, to receive the blessed body, each with a waxen taper in his hand, and carried it in ceremony to the church of Our Lady of the Mount, followed by a crowd of Christians, Mahometans, and Idolaters, who on this occasion seemed all to be joined in the same religion.

Don Alvarez was the only person who was wanting in his reverence to the saint: he was then actually at play in his palace, while the procession was passing by; and, at the noise of the people, putting his head out at the window, he miscalled the public devotion, by the names of silliness and foppery; after which, he set him again to gaming. But his impiety did not long remain unpunished, and the predictions of the man of God made haste to justify their truth.

The viceroy of the Indies, upon the complaints which were brought against Don Alvarez for his tyrannical proceedings, deprived him of the government of Malacca; and causing him to be brought to Goa as a prisoner of state, sent him to Portugal under a sufficient guard. There all his goods were confiscated to the king's exchequer; and for himself, he was condemned to perpetual imprisonment Before his departure from the Indies, he had gotten an obscene disease, which increased to that degree in Europe, that he died of it at last in a shameful manner, no remedy availing to his cure; the stench of his polluted body having first made him insupportable to all the world. As for Pereyra, who had sacrificed his whole estate for the benefit of souls, and propagation of the faith, though the governor had so unjustly made a seizure of his fortunes, yet King John III. restored him all with interest, and heaped his royal favours on him in succeeding years, according to the prediction of the Father.

But the devotion of the people failed not of an Immediate reward. The pestilence, which for some weeks had laid waste the town, as the saint had foretold not long before his death, in his letter to Father Francis Perez, on the sudden ceased; insomuch, that no infection was from thenceforward caught; and they, who had been infected, were cured, without taking any remedy. Besides this contagious disease, the famine raged to that degree, that multitudes of people daily died of hunger. This second judgment was likewise diverted at the same time; for, together with the vessel, which bore the sacred body, there came in a fleet of ships, which were laden with all manner of provisions, to supply the necessities of the town.

These so considerable favours ought to have obliged the inhabitants to have honoured the body of their benefactor with a sepulchre which was worthy of him. In the mean time, whether the fear of their governor withheld them, or that God permitted it for the greater glory of his servant, having taken the body out of the chest, they buried it without the church, where the common sort of people were interred; and, which was yet more shameful, they made the grave too scanty; so that crushing the body to give it entrance, they broke it somewhere about the shoulders, and there gushed out blood, which diffused a most fragrant odour. And farther, to carry their civility and discretion to the highest point, they trampled so hard upon the earth, which covered the blessed corpse, that they bruised it in many parts; as if it had been the destiny of that holy man to be tormented by the people of Malacca, both during his life, and after his decease. The sacred corpse remained thus without honour, till the month of August, when Father John Beyra came from Goa, in his return to the Moluccas, with two companions whom Gaspar Barzæus, the vice-provincial, had given him, pursuant to the orders of Father Xavier. This man, having always had a tender affection for the saint, was most sensibly afflicted for his death; and could not think of continuing his voyage to the Moluccas, till he had looked upon the body, of which so many wonders were related. Opening himself on that subject to James Pereyra, and two or three other friends of the dead apostle, they took up his body privately one night. The corpse was found entire, fresh, and still exhaling a sweet odour; neither had the dampness of the ground, after five months burial, made the least alteration in him: they found even the linen which was over his face tinctured with vermilion blood.

This surprising sight so wrought upon their minds, that they thought it their duty, not to lay it again into the ground, but rather to contrive the means of transporting it to Goa. Pereyra ordered a coffin to be made of a precious wood, and after they had garnished it with rich China damask, they put the corpse into it, wrapping it in cloth of gold, with a pillow of brocard underneath the head. The coffin was afterwards bestowed in a proper place, known only to the devoted friends of Father Xavier; and it pleased the Almighty to declare, by a visible miracle, that their zeal was acceptable to him: For a waxen taper, which they had lighted up before the coffin, and which naturally must have burnt out within ten hours, lasted eighteen days entire, burning day and night; and it was observed, that the droppings of the wax weighed more than the taper itself at the beginning.

In the mean time an occasion offered for the voyage of the Moluccas, while they were waiting for an opportunity of passing to Goa. Beyra, therefore, put to sea, more inflamed than ever with the zeal of souls; and filled with a double portion of an apostolic spirit, which the sight of the saint had inspired into him. But of the two companions which had been assigned for the mission of the Moluccas, he left one behind him at Malacca, to be a guardian of that holy treasure, and this was Emanuel Pavora. Peter de Alcaceva at the same time returned from Japan, whither he had been sent from Goa, for the affairs of that new Christianity. And both of them, not long after, carried the holy corpse along with them in the vessel of Lopez de Norogna.

The ship was so old and worn, and out of all repair, that none durst venture to embark upon her. But when once it was divulged, that it was to carry the corpse of Father Francis, every one made haste to get a corner in her, not doubting but there they might be safe. And the passengers had no cause to repent them of their confidence; for, in effect, God delivered them, more than once, miraculously from shipwreck.

A furious tempest, almost at their first setting out, cast them upon banks of sand, and the keel struck so far into it, that they could not get her off; when, against all human appearances, the wind coming about, and blowing full in their faces, disengaged the vessel; and, that it might manifestly appear to be the hand of God, the blast ceased that very moment when the keel was loosened from the sands.

Not long after, at the entry into the gulph of Ceylon, they struck impetuously against some hidden shelves, the rudder flying off with the fury of the stroke, the keel stuck fast within the rock; and it was a miracle that the vessel, being so crazy, did not split asunder. The mariners did that on this occasion, which is commonly put in practice in extremity of danger: They cut the masts with their hatchets, but that being of no effect, they were going to throw all their lading overboard, to ease the ship; but the fury of the waves, which beat upon her on every side, and outrageously tossed her, suffered them not to perform what they desired. Then they had their last recourse to the intercession of that saint, whose corpse they carried. Having drawn it out of the pilot's cabin, they fell on their knees about it with lighted flambeaux; and, as if Father Xavier had been yet living, and that he had beheld and heard them, they begged succour of him from that eminent destruction.

Their prayer was scarcely ended, when they heard a rumbling noise from underneath the vessel; and at the same time, perceived her following her course in open sea: from whence they concluded, that the rock was cleft in pieces, and had left a free passage for the ship.

They pursued their voyage cheerfully; and turning towards the cape of Comorine, landed at Cochin. The whole city came to pay their last duty to their instructor and beloved Father; and it is incredible what demonstrations of piety the people gave. From Cochin they set sail for Baticula. The wife of Antonio Rodriguez, one of the king's officers, who had long been sick, was in hope to recover, if she could see Father Francis. She caused herself to be carried to the ship, and at the sight of the dead saint, was restored to her health at the same moment. Not satisfied with this, she was desirous to have a little piece of the cope, with which the Father was habited; and it is wonderful what cures she effected by that precious relique.

The ship being now within twenty leagues of Goa, and being unable to make any farther way, because of the contrary winds, the captain went into the chalop, with some of his people, and got to the town by the help of oars, that himself might have the honour of bearing the first news to the viceroy, and the Fathers of the Society, that the blessed corpse was coming to them. Father Caspar Barzæus was already dead, and Father Melchior Nugnez declared his successor in his two offices, of rector of the college, and vice-provincial of the Indies, in virtue of the letter which Father Xavier had left sealed behind him when he went for China, and which was opened after the death of Gaspar, according to the orders of Xavier himself.

The viceroy immediately ordered a light galley for Nugnez; upon which he and three others of the Society embarking, together with four young men of the seminary, they set sail towards the vessel, to bear off the body of the saint. They received it with the honourable discharge of all the cannon, not only from the ship of Lopez, but from six other vessels which were in company, and which had been wind-bound towards Baticula. On the 15th of March, in the year 1554, the galley landed at Rebendar, which is within half a league of Goa; she remained there the rest of that day, and all the night; while they were making preparations in the town, for the solemn reception of the holy apostle of the Indies. The next morning, which was Friday in Passion week, six barks were seen to come, which were all illuminated with lighted torches, and pompously adorned, wherein was the flower of the Portuguese nobility. Twelve other barks attended them, with three hundred of the principal inhabitants, each of them holding a taper in his hand; and in every one of these barks, there was instrumental music of all sorts, and choirs of voices, which made an admirable harmony. The whole squadron was drawn up into two wings, to accompany the galley, which rowed betwixt them. The body of the saint was covered with cloth of gold, which was the present of Pereyra, and was placed upon the stern, under a noble canopy, with lighted flambeaux, and rich streamers waving on both sides of it,

In this equipage, they rowed towards Goa, but very softly, and in admirable order. All the town was gathered on the shore, in impatient expectation of their loving and good Father. When they perceived the vessel from afar, there was nothing to be heard but cries of joy, nothing to be seen but tears of devotion. Some, more impatient than the rest, threw themselves into the sea, and swimming up to the galley, accompanied it to the shore in the same posture.

The viceroy was there waiting for it, attended by his guards, the remaining part of the nobility, the council royal, and the magistrates, all in mourning. At the time when the holy corpse was landing, a company of young men, consecrated to the service of the altars, sung the _Benedictus Dominus Deus Israel._ In the mean while, they ordered the ceremony of the procession after this ensuing manner:--

Ninety children went foremost, in long white robes, with chaplets of flowers on their heads, and each of them holding in his hand an olive branch. The Brotherhood of Mercy followed them, with a magnificent standard. The clergy succeeded to the Brotherhood, and walked immediately before the corpse, which was carried by the fathers of the Society. The viceroy, with his court, closed up the ceremony, which was followed by an innumerable multitude of people. All the streets were hung with tapestry; and when the blessed corpse appeared, flowers were thrown upon it from all the windows, and from the tops of houses.

But nothing rendered the pomp more famous, than the miracles which at that time were wrought; for there seemed to breathe out from this holy body, a saving virtue, together with a celestial odour. Many sick persons, who had caused themselves to be carried out into the streets, were cured with only seeing it; and even some, who were not able to leave their beds, recovered their health with the bare invocation of his name. Jane Pereyra was of this number; after a sickness of three months, being almost reduced to a despair of life, she had no sooner implored the assistance of the saint, but she found herself in a perfect state of health.

Another young maiden, who was just at the point of death, and held the consecrated taper in her hand, having been recommended by her mother to the patronage of the saint, came suddenly to herself, and rose up well recovered, while the procession was passing by the house.

After many turns and windings, at last they proceeded to the college of St Paul; and there set down the coffin, in the great chapel of the church. A retrenchment had been made before the chapel, to keep off the crowd; but it was immediately broken down, notwithstanding the opposition of the guards, which were placed on purpose to defend it. To appease the tumult, they were forced to shew the saint three times successively, and to hold him upright, that he might more easily be seen by the longing multitude. It was also thought convenient to leave the body exposed to view, for three days together, for the comfort of the inhabitants, who were never weary with gazing on it; and who, in gazing, were pierced with a sensible devotion.

New miracles were wrought in presence of the holy body. The blind received their sight, those who were taken with the palsy recovered the use of their limbs, and the lepers became clean as babes. At the sight of these miraculous cures, the people published aloud all those wonderful operations, which they knew to have been performed by Father Xavier; and his old companion John Deyro, at that time a religious of the order of St Francis, related, with tears of tenderness and devotion, what the saint had prophesied of him, which was now accomplished. In the mean time, on that very day, which was Friday, the canons of the cathedral solemnly sung the high mass of the cross. The clay following, the religious of St Francis, whom the man of God had always honoured, and tenderly affected, came to sing the mass of the blessed Virgin, in the church of the Society.

When in this manner the public devotion had been accomplished, on Sunday night the coffin was placed on an eminence near the high altar, on the gospel side.

In this place I ought not to omit, that the vessel which had borne this sacred pledge to Goa, split asunder of itself, and sunk to the bottom, so soon as the merchandizes were unloaded, and all the passengers were come safe on shore; which was nothing less than a public declaration of Almighty God, that he had miraculously preserved her in favour of that holy treasure; and that a ship which had been employed on so pious an occasion, was never to be used on any secular account.

As soon as it was known in Europe that Father Xavier was dead, they began to speak of his canonization. And on this account, Don John the Third, King of Portugal, gave orders to the viceroy of the Indies, Don Francis Barreto, to make a verbal process of the life and miracles of the man of God. This was executed at Goa, at Cochin, at the coast of Fishery, at Malacca at the Moluccas, and other parts; and men of probity, who were also discerning and able persons, were sent upon the places, heard the witnesses, and examined the matters of fact, with all possible exactness.

It is to be acknowledged, that the people took it in evil part, that these informations were made; being fully satisfied of the holiness of the saint, and not being able to endure that it should be doubted in the least; in like manner, neither would they stay, till all the ecclesiastical proceedings were wholly ended, nor till the Holy See had first spoken of rendering him the worship due to saints; they invoked him already in their necessities, and particularly in all sorts of dangers. Some of them placed his picture in their oratories; and even the archbishop of Goa, Don Christopher de Lisbonne, (for the episcopal see had been erected into an archbishopric,) the archbishop, I say, wore on his breast an image of Xavier in little, which he often kissed with a reverent affection: and his devotion was not without reward; for, having been cruelly tormented with the stone, for a month together, he was freed immediately from it, and felt not any farther pains.

It also happened, that in many places of the Indies the new converts built churches in honour of Father Francis, through a precipitate and indiscreet devotion, which their good meaning and their zeal are only capable of excusing. Amongst those churches, there was one much celebrated, on the coast of Travancore. The Saracens having demolished it, together with eleven other ancient structures of piety, the Christians, who, by reason of their poverty, were not able to rebuild them all, restored only this one church, which was dearer to them than any of the rest.

For what remains, in what place soever any churches were dedicated to the Father, there never failed a wonderful concourse of people to honour the memory of the holy man; and, according to the relation of Francis Nugnez, vicar of Coulan, they were obliged to sink a well for the relief of poor pilgrims near the church, which was built in honour of him at that town. Nugnez also reports, "That those which had been consecrated to the apostles, and other saints, in a manner lost their titles, when once the image of St Xavier was there exposed; and that the people, turning all their devotion towards him, were wont to call them the churches of Father Francis."

But what was most to be admired, even the professed enemies of Jesus Christ paid him reverence after his decease, as well as during his life; calling him, "the man of prodigies, the friend of heaven, the master of nature, and the god of the world." Some of them undertook long voyages, and came to Goa, expressly to behold his body exempted from corruption, and which, only excepting motion, had all the appearance of life. There were amongst the Gentiles, who spoke of raising altars to him; and some people of the sect of Mahomet did, in effect, dedicate a mosque to him, on the western coast of

Comorine. The king of Travancore, though a Mahometan, built a magnificent temple to him; and the infidels had so great a veneration for that place, where the great Father was adored, that they durst not spit upon the ground, if we may believe the testimony of those who were natives of the country.

The Pagans had a custom, that, in confirmation of a truth, they would hold a red-hot iron in their hands, with other superstitions of the like nature; but after that Father Francis came to be held in so great veneration through the Indies, they swore solemnly by his name; and such an oath was generally received for the highest attestation of a truth. Neither did any of them forswear themselves unpunished after such an oath; and God authorized, by many proofs, this religious practice, even by manifest prodigies. Behold a terrible example of it: An Idolater owed a Christian a considerable sum of money; but as he denied his debt, and no legal proof could be made of it, the Christian obliged him to swear in the church, upon the image of St Francis: the Idolater made a false oath without the least scruple; but was scarcely got into his own house, when he began to void blood in abundance at his mouth, and died in a raging fit of madness, which had the resemblance of a man possessed, rather than of one who was distracted.

Neither was his memory less honoured in Japan than in the Indies. The Christians of the kingdom of Saxuma kept religiously a stone, on which he had often preached, and shewed it as a precious rarity. The house wherein he had lodged at Amanguchi, was respected as a sacred place; and was always preserved from ruin, amidst those bloody wars, which more than once had destroyed the town. For what remains, the Indians and Japonians were not the only people which honoured Father Xavier after his decease; the odour of his holy life expanded itself beyond the seas into other Heathen countries where he had never been. And Alphonso Leon Barbuda, who has travelled over all the coasts of Afric, reports, that in the kingdoms of Sofala, beyond the great river of Cuama, and in the isles about it, the name of Father Francis was in high repute; and that those Moors never mentioned him, but with the addition of a wonderful man So many illustrious testimonies, and so far above suspicion, engaged the king of Portugal anew to solicit the canonization of the saint; and in that prospect there was made an ample collection of his virtues, of which I present you with this following extract.

No exterior employments, how many, or how great soever, could divert the Father from the contemplation of celestial things. Being at Goa, his ordinary retirement, after dinner, was into the clock-house of the church, to avoid the interruption of any person; and there, during the space of two hours, he had a close communication with his God. But because he was not always master of himself on those occasions, so as to regulate his time, and that he was sometimes obliged to leave his privacy, he commanded a young man of the seminary of Sainte Foy, whose name was Andrew, to come and give him notice when the two hours, to which he was limited, were expired. One day, when the Father was to speak with the viceroy, Andrew, being come to advertise him, found him seated on a little chair, his hands across his breast, and his eyes fixed on heaven. When he had looked on him a while attentively, he at length called him; but finding that the Father answered not, he spoke yet louder, and made a noise. All this was to no purpose, Xavier continued immovable; and Andrew went his way, having some scruple to disturb the quiet of a man, who had the appearance of an angel, and seemed to enjoy the pleasures of the souls in paradise, He returned, nevertheless, about two hours after, and found him still in the same posture. The young man fearing that he should not comply with duty, if, coming the second time, he should not make himself be heard, began to pull the Father, and to jog him. Xavier at length returning to himself, was in a wonder at the first, that two hours should so soon be slipped away; but coming to know, that he had remained in that place beyond four hours, he went out with Andrew, to go to the palace of the viceroy. He had scarcely set his foot over the threshold, when he seemed to be ravished in spirit once again. After he had made some turns, without well knowing whither he went, he returned as night was beginning to come on, and said to his attendant, "My son, we will take another time to see the governor; it is the will of God, that this present day should be wholly his."

Another time, walking through the streets of the same city, his thoughts were so wholly taken up with God, that he perceived not a furious elephant, who, being broken loose, caused a general terror, and every man made haste out of his way. It was in vain to cry out to the Father, that he might avoid him; he heard nothing, and the enraged beast passed very near him without his knowledge.

In his voyages at sea, he continued earnestly in prayer, from midnight even to sun-rising, and that regularly. From thence it came almost to a proverb amongst the seamen, "That nothing was to be feared in the night, because Father Francis watched the vessel; and the tempests durst not trouble them, while he held conversation with God."

A man of Manapar, at whose house he lodged, and who observed him at divers hours of the night, found him always on his knees before a crucifix, and frequently beheld the chamber enlightened by the rays which darted from his countenance.

While he was sojourning among Christians, the small repose he gave to nature was commonly in the church; to the end he might be near the blessed sacrament, before which he prayed all the remainder of the night. But in countries where yet there were no churches built, he passed the night in the open air; and nothing so much elevated his soul to God as the view of heaven, spangled over, and sowed, as it were, with stars; and this we have from his own relation.

The Pope had permitted him, in consideration of his employments and apostolical labours, to say a breviary which was shorter than the Roman, and had but three lessons: it was called the "Office of the Cross," and was easily granted in those times to such who were overburdened with much business. But Xavier never made use of this permission, what affairs soever he was pressed withal, for the service of Almighty God: on the contrary, before the beginning of every canonical hour, he always said the hymn of _Veni, Creator Spiritus_; and it was observed, that while he said it, his countenance was enlightened, as if the Holy Ghost, whom he invoked, was visibly descended on him.

He daily celebrated the sacrifice of the mass with the same reverence and the same devotion with which he had said it the first time, and most ordinarily performed it at break of day. Those heavenly sweets which overflowed his soul at the altar, spread their mild inundations even over the assistants; and Antonio Andrada reported of himself, that, being then a young soldier, he found such an inward satisfaction when he served the Father, in serving at mass, that, in that consideration, he sought the occasions of performing the clerk's office.

In the midst of his conversations with secular men, the saint was often called aside of God, by certain sudden illuminations which obliged him to retire; and when afterwards they sought him, he was found before the holy sacrament, in some lonely place, engulphed in deep meditations, and frequently suspended in the air, with beams of glory round his countenance. Many ocular witnesses have deposed this matter of fact; but some have affirmed, that at first they have found him on his knees immovable; that they have afterwards observed, how by degrees he was mounted from the earth; and that then, being seized with a sacred horror, they could not stedfastly behold him, so bright and radiant was his countenance. Others have protested, that while he was speaking to them of the things of God, they could perceive him shooting upward, and distancing himself from them on the sudden, and his body raising itself on high of its own motion.

These extraordinary ravishments, which bore some manner of proportion to the glory of the blest above, happened to him from time to time during the sacrifice of the mass, when he came to pronounce the words of consecration; and he was beheld elevated in that manner, particularly at Meliapore and at Malacca. The same was frequently observed at Goa, while be was communicating the people; and what was remarkable, as it was then the custom to give the sacrament in kneeling, he appeared to be lifted from the earth in that humble posture.

For common extasies, he had them almost every day, especially at the altar, and after the sacrifice of the mass: insomuch, that many times they could not bring him to himself, with pulling him by the robe, and violently shaking him.

The delights which he enjoyed at such a time, are only to be comprehended by such souls, which have received from heaven the like favours. Nevertheless, it is evident, that if it be possible for man to enjoy on earth the felicities of heaven, it is then, when the soul, transported out of itself, is plunged, and as it were lost, in the abyss of God.

But it was not only in these extatic transports, that Xavier was intimately united to our Lord: In the midst of his labours, he had his soul recollected in God, without any dissipation caused by the multitude or intricacy of affairs; insomuch, that he remained entire in all he did, and at the same time whole in Him, for whose honour he was then employed.

This so close and so continual an union, could only proceed from a tender chanty: the divine love burning him up in such a manner, that his face was commonly on fire; and both for his interior and outward ardour, they were often forced to throw cold water into his bosom.

Frequently in preaching and in walking, he felt in himself such inward scorching, that, not being able to endure it, he was constrained to give himself air, by opening his cassock before his breast; and this he has been seen to do on many occasions, in the public places at Malacca and at Goa, in the garden of St Paul's college, and in the sandy walks of the sea-shore.

Almost every hour, words of life and fire burst and sallied as it were from out his mouth, which were indeed the holy sparkles of a burning heart. As for example, "O most Holy Trinity! O my Creator! O my Jesus! O Jesus, the desire of my soul!" He spoke these words in Latin, that he might not be understood by the common people: and being on the coast of Fishery, at the kingdom of Travancore, and at the Moluccas, he was heard to speak so many times every day these words, _O Sanctissima Trinitas!_ that the most idolatrous barbarians, when they found themselves in extreme dangers, or that they would express their amazement at any thing, pronounced those very words, without understanding any thing more of them than that they were holy and mysterious.

Even sleep itself had not the power to interrupt those tender aspirations; and all the night long he was heard to say, "O my Jesus, my soul's delight!" or other expressions as full of tenderness, which shewed the inclination of his heart. Being out of his senses by the violence of a burning fever, both at Mozambique and at Sancian, he spoke of God, and to God, with more fervency than ever; insomuch, that his delirium seemed only to be a redoubling of his love. He was so sensible of the interests of the Divine Majesty, that, being touched to the quick with the enormity of those crimes that were committed in the new world, he wrote to a friend of his, in these very terms:--"I have sometimes an abhorrence of my life, and would rather chuse to die than to behold so many outrages done to Jesus Christ, without being able either to hinder or to repair them."

For the rest, that he might always keep alive the fire of divine love, he had incessantly before his eyes the sufferings of our Lord. At the sight of the wounds and of the blood of a crucified God, he fell into sighs and tears, and languishments, and extasies of love. He was consumed with the zeal of returning his Saviour life for life; for martyrdom was his predominant passion, and his sentiments are a continual proof of it. "It sometimes happens, through a singular favour of the Divine Goodness," says he in one of his letters, "that for the service of God we run ourselves into the hazard of death. But we ought to bear in mind, that we are born mortal; and that a Christian is bound to desire nothing more than to lay down his life for Jesus Christ."

From thence proceeded that abundant joy which he conceived, when the faithful poured out their blood for faith; and he wrote to the Fathers at Rome, on occasion of the massacre of the baptized Manarois;-- "We are obliged to rejoice in Jesus Christ, that martyrs are not wanting, not even in our decaying times; and to give Him thanks, that, seeing so few persons make the right use of His grace for their salvation, He permits that the number of the happy shall be completed through the cruelty of men." "Admirable news," says he elsewhere, "is lately come from the Moluccas; they who labour there in the Lord's vineyard suffer exceedingly, and are in continual hazard of their lives I imagine that the Isles del Moro will give many martyrs to our Society, and they will soon be called the Isles of Martyrdom. Let our brethren then, who desire to shed their blood for Jesus Christ, be of good courage, and anticipate their future joy. For, behold at length a seminary of martyrdom is ready for them, and they will have wherewithal to satisfy their longings."

The same love which inspired him with the desire of dying for our Saviour, made him breathe after the sight and the possession of God. He spoke not but of paradise, and concluded almost all his letters with wishing there to meet his brethren.

But his charity was not confined to words and thoughts,--it shone out in his works and actions, and extended itself to the service of his neighbour. Xavier seemed to be only born for the relief of the distressed; he loved the sick with tenderness, and to attend them was what he called his pleasure: he sought out not only wherewithal to feed them but to feast them; and for that purpose begged from the Portuguese the most exquisite regalios, which were sent them out of Europe. He was not ashamed of going round the town with, a wallet on his back, begging linen for the wounded soldiers; he dressed their hurts, and did it with so much the more affection, when they were the most putrified and loathsome to the smell. If he happened to meet with any beggar who was sinking under sickness, he took him in his arms, bore him to the hospital, prepared his remedies, and dressed his meat with his own hands.

Though all the miserable were dear to him, yet he assisted the prisoners after a more particular manner, with the charities which he gathered for them; and in Goa, which was the common tribunal of the Indies, he employed one day in the week in doing good to such who were overwhelmed with debts. If he had not wherewithal to pay off their creditors entirely, he mollified them at least with his civilities, and obliged them sometimes to release one moiety of what was owing to them.

The poor, with one common voice, called him their Father, and he also regarded them as his children. Nothing was given him, but what passed through his hands into theirs, who were members of Jesus Christ; even so far as to deprive himself of necessaries. He heaped up, as I may call it, a treasury of alms, not only for the subsistence of the meaner sort, who are content with little, but for the maintenance of honourable families, which one or two shipwrecks had ruined all at once; and for the entertainment of many virgins of good parentage, whom poverty might necessitate to an infamous course of living.

The greatest part of the miracles, which on so many occasions were wrought by him, was only for the remedy of public calamities, or for the cure of particular persons; and it was in the same spirit, that, being one day greatly busied in hearing the confessions of the faithful at Goa, he departed, abruptly in appearance, out of the confessional, and from thence out of the church also, transported with some inward motion, which he could not possibly resist: after he had made many turns about the town, without knowing whither he went, he happened upon a stranger, and having tenderly embraced him, conducted him to the college of the Society. There that miserable creature, whom his despair was driving to lay violent hands upon himself, having more seriously reflected on his wicked resolution, pulled out the halter, which he had secretly about him, and with which he was going to have hanged himself, and gave it into the Father's hands. The saint, to whom it was revealed, that extreme misery had reduced the unhappy wretch to this dismal melancholy, gave him comfort, retained him in the college for some time, and at length dismissed him with a round sum of money, sufficient for the entertainment of his family. He recommended, without ceasing, his friends and benefactors to our Lord; he prayed both day and night for the prosperity of King John III. of Portugal, whom he called the true protector of all the Society: But the persecutors of the saint had a greater share in his devotions than any others; and at the same time when he was treated so unworthily by the governor of Malacca, he daily offered for him the sacrifice of the mass. He was used to say, that to render good for evil, was in some sort a divine revenge; and he revenged himself in that very sort on the governor of Comorine, which, in one of his letters is thus attested: "My dear brother in Jesus Christ, (thus he wrote to Father Mansilla,) I hear uncomfortable news, that the governor's ship is destroyed by fire; that his houses also are burnt down; that he is retired into an island, and has nothing left him, even for the necessary provisions of life. I desire you, out of Christian charity, to go with the soonest to his relief, with your Christians of Punical: get what barks you can together, and load them with all manner of provisions; I have written earnestly to the chief of the people, that they furnish you with all things necessary, and especially with fresh water, which, as you know, is very scarce in those desart islands. I would go in person to the assistance of the governor, if I thought my presence might be acceptable to him; but of late he hates me, and has written that he could not say, without giving scandal, all the evils I have done him. God and man can bear me witness, if ever I have done him the least prejudice."

His charity towards his neighbour has principally appeared in what he did for the conversion of souls. It is difficult to enumerate all his travels by land, and his voyages by sea; and if any one would take that pains, it might be thought he had scarce the leisure to do any thing but travel. Without mentioning his journey's from France to Italy, and from Italy to Portugal, he went from Lisbon to Mozambique, and from Mozambique to Melinda, to Socotoro, and in fine to Goa. From Goa he passed to Cape Comorine, and to the Fishing-coast, from thence to Cochin, and returning to Goa, came back to the coast of Fishery, entered far into the islands, and returned to the Fishery, from whence he travelled to the kingdom of Travancore, which is seated to the west.

After he had run over all these coasts, he was a second time at Cochin and at Goa; from Goa he took the way of Cambaya, and having crossed that whole region, which lies extended from the mouth of the river Indus, as far as Cochin, he made the tour of Cape Cori, and went to the islands of Ceylon, of Manar, and of Las Vaccas. There he took shipping for Negapatan, and from thence undertook the voyage of Meliapor, along the coasts of Coromandel. From Meliapor he set sail for Malacca, from Malacca he descended towards the equinoctial, which having passed, he entered into the southern hemisphere, as far as the Isle of Banda, and those of Amboyna, Nuliager, Ulate, Baranura, Rosalao, and others without name, unknown even to seamen and geographers.

In sequel of these voyages, he turned towards the Moluccas, was at Ternata, and passed from thence to the Isles del Moro. Went again to Ternata and Amboyna, repassed the equator, and returned to Malacca; from thence, by sea, he regained the port of Cochin; but immediately after his arrival departed for the coast of Fishery and Ceylon. After this he returned to Goa, and drew downward on the same coast for Bazain; from Bazain he returned once more to Goa and Cochin. He passed a-new from Goa to Cochin, and from Cochin to Goa; from thence following the coast as far as Cape Comorine, he set sail towards Malacca. Having there made some little stay, he continued his course northward, and coasting certain isles in sight of China, came at length to Japan. After he had made some courses there, during the space of two years, from Cangoxima to Firando, from. Firando to Amanguchi, from Amanguchi to Meaco, from Meaco back to Amanguchi, and from thence to Bungo, he put once more to sea, touched at the isle of Sancian, and was driven by tempest on the Isle of Mindanao, one of the Phillippinas. Once again he went to Malacca, and to Goa; from Goa, he repassed the fifth time to Malacca, and from thence arrived at Sancian, where death concluded all his travels.

Behold the sequel of the voyages of the Indian apostle Francis Xavier! I have omitted a vast number of islands and regions, where we are satisfied he carried the light of the gospel; I say I have not mentioned them, because the time is not precisely known, when he made these voyages. For what remains, I undertake not to reckon up the leagues which he has travelled, (the supputation would be difficult to make,) and content myself to say in general, that, according to the rules of our geographers, who have exactly measured the terrestrial globe, if all his courses were to be computed, they would be found to be many times exceeding the circumference of this world.

In the mean time, the least of his business, in all his travels, was to travel: And they who were best acquainted with him, report of him, what St Chrysostom said of the apostle St Paul, "That he ran through the world with an incredible swiftness, and as it were on the wing," yet not without labour, nor that labour without fruit, but preaching, baptizing, confessing, disputing with the Gentiles, rooting out Idolaters, reforming manners, and throughout establishing the Christian piety. His apostolical labours were attended with all the incommodities of life; and if those people were to be credited, who the most narrowly observed him, it was a continual miracle that he lived; or rather the greatest miracle of Xavier was not to have revived so many dead, but not to die himself of labour, during the incessant sweat of ten years toiling.

His zeal alone sustained him; but how painful soever were the functions of his ministry, he acquitted himself of them with so much promptitude and joy, that, by the relation of Father Melchior Nugnez, he seemed to do naturally all he did. These are the very words of Nugnez: "The Father, Master Francis, in labouring for the salvation of the Saracens and Idolaters, seemed to act not by any infused or acquired virtue, but by a natural motion: for he could neither live, nor take the least pleasure, but in evangelical employments; in them he found even his repose; and to him it was no labour to conduct others to the love and knowledge of his God."

Thus also, whensoever there was the least probability that the faith might be planted in any new country of the Gentiles, he flew thither in despite of all threatening difficulties. The certain number is not known of those whom he converted, but the received opinion amounts it to seven hundred thousand souls. Which notwithstanding, it ought not to be believed that he instructed them but lightly; for before he christened them, he gave them a thorough insight into all the principles of faith. According to their different conditions, his instructions were also different. He had some which were proper to youth, others for wives, for widows, for servants, and for masters. He never changed places till he had left behind him a solid establishment of faith, and capable of preserving itself on its own basis. And in effect, of all the countries which he made Christian, there is none to be found which relapsed into idolatry, excepting only the town of Tolo; and not that neither for any long continuance. But it is well known, that the people, who, during the space of fifteen or sixteen years, had not seen the face of any priest, or even of any Christian stranger, have been found instructed in religion, and as fervent in the practice of good works, as if they had but newly received baptism. It is known, that many of those converts were not less firm in their belief, than the prince of the isle of Rosalao, whom Pedro Martinez protests to have heard say, "That though all the world should arm against him, they should never be able to tear out of his heart that persuasion which Father Francis had inspired into him."

We know farther, that some of them having been made captives by the Pagans, have preserved their faith entire in the midst of Heathenism; and have chosen rather to lose their lives in torments, than renounce their Saviour Jesus Christ. The saint was accustomed to desire earnestly of God, the conversion of the Gentiles, in the sacrifice of the altar; and for that very end, said a most devout prayer, which he composed in Latin; and is thus rendered in our language.

"O eternal God, creator of all things, mercifully remember, that the souls of Infidels are the work of thy hands, and that they are created to thy resemblance. Behold, O Lord, how hell is filled with them, to the dishonour of thy name. Remember that Jesus Christ thy son, for their salvation, suffered a most cruel death; permit not, I beseech thee, that he should be despised by those Idolaters. Vouchsafe to be propitiated by the prayers of the church, thy most holy spouse, and call to mind thy own compassion. Forget, O Lord, their infidelity, and work in such manner, that at length they may acknowledge for their God, our Saviour Jesus Christ, whom thou hast sent into the world, and who is our salvation, our life, our resurrection, by whom we have been redeemed from hell, and to whom be all glory now and evermore. Amen."

The industry which the saint employed in converting the nations of the East, or in strengthening their conversion, was of various sorts. In those places where he preached the gospel, he erected crosses on the seashore, on hills, and in public passages, to the end, that the view of that sign of our salvation might give the Gentiles the curiosity to know the meaning of it, or to inspire them with religious thoughts, if they had already heard speak of Jesus Christ.

As it was impossible for him to preach always, or in all places, he writ many instructions relating to faith and to good manners, some more ample, and others more brief, but all in the languages of the converted nations; and it was by these instructions, in writing, that the children learned to read. The saint also composed devout hymns, and set the Lord's Prayer in musical numbers, to be sung, together with the Angelical Salutation, and the Apostles' Creed. By these means he banished those ribald songs and ballads, which the new Christians were accustomed to sing before they had received baptism; for those of Xavier were so pleasing, to men, women, and children, that they sung them day and night, both in their houses, and in the open fields.

But amongst all the means which the Father used for the conversion of Infidels, the most efficacious was this: So soon as he entered into a country of Idolaters, he endeavoured to gain to God those persons who were the most considerable, either for their dignity, or by their birth, and especially the sovereign; not only because the honour of Jesus Christ requires, that crowned-heads should be subject to him, but also, that, by the conversion of princes, the people are converted. So much authority there resides in the example of a monarch, over his subjects, in every nation of the world.

He was of easy conversation to all sorts of persons, but more familiar with the greatest sinners, not seeming to understand that they were keepers of mistresses, blasphemers, or sacrilegious persons. He was particularly free in his converse with soldiers, who are greater libertines, and more debauched, in the Indies than elsewhere; for, that they might the less suspect him, he kept them company; and because sometimes, when they saw him coming, they hid their cards and dice, he told them, "They were not of the clergy, neither could they continue praying all the day; that cheating, quarrelling, and swearing, were forbid to gamesters, but that play was not forbidden to a soldier." Sometimes he played at chess himself, out of compliance, when they whom he studied to withdraw from vice were lovers of that game; and a Portuguese gentleman, whose name was Don Diego Norogna, had once a very ill opinion of him for it. This cavalier, who had heard a report of Xavier, that he was a saint-like man, and desired much to have a sight of him, happened to be aboard of the same galley. Not knowing his person, he enquired which was he, but was much surprised to find him playing at chess with a private soldier; for he had formed in his imagination, the idea of a man who was recollected and austere, one who never appeared in public, but to discourse of eternity, or to work miracles: "What, in the name of God," said Norogna, "is this your saint! For my part, I believe not one syllable of his sanctity, and am much deceived if he be not as arrant a priest as any of his fellows." Don Pedro de Castro, his comrade, and cousin, took pains, to little purpose, to persuade Norogna of the wonderful things which had been wrought by Xavier: Norogna still adhered to his opinion, because he always found the Father cheerful, and in good humour. The whole company going ashore on the coast of Malabar, he perceived Xavier taking a walk by himself into a wood, and sent after him one of his servants to observe his actions: The servant found the man of God raised from the ground into the air; his eyes fixed on heaven, and rays about his countenance. He ran to give notice of his discovery to his master; who, upon the report, came thither, and was himself a witness of it. Then Norogna was satisfied that Xavier was truly a saint, and that his holiness was not incompatible with the gaiety of his conversation. By these methods the apostle of the Indies attracted the hearts of the soldiery to himself, before he gained them to our Lord.

He took almost the same measures with the merchants; for he seemed to be concerned for nothing more than for their interests: He gave his benediction to the vessels which they were sending out for traffic, and made many enquiries concerning the success of their affairs, as if he had been co-partner with them. But while he was discoursing with them of ports, of winds, and of merchandizes, he dexterously turned the conversation on the eternal gains of heaven: "How bent are our desires," said he, "on heaping up the frail and perishable treasures of this world, as if there were no other life besides this earthly being, nor other riches besides the gold of Japan, the silks of China, and the spices of the Moluccas! Ah, what profits it a man to gain the universe, and lose his soul?" These very words, which Father Ignatius had formerly used to Xavier, in order to loosen him from the world, were gotten familiar to him, and he had them frequently in his mouth. In respect of the new Christians, his conduct was altogether fatherly. He suffered their rough and barbarous behaviour; and required no more from them in the beginning, than what might be expected then from people of base extraction, and grown inveterate in vice As they were generally poor, he took a particular care of their families; and obtained from the king of Portugal, that the Paravas should be discharged from certain excessive yearly tributes. He protected them more than once from the fury of their neighbouring nations, who made war against them out of hatred to the faith, and induced the governor of the Indies to send a royal army to their relief; he saved them even from the violence of the officers, who despoiled them of their goods through avarice, and set bounds to the unjust exactions of those griping ministers, by threatening to complain of them both to King John the Third, and to the Cardinal Infante, who was grand inquisitor.

As the sin of impurity was the reigning vice in India amongst the Portuguese, he applied himself, in a particular manner, to withdraw them from their voluptuous living. The first rule of his proceeding was to insinuate himself into the favour, not only of the concubinarians, but of their mistresses; and he compassed this by the mildness of his aspect, by the obligingness of his words, and sometimes by good offices. Yet we cannot think that the conversions of sinners cost him only these addresses. Before he treated with them concerning the important business of their souls, he treated with God at the holy altars; but to render his prayers more efficacious, he joined them with all manner of austerities. Having notice that three Portuguese soldiers, belonging to the garrison of Amboyna, had lived for five years past in great debauchery, he got their good wills by his engaging carriage, and wrought so well, that these libertines, as wicked as they were, lodged him in their quarters during a whole Lent, so much they were charmed with his good humour. But while he appeared thus gay amongst them in his outward behaviour, for fear of giving them any disgust of his company, he underwent most rigorous penances to obtain the grace of their conversion, and used his body so unmercifully, that he was languishing for a month of those severities. When Xavier had reduced his penitents to that point at which he aimed, that is, when he had brought them to confession, they cost him not less pains than formerly. He always begged of God their perseverance with his tears; and frequently, when he had enjoined them some light penance, paid for them the remainder of their debts with bloody disciplining of his own body. But when he lighted on intractable and stubborn souls, he left them not off for their contumacy, but rather sought their good opinion; and, on occasion, shewed them a better countenance than usual, that thence they might be given to understand how ready he was for their reception.

When he went from Ternata to Amboyna, he left but two persons who were visibly engaged in vice: The first opportunity which the vessels had of repassing to Ternata, he writ expressly to one of his friends, that he should salute those two scandalous sinners with all tenderness from him, and let them know, that, upon the least sign which they should make him, he would return to hear their confessions.

But these condescensions, and this goodness of the apostle, had nothing in them of meanness, or of weakness; and he knew well enough to make use of severity when there was occasion for it. Thus, a lady who had accused herself in confession, to have looked upon a man with too alluring an eye, was thus answered by him: "You are unworthy that God should look on you; since, by those encouraging regards which you have given to a man, you have run the hazard of losing God." The lady was so pierced with these few words, that, during the rest of her life, she durst never look any man in the face.

By all these methods, Xavier made so many converts. But whatever he performed, he looked on it as no more than an essay; and he wrote, in the year 1549, that if God would be pleased to bestow on him yet ten years more of life, he despaired not but these small beginnings would be attended with more happy consequences. This ardent desire of extending farther the dominion of Jesus Christ, caused him to write those pressing letters to the king of Portugal, and Father Ignatius, that he might be furnished with a larger supply of missioners: he promised, in his letters, to sweeten the labour of the mission, by serving all his fellows, and loving them better than himself. The year he died, he writ, that when once he had subdued the empire of China, and that of Tartary, to the sceptre of Jesus Christ, he purposed to return into Europe by the north, that he might labour in the reduction of heretics, and restoration of discipline in manners; that after this he designed to go over into Africa, or to return into Asia, in quest of new kingdoms, where he might preach the gospel.

For what remains, though he was ever forming new designs, as if he were to live beyond an age, yet he laboured as if he had not a day to live, and so tugged at the work which he had in hand, that two or three days and nights passed over his head without once thinking to take the least manner of nourishment. In saying his office, it often happened to him to leave, for five or six times successively, the same canonical hour, for the good of souls, and he quitted it with the same promptitude that afterwards he resumed it: he broke off his very prayers when the most inconsiderable person had the least occasion for him; and ordered, when he was in the deepest of his retirements, that if any poor man, or even but a child, should desire to be instructed, he might be called from his devotions.

No man perhaps was ever known to have run more dangers, both by land and sea, without reckoning into the account the tempests which he suffered in ten years of almost continual navigation. It is known, that being at the Moluccas, and passing from isle to isle, he was thrice shipwrecked, though we are not certain of the time or places; and once he was for three days and nights together on a plank, at the mercy of the winds and waves. The barbarians have often shot their arrows at him, and more than once he fell into the hands of an enraged multitude. One day the Saracens pursued him, and endeavoured to have stoned him; and the Brachmans frequently sought after him to have murdered him, even to that point of merciless barbarity, as to get fire to all the houses where they imagined he might lie concealed. But none of all these dangers were able to affright him; and the apprehension of dying could never hinder him from performing his ordinary functions. It seemed that even dangers served to the redoubling of his courage, and that, by being too intrepid, he sometimes entered into the extreme of rashness. Being at Japan, he reprehended the king of Amanguchi so severely for the infamy and scandal of his vices, that Father John Fernandez, (who served him for interpreter, as being more conversant than the saint in the language of the court) was amazed and trembled in pronouncing what the Father put into his mouth; as we are given to understand in a letter written by the same Fernandez. Xavier, one day perceiving the fear of his companion, forbade him absolutely either to change or soften any of his words: "I obeyed him," says Fernandez, "but expected every moment when the barbarian should strike me with his scymiter, and confess my apprehensions of death were as much too great, as the concernment of Father Francis was too little."

In effect, he was so far from fearing death, that he looked on it as a most pleasing object. "If we die for so good a cause," said Xavier on another occasion, "we ought to place it amongst the greatest benefits we receive from God; and shall be very much obliged to those, who, freeing us from a continual death, such as is this mortal life, shall put us in possession of an eternal happiness: So that we are resolved to preach the truth amongst them, in despite of all their threatenings, and, encouraged by the hopes of divine assistance, obey the precept of our Saviour, who commands us to prefer the salvation of others above our lives."

In the most hazardous undertakings, he hoped all things from God, and from thence drew his assurance of daring all things. Behold what he says himself concerning his voyage of Japan: "We set out full of confidence in God, and hope, that, having him for our conductor, we shall triumph over all his enemies.

"As to what remains, we fear not to enter into the lists with the doctors of Japan; for what available knowledge can they have, who are ignorant of the only true God, and of his only Son our Lord Jesus? And besides, what can we justly apprehend, who have no other aim than the glory of God and Jesus Christ, the preaching of the gospel, and the salvation of souls? supposing that we were not only in a kingdom of barbarians, but in the very dominion of devils, and that naked and disarmed, neither the most cruel barbarity, nor the rage of hell, could hurt us without God's permission. We are afraid of nothing but offending God Almighty; and provided that we offend not him, we promise ourselves, through his assistance, an assured victory over all our enemies. Since he affords sufficient strength to every man for his service, and for avoiding sin, we hope his mercy will not be wanting to us. But as the sum of all consists in the good or evil use of his benefits, we also hope he will give us grace to employ ourselves for his glory, by the prayers of his spouse, and our holy mother the Church, and particularly by the intercession of our Society, and those who are well affected to it. Our greatest, comfort proceeds from this, that God beholds the scope of this our voyage, that our only aim is to make known the Creator of the universe to souls which are made after his own image; to bring those souls to give him the worship due to him, and to spread the Christian religion through all regions.

"With these encouragements, we doubt not but the issue of our voyage will be prosperous; and two things especially seem to assure us, that we shall vanquish all the opposition of hell; the one is the greatness of our holy enterprize, the other is the care of Divine Providence, whose dominion is of no less extent over devils than over men. I acknowledge, that in this voyage, I foresee not only great labours, but also dangers of almost inevitable death; and this imagination is frequently presented to my thoughts, that if those of our Society, who are endued with the greatest stock of knowledge, should come into the Indies, they would certainly accuse us of too much rashness, and would be apt to think, that, in exposing ourselves to these manifest dangers, we tempted God. Nevertheless, upon a more serious reflection, I cease to fear; and hope that the spirit of our Lord, which animates our Society, will regulate their judgments concerning it. For my own particular, I think continually on what I have heard our good Father Ignatius often say, that those of our Society ought to exert their utmost force in vanquishing themselves, and banish from them all those fears which usually hinder us from placing our whole confidence in God. For, though divine hope is purely and simply the grace of God, and that he dispenses it, according to his pleasure, nevertheless, they who endeavour to overcome themselves, receive it more frequently than others. As there is a manifest difference betwixt those, who, abounding with all things, trust in God, and those, who, being sufficiently provided with all necessaries, yet bereave themselves of them, in imitation of Jesus Christ; so is there also, in those who trust in God's providence, when they are out of danger, and those who, with the assistance of his grace, dare voluntarily expose themselves to the greatest hazards, which are in their proper choice and power to shun."

It was in the spirit of this holy confidence, that the saint, writing to Simon Rodriguez, speaks in this manner to him:--

"Our God holds in his hand the tempests which infest the seas of China and Japan; the rocks, the gulphs, and banks of sands, which are formidably known by so many shipwrecks, are all of them under his dominion. He is Sovereign over all those pirates which cruize the seas, and exercise their cruelties on the Portuguese: and for this reason I cannot fear them; I only fear lest God should punish me for being too pusillanimous in his service; and so little capable, through my own frailty, of extending the kingdom of his Son amongst those nations who know him not."

He speaks in the same spirit to the Fathers of Goa, in giving them an account of his arrival at Japan: "We are infinitely obliged to God, for permitting us to enter into those barbarous countries, where we are to be regardless, and in a manner forgetful of ourselves; for the enemies of the true religion, being masters every where, on whom can we rely, but on God alone? and to whom can we have recourse besides him? In our countries, where the Christian faith is flourishing, it happens, I know not how, that every thing hinders us from reposing ourselves on God; the love of our relations, the bonds of friendship, the conveniences of life, and the remedies which we use in sickness; but here, being distant from the place of our nativity, and living amongst barbarians, where all human succours are wanting to us, it is of absolute necessity that our confidence in God alone should be our aid."

But the saint perhaps never discoursed better on this subject, than in a letter written at his return from the Moluccas, after a dangerous navigation. His words are these: "It has pleased God, that we should not perish; it has also pleased him, to instruct us even by our dangers, and to make us know, by our own experience, how weak we are, when we rely only on ourselves, or on human succours. For when we come to understand the deceitfulness of our hopes, and are entirely diffident of human helps, we rely on God, who alone can deliver us out of those dangers, into which we have engaged ourselves on his account: we shall soon experience that he governs all things; and that the heavenly pleasures, which he confers on his servants on such occasions, ought to make us despise the greatest hazards; even death itself has nothing in it which is dreadful to them, who have a taste of those divine delights; and though, when we have escaped those perils of which we speak, we want words to express the horror of them, there remains in our heart a pleasing memory of the favours which God has done us; and that remembrance excites us, day and night, to labour in the service of so good a Master: we are also enlivened by it to honour him during the rest of our lives, hoping, that, out of his abundant mercy, he will bestow on us a new strength, and fresh vigour, to serve him faithfully and generously, even to our death."

"May it please the Divine Goodness," he says elsewhere, "that good men, whom the devil endeavours to affright in the service of God, might fear no other thing besides displeasing him, in leaving off what they have undertaken for his sake. If they would do this, how happy a life would they then lead! how much would they advance in virtue, knowing, by their own experience, that they can do nothing of themselves, but that they can do all things by the assistance of his grace!"

He said, "that our most stedfast hold in dangers and temptations, was to have a noble courage against the foe of our salvation, in a distrust of our own strength, but a firm reliance on our Lord, so that we should not only fear nothing under the conduct of such a general, but also should not doubt of victory." He said also further, "that, in those dangerous occasions, the want of confidence in God was more to be feared, than any assault of the enemy; and that we should run much greater hazard in the least distrust of the divine assistance, in the greatest dangers, than in exposing ourselves to those very dangers." He added, lastly, "that this danger was so much the more formidable, the more it was hidden, and the less that we perceived it."

These thoughts produced in the soul of this holy man an entire diffidence of himself, together with a perfect humility. He was the only discourse of the new world; Infidels and Christians gave him almost equal honour; and his power over nature was so great, that it was said to be a kind of miracle, when he performed no miracle But all this served only to raise confusion in him; because he found nothing in himself but his own nothingness; and being nothing in his own conceit, he could not comprehend, how it was possible for him to be esteemed. Writing to the doctor of Navarre, before his voyage to the Indies, he told him, "That it was a singular grace of heaven to know ourselves; and that, through the mercy of God, he knew himself to be good for nothing."

"Humbly beseech our Lord," he wrote from the Indies to Father Simon Rodriguez, "that I may have power to open the door of China to others; where I am, I have done but little." In many other passages of his letters, he calls himself an exceeding evil man; a great sinner; and conjures his brethren to employ their intercessions to God in his behalf. "Bring to pass, by your prayers," says he to one of them, "that though my sins have rendered me unworthy of the ministerial vocation, yet God may vouchsafe, out of his infinite goodness, to make use of me."

"I beseech you," says he to another, "to implore the heavenly assistance for us; and to the end you may do it with the greater fervency, I beseech our Lord, that he would give you to understand, how much I stand in need of your intercession."

"It is of extreme importance to my consolation," he writes to the fathers of Goa, "that you understand the wonderful perplexity in which I am. As God knows the multitude and heinousness of my sins, I have a thought which much torments me; it is, that God perhaps may not prosper our undertakings, if we do not amend our lives, and change our manners: it is necessary, on this account, to employ the prayers of all the religious of our Society, and of all our friends, in hope that, by their means, the Catholic church, which is the spouse of our Lord Jesus, will communicate her innumerable merits to us; and that the Author of all good will accumulate his graces on us, notwithstanding our offences."

He attributed all the fruits of his labours to an evident miracle of the Divine Power, which made use of so vile and weak an instrument as himself, to the end it might appear to be the work of God. He said, "that they who had great talents, ought to labour with great courage for the safety of souls; since he, who was wanting in all the qualities which are requisite to so high a calling, was not altogether unprofitable in his ministry."

As he had a mean opinion of himself, and that his own understanding was suspected by him, he frequently, by his letters, requested his brethren of Italy, and Portugal, to instruct him in the best method of preaching the gospel profitably. "I am going," said he, "to publish Jesus Christ, to people who are part Idolaters, and part Saracens; I conjure you, by Jesus Christ himself, to send me word, after what manner, and by what means, I may instruct them. For I am verily persuaded, that God will suggest those ways to you, which are most proper for the easy reduction of those people into his fold; and if I wander from the right path, while I am in expectation of your letters, I hope I shall return into it, when I shall have received them."

All that succeeded well to his endeavours in the service of our Lord, he attributed to the intercession of his brethren. "Your prayers," he writ to the Fathers at Rome, "have assuredly obtained for me the knowledge of my infinite offences; and withal the grace of unwearied labouring, in the conversion of Idolaters, notwithstanding the multitude of my sins."

But if the designs which he was always forming, for the advancement of religion, happened to be thwarted, he acknowledged no other reason of those crosses than his own sins, and complained only of himself.

As for those miracles which he continually wrought, they passed, in his opinion, as the effects of innocence in children, or for the fruits of faith in sick persons. And when, at the sight of a miraculous performance, the people were at any time about to give him particular honours, he ran to hide himself in the thickest of a forest; or when he could not steal away, he entered so far into the knowledge of himself, that he stood secure from the least temptation of vain glory. It even seemed, that the low opinion which he had of his own worth, in some sort blinded him, in relation to the wonders which he wrought, so that he perceived not they were miracles.

It was the common talk at Goa, that he had raised the dead on the coast of Fishery. After his return to Goa, James Borba and Cozmo Annez, his two intimate friends, requested him to inform them, for God's further glory, how those matters went; and particularly they enquired concerning the child who was drowned in the well. The holy man, at this request, hung down his head, and blushed exceedingly: when he was somewhat recovered of his bashfulness, "Jesus," said he, "what, I to raise the dead! can you believe these things of such a wretch as I am?" After which, modestly smiling, he went on, "Alas, poor sinner that I am! they set before me a child, whom they reported to be dead, and who perhaps was not; I commanded him, in the name of God, to arise; he arose indeed, and there was the miracle."

Ordognez Cevalio, who travelled almost round the world, tells us, in the relations of his voyages, that, in India, he happened to meet a Japanese, who informed him, in a discourse which they had together of these particulars: "Know," said he, "that being in Japan, a Bonza by profession, I was once at an assembly of our Bonzas, who, upon the report of so many miracles as were wrought by Father Francis Xavier, resolved to place him in the number of their gods; in order to which, they sent to him a kind of embassy; but the Father was seized with horror at the proposition of their deputies. Having spoken of God to them, after a most magnificent and elevated manner, he spake of himself in terms so humble, and with so much self-contempt, that all of us were much edified by his procedure; and the greatest part of us seriously reflecting, rather on his carriage than his words, from priests of idols, which we were, became the worshippers of Jesus Christ."

He shunned the offices of the Society, and believed himself unworthy of them. "I cannot tell you," wrote he from Cochin to Father Ignatius, "how much I stand obliged to the Japanese; in favour of whom, God has given me clearly to understand the infinite number of my sins; for till that time, I was so little recollected, and so far wandered out of myself, that I had not discovered, in the bottom of my heart, an abyss of imperfections and failings. It was not till my labours and sufferings in Japan, that I began at length to open my eyes, and to understand, with God's assistance, and by my own experience, that it is necessary for me to have one, who may watch over me, and govern me. May your holy charity be pleased, for this reason, to consider what it is you do, in ranging under my command so many saint-like souls of the fathers and brethren of our Society. I am so little endued with the qualities which are requisite for such a charge, and am so sensible that this is true, through God's mercy, that I may reasonably hope, that, instead of reposing on me the care of others, you will repose on others the care of me." He infinitely esteemed those missioners who were his seconds; and accounted his own pains for nothing, in comparison of theirs. After having related, what had been performed by Father Francis Perez in Malacca; "I confess, my brethren," said he to Paul de Camerino and Antonio Gomez, "that, seeing these things, I am ashamed of myself; and my own lazy cowardice makes me blush, in looking on a missioner, who, infirm and languishing as he is, yet labours without intermission in the salvation of souls." Xavier more than once repeats the same thing in his letter, with profound sentiments of esteem for Perez, and strange contempt of his own performances.

He recommends not any thing so much to the gospel-labourers as the knowledge of themselves, and shunning of pride; and we need only to open any of his letters, to behold his opinions on that subject,

"Cultivate humility with care, in all those things which depraved nature has in horror; and make sure, by the assistance of divine grace, to gain a thorough knowledge of yourselves; for that understanding of ourselves is the mother of Christian humility. Beware especially, lest the good opinion, which men have conceived of you, do not give you too much pleasure: for those vain delights are apt to make us negligent; and that negligence, as it were by a kind of enchantment, destroys the humility of our hearts, and introduces pride instead of it.

"Be distrustful of your proper strength, and build nothing upon human wisdom, nor on the esteem of men, By these means you will be in condition to bear whatsoever troubles shall happen to you; for God strengthens the humble, and gives him courage; he is proof against the greatest labours, and nothing can ever separate him from the charity of Jesus Christ; not the devil with his evil angels, nor the ocean with its tempests, nor the most brutal nations with all their barbarity. And if God sometimes permits that the devil put impediments in his way, or that the elements make war against him, he is persuaded, that it is only for the expiation of his sins, for the augmentation of his merits, and for the rendering him more humble.

"They who fervently desire to advance God's glory, ought to humble themselves, and be nothing in their own opinion; being diffident, even in the smallest matters, of their own abilities; to the end, that in great occasions, becoming much more diffident of themselves, through a principle of Christian humility, they may entirely confide in God; and this confidence may give them resolution; for he who knows that he is assisted from above, can never degenerate into weakness.

"Whatever you undertake will be acceptable in the sight of God, if there appear in your conduct a profound humility, and that you commit the care of your reputation into his hands; for he himself will not be wanting to give you both authority and reputation with men, when they are needful for you; and when he does it not, it is from his knowledge that you will not ascribe to him that which only can proceed from him. I comfort myself with thinking, that the sins of which you find yourselves guilty, and with which you daily upbraid your own consciences, produce in you an extreme horror of windy arrogance, and a great love of perfection; so that human praises will become your crosses, and be useful to admonish you of your failings.

"Take heed of yourselves, my dearest brethren; many ministers of the gospel, who have opened the way of heaven to other men, are tormented in hell for want of true humility, and for being carried away with a vain opinion of themselves; on the contrary, there is not to be found in hell one single soul which was sincerely humble."

These are the instructions which the saint gave in general to his brethren on the subject of humility; and, next, behold some particular admonitions which were addressed to some amongst them:--

"I conjure you to be humble and patient towards all the world," says he to Father Cyprian, who preached the gospel at Meliapore; "for, believe me, nothing is to be done by haughtiness and choler, when it cannot be accomplished by modesty and mildness." He continues; "We deceive ourselves, in exacting submission and respect from men, without any other title to it than being members of our Society, and without cultivating that virtue which has acquired us so great an authority in the world; as if we rather chose to recommend ourselves by that credit and reputation, than by the practice of humility and patience, and those other virtues by which our Society has maintained its dignity and honour with mankind."

"Be mindful," writes he to Father Barzaesus, who was rector of' the college of Goa, "to read frequently the instructions which I have left with you, particularly those which concern humility; and take an especial care in considering what God has done by you, and by all the labourers of the Society, that you do not forget yourself: for my own particular, I should be glad, that all of you would seriously think how many things God leaves undone, because you are wanting to him in your fidelity; and I would rather that consideration should employ your thoughts, than those great works which it has pleased our Lord to accomplish by your ministry; for the first reflection will cover you with confusion, and make you mindful of your weakness; but, instead of that, the second will puff you up with vanity, and expose you to the danger of having thoughts of arrogance."

This well-grounded humility in Xavier, was the principle of a perfect submission to the will of God. He never undertook any thing without consulting him before-hand; and the divine decrees were his only rule. "I have made continual prayers," says he, speaking of his voyage to Macassar, "to know what heaven requires of me; for I was firmly resolved not to be wanting on my part to fulfil the will of God, whensoever it should be made known to me. May it please our Lord," said he on the same subject, "that out of his goodness we might understand what he designs by us, to the end we might entirely conform ourselves to his holy will so soon as it shall be discovered to us; for he commands us to be always in a readiness to obey him at the first signal; and it becomes us to be as strangers in this world, always prepared to follow the voice of our conductor."

"I wish," said he, in another place, "that God would declare to us his most holy will, concerning the ministries and countries where I may best employ my labours for his glory. I am ready, by his grace, to execute those things which he makes me understand to be most pleasing to him, of whatsoever nature they may be; and, undoubtedly, he has admirable means of signifying his good pleasure to us; such as are our inward sentiments and heavenly illuminations, which leave no remaining scruple concerning the place to which he has designed us, nor what we are to undertake for his service. For we are like travellers, not fixed to any country through which we pass. It is our duty to be prepared to fly from one region to another, or rather into opposite regions, where the voice of heaven shall please to call us. East and west, north and south, are all indifferent to me, provided I may have an opportunity of advancing the glory of our Lord."

He says elsewhere, "I could wish, that you had ever in your mind this meditation, that a ready and obedient will, which is entirely devoted to God's service, is a more pleasing sacrifice to the Divine Majesty, than all the pomp and glitter of our noisy actions, without the interior disposition."

Being thoroughly convinced that the perfection of the creature consists in willing nothing but the will of the Creator, he spoke incessantly of God's good pleasure, and concluded almost all his letters with his desires of knowing and fulfilling it. He sacrificed all to that principle; even his ardent wishes to die for Jesus by the hands of the barbarians: for though he breathed after martyrdom, he well understood that the tender of our life is not acceptable to God, when he requires it not; and he was more fearful of displeasing him, than desirous of being a martyr for him. So that he died satisfied, when he expired in a poor cabin of a natural death, though he was at that very time on the point of carrying the faith into the kingdom of China: And it may be therefore said, that he sacrificed not only his own glory, but even that of Jesus Christ, to the good pleasure of God Almighty.

A man so submissive to the orders of heaven, could not possibly want submission in regard of his superior, who was to him in the place of God. He had for Father Ignatius, general of the Society of Jesus, a veneration and reverence, mixed with tenderness, which surpass imagination. He himself has expressed some part of his thoughts on that subject, and we cannot read them without being edified. In one of his letters, which begins in this manner, "My only dear Father, in the bowels of Jesus Christ;" he says at the conclusion, "Father of my soul, for whom I have a most profound respect, I write this to you upon my knees, as if you were present, and that I beheld you with my eyes." It was his custom to write to him in that posture; so high was the place which Ignatius held within his heart.

"God is my witness, my dearest Father," says he in another letter, "how much I wish to behold you in this life, that I might communicate to you many matters, which cannot be remedied without your aid; for there is no distance of places which can hinder me from obeying you. I conjure you, my best Father, to have some little consideration of us who are in the Indies, and who are your children. I conjure you, I say, to send hither some holy man, whose fervour may excite our lazy faintness. I hope, for the rest, that as you know the bottom of our souls, by an illumination from heaven, you will not be wanting to supply us with the means of awakening our languishing and drowsy virtue, and of inspiring us with the love of true perfection." In another of his letters, which is thus superscribed, "To Ignatius, my holy Father in Jesus Christ," he sends him word, that the letter which he received from his holy charity, at his return from Japan, had replenished him with joy; and that particularly he was most tenderly affected with the last words of it: "I am all yours, yours even to that degree, that it is impossible for me to forget you, Ignatius." "When I had read those words," said he, "the tears came flowing into my eyes, and gushing out of them; which makes me, that I cannot forbear writing them, and recalling to my memory that sincere and holy friendship which you always had, and still have, for me; nothing doubting, but that if God has delivered me from so many dangers, it has principally proceeded from your fatherly intercessions for me." He calls himself his son in all his letters, and thus subscribes himself in one: "The least of your children, and most distant from you, Francis Xavier." But the high ideas which Francis had of Ignatius, caused him frequently to ask his advice in relation to his own conduct. "You will do a charitable work," said he, "in writing to me a letter, full of spiritual instructions, as a legacy bequeathed to one who is the least of all your children, at the farthest distance from you, and who is as it were banished from your presence, by which I may partake some part of those abundant treasures which heaven has heaped upon you. I beseech you not to be too niggardly in the accomplishment of my desires." "I conjure you," says he elsewhere, "by the tender love of Jesus Christ, to give me the method which I ought to keep, in admitting those who are to be members of our Society; and write to me at large, considering the smallness of my talent, which is well known to you; for if you give me not your assistance, the poor ability which I have in these matters, will be the occasion of my losing many opportunities for the augmentation of God's glory."

In prescribing any thing that was difficult to his inferiors, he frequently intermixed the name of Ignatius: "I pray you by our Lord, and by Ignatius, the Father of our Society. I conjure you by the obedience, and by the love which you owe to our Father Ignatius." "Remember," said he farther, "to what degree, both great and small, respect our Father Ignatius."

With these sentiments, both of affection and esteem, he depended absolutely on his superior. "If I believed," says he, writing from the Indies to Father Simon Rodriguez, "that the strength of your body were equal to the vigour of your mind, I should invite you to pass the seas, and desire your company in this new world; I mean, if our Father Ignatius should approve and counsel such a voyage: For he is our parent, it behoves us to obey him; and it is not permitted us to make one step without his order."

In this manner, Xavier had recourse to Ignatius on all occasions, as much as the distance of places would permit; and the orders which he received, were to him inviolable laws. "You shall not suffer any one," so he writ to Gaspar Barzæus, rector of the college of Goa, "to receive the orders of priesthood, who is not sufficiently learned; and who has not given, for the space of many years, sufficient examples of his good life in our Society; because our Father Ignatius has expressly forbidden it." For the same reason he exactly observed the constitutions of the Society. "Make not haste," writes he in the same letter to Barzæus, "to receive children which are too young; and totally reject such sorts of people, whom Father Ignatius would have for ever excluded from our order." But nothing, perhaps, can more clearly discover how perfect the submission of Xavier was, than what his superior himself thought of it. At the time when Xavier died, Ignatius had thoughts of recalling him from the Indies; not doubting, but at the first notice of his orders, this zealous missioner would leave all things out of his obedience. And on this occasion he wrote to him a letter, bearing date the 28th of June, in the year 1553. Behold the passage which concerns the business of which we are speaking: "I add," says Ignatius in his letter, "that having in prospect the salvation of souls, and the greater service of our Lord, I have resolved to command you, in virtue of holy obedience, to return into Portugal with the first opportunity; and I command you this in the name of Christ. But that you may more easily satisfy those, who are desirous of retaining you in the Indies, for the good of those countries, I will present you with my reasons: You know, in the first place, of what weight are the orders of the king of Portugal, for the confirmation of religion in the East, for the propagation of it in, Guinea and Brasil; and you can rightly judge, that a prince so religious as he, will do all things necessary for the advancement of God's honour, and the conversion of people, if one of your ability and experience shall personally instruct him; And besides, it is of great importance, that the holy apostolical see should be informed of the present state of India, by some authentic witness; to the end, that Popes may issue out spiritual supplies, as well to the new as to the ancient Christianity of Asia; without which, neither the one nor the other can subsist, or cannot subsist without much trouble; and nobody is more proper than yourself for this, both in respect of your knowledge in the affairs of the new world, and of your reputation in these parts.

"You know, moreover, of what consequence it is, that the missioners, who are sent to the Indies, should be proper for the end proposed; and it is convenient, on that account, that you come to Portugal and Rome: for not only many more will be desirous of going on those missions, but you will make a better choice of missioners, and will see more clearly to what parts such and such are proper to be sent. You judge yourself of what consideration it is, not to be mistaken in these affairs; and whatsoever relation you can send us, your letters are not sufficient to give us a true notion of what labourers are fitting for the Indies. It is necessary that you, or some one as intelligent as you, should know and practise those who are designed for those countries. Besides what it will be in your power to do for the common benefit of the East, you will warm the zeal of the king of Portugal, in relation to Ethiopia, which has been under consideration for so many years, but nothing yet performed. You will also be of no little use to the affairs of Congo and Brasil, on which you can have no influence in India, for want of commerce betwixt them and you. But if you think your presence may be necessary, for the government of those of the Society who are in the Indies, you may govern them more easily from Portugal, than you can from China or Japan. For what remains, I remit you to the Father, Master Polanque, and recommend myself most cordially to your good prayers, beseeching the Divine Goodness to multiply his favours on you; to the end, that we may understand his most holy will, and that we may perfectly perform it."

Father Polanque, who was secretary to Father Ignatius, and confident to all his purposes, has given testimony, that the intention of the holy founder was to make Xavier general of the Society. The letter of Ignatius found Xavier dead. But we may judge of what he would have done, by what he writ before his death to Ignatius himself, who had testified so earnest a desire to see him: "Your holy charity," says he in his letter, "tells me, that you have an earnest desire to see me once again in this present life: God, who looks into the bottom of my heart, can tell how sensibly that mark of your tenderness has touched me. Truly, whenever that expression of yours returns to my remembrance, and it frequently returns, the tears come dropping from my eyes, and I cannot restrain them; while I revolve that happy thought, that once, yet once again it may be given me to embrace you. I confess, it appears difficult to compass my desires, but all things are possible to holy obedience."

Undoubtedly, if the letter of Ignatius had found Xavier alive, he had soon been seen in Europe; for having offered, of his own free motion, to leave the Indies, Japan, and China, and all the business which he had upon his hands, and having said, that the least beckoning of his superior should be sufficient for it, what would he not have done, when he had received a positive command to abandon all, and repass the seas?

His maxims of obedience shew clearly what his own submission was.

"There is nothing more certain, nor less subject to mistake, than always to be willing to obey. On the contrary, it is dangerous to live in complaisance to our own wills, and without following the motion of our superiors; for though we chance to perform any good action, yet if we never so little deviate from that which is commanded us, we may rest assured, that our action is rather vicious than good.

"The devil, by his malicious suggestions, tempts the greatest part of those who have devoted themselves to God's service: 'What make you there?' he secretly whispers; 'See you not that you do but lose your labour?' Resist that thought with all your strength; for it is capable not only of hindering you in the way to perfection, but also of seducing you from it: and let every one of you persuade himself, that he cannot better serve our Lord, than in that place where he is set by his superior. Be also satisfied, that when the time of God is come, he will inspire your superiors with thoughts of sending you to such places, where your labours shall abundantly succeed. In the mean time, you shall possess your souls in peace. By this means, you will well employ your precious time, though too many do not understand its value, and make great proficiencies in virtue. It is far otherwise with those restless souls, who do no good in those places where they wish to be, because they are not there; and are unprofitable both to themselves and others where they are, because they desire to be otherwhere.

"Perform, with great affection, what your superiors order you, in relation to domestic discipline, and suffer not yourself to be surprised with the suggestions of the evil spirit, who endeavours to persuade you, that some other employment would be fitter for you; his design is, that you should execute that office ill in which you are employed: I entreat you, therefore, by our Lord and Saviour Jesus Christ, to consider seriously, how you may overcome those temptations, which give you a distaste of your employment; and to meditate, more on that, than how to engage yourself in such laborious affairs, as are not commanded you. Let no man flatter himself; it is impossible to excel in great matters, before we arrive to excel in less: and it is a gross error, under the pretence of saving souls, to shake off the yoke of obedience, which is light and easy, and to take up a cross, which, without comparison, is more hard and heavy.

"It becomes you to submit your will and judgement to your governors; and to believe that God, will inspire them, in reference to you, with that, which will be most profitable to you. For the rest, beware of asking any thing with importunity, as some have done, who press their superiors with such earnestness, that they even tear from them that which they desire, though the thing which they demand be in itself pernicious; or if it be refused them, complain in public, that their life is odious to them: they perceive not, that their unhappiness proceeds from their neglect of their vow, and their endeavour to appropriate that will to themselves, which they have already consecrated to our Lord. In effect, the more such people live according to their own capricious fancy, the more uneasy and melancholy is their life."

The holy man was so thoroughly persuaded, that the perfection of the Society of Jesus consisted in obedience, that he frequently commanded his brethren, in virtue of their holy obedience, thereby to increase their merit.

"I pray you," said he to two missioners of Comorine, "to go to the Isles del Moro; and to the end you may the better have occasion of meriting by your obedience, I positively command you."

But it is impossible to relate, with what tenderness he loved the Society, or how much he concerned himself in all their interests, though of the smallest moment. Being in Portugal, before his voyage to the Indies, he wrote not any letters to Rome, wherein he did not testisfy his great desire to know what progress it made in Italy. Writing to the Fathers, Le Gay, and Laynez, he says thus: "Since our rule is confirmed, I earnestly desire to learn the names of those who are already received into our order, and of such as are upon the point of being admitted. He exhorts them, to thank the king of Portugal, for the design which his majesty had to build a college, or a house for the Society: and we ought to make this acknowlegment to the king," said he, "to engage him thereby to begin the building."

The news which he received from Father Ignatius, and the other Fathers who were at Rome, gave him infinite consolation. "I have received your letters, which I expected with much impatience; and have received them with that joy, which children ought to have in receiving some pleasing news from their mother. In effect, I learn from them the prosperous condition of all the Society, and the holy employments wherein you engage yourselves without intermission." He could scarcely moderate his joy, whensoever he thought on the establishment of the Society. Thus he wrote from the Indies to Rome: "Amongst all the favours which I have received from God in this present life, and which I receive daily, the most signal, and most sensible, is to have heard that the institute of our Society has been approved and confirmed by the authority of the Holy See I give immortal thanks to Jesus Christ, that he has been pleased his vicar should publicly establish the form of life, which he himself has prescribed in private to his servant, our Father Ignatius."

But Xavier also wished nothing more, than to see the Society increased; and he felt a redoubling of his joy, by the same proportion, when he had notice of their gaining new houses in the East, or when he heard, from Europe, of the foundation of new colleges.

To conclude, he had not less affection for the particular persons, who were members of the Society, than for the body of it. His brethren were ever present in his thoughts; and he thought it not enough to love them barely, without a continual remembrance of them. "I carry about with me (thus he writes to the Fathers at Rome) all your names, of your own handwriting, in your letters; and I carry them together with the solemn form of my profession." By which he signifies, not only how dear the sons of the Society were to him, but also how much he esteemed the honour of being one of their number.

The love which he bore to gospel-poverty, caused him to subsist on alms, and to beg his bread from door to door, when he might have had a better provision made for him. Being even in the college of Goa, which was well endowed, he sought his livelihood without the walls, the more to conform himself to the poverty of his blessed Saviour. He was always very meanly clothed, and most commonly had so many patches on his cassock, that the children of the idolaters derided him. He pieced up his tatters with his own hand, and never changed his habit till it was worn to rags; at least, if the honour of God, and the interest of religion, did not otherwise oblige him. At his return from Japan to Malacca, where he was received with so much honour, he wore on his back a torn cassock, and a rusty old hat on his head.

The Portuguese, beholding him always so ill apparelled, often desired him to give them leave to present him with a new habit; but seeing he would not be persuaded, they once devised a way of stealing his cassock while he was asleep. The trick succeeded, and Xavier, whose soul was wholly intent on God, put on a new habit, which they had laid in the place of his old garment, without discovering how they had served him. He passed the whole day in the same ignorance of the cheat, and it was not till the evening that he perceived it; for supping with Francis Payva, and other Portuguese, who were privy to the matter,--"It is perhaps to do honour to our table," said one amongst them, "that you are so spruce today, in your new habit." Then, casting his eyes upon his clothes, he was much surprised to find himself in so strange an equipage. At length, being made sensible of the prank which they had played him, he told them, smiling, "That it was no great wonder that this rich cassock, looking for a master in the dark, could not see its way to somebody who deserved it better."

As he lived most commonly amongst the poorer sort of Indians, who had nothing to bestow, and who, for the most part, went naked, he enjoyed his poverty without molestation. All his moveables were a mat, on which he lay sometimes, and a little table, whereon were his writings, and some little books, with a wooden crucifix, made of that which the Indians call the wood of St Thomas.

He cheerfully underwent the greatest hardships of poverty; and, writing from Japan to the Fathers of Goa, his words were these:--"Assist me, I beseech you, my dear brethren, in acknowledging to Almighty God the signal favour he has done me. I am at length arrived at Japan, where there is an extreme scarcity of all things, which I place amongst the greatest benefits of Providence."

Mortification is always the companion of poverty, in apostolical persons. Xavier bore Constantly along with him the instruments of penance; haircloth, chains of iron, and disciplines, pointed at the ends, and exceeding sharp. He treated his flesh with great severity, by the same motive which obliged St Paul, the apostle, to chastise his body, and to reduce it into servitude, lest, having preached to other men, he might himself become a reprobate.

At sea, the ship tackling served him for a bed; on land, a mat, or the earth itself. He eat so little, that one of his companions assures us, that, without a miracle, he could not have lived. Another tells us, that he seldom or never drank wine, unless at the tables of the Portuguese; for there he avoided singularity, and took what was given him. But, afterwards, he revenged himself on one of those repasts, by an abstinence of many days.

When he was at Cape Comorine, the viceroy; Don Alphonso de Sosa, sent him two barrels of excellent wine. He did not once taste of it, though he was then brought very low, through the labours of his ministry, but distributed the whole amongst the poor.

His ordinary nourishment, in the Indies, was rice boiled in water, or some little piece of salt fish; but during the two years and a half of his residence in Japan, he totally abstained from fish, for the better edification of that people; and wrote to the Fathers at Rome, "that he would rather choose to die of hunger, than to give any man the least occasion of scandal." He also says, "I count it for a signal favour, that God has brought me into a country destitute of all the comforts of life, and where, if I were so ill disposed, it would be impossible for me to pamper up my body with delicious fare." He perpetually travelled, by land, on foot, even in Japan, where the ways are asperous, and almost impassible; and often walked, with naked feet, in the greatest severity of winter.

"The hardships of so long a navigation," says he, "so long a sojourning amongst the Gentiles, in a country parched up with excessive heats, all these incommodities being suffered, as they ought to be, for the sake of Christ, are truly an abundant source of consolations: for myself, I am verily persuaded, that they, who love the cross of Jesus Christ, live happy in the midst of sufferings; and that it is a death, when they have no opportunities to suffer. For, can there be a more cruel death, than to live without Jesus Christ, after once we have tasted of him? Is any thing more hard, than to abandon him, that we may satisfy our own inclinations? Believe me, there is no other cross which is to be compared to that. How happy is it, on the other side, to live, in dying daily, and in conquering our passions, to search after, not our proper interests, but the interests of Jesus Christ?"

His interior mortification was the principle of these thoughts, in this holy man; from the first years of his conversion, his study was to gain an absolute conquest on himself; and he continued always to exhort others not to suffer themselves to be hurried away by the fury of their natural desires. He writes thus to the fathers and brethren of Coimbra, from Malacca:--"I have always present, in my thoughts, what I have heard from our holy Father Ignatius, that the true children of the Society of Jesus ought to labour exceedingly in overcoming of themselves.

"If you search our Lord in the spirit of truth," says he to the Jesuits of Goa, "and generously walk in those ways, which conduct you to him, the spiritual delights, which you taste in his service, will sweeten all those bitter agonies, which the conquest of yourselves will cost you. O my God, how grossly stupid is mankind not to comprehend, that, by a faint and cowardly resistance of the assaults of the devil, they deprive themselves of the most pure and sincere delights which life can give them."

By the daily practice of these maxims, Xavier came to be so absolute a master of his passions, that he knew not what it was to have the least motion of choler and impatience; and from thence proceeded partly, that tranquillity of soul, that equality of countenance, that perpetual cheerfulness, which rendered him so easy and so acceptable in all companies.

It is natural for a man, who is extremely mortified, to be chaste; and so was Xavier, to such a degree of perfection, that we have it certified from his ghostly fathers, and, amongst others, from the vicar of Meliapore, that he lived and died a virgin. From his youth upward he had an extreme horror for impurity; notwithstanding, that he was of a sanguine complexion, and naturally loved pleasure. While he was a student at Paris, and dwelt in the college of Sainte Barbe, his tutor in philosophy, who was a man lost in debauches, and who died of a dishonest disease, carried his scholars by night to brothel-houses. The abominable man did all he could towards the debauching of Francis Xavier, who was handsome, and well shaped, but he could never accomplish his wicked purpose; so much was the youth estranged from the uncleanness of all fleshly pleasures.

For what remains, nothing can more clearly make out his love to purity, than what happened to him once at Rome. Simon Rodriguez being fallen sick, Father Ignatius commanded Xavier to take care of him during his distemper. One night, the sick man awaking, saw Xavier, who was asleep at his bed's feet, thrusting out his arms in a dream, with the action of one who violently repels an enemy; he observed him even casting out blood in great abundance, through his nostrils, and at his mouth. Xavier himself awaking, with the labour of that struggling, Rodriguez enquired of him the cause of that extreme agitation, and the gushing of his blood. Xavier would not satisfy him at that time, and gave him no account of it, till he was just upon his departure to the Indies; for then being urged anew by Rodriguez, after he had obliged him to secrecy, "Know," said he, "my brother, master Simon, that God, out of his wonderful mercy, has done me the favour, to preserve me, even till this hour, in entire purity; and that very night I dreamed, that, lodging at an inn, an impudent woman would needs approach me: The motion of my arms was to thrust her from me, and to get rid of her; and the blood, which I threw out, proceeded from my agony."

But whatsoever detestation Xavier had, even for the shadow of a sin, he was always diffident of himself; and withdrew from all conversation of women, if charity obliged him not to take care of their conversion; and even on such occasions, he kept all imaginable measures, never entertaining them with discourse, unless in public places, and in sight of all the world; nor speaking with them of ought, but what was necessary, and then also sparing of his words, and with a grave, modest, and serious countenance. He would say, "That, in general conversation, we could not be too circumspect in our behaviour towards them; and that, however pious the intentions of their confessors were, there still remained more cause of fear to the directors in those entertainments, than of hope, that any good should result from them to the women-penitents."

Besides all this, he kept his senses curbed and recollected, examined his conscience often every day, and daily confessed himself when he had the convenience of a priest. By these means, he acquired such a purity of soul and body, that they who were of his intimate acquaintance, have declared, that they could never observe in him ought that was not within the rules of the exactest decency.

In like manner, he never forgave himself the least miscarriage; and it is incredible how far the tenderness of his conscience went on all occasions. In that vessel which carried him from Lisbon to the Indies, a child, who was of years which are capable of instruction, one day happened to die suddenly: Xavier immediately inquired if the child had been usually present at catechism, together with the ship's company? It was answered in the negative; and at the same moment the man of God, whose countenance commonly was cheerful, appeared extremely sad. The viceroy, Alphonso de Sosa, soon observed it; and knowing the cause of his affliction, asked the Father if he had any former knowledge that the child came not to catechism? "If I had known it," replied Xavier, "I had not failed to have brought him thither:" "But, why then," said the viceroy, "are you thus disquieted for a thing you know not, and of which you are no ways guilty?" "It is," replied the saint, "because I ought to upbraid myself with it as a fault, that I was ignorant that any person, who was embarked with me, wanted to be taught the Christian faith."

A body so chaste, and a mind so pure, could not have been but of one who was faithfully devoted to the Holy Virgin. The saint honoured and loved her all his life, with thoughts full of respect and tenderness. It was in the church of Mont Martre, dedicated to the mother of God, and on the day of her assumption, that he made his first vows. It was in that of Loretto that he had his first inspiration, and conceived his first desires of going to the Indies. He petitioned for nothing of our Lord, but by the intercession of his mother; and in the exposition which he made of the Christian doctrine, after addressing himself to Jesus to obtain the grace of a lively and constant faith, he failed not of addressing himself to Mary. He concluded all his instructions with the _Salve Regina_; he never undertook any thing but under her protection; and in all dangers, he had always recourse to the blessed Virgin as his patroness. For the rest, to shew that he depended on her, and made his glory of that dependence, he commonly wore a chaplet about his neck, to the end that Christians might take delight in seeing the chaplet; and made frequent use of it in the operation of his miracles.

When he passed whole nights at his devotions in churches, it was almost always before the image of the Virgin, and especially he offered his vows to her for the conversion of notorious sinners, and also for the remission of his own offences; as himself testifies in a letter of his, which shews not less his humility than his confidence in the intercession of the blessed Virgin: "I have taken the Queen of Heaven for my patroness, that, by her prayers I may obtain the pardon of my innumerable sins." He was particularly devoted to her immaculate conception, and made a vow to defend it to the utmost of his power.

In conversation he frequently spoke of the greatness of the blessed Mary, and attracted all men to her service. In fine, being just upon the point of drawing his last breath, he invoked her name with tender words, and besought her to shew herself his mother.

These are the principal virtues which were collected, to be presented to the Holy See. The archbishop of Goa, and all the bishops of India, seconded the designs of the king of Portugal, by acting on their side with the Pope, for the canonization of Xavier; but no one, in process of time, solicited with more splendour than the king of Bungo.

This prince, who was upon the point of being converted when Xavier left Japan, had no sooner lost the holy man, but he was regained by the Bonzas, and fell into all the disorders of which a Pagan can be capable. He confessed the Christian law to be the better; but said it was too rigorous, and that a young prince, as he was, born in the midst of pleasures, could not brook it. His luxury hindered him not from the love of arms, nor from being very brave; and he was so fortunate in war, that he reduced four or five kingdoms under his obedience. In the course of all his victories, the last words which Father Francis had said to him, concerning the vanity of the world, and the necessity of baptism, came into his remembrance: he made serious reflections on them, and was so deeply moved by them, that one day he appeared in public, with a chaplet about his neck, as it were to make an open profession of Christianity.

The effects were correspondent to the appearances: he had two idols in his palace of great value, which he worshipped every day, prostrating himself before them with his forehead touching the ground; these images he commanded to be thrown into the sea. After this, applying himself to the exercises of piety and penitence, he totally renounced his sensual pleasures, and was finally baptized by Father Cabira, of the Society of Jesus. At his baptism he took the name of Francis, in memory of the holy apostle Francis Xavier, whom he acknowledged for the Father of his soul, and whom he called by that title during the remainder of his life.

The king of Bungo had hitherto been so fortunate, that his prosperity passed into a proverb; but God was pleased to try him. Two months after his baptism, the most considerable of his subjects entering into a solemn league and covenant against him out of hatred to Christianity, and joining with his neighbouring princes, defeated him in a pitched battle, and despoiled him of all his estates. He endured his ill fortune with great constancy; and when he was upbraided by the Gentiles, that the change of his religion had been the cause of his ruin, he made a vow at the foot of the altar to live and die a Christian; adding, by a holy transport of zeal, that if all Japan, and all Europe, if the Father's of the Society, and the Pope himself, should renounce our Saviour Jesus Christ; yet, for his own particular, he would confess him to the last gasp; and be always ready, with God's assistance, to shed his blood, in testimony of his faith.

As the piety of this prince diminished nothing of his valour nor of his conduct, having gathered up the remainder of his troops, he restored himself by degrees, partly by force of arms, and partly by amicable ways of treaty. His principal care, after his re-establishment, was to banish idolatry out of his estates, and to restore the Catholic religion. His devotion led him to send a solemn embassy to Pope Gregory XIII. who at that time governed the church. Don Mancio, his ambassador, being arrived at Rome, with those of the king of Arima, and the prince of Omura, was not satisfied with bringing the obedience of the king, his master, to the vicar of Jesus Christ, by presenting him the letters of Don Francis, full of submission and respect to the Holy See; but he also petitioned him, in the name of his sovereign, to place the apostle of Japan amongst those saints whom the faithful honour; and declared to his Holiness, "That he could not do a greater favour to the king of Bungo."

In the mean time, the memory of Xavier was venerated more than ever through all Asia. An ambassador from the great Mogul being come to Goa, to desire some Fathers of the Society might be sent to explain the mysteries of Christianity to that emperor, asked permission to see the body of Father Francis; but he durst not approach it till first himself and all his train had taken off their shoes; after which ceremony, all of them having many times bowed themselves to the very ground, paid their respects to the saint with as much devotion as if they had not been Mahometans. The ships which passed in sight of Sancian saluted the place of his death with all their cannon: sometimes they landed on the island, only to view the spot of earth where he had been buried for two months and a half, and to bear away a turf of that holy ground; insomuch, that the Chinese entering into a belief, that there was some hidden treasure in the place, set guards of soldiers round about it to hinder it from being taken thence. One of the new Indian converts, and of the most devoted to the man of God, not content with seeing the place of his death, had also the curiosity to view that of his nativity; insomuch, that travelling through a vast extent of land, and passing through immense oceans, he arrived at the castle of Xavier: entering into the chamber where the saint was born, he fell upon his knees, and with great devotion kissed the floor, which he watered also with his tears. After this, without farther thought, or desire of seeing any thing besides in Europe, he took his way backwards to the Indies; and counted for a mighty treasure a little piece of stone, which he had loosened from the walls of the chamber, and carried away with him in the nature of a relick.

For what remains, a series of miracles was blazed abroad in all places. Five or six passengers, who had set sail from Malacca towards China, in the ship of Benedict Coeglio, fell sick, even to the point of death. So soon as they were set on shore at Sancian, they caused themselves to be carried to the meadow, where Xavier had been first interred; and there having covered their heads with that earth which once had touched his holy body, they were perfectly cured upon the spot.

Xavier appeared to divers people on the coast of Travancore, and that of Fishery; sometimes to heal them, or to comfort them in the agonies of death; at other times to deliver the prisoners, and to reduce sinners into the ways of heaven.

His name was propitious on the seas, in the most evident dangers. The ship of Emanuel de Sylva, going from Cochin, and having taken the way of Bengal, in the midst of the gulph there arose so furious a tempest, that they were constrained to cut the mast, and throw all the merchandizes overboard; when nothing less than shipwreck was expected, they all implored the aid of the apostle of the Indies, Francis Xavier. At the same instant, a wave, which was rolling on, and ready to break over the ship, like some vast mountain, went backward on the sudden, and dissipated into foam. The seamen and passengers, at the sight of so manifest a miracle, invoked the saint with loud voices, still as the tempest grew upon them; and the billows failed not of retiring always at the name of Xavier; but whenever they ceased from calling on him, the waves outrageously swelled, and beat the ship on every side.

It may almost be said, that the saint in person wrought these miracles; but it is inconceivable, how many were performed by the subscriptions of his letters, by the beads of his chaplet, by the pieces of his garments, and, finally, by every thing which had once been any way appertaining to him.

The crosses which he had erected with his own hand on sundry coasts, to be seen from far by mariners and travellers, were loaded with the vows and gifts, which Christians, Saracens, and Idolaters, had fastened to them daily, in acknowledgment of favours which they had received, through the intercession of the holy man. But the most celebrated of those crosses, was that at Cotata, whereon an image of Xavier was placed. A blind man received sight, by embracing of that cross; two sick men were cured on the instant, one of which, who was aged, had a settled palsy, and the other was dying of a bloody flux. Copies were made of that miraculous image at Cotata; and Gasper Gonçalez brought one of them to

Cochin. It was eleven of the clock at night when he entered into the port: an hour afterwards, the house of Christopher Miranda, adjoining to that of Gonçalez, happened to be on fire. The north-wind then blowing, and the building being almost all of wood, the burning began with mighty rage, and immediately a maid belonging to the house was burned. The neighbours, awakened with the cries of fire, cast their goods out at the windows in confusion; there being no probability of preserving the houses, because that of Miranda was the highest, and the burning coals which flew out on every side, together with the flames, which were driven by the wind, fell on the tops of the houses, that were only covered with bows of palm-trees, dry, and easy to take fire. In this extremity of danger, Gonçalez bethought himself of the holy image which he had brought; falling on his knees, accompanied by all his domestic servants, he held it upwards to the flames, and invoked Father Francis to his assistance. At the same instant the fire was extinguished of itself; and the town in this manner preserved from desolation, when it was ready to be burned to ashes.

A medal, which had on one side the image of the saint, and on the other that of the Holy Virgin holding the little Jesus, wrought yet more admirable effects. It was in the possession of a virtuous widow of Cochin, born at Tamuzay in China, and named Lucy de Vellanzan, who had formerly been instructed at Malacca in the mysteries of faith by Xavier himself; and who was aged an hundred and twenty years, when she was juridically interrogated, concerning the miracles which had been wrought by her medal. All infirm persons, who came to Lucy, received their cure so soon as she had made the sign of the cross with her medal over them; or when she had sprinkled them with water, wherein the medal had been dipt; in saying only these words, "In the name of Jesus, and of Father Francis, be your health restored."

"I have seen many," says an eye-witness, "who have been cured on the instant, by being only touched with that medal: Some, who being only putrified, ejected through the nose corrupted flesh, and matter of a most offensive scent; others, who were reduced to the meagerness of skeletons, by consumptions of many years; but the most celebrated cures, were those of Gonsalvo Rodriguez, Mary Dias, and Emanuel Fernandez Figheredo."

Rodriguez had a great imposthume on the left side, very near the heart, which had been breeding many months. The chirurgeons, for fear of exasperating the malady, by making an incision in so dangerous a part, endeavoured to dry up the humour, by applying other remedies; but the imposthume degenerated into a cancer, which gave the patient intolerable pains, and made him heart and stomach sick. Rodriguez having notice given him, what wonders were wrought by the Chinese Christian, by means of the medal of Father Xavier, went immediately to her, and kneeled before her. The Chinese only touched him thrice, and made the sign of the cross over him, according to her custom, and at the same moment the cancer vanished; the flesh returned to its natural colour, on the part where the ulcer had been formerly, and Rodriguez found himself as well as if nothing had ever ailed him.

Mary Dias was not only blind, but taken with the palsy over half her body, on the right side of it; so that her arm hung dead from her shoulder, and she had only the use of one leg: despairing of all natural remedies, she caused herself to be conveyed to Lucy's lodgings. The hospitable widow kept her in her house for the space of seven days; and washed her every of those days with the water wherein the medal had been dipt. On the seventh day, she made the sign of the cross over the eyes of the patient with the medal itself, and then Dias recovered her sight; her palsy, in like manner, left her, so that she was able to walk alone to the church of the Society, where she left her crutches.

As for Emanuel Gonçalez Figheredo, both his legs, for a long time, had been covered with ulcers, and were become so rotten, that worms were continually crawling out of them. The physicians, to divert the humours, put in practice all the secrets of their art, but without effect; on the contrary, the sinews were so shrunk up on one side, that one leg was shorter than the other. And for the last addition of misfortunes, Figheredo was seized with so terrible a lask, that, in a man of threescore years old, as he was, it was judged mortal. In effect, it had been so, but that he had immediate recourse to the medal of Xavier; he drank of the water wherein it had been dipped, after which he was entirely cured both of his ulcers and his disentery.

But that which was daily seen at Goa, blotted out the memory of the greatest prodigies which were done elsewhere. The body of the saint perpetually entire, the flesh tender, and of a lively colour, was a continued miracle. They who beheld the sacred corpse, could scarcely believe that the soul was separated from it; and Dias Carvaglio, who had known Xavier particularly in his life, seeing his body many years after he had been dead, found the features of his face so lively, and every part of him so fresh, that he could not forbear to cry out, and repeat it often, "Ah, he is alive!"

The vicar-general of Goa, Ambrosia Ribera, would himself examine, if the inwards were corresponding to the outward appearances. Having thrust his finger into the hurt which they gave the saint, when they interred him at Malacca, he saw blood and water issue out of it. The same experiment happened at another time to a brother of the Society.

The saint was one day publicly exposed, with his feet bare, at the importunity of the people, who through devotion petitioned to kiss them. A woman, who passionately desired to have a relick of Xavier, drawing near, as if it were to have kissed his foot, fastened her teeth in it, and bit off a little piece of flesh. The blood immediately ran in great abundance out of it; and of so pure a crimson, that the most healthful bodies could not send out a more living colour. The physicians, who visited the corpse from time to time, and who always deposed, that there could be nothing of natural in what they saw, judged, that the blood which came from a body deprived of heat, and issued from a part so distant from the heart as is the foot, could be no other than the effect of a celestial virtue; which not only preserved all parts of it from putrefaction, but also caused the humours to flow, and maintained them in the motion which only life infuses in them.

So many wonders, which spread through all the East, and were transmitted into every part of Europe, so moved the heart of Paul V. that he finally performed what his predecessor had designed. After a juridical examen of the virtues and miracles above-mentioned, he declared beatified Francis Xavier, priest of the Society of Jesus, by an express bull, dated the 25th of October, in the year 1619.

Gregory XV., who immediately succeeded Pope Paul V., canonized him afterwards in all the forms, and with all the procedures, which the church observes on the like occasions. The ceremony was performed at Rome on the 12th of March, in the year 1622. But as death prevented him from making the bull of the canonization, it was his successor Urban VIII. who finally accomplished it.

This bull bearing date the 6th of August, in the year 1623, is an epitome and panegyric of the miraculous life of the saint. It is there said, "That the new apostle of the Indies has spiritually received the blessing which God vouchsafed to the patriarch Abraham, that he was the father of many nations; and that he saw his children in Jesus Christ multiplied beyond the stars of heaven, and the sands of the sea: That, for the rest, his apostleship has had the signs of a divine vocation, such as are the gift of tongues, the gift of prophecy, the gift of miracles, with the evangelical virtues in all perfection."

The bull reports almost all the miracles which we have seen in his life, particularly the resurrections of the dead; and, amongst other miraculous cures, which were wrought after his decease, it observes those of Gonsalvo Fernandez, Mary Bias, and Emanuel Rodriguez Figheredo. It also mentions two famous cures, of which we have said nothing. One is of a blind man, who having prayed to God nine days successively, by the order of Xavier, who appeared to him, instantly recovered his sight. The other was of a leper, who being anointed, and rubbed over, with the oil of a lamp, which burned before the image of Xavier, was entirely cured. The Pope has added in his bull, "That the lamps which hung before the image, which was venerated at Cotata, often burned with holy-water, as if they had been full of oil, to the great astonishment of the heathens." The other miracles which we have related, and which are omitted in the bull, are contained in the acts of the process of the canonization.

Since the time that the Holy See has placed the apostle of the Indies in the number of the saints, it is incredible how much the public devotion has every where been augmented towards him. Cities have taken him for their patron and protector; altars have been erected, and incessant vows have been made to him; men have visited his tomb with more devotion than ever; and the chamber wherein he was born, has been converted into a chapel, to which pilgrims have resorted in great crowds, from all the quarters of the world.

For the rest, it was not in vain that they invoked him; and if I should take upon me to relate the miracles which have been lately done through his intercession, they would take up another volume as large as this. Neither shall I go about to make a recital of what things were wrought in succeeding years at Potamo, and Naples; but shall content myself to say, that in those places God was pleased to honour his servant by the performance of such wonders as might seem incredible, if those which preceded had not accustomed us to believe all things of St Xavier.

I shall even forbear to speak of the famous Father Mastrilli, who, being in the agony of death, was cured on the instant by the saint; and who, going to Japan by the order of the saint himself, to be there martyred, built him a magnificent sepulchre at Goa. It is enough for us to know, that never saint has been, perhaps, more honoured, nor more loved, in the church, than St Francis Xavier; and that even the enemies of the Society of Jesus have had a veneration and tenderness for him.

But these opinions are not confined to Catholics alone; the very heretics revere Xavier, and Baldeus speaks of him in these terms, in his History of the Indies: "If the religion of Xavier agreed with ours, we ought to esteem and reverence him as another St Paul; yet, notwithstanding the difference of religion, his zeal, his vigilance, and the sanctity of his manners, ought to stir up all good men, not to do the work of God negligently; for the gifts which Xavier had received, to execute the office of a minister and ambassador of Jesus Christ, were so eminent, that my soul is not able to express them. If I consider the patience and sweetness wherewith he presented, both to great and small, the holy and living waters of the gospel; if I regard the courage wherewith he suffered injuries and affronts; I am forced to cry out, with the apostle, Who is capable, like him, of these wonderful things!" Baldeus concludes the panegyric of the saint, with an apostrophe to the saint himself: "Might it please Almighty God," says he, "that being what you have been, you had been, or would have been, one of ours."

Richard Hackluyt, also a Protestant, and, which is more, a minister of England, commends Xavier without restriction:[1] "Sancian," says he, "is an island in the confines of China, and near the port of Canton, famous for the death of Francis Xavier, that worthy preacher of the gospel, and that divine teacher of the Indians, in what concerns religion; who, after great labours, after many injuries, and infinite crosses, undergone with great patience and joy, died in a cabin, on a desert mountain, on the second of

September, in the year 1552, destitute of all worldly conveniences, but accumulated with all sorts of spiritual blessings; having first made known Jesus Christ to many thousands of those Eastern people."[2] The modern histories of the Indies are filled with the excellent virtues, and miraculous operations, of that holy man.

[1: "The principal Navigations, Voyages, Discoveries, &c. of the English, &c." second part of the second volume.]

[2: The reader is referred to the original English for the words themselves; the translator not having the work by him.]

Monsieur Tavernier, who is endued with all the probity which a man can have, without the true religion, makes a step farther than these two historians, and speaks like a Catholic: "St Francis Xavier," says he, "ended in this place his mission, together with his life, after he had established the Christian faith, with an admirable progress in all places through which he passed, not only by his zeal, but also by his example, and by the holiness of his manners. He had never been in China, but there is great probability, that the religion which he had established in the isle of Niphon, extended itself into the neighbouring countries; and multiplyed by the cares of that holy man, who by a just title may be called the St Paul and true apostle of the Indies."

As to what remains, if Xavier was endued with all apostolical virtues, does it not follow, that the religion which he preached, was that of the apostles? Is there the least appearance, that a man, who was chosen by God to destroy idolatry and impiety in the new world, should be himself an idolater and a wicked man, in adoring Jesus Christ upon the altars, in invoking of the Holy Virgin, in engaging himself to God by vows, in desiring indulgences from the Pope, in using the sign of the cross and holy-water for the cure of the sick, in praying and saying masses for the dead? in fine, is it possible to believe, that this holy man, this new apostle, this second St Paul, continued all his life in the way of perdition, and, instead of enjoying at this present time the happiness of the saints, endures the torments of the damned? Let us then pronounce, concluding this work as we began it, that the life of St Francis Xavier is an authentic testimony of the truth of the gospel; and that we cannot strictly observe what God has wrought by the ministry of his servant, without a full satisfaction in this point, that the catholic, apostolic, and Roman church, is the church of our Saviour Jesus Christ.

John Dryden – A Short Biography

John Dryden was born on August 9th, 1631 in the village rectory of Aldwincle near Thrapston in Northamptonshire, where his maternal grandfather was Rector of All Saints Church.

Dryden was the eldest of fourteen children born to Erasmus Dryden and wife Mary Pickering, paternal grandson of Sir Erasmus Dryden, 1st Baronet (1553–1632) and wife Frances Wilkes, Puritan landowning gentry who supported the Puritan cause and Parliament.

As a boy Dryden lived in the nearby village of Titchmarsh, Northamptonshire where it is probable that he received his first education.

In 1644 he was sent to Westminster School as a King's Scholar where his headmaster was Dr. Richard Busby, a charismatic teacher but severe disciplinarian. Having recently been re-founded by Elizabeth I, Westminster now embraced a very different religious and political spirit encouraging royalism and high Anglicanism but as a humanist public school, it maintained a curriculum which trained pupils in the art of rhetoric and the presentation of arguments for both sides of a given issue. This skill would remain with Dryden and influence his later writing and thinking, as much of it displays these dialectical patterns.

His first published poem, whilst still at Westminster, was an elegy with a strong royalist flavour on the death of his schoolmate Henry, Lord Hastings from smallpox, and alludes to the execution of King Charles I, which took place on January 30th, 1649.

In 1650 Dryden was ready for University and travelled to Trinity College, Cambridge. Dryden's undergraduate years would almost certainly have followed the standard curriculum of classics, rhetoric, and mathematics.

Dryden obtained his BA in 1654, graduating top of the list for Trinity that year.

However family tragedy struck in June of the same year when Dryden's father died, leaving him some land which generated a small income, but not enough to live on.

Returning to London during The Protectorate, Dryden now obtained work with Cromwell's Secretary of State, John Thurloe. This may have been the result of influence exercised on his behalf by his cousin the Lord Chamberlain, Sir Gilbert Pickering.

At Cromwell's funeral on 23 November 1658 Dryden was in the company of the Puritan poets John Milton and Andrew Marvell. The setting was to be a sea change in English history. From Republic to Monarchy and from one set of lauded poets to what would soon become the Age of Dryden.

The start began later that year when Dryden published the first of his great poems, Heroic Stanzas (1658), a eulogy on Cromwell's death which is necessarily cautious and prudent in its emotional display.

With the Restoration of the Monarchy in 1660 Dryden celebrated in verse with Astraea Redux, an authentic royalist panegyric. In this work the interregnum is illustrated as a time of anarchy, and Charles is seen as the restorer of peace and order.

With the king now established Dryden moved quickly to place himself as the leading poet and critic of his day and transferred his allegiances to the new government.

Along with Astraea Redux, Dryden welcomed the new regime with two more panegyrics: To His Sacred Majesty: A Panegyric on his Coronation (1662) and To My Lord Chancellor (1662).

These panegyrics are occasional and written to celebrate events. Thus they are written for the nation rather than the self, but these and others put him in good standing for his eventual appointment as Poet Laureate, where a number of event poems would be required each year and speaking for the Nation and to the Nation would be the first order of duty.

These poems suggest that Dryden was looking to court a possible patron which would have given him an income and time to explore his creative ideas but no, his path instead would be to make a living in writing for publishers, not for the aristocracy, and thus ultimately for the reading public.

In November 1662 Dryden was proposed for membership in the Royal Society, and he was elected an early fellow. However, his inactivity and non payment of dues led to his expulsion in 1666.

On December 1st, 1663 Dryden married the Royalist sister of Sir Robert Howard—Lady Elizabeth Howard (died 1714). The marriage was at St. Swithin's, London, and the consent of the parents is noted on the license, though Lady Elizabeth was then about twenty-five. She was the object of some scandals, well or ill founded; it was said that Dryden had been bullied into the marriage by her brothers. A small estate in Wiltshire was settled upon them by her father. The lady's intellect and temper were apparently not good; her husband was treated as an inferior by those of her social status.

Dryden's works occasionally contain outbursts against the married state but also celebrations of the same. Little else is known of the intimate side of his marriage.

Both Dryden and his wife were warmly attached to their children. They had three sons: Charles (1666–1704), John (1668–1701), and Erasmus Henry (1669–1710). Lady Elizabeth Dryden survived her husband, but went insane soon after his death and died in 1714.

With the re-opening of the theatres after the Puritan ban, Dryden began to also write plays. His first play, The Wild Gallant, appeared in 1663 but was not successful. From 1668 on he was contracted to produce three plays a year for the King's Company, in which he became a shareholder. During the 1660s and '70s, theatrical writing was his main source of income. He led the way in Restoration comedy, his best-known works being Marriage à la Mode (1672), as well as heroic tragedy and regular tragedy, in which his greatest success was All for Love (1678). Dryden was never fully satisfied with his theatrical writings and frequently suggested that his talents were wasted on unworthy audiences.

Certainly therefore fame as a poet looked more rewarding. In 1667, around the same time his dramatic career began, he published Annus Mirabilis, a lengthy historical poem which described the English defeat of the Dutch naval fleet and the Great Fire of London in 1666. It was a modern epic in pentameter quatrains that established him as the pre-eminent poet of his generation, and was crucial in his attaining the posts of Poet Laureate (1668) and then historiographer royal (1670).

When the Great Plague of London closed the theatres in 1665 Dryden retreated to Wiltshire where he wrote Of Dramatick Poesie (1668), arguably the best of his unsystematic prefaces and essays. Dryden constantly defended his own literary practice, and Of Dramatick Poesie, the longest of his critical works, takes the form of a dialogue in which four characters—each based on a prominent contemporary, with Dryden himself as 'Neander'—debate the merits of classical, French and English drama.

He felt strongly about the relation of the poet to tradition and the creative process, and his heroic play Aureng-zebe (1675) has a prologue which denounces the use of rhyme in serious drama. His play All for Love (1678) was written in blank verse, and was to immediately follow Aureng-Zebe.

On December 18th, 1679 he was attacked in Rose Alley near his home in Covent Garden by thugs hired by fellow poet, John Wilmot, 2nd Earl of Rochester, with whom he had a long-standing conflict. Wilmot was constantly in and out of favour with the King and his own poetry was often bawdy, lewd, even obscene and made fun of the King who would often exile him from Court.

Dryden's greatest achievements were in satiric verse: the mock-heroic Mac Flecknoe, a more personal product of his Laureate years, was a lampoon circulated in manuscript and an attack on the playwright Thomas Shadwell. Dryden's main goal in the work is to "satirize Shadwell, ostensibly for his offenses against literature but more immediately we may suppose for his habitual badgering of him on the stage and in print." It is not a belittling form of satire, but rather one which makes his object great in ways which are unexpected, transferring the ridiculous into poetry. This line of satire continued with Absalom and Achitophel (1681) and The Medal (1682). Other major works from this period are the religious poems Religio Laici (1682), written from the position of a member of the Church of England; his 1683 edition of Plutarch's Lives, translated From the Greek by Several Hands in which he introduced the word biography to English readers; and The Hind and the Panther, (1687) which celebrates his conversion to Roman Catholicism.

He wrote Britannia Rediviva celebrating the birth of a son and heir to the Catholic King and Queen on June 10th, 1688. When later in the same year James II was deposed in the Glorious Revolution, Dryden's refusal to take the oaths of allegiance to the new monarchs, William and Mary, which left him out of favour at court and he had to leave his post as Poet Laureate. Thomas Shadwell, his despised rival, succeeded him. Dryden, England's greatest literary figure, was now forced to give up his public offices and live by the proceeds of his pen alone.

Dryden was an excellent translator with his own style which brought the ire of many critics. Many felt he would embellish or expand anything he felt short or curt. Dryden did not feel such expansion was a fault, arguing that as Latin is a naturally concise language it cannot be duly represented by a comparable number of words in the much larger English vocabulary. He continued with his task of translating works by Horace, Juvenal, Ovid, Lucretius, and Theocritus, a task which he found far more satisfying than writing for the stage.

In 1694 he began work on what would be his most ambitious and defining work as translator, The Works of Virgil (1697), which was published by subscription. The publication of the translation of Virgil was a national event and brought Dryden the sum of £1,400.

His final translations appeared in the volume Fables Ancient and Modern (1700), a series of episodes from Homer, Ovid, and Boccaccio, as well as modernised adaptations from Geoffrey Chaucer interspersed with Dryden's own poems. As a translator, he made great literary works in the older languages available to readers of English.

John Dryden died on May 12th, 1700, and was initially buried in St. Anne's cemetery in Soho, before being exhumed and reburied in Westminster Abbey ten days later. He was the subject of poetic eulogies, such as Luctus Brittannici: or the Tears of the British Muses; for the Death of John Dryden, Esq. (London, 1700), and The Nine Muses.

He is seen as dominating the literary life of Restoration England to such a point that the period came to be known in literary circles as the Age of Dryden. Walter Scott called him "Glorious John."

Dryden was the dominant literary figure and influence of his age. He established the heroic couplet as a standard form of English poetry by writing successful satires, religious pieces, fables, epigrams, compliments, prologues, and plays with it; he also introduced the alexandrine and triplet into the form. In his poems, translations, and criticism, he established a poetic diction appropriate to the heroic couplet—Auden referred to him as "the master of the middle style"—that was a model for his contemporaries and for much of the 18th century. The considerable loss felt by the English literary community at his death was evident in the elegies written about him. Dryden's heroic couplet went on to become the dominant poetic form of the 18th century.

What Dryden achieved in his poetry was neither the emotional excitement of the early nineteenth-century romantics nor the intellectual complexities of the metaphysicals. Although he uses formal structures such as heroic couplets, he tried to recreate the natural rhythm of speech, and he knew that different subjects need different kinds of verse. In his preface to Religio Laici he says that "the expressions of a poem designed purely for instruction ought to be plain and natural, yet majestic... The florid, elevated and figurative way is for the passions; for (these) are begotten in the soul by showing the objects out of their true proportion.... A man is to be cheated into passion, but to be reasoned into truth."

Perhaps the following illustrates Dryden and his life—"The way I have taken, is not so streight as Metaphrase, nor so loose as Paraphrase: Some things too I have omitted, and sometimes added of my own. Yet the omissions I hope, are but of Circumstances, and such as wou'd have no grace in English; and the Addition, I also hope, are easily deduc'd from Virgil's Sense. They will seem (at least I have the Vanity to think so), not struck into him, but growing out of him".

John Dryden – A Concise Bibliography

Astraea Redux, 1660
The Wild Gallant (comedy), 1663
The Indian Emperour (tragedy), 1665
Annus Mirabilis (poem), 1667
The Enchanted Island (comedy), 1667, with William D'Avenant from Shakespeare's The Tempest
Secret Love, or The Maiden Queen, 1667
An Essay of Dramatick Poesie, 1668
An Evening's Love (comedy), 1668
Tyrannick Love (tragedy), 1669
The Conquest of Granada, 1670
The Assignation, or Love in a Nunnery, 1672
Marriage à la mode, 1672
Amboyna, or the Cruelties of the Dutch to the English Merchants, 1673
The Mistaken Husband (comedy), 1674
Aureng-zebe, 1675
All for Love, 1678
Oedipus (heroic drama), 1679, an adaptation with Nathaniel Lee of Sophocles' Oedipus
Absalom and Achitophel, 1681
The Spanish Fryar, 1681
Mac Flecknoe, 1682
The Medal, 1682
Religio Laici, 1682

To the Memory of Mr. Oldham, 1684
Threnodia Augustalis, 1685
The Hind and the Panther, 1687
A Song for St. Cecilia's Day, 1687
Britannia Rediviva, 1688, written to mark the birth of a Prince of Wales.
Amphitryon, 1690
Don Sebastian (play), 1690
Creator Spirit, by whose aid, 1690. Translation of Rabanus Maurus' Veni Creator Spiritus
King Arthur, 1691
Cleomenes, 1692
The Art of Satire, 1693
Love Triumphant, 1694
The Works of Virgil, 1697
Alexander's Feast, 1697
Fables, Ancient and Modern, 1700

9 781785 438738